Aging and
the Welfare-State Crisis

The University of Delaware Press Series
The Family in Interdisciplinary Perspective
General Editor:
Tamara Hareven, Unidel Professor of Family Studies and History

Charbonneau, Hubert, Bertrand Desjardins, André Guillemette, Yves Landry, Jacques Legare, and François Nault; Paola Colozzo (trans.). *The First French Canadians: Pioneers in the St. Lawrence Valley*

De Singly, François. *Modern Marriage: A Sociological Look at Its Costs to Women*

Guillemard, Anne-Marie. *Aging and the Welfare-State Crisis*

Jussen, Bernard; Pamela Selwyn (trans.). *Spiritual Kinship as Social Practice*

Aging and the Welfare-State Crisis

Anne-Marie Guillemard

DELAWARE

Newark: University of Delaware Press
London: Associated University Presses

Associated University Presses
440 Forsgate Drive
Cranbury, NJ 08512

Associated University Presses
16 Barter Street
London WC1A 2AH, England

Associated University Presses
P.O. Box 338, Port Credit
Mississauga, Ontario
Canada L5G 4L8

The paper used in this publication meets the requirements
of the American National Standard for Permanence of Paper
for Printed Library Materials Z39.48-1984.

Library of Congress Cataloging-in-Publication Data

Guillemard, Anne Marie.
[Déclin du social. English]
Aging and the welfare-state crisis / Anne-Marie Guillemard.
p. cm.—(The University of Delaware Press series, The family in interdisciplinary perspective)
Includes bibliographical references.
ISBN 0-87413-594-X (alk. paper)
1. Aged—Government policy—France—History—20th century. 2. Retirement—France—History—20th century. 3. Age and employment—France—History—20th century. 4. Old age pensions —France—History—20th century. I. Title. II. Series.
HQ1064.F7G82713 2000
305.26'0944—dc21 99-12864
CIP

PRINTED IN THE UNITED STATES OF AMERICA

Contents

Foreword to the English Edition
MANUEL CASTELLS 7

Foreword to the Original French Edition
ALAIN TOURAINE 9

Acknowledgments 15

Introduction 17

1. Old Age and Retirement: Developing the Right to Retirement 29
2. Old Age and Ways of Life: The Emergence of a Policy of Social Integration of the Elderly 89
3. Old Age and Employment: A Sharp Rise in the Adoption of Early-Exit Schemes 169
4. The Elaboration of Policies for Old Age, and the Crisis that Ensued: Clues for an Interpretation 228

Appendix: Demographic and Economic Data on Aging 277

Notes 288

Glossary 320

Bibliography 334

Index 348

Foreword to the English Edition

The demographic and cultural transformation of old age in the informational society is one of the most decisive trends affecting our world and our lives. The rapid increase in the proportion of the population over sixty-five and, moreover, the emergence of a sizable group of citizens over eighty (the fourth age) have modified the notion of life cycle and opened up a new realm of human experience. Technological progress in health care and declining fertility rates have combined to create a new age profile in our societies. The growth of the old-age population and the increasing cost of health care appear to threaten the welfare state in its entirety, too. In the United States, projections of public-finance statisticians predict the bankruptcy of social security within the next two decades. Intergenerational solidarity seems to be breaking down, both at the personal and at the social level. On a personal level, the crisis of the traditional, nuclear family weakens the commitment toward old people. On a social level, younger workers, concerned about the stability of their own jobs, and lacking financial security because of slow growth of real wages, are increasingly reluctant to pay for their elders, while elderly voters increasingly are turning against public financing of schools and child care. Thus, the transformation of old age, which is at the heart of the crisis of the welfare state, will probably be the most important question of social policy in years to come. It certainly is the one that will affect our lives most directly.

However, most social-science analyses are not up to the task of correctly diagnosing the problem in order to be able to offer adequate treatment. This is because the new condition of aging is not a mere demographic phenomenon, but a sociocultural one. Because social policies and public finance depend on politics, the relationship between the state and society is also affected. Furthermore, the relationship between aging and the economy is highly dependent on the relationship between employment, retirement, and patterns of entry and exit in the labor market. A proper assessment of the social impacts of the new structure of aging requires an in-depth sociological analysis combining all the elements mentioned above. Hence, the extraordinary importance of Professor Guillemard's work.

Anne-Marie Guillemard has been at the forefront of European sociology of aging and social policies for the last twenty-five years. Her first book *(Retirement: A Social Death),* was the first quantitative sociological analysis ever conducted in France on the social determinants of behavior during retirement. She showed how class and cultural attributes during the work life largely determined the last stage of existence. This intimate connection between work and retirement runs through Guillemard's research, and I think it is an essential analytical element to understand the old-age condition, particularly in this time of full transformation of labor arrangements.

A second theme was introduced in her work *La Vieillesse et l'Etat* (Old Age and the State): the interplay between politics, culture, and state institutions in the design and implementation of social policies. *Aging and the Welfare-State Crisis* brings together the structural and political threads of her theory, showing their complex interplay in a fine-grain analysis whose cognitive value goes well beyond the French context that she studied.

Guillemard's additional value lies in her linking of theory and practice, sociological research and a personal acquaintance with social policy and business problems. While she is a professor of sociology in the Sorbonne, she has always been close to practice, as a consultant to pension funds, as an advisor to the French government, and as president of the European Union's Observatory on Aging. While unequivocally French, she has also broad international experience, both as founder and first president of the International Sociological Association's Research Committee on Sociology of Aging and as a frequent lecturer at leading universities around the world. Her practical experience and her international understanding are reflected in the pages of this book. While dealing with France, she thinks about the world, at least about the industrialized world. And while discussing issues on the basis of rigorous research, she never loses the perspective of what is to be done.

This is an extremely important book: for sociology, for society, and for you.

MANUEL CASTELLS

Foreword to the Original French Edition

What purpose does the field of sociology serve? Between descriptions that are always a step behind reality, like last year's train schedule and general analyses that are somewhere between theories and opinions, sociology's middle ground covers the knowledge of *policies.* It is more than just politics, however, since politics refers to society, government, and the state—notions that I fear both impose the idea of a logic and a mechanism of systems, as well as revealing the fascination that intellectuals, people who think and have doubts, have often had for princes, who are supposedly men of action and decision. Sociology involves the knowledge of policies, i.e., the constructions by various actors, social groups, politicians, and central powers, but also trends of thought, beliefs, political groups, ways of organizing experience and of managing time and space, age, sex, work and money, and days of celebration and mourning. Would it be more appropriate to speak in terms of *political culture?* The term seems awkward, since *culture* designates the construction of relationships that are not limited to social matters, whereas *political* implies the production and application of institutional norms that regulate social interaction. However, the social matters that sociologists study are in between culture and politics.

It would therefore seem that sociology is largely dedicated to studying economic, social, scientific, educational, urban, and family policies—the production of social organization. And yet, that isn't the case. Why? Certainly because the privileged object of sociological study, while easy to define, is not so easy to apprehend. That's because it doesn't appear to be a social object at all. Sociologists doing research first study texts that refer, on the one hand, to an ideology, and, on the other, to the workings of government and organizations. Once defined, political questions—the desired object—immediately drop out of the picture. There are those who suggest concentrating on how organizations function; lawyers situate particular texts within the framework of regulations and the evolution of the law; political analysts reconstruct the forces at work that led to a decision. The study of social or economic policy seems to begin by splitting its object into politics and the network of decision making, on the one hand, and labor or health and welfare, on the other.

Anne-Marie Guillemard, however, does quite the opposite by pulling together all the threads so often separated. She never speaks of policies for the aging without discussing aging itself. Or rather, since she has already written a book on the topic, *La retraite, une mort sociale* (Retirement: A Social Death), she chose straightaway to define policies for the aging as social constructions of all the practices and representations that make up aging as a social fact. In so doing, she shows us that it isn't a simple matter of alleviating the worst poverty, but rather of constructing a major part of the policy itself, since it is impossible to discuss aging without also dealing with retirement, illness, the family, the state, taxes—simply put, with the welfare state, and, more concretely, with massive quantities of people and money. If one had to define Europe in today's world, one could say that it is the part of the planet where the two basic values are progress in production and the welfare state. Obviously, analyzing old-age policy must go beyond explanations of laws, government measures, and their consequences and must include the use that the society makes of its most precious commodity, human life.

If we adopt this approach, it is hard to make headway without resorting to a historical method, that is to say, without linking policy on aging with other political decisions and social relationships that make up what we call a society (if we strip the word of any explanatory quality). Anne-Marie Guillemard was nearly obliged from the outset to take the widest possible analysis because the French welfare state was not created as a comprehensive assistance program or economic mechanism (like the Beveridge Plan), but rather as a giant social and national reconstruction project that included extending a "social citizenship" to the working class that employers and the government had previously denied them. The agreement between General de Gaulle and the Communist Party (associated with the CGT trade union at the height of its power) was based on this broad conception of the Republic's reconstruction, which included not only an institutional dimension but also a social one. It was this enormous project, put in place by one of the most renowned public service figures, Pierre Laroque, that created one of the first public policies dealing with aging that Anne-Marie Guillemard encounters in her historical study. At that point in time, the chief criterion was not age but work; old age was less of an issue than retirement, and the creation of the welfare state was part of the labor movement's overall agenda. By associating the words *republic* and *labor movement* one gets a representation of French social life that has dominated our history since the 1930s and the Popular Front.

The central theme of Anne-Marie Guillemard's book emerges clearly from this lofty point of departure: the slow unraveling of republican and labor culture in the course of half a century. Does a new old-age policy replace it, marking the creation of a new culture? Or are we witnessing the deterioration of the image of social causes and its replacement by an incoherent set of economic constraints, the accepting of social inequality and speeches as vague as they are generous? It is a matter of great importance and cannot be explained by bureaucratic red tape or the government's lack of resolve. We are confronted with three major factors: social pressure groups, the end of economic growth, and the change in organizations and values.

I will now return to the author's analyses in a slightly different order than her own in order to highlight the sequence of her work in two stages: first the crisis of the republican and social-oriented model, and then the search for a new model.

The crisis of the model put in place after World War II was caused primarily by ongoing social inequality. Anne-Marie Guillemard pointed out in her first book that different social groups are as unequal when it comes to retirement as they are in terms of working conditions and pay. Given a system mainly dedicated to providing the mere minimum and protecting the greatest number of elderly workers from poverty and overwork, economic growth allowed the highest-paid and the best-organized employees to maintain their social standard upon retirement. The pension system diversified and became fragmented, and supplementary pension schemes multiplied. Agreements between companies and unions added to and modified legal interventions. This was a normal—and even encouraging—development, since the growing French economy has continually spent more of its GNP on social policies. If one were to define the French middle class today, wouldn't it be necessary to describe it as being made up of all those who are insured, i.e., those who consider themselves protected against accidents, or that it is comprised of all the people who receive (or will receive) supplemental pension payments? Nevertheless, the idea of equality is fading. Anne-Marie Guillemard alerts us to the fact that pension payments do not create an effect of redistribution because of the inequality inherent in dying.

If economic growth exceeded the original spirit of the welfare state while improving the living conditions of retired people, the effects of the subsequent economic crisis were more brutal. And this is the tour de force of Anne-Marie Guillemard's book, which at times takes the tone of an indictment: according to her, concern for the elderly and the desire to humanize that part of a person's life that constitutes old age are dwindling. Instead, the only thing that seems to matter is unemployment statistics. Work for all is no longer an objective; the beginning and end of the age curb are truncated. Young unemployed people suddenly become "students" and "trainees," and elderly unemployed people are "preretirees." According to Anne-Marie

Guillemard, retirees, the elderly, or senior citizens—whatever we choose to call them—are now invisible; all attention is focused on the nearly one million people who have taken an "early retirement." If the debate is shifted to the effects of an early retirement on a fifty-five-year-old man or woman, who is going to worry about what retirement and old age mean for someone in their seventies? The very idea of a policy for the elderly loses all meaning, since the secretary in charge of old-age policies has no power to resolve the problems posed by increasing unemployment. Social policy becomes a mere appendix to measures designed to adapt to unemployment, which by definition is the wrong way to proceed.

But blaming the government is not in order, since public opinion approves of its policy for a number of reasons. For one, it is better to reduce the income of people who no longer have dependent children than of those in the middle of their careers and who have families to care for; for another, many people strongly favor lowering the retirement age, especially those who are not likely to live long after they stop working.

Yet this particular form of labor division is far from an acceptable solution: first, because many people who opt for preretirement feel as if they have in reality lost their jobs and have drifted out of the mainstream of society, especially after the initial months. Second, such stopgap measures hide the fact that we are headed toward an impossible situation in which either what working people pay into the retirement fund will have to be doubled in order to maintain current retirement benefits, or, if that option is rejected, pensions will have to be cut in half. The public should not be fooled into believing that it is possible both to greatly reduce their working life and to maintain a standard of living that supposes a major reallocation of resources toward health, education, and retirement expenses.

How far we have come since 1945! After the war the goal was to secure at least a minimal retirement for older workers; this constituted a positive, though limited, social policy. Today we are letting ourselves be led, eyes closed, toward a world in which the product of our labor will no longer pay for the collective benefits of the welfare state to which we have become so attached. The worst part of it is that apparently no solution is being sought as long as the rate of unemployment stays high. The retirement age could be adjusted so that everyone had the same number of years of rest and, more important, so that those who had the hardest, most tedious, and poorly paid jobs could work less. Also, a period in the middle of a person's working life could be set aside for child raising. But why dream on when all discussion of old age has completely vanished? The only thing that counts now is what is called (in bad faith) social programs for the unemployed.

The present situation has only one advantage: it shows us in retrospect how feeble the grand declarations on aging and on the choices available to retirees really were. Not to discount the different activities organized by various municipalities and organisms both public and private, but the assistance provided is possible only in a rich society in which most people in fact never encounter poverty or poorhouses and old people's homes. In the final part of her historical analysis Anne-Marie Guillemard sensitizes us to both the innovativeness of the themes introduced by certain groups and amplified by the Laroque Commission, as well as the fragility of the results obtained. For aging cannot be endowed with a cultural content if the aging do not exercise socially defined functions. What is needed is a conception of "function" that may not always involve productivity but at least implies utility—that creates social roles comprising responsibilities, results, and payment of one type or another. If a student can get a grant, a young worker or employee can be paid to undergo training, why should the elderly not be similarly paid for courses, mutual assistance, baby-sitting, running associations, etc.? Today the boundary between what is and is not considered work is more absolute than ever, and, despite all declarations, the rejection of those who do not work is extreme. And yet it is within our power to escape from this current nonsensical state and reconstruct the integrity of human life.

Rather than go any further, let us reflect on this bitter taste of regressive social policies. Of course today's policies cannot be sustained by ideas from half a century ago, but new ideas can be invented. However, current policies amount to nothing more than attempts to plug up unemployment.

When you finish this book, what will you be left with apart from this bitterness and rage that one day ought to help recreate a policy for the aging? For one thing, the idea that our society will suffocate unless it breathes with its two lungs—economic growth *and* security. It is equally dangerous to dream of a society in which no one has to work as it is to believe that social security must be sacrificed in order to reestablish economic growth. Both are ways of sinking into a state of savagery. Secondly, and above all, the realization that the scope of political debate has become incredibly narrow and impoverished. The intensity of the present economic crisis is no excuse. What kind of democracy is it that is obsessed with external constraints, the price of oil, the exchange rate of the dollar, the balance of trade, and inflation? As if the art of politics consisted of nothing more than regaining economic balance, as if the collective will could not possibly be carried out or social and political debates served no purpose and the economy responded to laws beyond human influence. Everyone knows perfectly well that economic constraints exist and that increases in distributable resources depend on production and productivity. But this awareness we have acquired of economic constraints must be balanced and complemented by a comparable consciousness of social demands, of the new forms of social and cultural participation that are possible and necessary. To reject the old and young and to condemn them to an inferior status is incompatible with democracy, for a democracy is sick when a society hides an important part of its own reality from itself.

Anne-Marie Guillemard's book is good social history and good sociology. Moreover, it is an appeal for information, a call for debate and for the invention of new policies. It is one of those books that effectively convinces us that sociology can indeed be useful.

ALAIN TOURAINE

Acknowledgments

The English translation of this book was made possible in part by a grant from the French Ministry of Culture.

It was translated from the French by Michael Cunningham; kindly revised by Raymond Maniccacci, Christopher Mierzejewski, and the author.

Thanks to Jean-Philippe Viriot-Durandal for compiling the glossary for the English edition.

My deep gratitude goes to Professor Tamara K. Hareven, general editor of the series, who has made this book available to English readers.

I would also like to thank Christine Colpin, in Paris, and Christine Retz at AUP for their perseverance and professionalism in proofreading the book.

* * *

This book was first published as *Le déclin du social: formation et crise des politiques de la vieillesse,* published by the Presses Universitaires de France, Paris, 1986.

Introduction

The last fifteen years have been marked by a remarkable expansion in the field of social policy, and in most industrialized countries new elements in the management of social risks have been gradually introduced alongside traditional legislation covering the poor. Initially, this management was somewhat crude, as it dealt exclusively with the largest risks faced by the most vulnerable sections of the population. Only later did it broaden its scope to provide universal coverage and diversify its fields of activity. The state had shifted away from being merely a protector. By this stage, it made much more sense to refer to it as a welfare state that dealt with both the prevention and the coverage of risks and exclusions, and that, by redistributing resources, even became an agent for transforming living environments and lifestyles. Almost everywhere today, the welfare state is in crisis, and there is much anxiety about its future. The controversies that this arouses are on a par with the vitally important place hitherto occupied by social protection in the social and economic mechanisms of industrially developed countries.

The idea for this book was based on such an analysis. It encourages the reader to question the social dynamics that lie at the heart of this unprecedented development in social policy. It also makes out a strong case for clarifying how this policy is formed and transformed, by simultaneously altering the lifestyles and social status of target populations.

We can only hope to address the problems at hand by a detailed, in-depth study of a particular social policy, a study that makes it possible both to reconstruct the play of social forces that figured in its foundation and to piece together the interactive effect on behavior and attitudes. Accordingly, this book deals with the rise and fall of social welfare through an analysis of the way in which policies for the elderly have developed, and of the crisis that currently envelops them.

Until now, the idea of a policy for the elderly has been curiously neglected by social policy analysts, despite the fact that it is a popular research field among those who are eager to explain the societal phenomenon of the extraordinary growth of social protection and the difficulties it is currently facing. There are two reasons for this. First, old-age benefits constitute the biggest item in the social expenditure of industrial countries. In the seven leading OECD countries in 1981 (United States, Japan, Germany, Canada, France, Italy, and the United Kingdom) such benefits represented approximately 35 percent of total expenditure, followed by health (23 percent) and education (24 percent), with unemployment insurance accounting for 5 percent (see table 1 in the appendix). In Europe (see table 3 in the appendix), almost half of all social expenditure is on the elderly (46 percent in 1989 within European Union). Spending on the elderly is also the area that has undergone the most structural growth since 1960. While old-age expenditure has moved up 10 points from 1960 to 1994 in France, an increase greatly in excess of population aging, health has risen by only 1 point, and employment by 7 points during the same period, while family benefits have fallen by 18.3 points (see table 2 in the appendix).

Second, the choice of policies for the aging as a major research field provides an interesting opportunity to carry out background analysis into the implications of one of the major changes to have taken place in the last hundred years: the fact that we now live longer. Life expectancy at birth has risen from a little over forty-five in 1900 to seventy-five today (see table 4 in the appendix for changes in life expectancy at different ages in France). Aging is no longer the lot of a few people in each generation; it has become something that everyone can look forward to objectively.

As a new stage in the life course emerged, collective strategies concerning time were changing horizons, as were ideas about risks and security. The extension of the collective time framework to include a complete life cycle has given individuals, and not just the family unit, a real future; the sole, controllable future is no longer limited to that of the family and the preservation of its heritage. It is precisely because of this new temporal horizon that aging has been able to break free from the private family setting and emerge as a "social problem" requiring a whole series of specific orientations and interventions.

The formation of a policy for the elderly clearly takes place in the context of an overall change in social frameworks, and the policy itself plays a role in the way these frameworks are restructured. It is not the aim of this book to limit the analysis of the policies to a political context, but rather to focus on them in the context of their dialectical relationships with social organization as a whole—that is to say, the organization of ages, life course, and the structure of social classes and intergenerational relationships. One of the objectives underlying this research is to follow up work on the social construction/reconstruction of the reality of aging, a phenomenon inherent to the development of policies on old age. In practice, as the management of policies for the elderly has been socialized, political mechanisms have played a central role in this work on social construction. This had previously operated in interactions within the immediate and extended family and in the community. It is clear that a sociological study of government policy for the elderly, together with an examination of the configurations of social relationships that form the basis of this policy, provides an excellent opportunity to study the central social mechanisms whereby the experience of aging is fashioned. It is also surely a way of identifying one of the main processes whereby a society "produces" its elderly population.

This book attempts to understand national policies and aging, its social status and its attitudes, in a single intellectual sweep. This approach has guided the way in which the issue has been taken up and how it has led to a definition of policies for the aging.

Unlike many writers on social policy, I have not chosen to look at particular decisions taken by the state. Instead, I have opted to study the whole of the fluid process through which a piece of social policy passes. This has led me to examine the way in which, before a public decision is taken, various social forces first confront one another and negotiate how a social problem is to be defined, and then demand that a program of public intervention be drawn up. This book does not look upon policies for the elderly solely as a decision-making process, but also as a negotiated process of producing definitions.[1] Under this heading, I seek to establish which conceptions of age, and which definitions of old age, are involved in the struggles waged by social players with key roles in the formation of policies for the elderly.

The fundamental analytical principle has informed my wide-ranging definition of policy for the elderly. *By "policy for the elderly," I mean all public interventions that explicitly or implicitly structure the relationships between old age and society.* Two observations are necessary here. First, my definition represents a wish to reject all a priori definitions of old age. The reason for that is that it enables me to concentrate on both the interactive processes that occur between state action and on the configuration of relationships existing at any one time between old age and society.

Second, in the context of policies for the elderly, the proposed definition incorporates all major issues around which state intervention is organized. It is not therefore confined to the administrative definition prevailing at any given time. This decision to look to all public interventions on old age is linked to an analytical principle, and not to any desire to carry out exhaustive research. In fact, it is essential to take all controversies over old-age issues into account if we are to keep pace, over an extended period of time, with the movements from one theater of confrontation to another and with the players most actively involved. It is the price we have to pay for being able to reconstruct the polemics articulated by the various players, each of whom seeks to impose his or her definition of policy for the elderly and to shift the debate to suit his or her own interests and sense of rationality. Mine is the only analytical approach that facilitates a construction of the social dynamic essential to the formation of a piece of social policy. The decision to take all the discussions and interventions on old age into account distinguishes this book from other studies on the subject in France and abroad; the latter analyze old age in a fragmentary manner, for example only dealing with policies covering pensions or home-care arrangements.

The following propositions may clarify the theoretical framework informing this research.

1. In broad terms, government interventions with regard the relationship between old age and society may be reconstructed on the basis of three major political axes. These represent the fundamental issues that have structured debate on the question of managing old-age matters for the last hundred years.

The first issue is that of *old age as a social entitlement to a pension*, and is central to the pensions debate. The growth of social security, the development of supplementary pension schemes, and successive reforms to the French social security old-age benefits require no less analysis than the decisions that have resulted from contradictory reports produced by the leading players involved in this issue.

The second issue is that of *old age as a specific way of life*. Disagreements between the actors focus on the definition of a way of life for the elderly and on how to implement it. Measures taken to provide social housing and home-care arrangements reflect the way in which debate on this subject has moved.

The third issue is that of *the level and mode of participation of older workers in the labor market*. It is central to the discussions that have informed employment policies for workers who are getting older.

It flows from this that the formation and transformation of policies for the elderly may be understood on the basis of a reconstruction of the range of social players in conflict over each of the fundamental issues. I also analyze the polemic that developed between the actors, sometimes resulting from arguments over the terms of the issues at stake.

2. This entire analytical process is organized on the basis of a flexible theoretical framework that seeks to build a bridge between two theoretical perspectives. One sees social policy as the reflection of conflictual class

relationship. The other is closer to sociology of bureaucracy, and looks upon social policy as the expression of the functioning of state organization, and of the degree of fusion or dissociation between the various legislative, executive, and administrative powers.

My line of inquiry is not susceptible to an analysis that sees state policies as simple reflection of the ruling class's economic, political and ideological interests. However, from a perspective that takes class relationships into account, it does seek to clarify the relations that exist between state orientations and social interests. The wish to focus on the social roots of those involved in policy for the elderly and to make sense of the class content of public actions distinguishes my approach from more pluralist currents. For the latter, the actors are independent strategists who boast varying amounts of influence, power, and authority, and are not located in class relations. However, my explanation for the way that policies for the elderly have been formed is not confined simply to a consideration of class actors. I shall also attempt to identify the peripheral actors involved in the development of state interventions.

Lastly, my approach seeks to take into account the extent to which public interventions are indebted to the functioning of the state apparatus. Many of the characteristics of public decisions can be understood in light of the government's standardized models for action, or as a function of the alliances and rivalries that can spring up between administrative sections involved either at the center or on the periphery. However, I shall not restrict myself to an organizational analysis of social policy that represents the state as an administrative machine situated outside social relationships. That would do no more than postulate strong independence of the administrative and executive levels. On the contrary, I believe it is vital to look at the margin of fluctuating independence that the state enjoys with regard to society. The proposition underpinning this book is that government interventions reflect the tensions and relentless changes that mark the dialectic between the order of the state and the order of social relations. Action by the state is therefore rooted in social relations, although it never completely merges into it, and it is evidence of its own dynamic as a piece of social relations. Clarifying the development of policies for the elderly is therefore based on a study of the mobile, complex negotiations that take place unceasingly between state and social interest.

3. Policies are not simply the end product of social processes. Once they have been produced, policies for the elderly metamorphose into the network of relations constantly built up between the elderly and society.

This book will endeavor to trace the entire feedback process whereby policies that are implemented represent a redefining of the life course. They also correspond to a restructuring of the lifestyles of the elderly, and in return occasion a rearrangement of social relations and of the issues that dominate the formation of public interventions.

The work method that I have adopted reflects my research intentions. The central analysis focuses on French policy for the elderly between 1945 and 1981. Investigation into the period prior to 1945 was based on work on secondary data analysis.

For the most part, the empirical material on which this book is based consists of my own original research. A summary of the main components follows.

1. Analysis of the development of policies for the elderly in France was carried out on the basis of a wide range of data which aimed both to identify the various collective actors in conflict about each of the issues, and to piece together their polemical relationships and their effective roles in the process of delivering public decisions. Over two hundred in-depth interviews were carried out with individuals who worked inside and outside the state, and who had national or local roles in the development of policy for the elderly during the period 1945–81. The information gathered in the course of these interviews has been expanded and cross-checked against a corpus of documentary material that included the following elements:

• a content analysis of articles on old age and pensions that have appeared in the main journals published by trade unions and employers' associations during the period 1945–81;[2]

• an analysis of debates during that period in the Parliament and the Economic and Social Council (CES) on issues relating to pensions and old age;

• an analysis of public reports relating to old age and pensions, produced by various departments of the state including the commissions of the Commissariat du Plan and the Ministry of Health, Social Security and General Inspection of Social Affairs (IGAS);

• a quantified content analysis of articles published in *Le Monde* on pensions, old age, and the employment of older people during the period 1946–75.

The aim of this content analysis has been to produce a synthetic, empirical study of the varying themes that informed public debate on old age over thirty years, and based on a homogeneous corpus of articles in a daily newspaper. This diachronic approach has facilitated a posteriori periodizations of the debate that can be compared to periodizations obtained by other means. The approach has made it possible not only to follow changes in the debate on old age, but also to identify the experts and social groups that are the agents of this change.

The above systematic data are complemented by other material:

• information from participative observations that I have carried out on the many occasions I have played a central or peripheral role in drawing up orientations and decisions in the field of policy for the elderly, and particularly for the preparatory commissions of the Commissariat du Plan leading up to the Seventh and Eighth Plans;

• specific data on employment policies covering older workers, which data were collected in the course of a study carried out in nine leading companies in the Rhône-Alpes Region, and were drawn from interviews with managers and members of Work Councils (CE);

• lastly, data concerning the origin and operation of facilities and services measures administered locally to manage old age derived from an empirical study of at least ten local authorities.

2. The study of interactions between political measures and the field of attitudes and behavior is essentially based on two empirical surveys.

The first of these was based on the interface between the elderly population and local facilities. It evaluated the effect on elderly people of facilities and home-care arrangements introduced as a part of new orientations of the policy covering elderly people's ways of life. The second was a questionnaire-based survey of a sample of 360 early exiters from the labor market, the aim of which was to consider the impact of employment policies.

A large amount of varied data has been collected specifically for the purposes of my research. The data have not been used exclusively for reasons of verification, as the classical procedure of hypothesis and deduction would demand. My approach has been more inductive. Empirical studies carried out within a provisional theoretical framework have been as likely to prompt new theoretical questions, or to rectify the provisional explanatory scheme, as they have been to provide validation or proof. To a certain extent, my approach is closer to that of social history. I have patiently reconstructed the play of social and political forces according to which this or that political decision has developed, on the basis of cross-fertilizing and regrouping my various sources of information. These sources make it possible to identify the leading players, and the polemics and issues in which they are involved, and also to integrate into the analytical scheme the attitudes adopted by elderly people and their level of expectations. However, it has not been my intention to be descriptive. I aim to produce a formal framework that provides an understanding of the fundamental social processes through which French policy for the elderly has been formed and transformed. With this aim in mind, the research strategy guiding my work has been as follows.

My subject, policy for the elderly, has been subdivided into three main constituent elements: pensions policy, policy on the way of life of elderly people, and employment policy for older workers. These correspond to the three main issues around which debate on policy for the elderly is essentially structured. Each of these fundamental themes is evident with greater or lesser intensity in the course of the forty years that my research has focused on. During the first stage, the analytical procedure involved the introduction of a periodization of government interventions for each of the three components, using the data in my possession. This initial approach enabled me to select the most relevant time-spaces before proceeding to an in-depth analysis of the action at the very root of public decisions on each of the issues. Time-spaces considered to be relevant included those in which an overall shift in public orientations could be observed, and in which new political practice was developing in different ways. My intention was to concentrate my analysis on the point where the process of producing policies for the elderly became more comprehensible as a result of being transformed. There is, of course, something arbitrary about any attempt at periodization. For the analysis of the logic underlying state action, I have deliberately highlighted legislative, regulatory, and budgetary acts as chronological markers. In fact, they represent the institutionalizing of the new philosophies.

The second stage saw the reconstruction, on the basis of my empirical data, of configurations of social relations that engendered the new public philosophy under each of the headings for the relevant period. The demonstration procedure occupied one last stage during which the relevance and comprehensiveness of the explanatory model for each of the issues were tested by checking their capacity to explain other aspects of government orientations.

The first three chapters of the book are devoted to an analysis of the dynamics involved in the production of policies for the elderly around each of the fundamental issues. Their internal structures reflect the stages of the above demonstration procedure. There is also an assessment of policies that have already been implemented. The first chapter deals with the development of pension schemes. The period runs from 1945, when the French social security pension system was set up, to 1961. However, as I wish to analyze the formation of the system of actors in conflict about the "social right to a pension" issue, I also look at the establishment of pension schemes from the second half of the nineteenth century onwards. The second chapter contains an analysis of the process whereby a policy covering the way of life of elderly people is produced, and focuses on the period when a policy of old-age social integration was drawn up and implemented (1960–75). The third chapter studies the social dynamic of employment policies for older workers on the basis of pre-retirement measures introduced and developed during the period 1972–85. The last chapter brings together the results of the whole research, and comes up with an interpretation of the development of policies for the elderly and of the crisis that they are currently facing. My view is that the history of social protection of the elderly contains an underlying decline in social welfare. The very existence of social policies is under review, not for purely economic or demographic reasons, but because the overwhelming consensus on which the elderly have relied is collapsing. We seem to have come to the end of an era for one kind of social protection. The restructuring of the welfare state is now high on the agenda.

The overall aims of this book are threefold. On an intellectual level, the aim is to seek a better understanding of the way in which social policies are formed within a social dynamic that variously combines social relations and departments of the state. The aim is also to analyze how they mold and transform the environment in which they operate. Such an understanding can only come, I believe, from research firmly rooted in a way of observing reality that is not only rigorous and painstaking, but also rejects dogmatism and avoids empiricism. In addition to developing speculative ideas, this book also throws further light on the crisis in the welfare state that is currently faced by industrially developed countries, and contributes elements of sociological knowledge that might be useful for decision making. Lastly, even though I have been involved in work of an intellectual nature, it is not possible to inhabit the world of old age and its associated problems for so many years—or to study the consequences of political orientations and observe the damage that some of them will cause, or are already causing—without nurturing the hope that this book may help to transform the relations that now exist between the state, the elderly, and society, and help to break the "conspiracy of silence" that surrounds the fate of the elderly in our societies.

Aging and the Welfare-State Crisis

1

Old Age and Retirement: Developing the Right to Retirement

Today retirement is closely associated with old age. The passage from the status of worker to that of retiree is seen as an important social sign of entry into the final life stage. Once retirement begins, it plays a key role in redefining the last life stage and endows that stage with a particular form and content. Yet retirement is a very recent social phenomenon. Today's retirees are the first generation to benefit from retirement; few of their parents, unless they were civil servants, had adequate replacement income on which to live in their old age.

This chapter will seek to reconstruct the interplay of social forces whereby retirement was developed as a new, work-related social right, and later became universally available, before ultimately fragmenting.

The pension legislation that was passed at the turn of the century in France reflected the emergence of a new form of public management of old age; it also represented a new way in which the state structured the relationship between old age and society. Public intervention had previously been limited to helping only the population's most disadvantaged sections, irrespective of age—in other words, those who had no family or private support networks and had only the state to fall back on in case of sickness or disability. By instituting retirement in the form of a compulsory insurance scheme that gave workers the right to a pension and ensured that they received a replacement income when they reached retirement age, the state redefined the place of old age in society and the system of exchanges of which it formed a part. Economic security in old age was no longer an individual responsibility, but a collective one. A new form of solidarity, which was now bureaucratic, and no longer domestic or communal, was established.

Insofar as retirement policy is defined as the restructuring by the state of the relationship between the elderly and society based on the recognition of a work-related social right, what was the social dynamic that led to its institution? Who were the actors that confronted one another about this issue of retirement as a new work-related social right? What configurations of social relationships were embodied in the various forms that pensions successively adopted? These are the main questions that this chapter will attempt to answer.

The first part deals with the reconstruction of the social processes by which retirement, as a new work-related social right, was progressively devised. The second part concentrates on the creation and development of French pension policy since 1945. There will be an analysis of the interplay of social forces that led to the elaboration of a universal right to retirement within the framework of the French social security system in 1945, and an examination of the occupational segmentation of this right between 1948 and 1961. This detailed analysis of the production of retirement policies will run until 1961, when the French retirement system may be said to have reached its definitive form. Complementary pensions became almost universally available following the ARRCO[1] agreement of 1961, and gave France a two-tiered pension system. Subsequent public interventions between 1962 and 1981 took the form of minor adjustments and involved no major upheavals.

The ordinances of 1967 brought about important changes in the organization of social security: they established a new balance of forces by introducing equal representation and distinguishing between the different risks covered, but the general pension structure was unaffected. Similarly, the Boulin Act[2] of 1971 changed only the way pensions were calculated as a percentage of average income.

The Emergence of Retirement as a New Work-Related Social Right

The Rise of the Industrial Proletariat and the First Fissures in a Social Security System Based on Property

The first pension schemes were available only to civil servants and employees of the state and other public bodies.[3] The concept of retirement considered as a new, work-related social right is closely linked to the history of manual workers' pensions.[4] The debates, issues, and contradictions initiated by the emergence of an industrial proletariat owning nothing but its labor, and whose only resource was the hire of this labor power, led to the development of new forms of safekeeping that included pensions and were no longer based on property but on work. The advent of capitalistic relations of production uprooted individuals from their primary support networks, turning them into a labor power commodity, and raised the question of how they would survive when they became too old to work.

Throughout the nineteenth century, various ways were found to meet the security needs of a burgeoning working class, all of them stemming from the dominant property-based concept. The only way to build up capital to rely upon in old age, at least for those who had no belongings, was savings on income. This principle was applied in public policy, and gave birth to a law on 18 June 1850 and to the creation of the Caisse Nationale de Retraite pour la Vieillesse (National Old-Age Retirement Fund).

This first state pension-related intervention involved setting up a specific institutional framework warranting the payment of interest on capital set aside for this purpose. The intention was to correct the previous failure of the mutual insurance system *(mutualité),* by providing workers with a structure that would warrant them pensions in return for contributions. The aim of the National Old-Age Retirement Fund was therefore to encourage the so-called voluntary providence *(prévoyance)* based on individual savings and eventually subsidized by the state. Every individual had to take charge of his or her own risks, and security was to rely on property or its functional equivalent, savings, for those who had nothing to trade besides their labor.

This "providence" enabled the proletariat to cope with the uncertainties of life. The role of public assistance measures then available to improvident citizens was to dissuade; they were designed to inculcate the virtue of saving in those who were obliged to have recourse to such assistance, and also in those outside the system.[5]

As the conservative concept of security based on voluntary saving was put into practice, however, its flaws began to emerge. Of all risks, old age was probably the one for which voluntary provision was most inadequate. This was partly because it was far off, so that a long time had to pass before people could reap the rewards of their efforts, and partly because it was technically difficult to manage reserves of the size needed to guarantee a future pension requiring a large number of contributors. For these reasons, the problem of workers' pensions was probably an important factor in the move from a policy of saving to one based on insurance.

Furthermore, a system that made the security of the working class dependent on saving meant that protection was circumscribed by the amount of wages, which, in most cases, could merely maintain workforce capacities. The working class was consequently excluded from the very provisions that had been designed for them. The Old-Age Fund was a good illustration of this problem. It had been intended to cater to blue-collar workers, but instead mainly attracted a better-off, petit- and middle-bourgeois clientele. The working class was therefore excluded from the system designed to protect it, because this system did not in principle recognize the condition of the working class as permanent. The system was based on the idea that the future of the proletariat lay in its members escaping from their condition by building up capital, which would enable them either to become independent or to have an income in old age. Wage earning was considered an inferior, albeit temporary, status, and escape was possible if determined efforts were made to rise through the social hierarchy. An argument put forward by conservatives, who were opposed to the principle of a legal obligation to contribute to a pension fund, was that such a provision would immediately divide the nation into classes.

This view is clearly stated in a speech made in the Chamber of Deputies by a conservative deputy for Paris during an early debate on draft legislation that ultimately became the Factory and Agricultural Workers' Pensions Act of 1910:

> When you give a worker legal advice that obliges him to put his savings into your pension fund, you are preventing him from doing many other things he might have preferred to do. In the country, he might have bought a field, a house, or livestock; in the town, tools or a little shop. He would have become an employer. ("Hear, hear!" from the right and other benches.) You, on the other hand, make him remain an employee by insisting that he spends his tiny amount of capital on one thing and one thing only, and oblige him to invest it in a particular way. What is wrong with your draft law, gentlemen, is that it divides people into two classes and separates them into two camps: employers and employed. In practice, the two camps infiltrate one another and the two classes mingle. You will search in vain on your lists of pensioners for a worker with savings; he has become an employer and joined the middle class without telling you, and without any help from you.[6]

However, the idea of society being divided into two conflicting parts that so terrified the Chamber of Deputies had already become a social reality as a result of industrialization. Wage earners ceased to be a marginal group enjoying a transitory status, and employees of large enterprises soon gave up any idea of changing their condition. The growth of big industry gradually reduced the range of options open to workers for leaving the working class and profoundly altered the way they moved from one occupation to another within the production system. In the early years of the nineteenth century, few workers had remained in factory jobs after the age of thirty or thirty-five. Such employment had been a stepping-stone to becoming a master craftsman or a self-employed worker in industry, agriculture, or commerce. However, from the middle of the century onwards, there emerged a new worker life cycle typical of big industry: workers no longer left the factory to make their fortunes, but instead remained wage earners for life. Promotion within the factory hierarchy replaced previous occupational mobility, which involved the movement of the workforce from large industrial organizations to more traditional activities, such as crafts, which offered a chance of independence and provided a refuge for workers who had failed to achieve autonomy. In the new context of big industry, however, a protection system based on savings or its functional equivalents was to appear as increasingly inadequate.

Once the worker ceased to be, according to the words of Auguste Comte, a nomad "camping in society without being part of it," but had a consolidated status as worker, it became increasingly apparent that it was inappropriate to base his or her security on individual ownership, particularly in a property-based system, when the main characteristic of the working class was a permanent lack of property. Subsidized individual assistance and provident funds, most of them established by employers after the setting up of the National Old-Age Retirement Fund, experienced many problems, mainly with retirement, which demonstrated that the liberal answer to the working-class old-age security problem was contradictory and ineffective. The number of retirees remained insignificant. There were 306,370 pensions paid out on 31 December 1899, when, according to the 1901 census, there were 3,157,000 people aged sixty-five and over.[7] According to a survey carried out in 1898 by the Labor Office (Office du Travail), approximately 560,000 people out of a total of 6,560,000 workers were contributing to private pension funds at that time.[8]

Therefore, fewer than 10 percent of workers in the private sector had any prospect of retirement and, as a later section will show, even the pensions that awaited them were very small[9] and as we will show hereafter, precarious. In fact, apart from employees in the mining and railway industries, only a tiny proportion of the working population (3–4 percent) qualified for a pension at all, and most of them were employed by large companies. As far as retirement for working-class people was concerned, the conservative notion of security, which was based on individual responsibility and dependent on what each person owned or had been able to save, was a resounding failure. As a result of the inadequacy of the individual provision policy, even when subsidized, and the theoretical criticism and reactions it provoked in practice, another social security system began to take shape at the end of the nineteenth century, leading to the institutionalization of retirement. Far from being based on a negation of the proletarian condition, as individual provision had been, the new social security system was organized around the slow elaboration of a worker status in which retirement played an essential part. A work-based right to security developed alongside the property-based right, and provided a basis for security for those whose social position was defined solely by the possession of labor potential to be traded on the market. As wage earners moved from a marginal to a dominant position in society, measures taken initially to protect them were extended to the whole population, though not without some resistance.

At first, the owner status inspired security policies; later, the wage-earner status became the basic criterion, and retirement schemes for the self-employed and employers in the second half of the twentieth century were modeled on those of wage earners. The next section examines the interplay of social forces that slowly led to the institutionalization of workers' social right to retirement. These considerations about the origins of retirement are essential to understanding the social roots of this right, which did not reach its full expression until social security was set up in 1945.

Retirement for the Working Class is Developed at the Point where Employers' Strategies and Workers' Struggles Meet

Strictly speaking, no serious social and political history of pensions in France had been written at this stage.[10] However, historical research on the premises of the French social security system and the analysis of employers' policies and workers' campaigns concerning retirement (such as that in Rolande Trempé's work on miners) suggest that planned retirement was invented at the point where employers' strategies and workers' struggles met. Careful examination of this period shows that planned retirement cannot be explained by determinism alone; to be more precise, it was not simply brought about by slow, irresistible pressure by the working-class movement. Henri Hatzfeld has shown that the birth of social insurance *(assurance sociale)* cannot be considered only as a working-class achievement; it would be equally simplistic to view the history of planned retirement as a chronicle of the victories and defeats of class struggle. In fact, the retirement matrix was much more complex: industrialization had inspired the nascent working class with new aspirations to security and, simultaneously, prompted new demands in the emerging sector of big business. The resulting dialectical interplay of the two movements, the new modes of rationality and changes in thinking, formed the basis for the establishment of the working class's social right to retirement. This social right was later partly incorporated into the Social Insurance Act of 1930, and became universal in 1945. All the research on this subject[11] shows that big business and the social relations that developed within it provided the main framework for this transformation. By contrast, small businesses and their employees appear to have had a restraining effect.

THE WORKING CLASS AND PENSIONS

Retirement was too far over the horizon in the minds of working-class people, and it was therefore not a major issue for them at the turn of the century. For the working class, old age was not so much a specific risk as a form of work disability. The fact that the workers' mutual insurance system paid little attention to security in old age is evidence of this. Even when it first came into existence as restrictions on the right of association were being lifted, the workers' mutual insurance system considered pensions as being of secondary importance. Instead, it confined its attention to health insurance; one of the main reasons for this was the decree of 26 March 1852, which, until it was amended several years later, stipulated that mutual benefit societies could only allocate to retirement those sums of money that had not been used to cover sickness expenses. Only approved mutual benefit societies, of which workers were very wary, had enough funds to pay their members modest pensions, and even they were not always able to do so. Moreover, at the suggestion of benefactor members, these pensions were restricted to the "deserving poor." Ten years after the Mutuality Charter was adopted in 1898, mutualist pensions were still few in number and precarious: there appear to have been about 130,000 pensioners in 1908, and the average pension varied between seventy and one hundred francs.[12] There were two main reasons for these poor figures: one was technical, and the other was linked to the working culture of the period.

From a technical standpoint, old-age coverage required the immobilization of much more capital than was needed for health insurance. This meant that the amount of capital that had to be built up was substantially out of proportion to the options open to members. From a cultural standpoint, the long delay involved in setting up a pension scheme, between the payment of premiums and the receipt of a pension, was incompatible with the circumstances of the industrial proletariat. Their condition was characterized by unpredictability, and this did not foster the kind of attitude toward time that was necessary for the patient accumulation of a pension. As Antoine Prost noted, "[T]he security of old age crowns the security of an entire lifetime."[13] Retirement was so far off that it was simply out of sight for the still itinerant workers of the second half of the nineteenth century. The immediate future was uncertain enough due to job insecurity, the specter of illness, and the arbitrary behavior of employers. Accordingly, workers' mutual benefit societies concentrated on relieving the immediate risks that workers faced daily, such as unemployment, illness, and disputes with employers. Retirement came a long way down the list of priorities, and saving was often superseded by the need to resist the attacks of employers, with mutual aid funds going to support strikers.

In his history of attitudes towards old age, which was based on the situation in France, Peter N. Stearns notes that "retirement was completely alien to working-class culture."[14] He contrasts the attitudes of lower-grade civil servants and state employees—who enjoyed job security and the early introduction of pensions, and included retirement in their life plans at a very early stage—with those of the urban proletariat, whom he sees as trapped in a vicious circle of unplanned, and therefore unorganized, retirement that led inevitably to disaster in old age. This disaster further reinforced working-class collective reluctance to anticipate the effects of age, and stressed powerlessness and fatalism.

Industrialization, with the migrations and urbanization that accompanied it, led to the formation of a large urban proletariat. Workers were now cut off from all the occupational or local support they had had in their rural communities, either from their families and friends or from personal relationships with employers. This urban proletariat had nothing to fall back on in the event of incapacity for work, and experience of capitalist insecurity raised its consciousness and encouraged new aspirations. These were expressed in vigorous statements of principle such as "Society must take responsibility for all who are incapable of work." For a proletariat that owned nothing but its labor, security could not be based on property. Society owed a social debt to those who had given or had already given their best. "It is natural that any citizen who has given society his share of work and strength should receive from it the wherewithal to live a decent life when his strength fails or he becomes unfit for work."[15] The working class was claiming a work-based right to security, which was the premise of future labor law.

Workers' insecurity was not an individual responsibility; it was a social problem. Society, as it was then, compelled workers to take risks, and it had a social duty to compensate them. By devoting their lives to creating wealth, workers acquired a right as creditors towards society. Their work entitled them to a social right to security. But insofar as work was their only source of security, the fight for the *right to work* rather than for the right to retirement became more fundamental to them. In fact, this aim became central to working-class action.

Agreement was unanimous on these fundamental principles among working-class people, but there was disagreement over the implementation of the work-based right to security. In big companies, where production was beginning to be rationalized, workers fought for a compulsory insurance system funded by employer and employee contributions and by a state grant. Rolande Trempé has described the early, hard-fought battles of workers employed by big companies to gain a measure of control over the pension and social benefit funds set up for them under the law.[16]

Railway workers adopted a similar approach. An analysis of the strategies adopted by big companies, where work management was a prime consideration, sheds light on these workers' views of retirement. Both in smaller businesses, which employed mainly skilled workers, and in labor unions, which included a larger proportion of such workers, retirement was of little importance in day-to-day activities, and was envisioned in the context of a revolutionary problematic issue of class struggle and the abolition of the wage system. Workers' contributions to security were dismissed out of hand, and their statutory obligation to contribute was condemned as "legalized theft," as Jules Guesde phrased it when he argued against the Pension Act of 1910. The employer's contribution was similarly rejected on the grounds that this too was ultimately taken from wages and constituted a form of capitalist superexploitation. When workers' associations were consulted in 1901, after the first abortive draft law on the Factory and Agricultural Workers' Pensions Bill, they opposed the law and rejected the worker's compulsory contribution. For this and other reasons, the Confédération Générale du Travail (CGT) similarly opposed the Factory and Agricultural Workers' Pensions Act of 1910, which it called the "pension swindle." Insofar as any precise formula can be said to have emerged from the positions adopted by this section of the working class, they opted for a solidarity system funded out of taxation,[17] the borderline between assistance and insurance being often hazy. There was a clear demand for a social right to subsistence in old age or in the event of incapacity for work, and the public authorities and the law were clearly expected to intervene to this effect. However, there was no general agreement as to whether this right should be conditional and exercised only in the event of incapacity for work or extreme poverty (and this would have to be proved), or whether it was a right to insurance to which all workers were fully entitled after a given age.

The working class made a powerful claim for a right to subsistence *(droit à l'existence)* acquired through work; the demand was made on behalf of all those who were no longer able to work, especially as a result of old age, but workers themselves were divided on how the right should be applied. This claim was accompanied by another working-class campaign that aimed to limit capitalist exploitation of the workforce by reducing the length of both the working day and a person's working life. This was no longer a statement of a right to subsistence when one no longer had the strength to work, but the demand for a right to a period of rest; in a way, it ran parallel to the right to work, and was similarly based on the work that the employee had performed. The claim was given a radical formulation by Paul Lafargue in a pamphlet published in 1880; it denounced the right to work as a "disastrous dogma," and called on the proletariat to rise up in order to gain recognition of its "right to laziness,"[18] Lafargue argued that support for the right to work condemned the working class to perpetual alienation, and led only to "the right to misery." Instead of sinking voluntarily into "industrial slavery," the proletariat should affirm its right to pleasure. In effect, Lafargue was declaiming the subversive principle that workers' lives amounted to more than mere labor and survival, and that workers themselves did more than provide the workforce and ensure its restoration. They had a right to rest and leisure. The demand was for a work-based right not to work. Lafargue, the instigator of the right to leisure, suggested that "an iron law should be forged forbidding all men from working more than three hours a day." This was still a utopian dream, but he believed that it could be turned into reality through the development of industrial machinery.

Rolande Trempé describes miners setting out in their 1882 Grievance Register the principle of retirement after twenty-five years' work in mines, irrespective of age. As one of their representatives said, "Only those who have spent their lives surviving the poisonous air of the galleries, the explosions and the cave-ins are competent to say that twenty-five years of such an existence gives them an unalienable right to rest."[19] In this case, the right to a period of rest at the end of the working life was clearly claimed as a compensation for the alienating and atrocious working conditions. The miners' struggle for pensions around the time of the 1884 act on miners' pensions has echoes in the debate during the 1960s and 1970s about the age of retirement. What the working class was demanding was the right to social recognition and pleasure to compensate for alienation. Alienation at work and the right to a period of rest went hand in hand. In a way, the working-class demand for a right to a period of rest to compensate for alienation at work contained the germ of a form of acceptance of this alienation. By focusing on the amount of time worked, the working class sought to limit exploitation rather than challenge it. For the most part, this struggle was quite separate from struggles to improve working conditions, to control the work processes, and, more generally, to humanize the workplace.

The entire working-class perspective on retirement was later structured around two axes that, as we have already demonstrated, were already present to a greater or lesser extent in working-class consciousness at the turn of the century: the demand for a right to subsistence in old age in exchange for work performed, and the demand for a right to a period of rest to compensate for alienation at work. For some, the latter objective took the form of a demand for an effective right to a period of rest at the end of life. In the case of the miners, it found concrete form in a struggle—a very modern struggle, in some respects—over retirement age, which they felt had been set too high by the legislation of 1884. This preoccupation with the retirement threshold found expression in the militant workers' hostility to the Factory and Agricultural Workers' Pension Act: they fiercely opposed the setting of retirement age at sixty-five, calling it "a law for the dead."

The following examination of employers' strategies for retirement will attempt to show how the interplay of these aspirations of working people and some positions adopted by the employers brought about shifts in working-class perspectives.

EMPLOYER STRATEGIES

Employers do not appear to have been any more united than workers in their attitudes and behavior with respect to retirement. Again, it was in the world of big business that retirement took clearest shape. Employers in preindustrial small businesses remained sympathetic to conservative doctrine, and saw security exclusively as the result of optional saving; by contrast, employers in big companies, who had to deal with the problems of organizing a large workforce, pragmatically transformed the system of responsibility for security, and at the same time introduced age discrimination among workers. The development of the idea of a working-class pension in the form of a deferred wage stemmed from this two-pronged approach by the big employers and the new strategies it stimulated among workers. In the end, the social right to retirement seems to have resulted less from a workers' victory than from a complex intermingling of workers' aspirations and demands with the new management needs of a rising big industry.

The advent of big business created new workforce needs. Such businesses needed a new type of worker who had to be recruited, trained, and kept in the same workplace. They also needed to have greater control over workforce mobility through big business hierarchy in order to remove impediments to improved productivity. The contract for hire of services, which had hitherto been widely used and expressed no more than the intent to pay wages in return for work, was obviously inadequate to meet the new requirements. It provided the company with a workforce, but did not properly address the issues of quality control and the regularity and intensity of work, factors that were becoming fundamental to the effective functioning and development of large-scale industry. The introduction of new methods of payment (piecework rather than payment by the day) and the control of jobs, which were no longer a worker's inheritance, increased management's power over the organization of work. Welfare institutions and pension funds were also set up as new instruments for workforce management. They provided a working population anxious for security with benefits that were additional to wages, and could be modulated according to the management imperatives of large companies.

Retirement as an instrument for achieving worker discipline. The emerging big businesses were more closely geared to organization than to the manufacture of goods, and were looking for a new type of worker. They no longer wanted skilled workers concerned for their professional autonomy and largely itinerant, of whom Denis Poulot has provided such a vivid portrait.[20] They were trying to develop a new kind of worker prepared to relinquish autonomy and be integrated into an organization, submitting to its rules, discipline, and working methods. In short, the big companies no longer wanted a member of the proletariat; they wanted a wage earner. Now that the work was integrated, divided, and specialized, it required regularity, punctuality, and loyalty; workforce mobility was ill-suited to such needs. The pension schemes set up and managed by employers allowed them to threaten the workforce with loss of pension rights, and thus became a way of subjecting employees to the discipline and constraints required for the smooth functioning and development of the particular industry. They were also a useful recruiting tool, since potential staff were attracted by the prospect of security in old age.[21] In the case of the Carmaux miners, Rolande Trempé writes that the promise of a pension was seen by managers as a means of recruiting workers who otherwise found mining unappealing. It also enabled the company to put a stop to any suggestion of staff instability that might be prejudicial to the smooth running of the business. In fact, there was considerable worker mobility[22] at a time when "the stability and hard work of the workers were as necessary to the mine's prosperity as improvements to miners' existence."[23] The fact that the company insisted on twenty-five to thirty years' continuous service before granting a pension is a measure of the pressure that the scheme exerted on workers; it meant that they had to devote almost their entire working lives to the same company. William Graebner describes the way retirement was used by some large American companies, such as Du Pont and General Electric, at the start of the century as a way of reducing workforce mobility and promoting company loyalty.[24] First and foremost, big firms wanted to make workers give up their dreams of independence by offering them advantages that could compete with the attractions of paths traditionally followed by the working class; these paths involved workers leaving their jobs when they were in their prime and best equipped to serve the company to work as self-employed contractors in order to build up savings. Big companies thought that the prospect of a pension in old age might make employees hesitate and realize that it was risky to leave their jobs; instead, a pension could give them a form of security comparable to the hypothetical fortune they might make by embarking on a new occupation. Besides, pension entitlement was an incentive to relinquish other, concurrent work. Retirement benefits therefore encouraged them to stay with the company throughout their working lives, and to devote the whole of their labor to it.

Retirement as a means of managing workforce mobility inside large companies. New production methods incorporated the scientific organization of work and mechanization and, because labor was used more rationally to increase productivity, they were the origin of a new social conception of the worker as aging. The intensification of work, and the accelerated pace at which it was performed following the introduction of Taylorism, or scientific management, showed that older workers could no longer meet the requirements of the work process and that their output fell short of the optimum level set up by the company; this performance was customarily compared with the productivity of a young worker in good physical condition. These developments led to a new classification of workers based on age and the formation of the new category of older worker. They were also accompanied by the implementation of new, rational policies for recruiting and managing workers. The need for increased productivity led to the selection of workers who were likely to be the most productive, and the rejection of those least able to adapt to the new demands. Retirement was therefore used by employers to get rid of older workers whose output was low.

In his study of the history of retirement in the United States, William Graebner provides numerous instances of the link between retirement and what he calls the phenomenon of age discrimination in the workforce: "Retirement and age discrimination emerged as important phenomena at the same time, and not coincidentally. Retirement was one of several means available to a business culture committed to restructuring the age components of the work force."[25] According to Graebner, the origins of age discrimination were twofold: the workers' struggles for a shorter working day in the United States in the late nineteenth and early twentieth centuries, and the employers' strategies that these prompted in terms of mechanization and the intensification of labor. One effect of changes in working practices and the resulting pressures on workers was that occupational aging now preceded physiological aging and the inability to work, and this in turn led to an economic definition of old age according to which older workers were unproductive and unadaptable. This definition meant that it was economically difficult for industry to keep older workers on, and they were thereafter seen as a burden on the company. It also encouraged employers to consider means of reducing wage costs by getting rid of older workers who were overpaid in relation to their output.

The labeling of a group of workers as "older" was socially constructed on the observation of a drop in performance statistically related to age. This definition of the elderly worker depended on the particular company and the organization of the work, and proposed a new social construct of the reality of old age that no longer meant a physical inability to work. In fact, there was no longer any confusion of age with illness or incapacity for work; age was instead associated with a socially constructed inability to work that was shortly afterwards sanctioned by retirement. This produced a new phase in the life cycle in which a worker was too old for the labor market, but was not yet completely incapable and physically worn out. This notion stemmed from the diffusion of scientific work organization and the new economic structure that it brought about. It was also in line with the economic thinking of employers, who put it into practice by introducing management systems based on criteria that took account of such factors as age limits on recruitment, promotion, and retirement. Peter Stearns's study of the process of industrialization in Europe from 1890 to 1914[26] clearly shows the impact that changes in production methods had on the emergence of a process of occupational aging. He also describes procedures, such as speed and eyesight tests, that companies used to establish objective proof of the aging process in some jobs. In short, professional devaluation went hand in hand with discrimination.

In this new perspective on productivity, retirement was seen not only as a rational means of getting rid of older, unproductive workers, who therefore added to production costs, but also more generally as a way of opening up promotion and recruitment prospects for younger, more efficient generations of workers. As Ronald Melchers explains,[27] the setting up of a pension by the Blanzy Mining Company at Montceau-les-Mines enabled management to accelerate employees' mobility through the mining hierarchy by enabling younger workers earlier access to better-paid posts. This was more advantageous to the company than across-the-board wage increases.

In this way, the institution of pensions enabled companies to control the flow of workers without having recourse either to downgrading, which was often taken badly, or to layoffs, which were unlikely to encourage the kind of company loyalty that the firm wanted to promote. As managers at the Carmaux coal mines realized, it would be "deplorable if it began to be known that employees could work for the company for many years, and go hungry in their old age."[28]

Retirement pensions therefore proved to be a highly useful tool, not only for getting rid of older, less productive workers, but also for exerting better control over the whole mobility of the workforce through the company hierarchy. The development of retirement appears to have responded to two successive strategies adopted by companies undergoing the process of industrialization. As large companies developed, they initially sought to retain and discipline staff paternalistically by trying to make them give up dreams of autonomy and binding them inextricably to the factory's interests. Later on, however, pensions were used more pragmatically to resolve the contradictions brought about by the lack of mobility of workers who were now tending to grow old in their jobs, a process leading to an accelerated aging of the workforce as a whole when expansion tailed off: this triggered a decline in productivity and workers' adaptability to technological change, and restrained mobility within the company. In such circumstances, pensions allowed managers to regulate the mobility of workers and to use them in a more rational way. Ronald Melchers's study of the wages and social policies of two large companies, Schneider at Le Creusot and the Blanzy Mining Company at Montceau-les-Mines, between 1836 and 1914 provides an excellent account of these two phases in employers' use of retirement.

Transforming the system of responsibility and the emergence of a new wage-related form of security. Strategies used by employers to establish the practice of retirement led to a new wage-related form of security. This evolution initiated a responsibility concept that became the basis of future developments in social insurance. The notion of responsibility, which was the cornerstone of the providence policy, relied on the principle that it was up to the individual to make provision for the hazards of life. It is true that under the terms of the new pension schemes developed by large companies, retirement was often less of a right than a favor granted to the wage-worker as a return for his loyalty and obedience; but it did imply that employers assumed responsibility for their workers' security. Employers no longer simply paid wages in exchange for work; under given conditions, they also dispensed security. The responsibility system was thus deeply altered. Workers' individual responsibility for providing for their old age was, for the first time, transferred to someone else, in this instance the employer.

As François Ewald has stressed in his analysis of the formation of the notion of industrial injury, which he sees as the origin of social insurance institutions in France, this shift in responsibility led to the development of the wage earner's status of being legally dependent on another person. The modern idea of an employment contract was emerging. "The employer will no longer only be responsible for paying for the labor that someone else has temporarily hired him according to the laws of supply and demand. He will also be the person answerable for ensuring the worker's security."[29] The state merely transformed this shift in responsibility into a legal obligation. The principle of a legal obligation in the wage relationship was established by the Industrial Injuries Act of 9 April 1898 and the Factory and Agricultural Workers' Pensions Act of 5 April 1910. Wages henceforth found a correlate in the right to security, and security was no longer based on property or savings. A work-based right to security was developing alongside the property-based right; meanwhile, pensions were emerging, which were no longer to be considered as an income from individual savings, but as a new work-related social right. This wage-related form of security was first outlined in employers' pension funds. It acquired a legal footing only because employers' ideas met and stimulated some demands put forward by workers.

RETIREMENT ANSWERS DIFFERENT NEEDS

The introduction of pensions was the pivot for new demands faced by large companies with respect to workforce management, stemming from the awareness, aspirations, and struggles of that section of the working class most directly affected by the process of change.

Retirement provisions had originally been developed by employers to ensure that their workers stayed put in the emerging large industries. They also met the new need for security voiced by workers who were now growing old in factory jobs and, with the onset of industrialization, were beginning to find out what old age was like without savings. Employers and workers in large companies then confronted one another on the question of the management of social benefit and pension funds. Employers wanted to vary the benefits according to the demands of workforce management and were therefore also anxious to retain control over the provident institutions they had set up and keep them exclusively linked to the company. It followed that pensions were viewed more as a form of largesse than a right even though from 1850 onwards many companies made the employee's contribution a compulsory clause in the employment contract. The highly arbitrary behavior of employers in this respect[30] encouraged many sections of the working class to take action in order to enjoy as a right benefits that had hitherto been given only as a reward.

Beginning in 1850, mine workers took action against the unsatisfactory manner in which their pension funds were run; this action ranged from strikes to parliamentary interventions and culminated during the 1880–1914 period.[31] One of the main aims of these struggles was that there should be state intervention to turn what was still little more than employers' largesse into a statutory security policy. As the large companies became less concerned with hanging onto workers and "civilizing" them, and more anxious to use them in a rational way in order to achieve greater productivity, the antagonism between managers and workers took on a new form. Workers' aspirations to, and campaigns for, the right to retirement were reinforced and broadened by two factors: the precarious situation of older workers in companies where the work was organized along scientific lines, and the difficulties they faced in fulfilling new work demands. Workers in large industrial firms wanted a retirement system founded on legally based, impersonal rules that gave older employees a real guarantee and effective protection from the arbitrary views of employers and the discretionary practices of managers. Retirement was now an eminently desirable institution for both parties. It was a way of raising the quality and profitability of the work as far as the employer was concerned, and a vital safety net for older workers in large companies as their jobs became less secure. It may well be that the differences observed by Henri Hatzfeld between the "reformist" tendencies of workers in large companies who fought for pensions at a very early stage and the revolutionary positions of employees in medium-sized establishments who denounced "the pensions swindle" originated in the former group's experiences of age discrimination. In a broader sense, it is possible to understand the development of the working-class perspective on pensions on the basis of Alain Touraine's analyses of working-class consciousness and the changes that it underwent as work organization progressed.[32] The proletariat's marginality meant that it could develop only a simple awareness of exclusion and a global revolutionary opposition to the whole social system; "proletarian consciousness" was in decline. The working class was now increasingly embroiled in the technical and bureaucratic organization of large-scale industry,[33] and was developing a new "wage consciousness." Action took the form of broader-based and more conflictual participation in industrial society and greater involvement in negotiations.

More workers were now prepared to exchange a general reduction of professional autonomy for pay increases, and especially for the creation of a social right to retirement based equally on work and property. Similarly, large companies in the process of reorganization were no longer so anxious to retain absolute control over social institutions that had been set up for workers. This reflected a move from paternalism to a more technical form of management of social matters. Even before the turn of the century, the Creusot factory employed outside agencies to manage its social affairs according to the principles of commercial insurance.[34]

The introduction of pensions in the form of compulsory insurance allowed employers to depersonalize relations with their employees. With insurance schemes, communal solidarity based on the domestic community or the working community gave way to a form of statistical solidarity that was abstract, legal, and anonymous. The company could therefore get rid of older workers solely on the grounds of economic rationality, and not take account of any interpersonal or employer-employee links that might get in the way, or have a dysfunctional effect on the firm.

Both sides seem to have gone beyond the principles of liberal individualism. A battle was in progress for the control of nascent institutions of protection, but a meeting point was emerging. Although the two parties had different needs, they both wanted to depersonalize employer-employee relations and construct a system of impersonal rules. Personal relationships had to bow to bureaucracy. From now on, both sides aspired to the development of an employee status of which retirement would be a fundamental part and, more generally, to a bureaucratization of society as Weber understood it.

FROM FACTORY AND AGRICULTURAL WORKERS' PENSIONS ACT OF 1910 TO THE SOCIAL INSURANCE OF 1930: STATE INTERVENTION GIVES SHAPE TO AN AGREEMENT ON PENSIONS

An earlier section has described how, between 1910 and 1930, there had been an improvement in social conditions facilitating convergence of the conflicting views of employers and trade unions on the question of retirement. There was now a broader social basis for agreement between the two sides, and progressively less opposition to the principle of compulsory retirement insurance. Instead, argument focused on the form the insurance would take and the managerial rights that each side would enjoy; the legal forms successively adopted by retirement reflected this shift. These appear as the imposition by the state of successive agreements between the two camps: on one hand, employers were trying to subordinate the treatment of old age to the demands of production and the production system; on the other, the working class was, for many reasons, increasingly concerned with the construction of a right to retirement, and its needs could only be met through the state by the setting up of a new employment law. The Factory and Agricultural Workers' Pensions Act of 5 April 1910 was the first piece of legislation to posit the principle of a right to retirement involving compulsory insurance, and it introduced a wage-related form of security in old age based on employers' and employees' contributions, to which a state contribution was added. However, this first attempt was unsuccessful.[35] The law failed because it ran into fierce opposition from liberals, and did not win strong working-class support, or even manage to unite the Left. Its legislative framework was very largely influenced by new social technologies developed by large companies to deal with retirement. In particular, it legalized the employers' formula for security based exclusively on wages, by deferring part of it to security in old age. It was a minimum framework that was fixed at the tolerance threshold of small industry, a threshold that many large companies had already gone beyond. The coverage it provided in old age was consequently derisory, giving workers who had contributed for thirty years hardly any more than the 1905 Act had given them in assistance benefits.

What had been out of the question in 1910 became possible in 1930. The Social Insurance Act of 30 April 1930 established a social right to retirement for the working class. It was a funded plan and guaranteed a pension from the age of sixty onward, after thirty years' contributions, to workers whose wages were below a certain ceiling. There was a striking contrast between the hostile attitudes of working-class people towards the pensions legislation of 1910 and the active part that many played in drawing up Social Insurance Act.[36] The interests of small and large companies were quite different, but the employers were relatively united during the social insurance negotiations. The use of retirement as a means of managing workforce mobility had become more widespread[37] and, in these circumstances, employers no longer resisted the principle of compulsory insurance. On one hand, they wanted state intervention to provide simply a minimum framework that fixed small old-age pensions; this left large companies enough room to develop forms of voluntary provision that they themselves controlled. On the other hand, they sought to preserve their managerial rights over the structures; they could then keep a measure of control over social institutions, which were also instruments for managing the workforce. Employers were relatively satisfied with the Social Insurance Act as far as their two main objectives were concerned.

First, the fear of a monstrous state institution managing every aspect of social insurance was removed by separate management of risks, a multiplicity of funds, and the importance accorded to mutual insurance. Second, the increased cost to industry was kept within very strict limits at the expense of the level rate of pensions: as Guy Perrin has noted,[38] workers were under some form of obligation to "help themselves." Benefits were still essentially tied to the limitations of the preexisting price of the workforce[39] so there was only restricted coverage in old age for the lowest-paid workers.[40] The low level of replacement income was further aggravated by financial instability and inflation.

The principle of a worker's right to relaxation and rest at the end of his or her life had gained ground, and acquired a legal basis under the social insurance system. It remained largely a theoretical entitlement, however, and concerned only those still in employment. A worker's right to retirement had been established, but it was open only to a minority. Old age and retirement were still far from synonymous; older people still relied on public assistance, or else they carried on working. In the mid-1930s, almost as many old people were receiving welfare benefits as pensions. There are no precise figures for the period, but at that time there were probably between 750,000 and 1,000,000 pensioners,[41] and approximately 750,000 recipients of benefits. The million or so pensioners represented only about 25 percent of people aged sixty-five and over (4,100,000 according to the 1936 census), and the overwhelming majority were miners, railway workers, and employees of the state and local authorities. The industrial workers who received social insurance pensions in 1935 made up only a tiny proportion of pensioners.[42]

As employment rates for older members of society at this time show, the predominant way of life for the aging population was to carry on working, at least part-time.[43] However, there was a gradual decline in the rate between 1906 and 1936, and this can probably be blamed on the equally slow development of pensions. (See table 1.1.)[44]

Table 1.1. Changes in the Rates of Employment of Older Men between 1906 and 1936 (All Jobs)

Age	1906	1926	1931	1936
60–64	85	82	81	74
65–69	78	74	72	65
70 and over	57	53	50	45
60 and over	73	69	67	61

For the working class, which was alone affected by the right to retirement set up under social insurance, the rate of employment in 1936 for sixty- to sixty-four-year-olds was 62 percent; for the self-employed and for small employers, it was close to 100 percent. In the period leading up to the Second World War, therefore, the elderly population had little access to any old-age insurance. On the other hand, a new life cycle was emerging for those workers beginning to enjoy protection in their old age. For them, the final life stage took the form of leisure supported by a pension. However, these new social constructs of old age did not really come into effect until after the Second World War, when pensions became universally available.

From Universal Provision to Fragmentation of Workers' Right to Retirement—Social and Political Forces for Retirement after 1945

Retirement as a Universal Employment Right: The Development of the French Social Security System (1945–1946)

After the French social security system[45] was founded in 1945, the right to retirement, which included a right to subsistence in old age and the right to a period of rest in one's declining years, became a universal employment right. As far as old age and a number of other risks were concerned, there was now real solidarity among all workers, irrespective of category or status. France was abandoning one-class solidarity, the form that had been linked to social insurance and that tended toward the inevitable reintroduction of public assistance. The ideal of the French social security system was universality on two fronts: it covered protected individuals, since it had to look after all of the nation's workers; and it covered the allowable risks, since it had to give the widest possible protection against all life hazards that could affect the ability of individuals to meet their own and their families' needs through work. It was also characterized by a single structure,[46] but complete historical analysis of the foundation of the French social security system is outside the scope of this study.

Instead, this book will restrict itself to identifying the main elements necessary for the making of a comprehensive and universal right to retirement. The establishment of this universal right should be seen as an expression of working-class power that operated in both labor union and political terms. For retirement to be fully understood, it has to be viewed in the sociopolitical context of the Liberation.

THE SOCIOPOLITICAL CONTEXT OF THE LIBERATION

French social security was set up in the unique context of the Liberation, which was itself characterized by the strong, united dynamic of the forces that had fought together during the Resistance. As many as 80 percent of the seats in the First Constitutional Assembly were held by the three main parties to which these forces belonged: the MRP (Mouvement Républicain Populaire—Popular Republican Movement), the SFIO (Section Française de l'Internationale Ouvrière—French Section of the Workers' International), and the PCF (Parti Communiste Français—French Communist Party). In effect, these groups joined together to form a three-party government. They were able to act in relative harmony, and set up social security in accordance with the program established by the National Resistance Council (Conseil National de la Résistance); the situation was also notable for a marked preponderance of left-wing forces. The Socialist and Communist bloc commanded a majority in the country until the summer of 1946; the Communist Party was the largest party in France and there were also Communist ministers in the government. The labor unions, too, played a key role in the life of the nation and were closely associated with the country's political and economic life. Many labor unionists held seats in the Assemblies. The working class was held in the very highest regard because of its major contribution to the Resistance and victory in the Second World War. It was a dominant force in society, its interests were well represented within the political system, and it had penetrated the administration and established its own representation in the government.

By contrast, the military rout of 1940 and the lukewarm patriotism shown by a large number of employers had discredited the business world. The conservatives and moderates had frequently been compromised by the Vichy government, and were temporarily in eclipse; meanwhile, company managers were disorganized[47] and remained on the sidelines, and their political influence was almost nonexistent.

French social security system—hereafter designated as "social security," unless otherwise specified—was set up, "if not in opposition to the employers, at least in their absence,"[48] as will be shown later, they adopted it with resignation[49] and, to say the least, "without conviction."[50] It was born of a union of left-wing forces at the time of the Liberation, and reflected the influence of labor unions in national life. However, to understand how social security became a fundamental public reform it is necessary to acknowledge how important it was at that time for the state to restore its authority and unite the nation. "The special circumstances of the aftermath of war provided an unprecedented and unrepeatable opportunity to reform the social security system"; and the opportunity was seized by a government whose plans were sufficiently well-founded and clear to leave room "for no retreats on matters of principle, and only strategic and tactical withdrawals."[51] From June 1944 onward, General de Gaulle and the provisional government were preoccupied with getting the state back on its feet; this effort was felt to be a sine qua non for the reconstruction of the country.[52]

The profound upheavals that the country had just undergone and the concomitant breakdown in political, administrative, social, and moral life demanded an act of social renewal that offered an image of the future and would, in turn, harness the nation's forces and rebuild national unity. After the harrowing experience of war, it was important to redefine the social bond that should unite citizens with one another and with their government. The system of reciprocal debt between citizens and the state needed to be reformulated, so that the latter could confirm its legitimacy by restoring confidence in its capacity for social overview. The state then became the agent of profound social change, asserting itself as a welfare state and effecting a redistribution of national revenues. At a time when the workers were seen as the essential architects of victory, national cohesion was out of the question unless their condition was improved and they were integrated morally and socially into the nation.[53]

The setting up of social security was one of the main ways in which the state restored its legitimacy and reestablished social order.[54] Several analysts of social policy have pointed to the links between the "warfare" state and the "welfare" state.[55] The global conflicts in which Western democracies had become embroiled obliged them to further justify their actions by outlining a plan for a new, fairer, more egalitarian, and more interdependent society that would be capable of restoring national consensus. The principles of solidarity and state intervention that had operated in wartime were then transposed to peacetime and were used to achieve economic reconstruction and an extension to social well-being. The program drawn up by the National Resistance Council during the spring of 1944 was in keeping with these principles. It transmuted the union and fraternity of earlier fighting into future promises, and outlined a new plan for society based on the construction of real economic and social democracy.

In economic terms, there were forecasts for the growth and for a planned organization of production, the restoration to the nation of the principal sources of energy and credit, and workers' participation in management; on the social front, there was a commitment to the right to work, retirement, education, and culture. There was also the announcement of a comprehensive social security system "aimed at providing all workers and their families with the wherewithal for living whenever they were unable to procure it through work. Management was to be in the hands of representatives of those affected and the state."[56] The new social security substantially broadened the notions of social risk and the state's role in managing this risk; these had previously formed the basis of social insurance. The objective was no longer simply to improve the situation of the workers, but to build a new social order through "a redistribution of national revenues within a vast national organization of compulsory mutual aid covering a wide range of people and risks."[57] The ordinance of 4 October 1945, which was the cornerstone of the French social security plan, contained a statement that set out the scheme's aims and clearly articulated this broad ambition: "Finding its justification in an elementary desire for justice, [social security] answers workers' need to be free from uncertainty about the future, and from the constant uncertainty that engenders a feeling of inferiority; this is the true, underlying basis of class distinction between the 'haves', who are sure of themselves and their future, and the workers who are permanently cowering under the threat of poverty."[58]

The establishment of social security hinged on the development of a new social pact that would serve as the basis for the modern welfare state. In exchange for a new redistributive social state and a bigger say in managing the system, workers' collaboration in rebuilding the country was assured. The working class thereupon threw itself enthusiastically into the "battle for production." It agreed to work within the capitalist production system, and called off its campaign for the abolition of wages, and even for improved working conditions and control of the work process, in exchange for a state that would redistribute national revenues and guarantee security.

In the immediate aftermath of war, there was overall identification between the new demands for social equity and the imperatives of reconstruction and economic growth. Under the French social security plan, economic efficiency and social progress converged along Keynesian lines; this contributed to the renewal of the workforce, which was essential to the country's recovery,[59] while at the same time redistributing national revenues to the advantage of workers and giving them wide-ranging powers in the plan's management.

With the establishment of the social security system, state activity in the field of social protection reflected the influence of left-wing parties at the time of the Liberation and the power of the labor union movement, which had emerged from the Resistance with renewed strength.[60] Social insurance had come into being in a climate notable for social initiatives taken by big employers, but social security reflected the deep penetration of labor interests in the political system and the state.

The French social security plan followed the philosophy of the labor union movement. This can be seen at three distinct levels:

- the principles of organization were essentially in keeping with the basic aims of the working class;
- the labor union movement and the bodies that gave it political expression were an essential driving force at every stage of the plan's genesis;
- and labor unions played a key role in setting the new scheme in motion.

ORGANIZING PRINCIPLES IN LINE WITH LABOR UNION POSITIONS

The organizing principles adopted for social security in 1945 included a number of points that reflected demands that the working class had articulated during the campaign for social insurance.

First, a pay-as-you-go system replaced the funding system, which had been consistently and vigorously opposed by the working class. The preference for pay-as-you-go at the time of the Liberation undoubtedly owed much to the experience of inflation, to impoverishment across the country at large, and, above all, to the "failure" of social insurance; the latter institution had been funding retirement pensions since 14 March 1941 without a review of old-age insurance. Moreover, the principle of pay-as-you-go was very much in line with working-class perspectives. It made it possible to claim that protection should be based on the criterion of workers' needs, and no longer on their ability to pay. It established the concept of solidarity, since contributions were no longer funded but immediately passed on to beneficiaries. It also made social needs a priority, and the ability to meet these needs was no longer limited by the amount received in contributions, as happened with insurance plans; instead, it was covered by a major redistribution of national revenues. The pay-as-you-go principle of distribution made the notion of need rather than the availability of resources central to determining expenditure. This philosophy was fundamentally at odds with the employers' position and offended their entrepreneurial instincts and liberal ideas.[61] As businessmen, they found it difficult to accept that expenditure should be fixed according to need rather than income. Furthermore, as supporters of a liberal system, they were hostile to the confusion that, in their opinion, social security was introducing between social policy and income policy. They also deplored the abandonment of traditional methods of insurance along with the notion of covering risks, and their replacement by the principle of a vast redistribution of national revenues. They felt that the new system was very expensive. As a 1951 report by the UIMM (Union des Industries Métallurgiques et Minières—Union of Metalworking and Mining Industries) shows, they believed that there was reason to "fear that social security carried within it the seeds of its own destruction, since it replaced the notion of covering risks with that of redistributing income; the only restraint was the satisfaction of the needs themselves, and these were always liable to expand."[62]

Second, the principles on which the organization and management of social security were based reflected the expectations of working-class people. As regards organization, the principle of a single system fulfilled an old ambition of the workers to secure recognition of society's indebtedness to them. This would protect them from all risks of sickness, old age, and accidents that might threaten their own living standards and those of their families.[63] The social security plan set up a vast, national solidarity scheme that covered a wide range of risks, and was designed to include the whole population. This single design ran directly counter to the wishes of the employers, who had always advocated that the risks should be separated, and each managed independently and judiciously.[64] The working-class movement had consistently called for a broad-based organization that dealt with all risks, but its position fluctuated more with regard to the organizational principle of a single fund. The CGT had argued for a large number of social insurance funds: it feared a state takeover of the plan, and wanted to preserve working-class autonomy in fund management. However, after the Liberation, militants who had been the most ardent supporters of social insurance, such as Georges Buisson, came out strongly in favor of a single fund; they denounced the bureaucratization that followed the adoption of multiple funds under social insurance as cumbersome, complicated, and costly. The minority group in the CGTU was already criticizing the 1930 act for giving too much weight to the principle of mutual insurance, and they argued for a unified organization.[65] Only the CFTC remained hostile to the principle of a single fund and, after joining forces with the MRP, it achieved a dual system consisting of social security and family allowance funds.[66]

Third, the social security plan established as a principle that the institution should be managed by those directly affected and, in the tradition of mutual insurance, it invited workers to take responsibility for managing institutions that had been set up for them. In this way, social security responded to a standing labor union preoccupation: that social protection should be managed by the workers themselves.[67] At the time of the Liberation, this position of the labor unions was further influenced and reinforced by the Soviet model of social insurance, the management of which had been in the hands of company-based labor union sections for several years.[68] By establishing social security as an autonomous organization in order to "avoid any danger of bureaucratic statism"[69] and by giving the majority of the seats on the management committees to labor unions as representatives of the workers,[70] the French social security plan did as the unions had asked.

The social security plan enabled the labor unions to be masters of the new institution. This was a major innovation. It is true that the principle of mutual insurance had already influenced the Social Insurance Act, but the beneficiaries had never had responsibility for the prewar institutions.[71] Furthermore, under the new organization, private insurance companies, which had managed industrial injuries, and employer-run compensation funds, which had administered family allowances, were permanently excluded from the management of social protection. The employers strongly objected to the distribution of power within the social security institutions: in their view, it made it quite impossible for them to exercise what remained of their share of responsibility, and they argued consistently for "balanced" representation of employers and workers on the management committees. They eventually won the day with the ordinances of 1967, which introduced equal representation in the social security structure; but, for the time being, their removal from the political scene obliged employers to accept the new principles as they were. They bowed to the principle of democratic management, which was too widely accepted to be questioned, and they fell back on criticism of the way the system worked; moreover, as will be demonstrated later, they systematically supported all opposition to social security, particularly as far as the generalization of the single fund was concerned. Unexpectedly, given their aversion to all forms of state intervention, the employers also supported administrative supervision of social security; this had been rejected by the unions, but the employers may have seen it as a way of counterbalancing union power.

It began to be clear that the principles adopted for the organization of social security mirrored the fundamental aspirations of the working class and were radically opposed to the wishes of the employers. However, the new united administrative labor unionism of the Liberation now unanimously accepted the funding of social protection by deductions from wages, although this was a system that had long been repudiated, at least by the unified, minority fraction of the CGT, which was now in the majority. It also tolerated the omission of unemployment, a risk of the very highest importance to the working class, from the new system of solidarity under construction. These few concessions confirm that the setting up of social security was in the nature of a social pact. A new, broader right to retirement was being established by the state. This sanctioned the labor unions' predominant position; in exchange, they accepted their position in the capitalist production system and limited their campaign on questions of redistribution and wages.

THE LABOR UNION MOVEMENT AS A DRIVING FORCE BEHIND THE SETTING UP OF SOCIAL SECURITY

The birth of social security was marked by an ever-present labor union movement. In particular, the reunited CGT, by far the most powerful union, worked closely with the Communist Party[72] and the SFIO, and was involved in every stage of its genesis.

Since the spring of 1944, the CGT had participated in drawing up the National Resistance Council's economic and social program, the aims of which served to inspire the administration's plan. This chapter has already demonstrated how this council was preoccupied with fulfilling workers' aspirations to security, but our research has shown that there were also direct links between a number of senior members of the Social Security General Direction and the CGT. It is, therefore, not surprising that the principles and broad thrusts of the general plan drawn up by the administration met the union's requirements and that the CGT was consequently its most reliable supporter and most active defender.

However, it would be wrong to conclude that the only time the administration carried out labor union wishes was while it was setting up social security. According to the then-director general of social security, Pierre Laroque, the administration of social insurance was in good health and had the benefit of a young, dynamic team. The role it played in setting up social security was more that of catalyst or midwife.

The proceedings of the special commission set up in June 1945 to carry out a preliminary examination of the organization of social security describe the CGT as defending the administration against attacks from the various bodies opposed to the principle of a single administrative management.[73] The main critics of a single organization were the employers,[74] mutual benefit societies, and Christian groups. The employers attempted to head off the integration of industrial injuries into the social security plan and, along with the mutualists and Christians, defended the autonomous management of family allowances.

When the administration asked the Provisional Consultative Assembly to give its verdict on the planned reform, it had powerful backing from the Commission du Travail des Affaires Sociales (Workers Social Affairs Commission), which was chaired by Ambroise Croizat, a Communist representative who shortly afterwards supported the plan again as minister of labor and social security. The bill was introduced by Georges Buisson, general secretary of the CGT and a member of the confederate section. The commission viewed the administration's plan very favorably and supported its initial proposals with great enthusiasm, though blaming it for the concessions it had felt obliged to make and the compromises it had accepted following the special commission's deliberations. It further rejected a proposal submitted by opponents of various aspects of the social security plan; this proposal by moderate, conservative, and Christian Democrat members of the Provisional Consultative Assembly was a delaying tactic aimed at reducing the scope of the government's plan.

The commission's report was debated by the Assembly on 31 July 1945. Left-wing parties again united in defense of the plan against the conservatives; meanwhile, the latter attempted to defend plurality of funds by a tactical withdrawal that enabled them to avoid the financial concentration of a single fund and political control of this powerful body by the unions. They therefore supported the MRP in its fierce opposition to the single fund, which aimed to preserve the autonomy of family and birth-rate policy. The MRP succeeded in separating the family allowance fund from other risks, and the government's plan was finally adopted by the Provisional Consultative Assembly by nineteen votes to one (PRL [Parti Républicain de la Liberté—Republican Liberty Party]) with eighty-four abstentions (mostly MRP representatives and CFTC members). The ordinance dealing with the organization of social security was promulgated on 4 October 1945, shortly after the publication of the report by the workers commission that was set up by Georges Buisson.

The First Constituent Assembly, which was elected on 21 October 1945 and was the forerunner of the three-party government that came to power shortly afterwards,[75] saw the same Communist and Socialist majority repel the attacks of the MRP. The latter was better equipped than before to ensure that its views on social security prevailed, and it was now joined by conservative, PRL, and radical elements. However, the MRP's repeated requests for application of the ordinances to be postponed from 1 July 1946 to 1 January 1947 were opposed: "The MRP's hostile attitude toward the ordinance of 4 October 1945 and the scheme contained therein was counterbalanced by the enthusiasm with which the Communists and CGT supported its implementation."[76]

There was no lack of opposition to, or disagreement about, the social security plan, but no party was prepared to make its hostility public. As a result, the confrontation focused strategically on organizational problems. This explains the disagreements that divided political parties over how to organize social security and their unanimous commitment to support its universal application in the spring of 1946. This generalization was prompted by the alarming situation of the elderly, just as future fragmentations of social protection were caused by the pension question. In response to legislative pressure in favor of universal application, the government introduced a bill countersigned by socialist ministers and Ambroise Croizat. A communist representative then reported the workers commission's unanimous assent to the First Constituent Assembly, which adopted the bill unanimously. The old-age pension extension was to become effective when the index of the industrial population reached 110, starting from a base of 100 in 1938; for other risks, this was delayed until the index reached 125. The 22 May 1946 act, generally known as the Croizat Act, thus established a gradual generalization of social security. The public perception was that "this law deals in the first instance with an extension to the old-age pension"; this was a reference to the AVTS (*allocation aux vieux travailleurs salariés*—older salaried workers' benefit). At the time, all French citizens over the age of sixty-five were referred to as old ("aged").[77] The consequences of this measure were far-reaching, since its application more than doubled the number of older workers receiving an allowance; around 1,800,000 new beneficiaries were added to the 1,700,000 recipients of the AVTS. Of the 4.5 million people in the country who were entitled to the minimum allowance, 3.5 million actually drew it; this gives some idea of the poor conditions in which the elderly lived after the war. The scale of the problem explains two things: first, the many calls from the most representative parties in the Assembly for rapid government action to support those who had previously been known as the *économiquement faibles* (lower-income groups, i.e., elderly people living on a small private income and ruined by inflation); second, the preparation by the government, in response to these pressures, of a bill to provide lower-income groups with public assistance; this came into effect during the summer of 1946 after the Second Constituent Assembly had been elected. This bill proposed only slight improvements of a fiscal nature. The preamble stated that the extension of the old-age pension to everyone over the age of sixty-five would probably have been the best way to remedy the plight of the elderly, but that the state of the economy was such that the extension could not be put into effect right away; it would have to wait until production recovered more fully. The Finance Commission amended the bill considerably to meet the demands of the Communist Party, which had asked for clauses in the 22 May act relating to old age insurance to come into effect earlier (on 1 January 1947). The assembly adopted the bill unanimously, and the act on the general application of old-age insurance was promulgated on 13 September 1946.[78] Ambroise Croizat, the Communist Party, and the CGT publicly took credit for the measure, notwithstanding its unanimous adoption by the assembly, and despite the frenzy that their behavior had triggered among the representatives of a three-party government in the process of breaking up. The CGT's identification with measures adopted for the general application of old-age insurance was featured in the columns of *Le Peuple* (The people). An article entitled "Il y a de la joie chez nos bons vieux" (Our old people have something to rejoice about) on 19 October 1946 stated:

> The old people of France praise Croizat, the CGT, and the Union Nationale des Vieux Travailleurs de France (National Union of Older Workers in France) for the tenacity they have shown in remedying the plight of older workers. The excellent new legislation comprises:
>
> - the 22 May 1946 act;
> - the 19 July 1946 decree on older women who have five children and have brought them up to the age of 16;
> - the 13 September 1946 act dealing with the interim pension.

Similarly, *Le Peuple* published the following under the headline "Que la CGT soit fière!" (The CGT can be proud of itself!) on 9 November 1946:

> Ambroise Croizat, metallurgist turned minister of labor and social security, a man of the people, was well qualified to defend those who had suffered, labored, and been exploited all their lifetime and were never able to enjoy

the sound pleasures of life. Often old before their time, they despaired of ever being able to enjoy their old age.

They can now. Admittedly, there are still gaps, but we have every reason to hope that we can fill them, and correct the faults, weaknesses, and errors in existing legislation as we go along.

To recapitulate:

• The Social Security Act of 22 May 1946, and what was already a legal right: (a) an interim pension for those on lower incomes of 700 francs a month, or 2,100 a quarter; it may not be much but it is a start, and will go some way toward improving the situation of those who have had nothing until now and who are enduring enormous hardship; (b) the certainty of an old-age benefit from 1 April 1947 onwards, with payment starting on 1 July 1947; (c) an allowance for older mothers who have five children and have brought them up to the age of sixteen if they are wives or widows of wage earners; (d) exemption from property tax for recipients of the above-mentioned interim pension; the 22 May act leaves open the question of the payment of sickness insurance benefits (medical and pharmaceutical);

• The 13 September act, which puts the Interim Benefit into effect;

• The 7 October act, which gives a general increase to all recipients of the allowances given to older workers and to women who have brought three children up to the age of sixteen.

What other minister of labor could point to such a positive record? Not one!

The CGT's total support of the social security plan[79] and its triumphalist behavior were in marked contrast to the CFTC's more reserved, critical posture during this period. The columns of its journal, *Syndicalisme,* launched a wide-ranging offensive: it demanded "a real social security law" that did not stop short at a "state takeover of a few existing institutions" (10 November 1945); it said that what the government was doing for older workers was inadequate (20 June 1946); it called for a campaign to help the elderly in conjunction with the Comité d'Entraide Sociale (Committee for Mutual Aid) (21–27 November 1946); and it attacked the CGT and the Communist Party under the headline "Trompe-t-on les vieux?" (Are the elderly being taken for a ride?) (15–21 August 1946). At this time, Christian labor unionism was mainly preoccupied with preserving labor union pluralism; the main thrust of its action was therefore aimed at the single fund, which it considered to be a threat to pluralism, given the CGT's dominant position in social security.

This chapter has described how it took two and a half years to build the basic framework of social security, from the National Resistance Council program in the spring of 1944 to the generalization of the old-age pension in the autumn of 1946. Throughout this period, the labor unions, particularly the most powerful of them, the CGT,[80] played a decisive role alongside left-wing political parties in the institution's foundation. The CGT had close ties with the Communist Party and was one of the most ardent defenders of the new social security plan. This chapter has shown that it constantly supported the plan, which had been drawn up by the administration, and unfailingly backed the projects of a government whose minister of labor and social security was also a Communist. The CGT was not only the key driving force behind social security, but also the brains behind its implementation.

THE PREDOMINANT ROLE PLAYED BY LABOR UNIONS IN BRINGING SOCIAL SECURITY INTO EXISTENCE

In 1955, Pierre Laroque, a major participant and observer of the period, wrote of labor union involvement in the following terms: "Until the first elections in 1947, the CGT had an absolute majority on almost all the management committees. CGT representatives formed dynamic and effective groups, and played a leading role in setting up the new organization. It owes them a great debt of gratitude."[81] The administration's project required a large number of complex administrative procedures to be carried out within an extremely short time, because the ordinances of October 1945 laid down that that plan was to come into effect on 1 July 1946: several hundred mutualist funds from the social insurance system of 1930 had to be merged into several dozen entirely new *département*-based and regional funds; "workplace accident" branches needed to be integrated; staff required regrading; and administrators had to be appointed and management teams put together.[82] These tasks were completed in time, thanks to the administrators and the efficiency of CGT activists. The administration needed the cooperation of the most powerful, most representative, and best-organized confederated union, and the CGT was capable of mobilizing a large number of disciplined, hard-working activists. For its part, the CGT used the situation for a variety of purposes: establishing a de facto virtual monopoly on social security (i.e., having a majority of seats on the committees); occupying the most important posts in the hierarchy; federating social security bodies; and making Henri Raynaud president of the federation, in charge of defending social security legislation and dealing with the supervisory administration at the national level.[83] It is worth noting that the CFTC made things easier for the CGT during this initial period by refusing to cooperate with the establishment of the "single fund" and turning down the offer of representation on its management committees.[84]

In the first social security elections on 25 February 1947, the CGT won 60 percent of the votes and retained its majority on most of the management committees, but with the CFTC receiving 26 percent, its influence was now waning. The constructive role played by the CGT throughout the brief period when social security was being set up explains the union's strong identification with the institution. This powerful bond uniting social security to the union was to endure: at the celebrations marking the thirtieth anniversary in 1975, social security was presented by the union as "a child of the CGT."[85] This explains why the union has often tried to assume the role of social security watchdog and guardian, and thereby aroused the hostility of its partners; a later section will examine this in further detail.

With the introduction of elections to management committees and the appearance of labor union pluralism in the system of social security management, the other confederated unions duly developed an enthusiasm for the institution and defended it against attempts at reform.

RETIREMENT AS A UNIVERSAL WORK-RELATED SOCIAL RIGHT AND AS AN EXPRESSION OF LABOR-UNION PHILOSOPHY

The foregoing analysis of the fundamental principles, genesis, and application of social security has shown how the institution reflected working-class thinking and activity. It also described the eclipse of employers and conservative political forces. Public policy on aging in 1945 introduced a social right to retirement for all workers. The right to subsistence and to a period of rest in later life was being demanded with increasing frequency by the working class, and it now had a basis in law.

The birth of social security, and the concomitant establishment of a universal and democratically managed right to retirement, reflected the labor union movement's power in the immediate postwar period and its political, economic, and social influence. However, this power would not have been enough to ensure success for its views on security if the unions had not established themselves deep inside the politico-administrative system.

At the time of the Liberation, the state, as mentioned, needed to restore its authority and legitimacy. It did so by reaffirming its protective role and turning itself into a welfare state, redistributing national revenues to the advantage of a powerful working-class movement whose cooperation was essential to the country's reconstruction. Working-class action was strongly conditioned by social interests represented in a political system that was almost structured by tripartism, and was largely dominated by the two political parties, the SFIO and the Communist Party, which most directly represented workers' interests. Three parties dominated the Constituent Assemblies and governed. The power of the working class was thus not only expressed in society, but was also to be found in the state. The Communists, who had a majority in the reunited CGT, had seats in government, and the labor union movement had also penetrated the administration. It is, therefore, hardly surprising that pension policy implemented at this time incorporated most labor union interests.

Occupational Segmentation of the Right to Retirement from 1947

A NEW SOCIOPOLITICAL CONJUNCTURE

Until almost halfway through the twentieth century, workers' pensions played a key role in the construction and rationalization of a new pay-related form of security, but paradoxically, they then triggered the permanent collapse of the plan for a unified social security scheme extended to the whole nation.

The 13 September 1946 act, which provided for old-age insurance to be generally available to all French citizens, accelerated the development of special occupational plans, and this in turn led to the fragmentation of the right to retirement. After being the spearhead of extended working-class security—and probably for that very reason—the issue of pensions was now a key element of the movement to break it up.

It was the question of retirement that united the traditional middle classes against the general application of social security. In order to defend their special pension rights, cadres (managerial staff) set up their own complementary plan, and introduced a two-tiered old-age insurance scheme that clearly implied an occupational stratification of old-age coverage. These initial reverses inflicted on the principle of united national solidarity were made worse by the establishment of complementary schemes for employees who were noncadres and their more widespread availability in the late 1950s. This section will now analyze the social dynamic that governed the fragmentation of the right to retirement.

The new dynamic took root because the specific conjuncture of social and political forces that facilitated the setting up of social security at the time of the Liberation had faded away. This decay took place in two ways:

1. The gradual weakening of ties forged during the Resistance among the three governing parties, and the reappearance of moderates and conservatives on the political scene, led to the break up of the tripartite coalition. This was followed by tenuous alliances between the SFIO and moderate center parties that were constantly collapsing; the result was a weak executive body that was acutely subservient to a parliament in which a wide range of social interests were expressed, but where those of the traditional and new middle classes were predominant.

2. The international situation, particularly the Cold War, caused a deep

rift in the labor union movement; this led to a marked drop in membership and a weaker structure. This decline in the power of the working-class movement in society was accompanied by a decline of its political influence within the state, a phenomenon marked by the departure of Communist ministers from the Ramadier government in May 1947 and the radicalization of the CGT.

In such a setting, there was an inexorable breakdown in the administration-CGT alliance that had played a major role in making the right to retirement universal. At the same time, the traditional and new middle classes established a front opposing it. This front found an extended parliamentary support as the developing political situation gave them more influence in the National Assembly. It also benefited from the support of employers ever anxious to limit the scope, and slow down the development, of a plan that had been imposed on it. The result of these changes was one of the first reversals for the right to retirement, which became less a common employment right than a right that could be varied according to each occupational group. These first blows to the principle of a universal right to retirement marked the evolution of a new balance of power among the three main agents of pension policy: the labor unions, the employers, and the state. It survived, one way or another, until the early 1960s. The new balance of forces stimulated an increase in the number of basic plans, as well as the emergence and proliferation of complementary plans. At the same time, it heralded a period of stagnation and cutbacks in the general scheme, which was now moving in the direction of a minimum plan.

THE FIRST BODY BLOWS: THE OPPOSITION FRONT FORMED BY THE TRADITIONAL AND NEW MIDDLE CLASSES

Special occupational plans and defeat for the universal right to retirement. The year 1947 witnessed some major political splits, and also saw the end of the universal right to retirement. The fragmentation of the social protection system by professional groups now prevailed over the idea of a single social security plan based on nationwide solidarity. The cadres' keen opposition to the government's plan since 1945 deepened in January 1947 with the publication of a decree that registered them in the social security plan.

A new confederation, the CGC (Confédération Générale des Cadres—General Confederation of Cadres), established a common front with the self-employed,[86] who also had to make old-age payments after 1 January 1947; this had been a provision of the 13 September 1946 act that made old-age insurance generally available. The prewar confederation of the middle classes was now reborn in the form of a national committee (Comité

National de Liaison et d'Action des Classes Moyennes—National Middle-Class Liaison and Action Committee) whose specific objective was to oppose the extension of old-age insurance.[87] On a broader front, it tried to become a body that opposed the forces that had come out of the Resistance, particularly the CGT and the Communist Party, in order to demonstrate that the middle classes could take on the political strength of the working class. Although the struggles waged by the cadres and the self-employed against old-age insurance did not follow exactly the same pattern or end in the same way, they had many points in common over and above the fact that they had formed an alliance of forces.

For these occupational groups, it was above all a question of preserving and publicizing their particular needs by refusing to be confused with the generality of wage earners in a single social security plan. This was particularly important as high inflation and monetary upheavals resulting from the war had wiped out their retirement savings. A great many older craft workers and shopkeepers had been left without any money, and even cadres had been driven to ask for the older workers' pension.[88] Workers in these categories were acutely aware of their distinctiveness and felt that they were in danger of being lumped together with the common run of worker and receiving only a uniform minimum pension.

The cadres were particularly sensitive on this point. The abolition of the earnings ceiling under the ordinances of 1945 meant the disappearance of their "respectability threshold,"[89] which had been the basis for an important set of social benefits organized by the employers.[90] The decision to abolish the earnings ceiling in fact imperiled their very existence, as the fixing of this ceiling had been a decisive factor in the construction of the social definition and identity of the cadres.[91] The CGC, which was formed in October 1944 but was not recognized as a representative body until 1946, ran a campaign opposing the disappearance of the cadres' special pension plan and supporting an autonomous scheme. In other words, pensions were acquiring an almost existential importance for cadres. Indeed, retirement remained one of the CGC's favorite themes for many years. On 24 June 1945, at its first national congress, the CGC general secretary had vigorously opposed the assimilation of cadres with other workers in the general old-age insurance plan, and had argued for differential treatment.

> We have neither the same mentality as small pensioners nor are we governed by the same rules. We suggest that, after years of loyal service, it should not be your ambition to retire to the country where you can top up your small pensions with a new job. We are not proposing that cadres worthy of the name should have this as their ambition. . . . When these men reach an age when they can no longer work, it is quite wrong to reserve for them a position that prevents them from having the status they enjoyed be-

fore, and force them to hide their poverty away in the depths of the countryside. It is therefore vitally necessary for cadres to receive a decent pension at the end of their working lives so that they can go on enjoying the same standard of living as before. . . . To achieve this, funded plans must be abandoned at once. We know their advantages. We know that the money deposited in them yields a profit and that we can gradually become entitled to larger sums than we have actually invested. But we are all aware of the sad experiences of the last few years. We know that devaluation has followed devaluation, that the value of money has gone down daily, that those of you who thought that a little pension of twenty thousand francs was ample for your needs now have hardly enough to live on for a month. It is therefore absolutely vital to replace this system with a pay-as-you-go plan that allows the real resources to be shared constantly among all members. The CGC was surely the first to study a complete plan, and to study it in depth, and we have finally come up with the following proposal: that a deduction of approximately 16 percent would provide a pension amounting to 60 percent of average salary or 50 percent of salary over the final few years. . . . What I am trying to say is that we also need to build up a bloc to oppose any government measure that aims at a uniform pension for all French citizens. . . . As for ourselves, we do not think everyone should get the same pension. Here too, each person's individual efforts should be taken into account and if one supervisor has worked harder than another, he ought to be able to get a better pension, and the same is true for everyone. We should therefore avoid moving in the direction of uniformity, and this is a point of view that we, as cadres, need to defend, because we can say with justifiable pride that we are not the kind of people who can be absorbed into a single mass. On the contrary, we are an elite that must rise above the masses; it is therefore legitimate for this elite to enjoy special conditions.[92]

The main problem for cadres was how to maintain their position in the hierarchy and thereby preserve their standard of living in retirement.[93] They perceived the redistributive aspect of the new social security system as an extra tax that cadres would have to pay without getting much benefit in return. Indeed, given that they had joined very recently, they could hope to draw only 40 percent of earnings up to a ceiling—already considerably lower than a cadre's real salary—when they retired after paying contributions for thirty years.[94] They wanted an insurance scheme, not a system of vertical redistribution.

The efforts of the self-employed not to be included in the social security old-age insurance system were also based on a defense of their professional autonomy: they objected to being placed in a single scheme with wage earners. They still regarded wage earners as semislaves who had been unable or unwilling to make the effort to free themselves from their alienated condition by climbing patiently up the social ladder until they could set up in business on their own. In the eyes of the self-employed, old-age insurance was all very well for those who were improvident and irresponsible enough not to have provided for their old age, but it ran totally counter to the small employer's ethic. The hostility of small employers towards social security was part of a rearguard action on security that they had been fighting since the early part of the century; Henri Hatzfeld's work on the origins of social protection has illustrated this with great skill. Small employers had always "had a braking effect" on the development of modern forms of social protection. As Hatzfeld makes clear, the stakes were high: "[I]t was above all a question of defending a type of society in which small property played an essential part."[95] By contrast, social security contained the seeds of another type of social organization, one founded on bureaucratic relationships and the regulatory intervention of the state; within it, individualism and entrepreneurial freedom were severely restricted.

Immediately after the Second World War, the self-employed still had every reason to believe in their individual ability to solve their problems of security.[96] Small business rediscovered a vitality that had long been lacking, and there were a number of spectacular successes. In these circumstances, there was little reason for small employers to agree to amalgamate with wage earners and be obliged to pay what they considered to be exorbitant sums for a form of interclass solidarity. This was the exact opposite of what they saw as their specific nature and identity, and it threatened their very existence; there was even less reason if, on joining the great structure made by and for the workers, they found themselves in a minority on the committees; as this chapter has shown, these were dominated by the labor unions. Like the cadres, workers were rejecting not so much the principle of compulsory insurance as the pay-as-you-go principle that characterized social security. Like them, they rejected national solidarity and opted for an occupationally based autonomous security plan, although they also hoped that the state would develop a policy of financial assistance that could see to the needs of the many elderly people who had no means of support. The resistance of the traditional and new middle classes to the general application of social security was based on the same preoccupation with defending specific socioprofessional plans. It could count on support from the same forces and alliances, even though the struggles were being fought in different ways and were achieving different ends.

Support for this middle-class opposition came from three main sources. First were the large employers. Then there were organizations such as the MRP and the CFTC, which, although sympathetic to social security, had always been opposed to the single fund and saw support for the middle-class campaign as a way of defeating this principle. Last, there were all the forces opposed to the Socialist and Communist majority that had come to power at the time of the Liberation; these attempted to halt the process of "extreme Socialist measures" that it had set in motion.

Action taken by cadres and the birth of the complementary pension plan: the National Agreement of 14 March 1947. As soon as the ordinances of October 1945 were published, the CGC embarked on a campaign that opposed the compulsory transfer of cadres and defended both their acquired rights and the survival of their private plan. It was later joined by the CFTC.[97] Then, on 12 December 1945, the CDIC (Comité de Défense du Personnel des Ingénieurs et Cadres Bénéficiant d'un Régime Particulier—Defense Committee for Engineers and Cadres belonging to a Special Plan) was set up, and it ran a campaign of sustained collective action until the signing of the 1947 agreement. The employers' intervention was decisive in the final phase of this conflict. The CDIC's defense of cadres' acquired rights might well not have defeated the united front formed by the confederal cartel of CGT cadres,[98] the government, and the administration, if the CNPF had not proposed a complementary pension plan. This safeguarded the cadres' benefits and kept them on the social security register, and it was also acceptable to the CGT cartel and the government. Negotiations on the CNPF's proposals culminated in the signing of the National Collective Agreement of 14 March 1947 between the CNPF and the labor unions (CGT, CFTC, and CGC); it was this that gave birth to the cadres' pension and savings plan.

The employers' motives for intervening now were the same as when they had set up the cadres' insurance scheme in 1937: they wished to reaffirm their proximity to employers and senior managers[99] at a time when their employed status was drawing closer to that of working people, and they wanted to ensure their loyalty.[100] There was probably an additional, related aim of encouraging labor unionism among cadres by helping the CGC to become established.

The employers' role in this conflict also shows their general attitude towards the new organization of social security:

• They were opposed to the principle of redistribution of national revenues on which the system was founded. The setting up of a complementary plan enabled them to reintroduce insurance methods, which they preferred, and allowed them to restore the role of the insurance companies; the latter had been excluded from the management of social protection under the terms of the ordinances.

• As the employers had only a minority of seats on the social security management committees, and therefore very little power, the new system of equal representation gave them more control over the management of wage-related welfare benefits.

• They were also opposed to the general application of social security, a development that they saw as a "state takeover," and argued for the idea of a social security system with separate categories for different occupational groups. The employers therefore supported, more or less directly, all movements opposed to general application, and worked tirelessly for the occupational fragmentation of solidarity. As far as the cadres were concerned, this fragmentation was partly achieved by setting up a complementary plan, and noncadres were not slow to benefit from this initiative. There was complete fragmentation in the case of the self-employed, and this effectively halted the generalization of social security.

Action taken by the self-employed for autonomous pension plans: the 17 January 1948 act. The passing of the 13 September 1946 act, which brought forward the general application of old-age insurance, met with vehement opposition from the many professional organizations concerned; their response took the form of public meetings, interventions, and the publication of tracts.

The successful campaign of the self-employed culminated in the 17 January 1948 act. This established a number of pension funds based on narrow professional solidarity, but these soon proved ineffective. Four autonomous pension schemes were then set up for shopkeepers and industrialists (ORGANIC),[101] craft workers (CANCAVA),[102] members of the liberal professions, and farmers.[103] It was a triumph for the segmentation of solidarity on a narrow occupational basis. The fundamental principles of the general social security plan were discredited, and the single fund and extensive redistribution of national revenue to the whole population fell apart, with social security confined to wage earners. This middle-class opposition had succeeded because of the favorable political climate in which it had been operating.

The elections to the legislature of 10 November 1946 left the Communists and Socialists in a minority, while the Right and Center both increased their votes.[104] While the three-party government held onto its majority, it was deeply divided ideologically. It collapsed a few months later, on 5 May 1947, with the Communist ministers walking out of the Ramadier government. A third force made up of fragile alliances then appeared on the scene. In order to form a government, the Christian Democrats and SFIO had to join forces with the Center and Right; the latter groupings held the balance of power, and were therefore in a position to ensure that their views were adopted. The middle classes now gained influence in the political system;[105] they also became a more powerful force in society with the setting up of the National Middle-Class Liaison and Action Committee, a new body that brought together the old and new middle classes.

The middle classes had the backing of the National Assembly and refused to obey the law and pay contributions. They also enjoyed continuous and discreet support from large employers ever anxious to check the extension of a system of social protection about which it had grave reservations. However, they were not in a position to express these reservations freely,[106] partly because of the broad-based popular movement that supported the setting up of social security and partly because they were poorly represented in the assembly. In this context, it was Parliament that held the key to power.

The first damaging blow to workers' universal and unified right to retirement was delivered by the traditional and new middle classes, when the universal right was targeted for certain occupational categories. The support that the middle classes found in their struggle for special pension rights made it clear that a new balance of power was now in existence. This soon manifested itself in a proliferation of complementary plans for noncadres and these gave rise to a wide range of occupational plans inspired by the system used by cadres.

EMERGENCE AND SPREAD OF COMPLEMENTARY PENSION PLANS FOR NONCADRES BETWEEN 1948 AND 1961; LABOR UNION DISILLUSIONMENT WITH WHAT HAD BEEN ACHIEVED

A right to a period of rest or the right to poverty? A previous section of this book has described the key role played by the working class in the birth of social security, but the end of 1947 heralded a period of disillusionment: the "right to a period of rest" achieved for older workers also turned out to be a "right to poverty."[107] Gaps in provision for the elderly, which were becoming increasingly intolerable with the end of postwar shortages and the beginnings of growth in the early 1950s, were due to two main factors. First, under the 1945 ordinances, old age had been sacrificed to the imperatives of reconstruction. Priority was given equally to the needs of the labor force and to ensuring its renewal through the implementation of a policy supporting a rising birth rate. From the start, old-age pensions did not provide an adequate income; in fact, no pensioner could hope to receive a full pension before 1960, since it required thirty years of contributions.

Second, and taking into account the fact that it was far from generous in the early stages, old-age coverage suffered more than other programs of the French social security system from the stagnation that affected the general scheme and the resulting competition between risks. Not only was there no notable improvement in old-age benefits during this period, but they never reached even the minimum level that had been fixed by Directorate of Social Security experts in 1945. Senior officials had estimated that there needed to be a 9 percent contribution from wages to fund old-age benefits, but this was ignored, and it never went higher than 7 percent.[108] The excess could have been used to build up reserves to provide credit for years of service for retirees who had not contributed (as complementary plans were later to do), thus permitting an immediate improvement in benefits. Instead, it was used to mop up deficits in other risks—first family allowances, and later health insurance—whose costs were rising rapidly. This had the advantage of allowing the increase in the rate of social contributions to be more or less contained, and old-age insurance accordingly acted as a minimum assistance scheme during this period.

According to a survey of nine hundred retirees carried out in July 1946, nearly half were dissatisfied with their material situation,[109] with only 29 percent expressing satisfaction. In 1948, out of the 2,200,000 old-age pensioners in the general scheme, nearly half of them (1,015,000) received no more than a noncontributory pension, the AVTS. By law, pensioners were supposed to receive a sum rising to 40 percent of wages over their final ten years; however, in 1957, when the pensions of those who had been contributing since 1930 were approaching maturity,[110] they still only represented 25 percent of average pensionable salary.

These figures give an indication of the appalling living conditions of noncadres, whose only replacement income on retirement was old-age insurance. This was usually very close to the minimum set by the noncontributory benefit for older workers.[111] Given this dreadful poverty, the labor unions were forced into a double maneuver; they had to defend a vital minimum standard for older workers, or "life's victims"[112] as they were called, and to seek an improved right to retirement for those still working; furthermore, these better retirement rights had to be more than just a "right to charity." This dual strategy structured labor union action throughout the period.

An analysis of the labor union press throws light on what lay behind these two issues that were at the forefront of all three unions' activities throughout the period under examination. Virtually all the articles on old age or retirement dealt with them. The headlines alone are a good indication of what the unions' central preoccupations were; the most important of CGT and CFTC concerns are set out below. Much space was devoted to a guaranteed minimum right for the elderly, and it featured in over 50 percent of all articles.

Headlines in *Le Peuple* included the following:

"The elderly are tired of waiting" (26 December 1949)

"What happened to the 120 billion francs that belonged to the elderly?" (Henri Raynaud, 1 January 1951; article dealing with the fact that part of the

9 percent assigned to old-age insurance was redirected to health insurance)

"Urgent need to raise the AVTS. Another 40 billion francs should be given to older workers" (1 June 1952)

"No more misery for older workers!" (1 October 1957)

Syndicalisme, the journal of the CFTC, placed even greater emphasis on the minimum right following the union's 1954 bill on setting up a Fonds National Vieillesse (National Old-Age Fund), a national retirement pension financed out of taxes:

"The state is not giving our old people the right to subsistence" (1948)

"Old-age insurance consigns the elderly to the scrap-heap" (1951)

"The CFTC bill: a solution to the poverty of the elderly" (1954)

"Make way for the elderly! This is the progress that we need to make if we are to do away with the grinding poverty of the elderly" (1955)

"The National Old-Age Fund, and the struggle for a decent minimum for all retired people" (1956)

The second dominant theme of the period was the campaign to defend and improve the right to retirement. It took on a new dimension in the early 1950s. The CGT relentlessly criticized the inadequacy of old-age provision under social security, and repeatedly made the point that a percentage of the contributions earmarked for old age was redirected mainly to health benefits. The other confederations also defended the working-class achievement of setting up social security and argued for improved pensions and a lower retirement age. Furthermore, they initiated negotiations with the employers about complementary schemes earlier than the CGT, which continued to voice its reservations about the "setting up of 'in-house' pension schemes" (*Le Peuple*, 7 February 1952).

This two-pronged union action necessitated by the deplorable situation of older workers had its contradictions. There was a danger, for example, that the campaign to give the elderly population a minimum living standard would, if successful, absorb all public finance in the area of old age, and ultimately transform old-age provision into provision of a basic minimum. This danger was accentuated by the fact that such an objective suited both the employers, who hoped to see the general scheme evolve into a minimum scheme, and the unwaged, who would be the first to benefit from measures incorporating a guaranteed minimum.[113] This concordance destabilized state action, and precipitated the transformation of the general scheme into a basic minimum scheme. This development was, of course, contrary to the second labor union aim, which was to defend and extend the working-class achievement of a general right to retirement.

Retirees could not be allowed any longer to "live on a pittance";[114] retirement had to provide an adequate pension that guaranteed a real right to subsistence and to a period of rest in old age.

Growing impatience. Accelerated work processes, combined with incipient growth in the economy, intensified workers' struggles against alienation and exploitation. These frequently took the form of requests for a reduction in working hours. More particularly, however, they involved a demand for an extension of the right to a period of rest at the end of the working life; this included both an improvement in the level of pensions and a lower age of entitlement to retirement on a full pension. All the labor unions adopted this claim in the early 1950s. From that time onwards, they called repeatedly for improvements in old-age provision under the general scheme. This demand broke down as follows:

1. lowering the age of retirement on full pension to sixty for men and fifty-five for women;
2. increasing the full rate from 40 percent to 50 percent of average wages, and raising the contributions ceiling;
3. fixing a minimum guaranteed pension at 50 percent of the minimum guaranteed interprofessional wage.[115]

The unions considered that higher productivity encroached on the hard-won right to retirement, in that accelerated work rates forced older workers to withdraw sooner from the alienation of capitalist relations.[116] To quote Henri Raynaud, secretary general of the CGT: "At a time when the intensification of working conditions and methods is leading to premature exhaustion, and making it difficult for redundant workers to find work after the age of fifty, the demand for retirement at 60 is the most widely supported of all workers' demands."[117]

While it was defensible, "given the state of the economy, to ask the workers to redouble their efforts" in 1945, it was no longer justified as the economy picked up, "especially as the rate of production [was] becoming increasingly exhausting and piecework [was] becoming the norm."[118] Given these working conditions, the preservation of the right to retirement at the end of the working life meant a lower retirement age.[119] The extension of the right to retirement and the lowering of retirement age now became increasingly important issues for labor unions, and this development was accompanied by a growing contradiction between acceleration in the pace of work, which made it difficult to carry on working after a certain age, and stagnation in pensions, which obliged elderly people to carry on in employment.[120] The unions were also losing patience with a general scheme that was no longer making any headway.

Ambivalent demands. The union emphasis on lowering the retirement age in the early 1950s underlines the ambivalent nature of this demand. Bringing forward retirement age might have been seen as a dynamic demand designed to extend the right to a period of rest at the end of the working life, based on the work actually performed during that time. In fact, it showed a certain defeatism on the workers' part. This chapter has already shown how the origins of the demand lay in the deterioration of working conditions, and in the difficulties that older workers increasingly faced in doing their jobs and in remaining on the labor market. It was as if the labor unions were banking on retirement because they had failed to improve working conditions and vary them according to the employee's age. In other words, retirement now had the task of compensating for a lifetime of injustice and toil. However, there was also the danger that this revenge for a lifetime of alienating work was an illusion. It is well established that life in retirement is always an exact reproduction of one's former working life and leisure time.[121] This suggests that the demand for a lower retirement age was less an attempt to win the right to a period of rest than an acknowledgment of impotence and failure at dealing with poor working conditions. Moreover, this approach to retirement reduced it to the status of a counterpart, or inverted image, of work. It avoided any examination of what retirement itself is like, and encouraged people to underestimate the problems associated with it. Significantly, throughout the period 1945–75, the labor union press dealt with old age only in terms of the struggle to maintain and extend the right to retirement, and action in defense of old people's right to subsistence and thus access to a minimum income. Labor union campaigns focused on the level of pensions and the lower age at which they should be granted. Articles in *Le Monde* between 1946 and 1975 indicate that each time labor union voices were raised in the general debate about old age, they mainly referred to demands or action regarding pension schemes and/or the age of retirement.[122] Another theme was the defense of elderly people's standard of living; this reflected impatience with, and disappointment at, the inadequacies of the retirement system. Employment was not raised as a labor union issue until late in the debate, in 1972.[123]

On the other hand, there were hardly any labor union interventions whatsoever relating to the way of life of the elderly. Of the lifestyle aspects most frequently denounced by the labor unions, as featured in *Le Monde,* the two main themes throughout the period were late retirement age and the inadequacy of pensions. The unions also joined forces with other bodies such as opposition parties, charitable associations, and specialists to criticize the low level of public spending on old age and the atrocious living conditions imposed on the elderly population. By contrast, neither the guillotine effect of retirement nor the isolated or marginalized situation of the elderly figured in any of the labor union criticism.

It is therefore clear from an analysis of *Le Monde* that the most appropriate issues for labor union intervention were the elderly population's right to retirement and right to subsistence. The place of old age in the system of transfers and its role in the redistribution of resources were central to labor union perspectives. By contrast, lifestyle problems, as distinct from the standard of living, were constantly underestimated.

Marking time in an impasse. While the combination of disgraceful treatment of the elderly and accelerated work rates made an extended right to retirement even more urgent, old-age provision under the general scheme was stagnating. No measures were taken to stop deficits in health insurance from being made good at the expense of old-age insurance. The labor union press constantly expressed indignation at this situation throughout the period 1950–60 and denounced the large sums of which the elderly were "defrauded."[124] As far as retirement age was concerned, the authorities seemed disinclined to lower it. On the contrary, they issued a number of disturbing statements about the continued growth of the elderly population in France, and the increasingly heavy burden on the adult population that resulted from this, and called for the working life to be extended.[125]

Old-age insurance ran into two kinds of problems: deterioration, and ultimately paralysis, in the internal functioning of the institution; and a new balance of power on the political scene, facilitating the survival of defensive majorities that were capable of blocking regression but incapable of stimulating improvement.

Deterioration in the way social security operated. During the institution's first few years of existence, there continued to be cooperation between the administration and the CGT. However, relations between the management committees and the state went into a downward spiral. There were two main reasons for this. First, labor unions became increasingly confrontational: this was particularly noticeable after the 1950 social security elections in which the CGT lost majority control. The union changed its attitude completely and became very critical and hostile,[126] and this in turn led to the formation of anti-CGT alliances between non-Communists on the committees. Unremitting interunion rivalry also diminished the administrators' sense of responsibility, and social security became less successful at fulfilling its objectives, and even changed its aims. Second, this led to increasingly suspicious supervision by the state from 1950 onwards,[127] especially as the minister of finance could not ignore the escalating sums involved. As time went by, his interventions became increasingly forceful. This closer supervision took two main forms: regulations that gradually took control of the funds' budgets, and reform in the way social security worked. The latter was imposed by the 1960 decrees and was, in the words of Antoinette Catrice-Lorey, "an external response to a situation that had deteriorated. "

Increasingly fierce interventions by the state met with "provocative" and "guerrilla" responses from the managers, and the result was that "supervision" and the "institution" were isolated and became rival forces.[128] The permanent confrontation meant that all initiatives were blocked at the level of the institution itself. Old-age coverage ground to a halt, and workers' confidence in the general scheme faltered; moreover, some people even began to feel that company-level and sectoral complementary plans, over which the state had very little control, were preferable to a scheme in which the "power to prevent" was of more significance than the principle of social democracy that had inspired its foundation.

Labor union claims grind to a halt. The unions never succeeded in extending the right to retirement. In fact, none of their claims relating to old-age insurance ever became law, and the Boulin Act of 1971 was the first piece of favorable legislation. Between 1948 and 1960, the only public policy to see the light of day related to minimum old-age provision; even here, the process was laborious, and culminated in the adoption in 1955 of the National Old-Age Fund. This was an essentially symbolic measure taken on the eve of the elections, and was reformulated into the National Solidarity Fund under the 26 July 1956 Act. The latter legislation was innovative in that it was based on the principle of solidarity, but it was hardly any more generous than the basic statutory public assistance.

Significantly, even in the public debate on old age as presented in *Le Monde*, the unions were no longer able to win the day on old age or their definition of the right to retirement. In 1946 and 1947, the debate had centered on retirement policy (70 percent of articles in 1946, 38 percent of articles in 1947), but from 1948 onward there was a new dominant theme. In 1948 and 1949, the policy of minimum old-age provision and the question of noncontributory allowances came to the fore and featured in 60 percent of articles. These questions were usually presented for public debate by political institutions such as the government, assemblies, and political parties, and very rarely by the labor unions, but this nonetheless marked the high point in the popularity of pensions; retirement policy took second place with 40 percent of articles. From 1950 to 1959, the gap between the two themes widened: the policy of noncontributory allowances occupied most of the debate, and was the one most frequently referred to;

meanwhile, the question of pensions figured in the public debate mainly as a result of labor union claims and came only second or third. During the period 1951–54, 26 percent of articles dealt with retirement (in terms of policy or demands) compared with around 11 percent for the period 1955–59.

During the period under examination, therefore, the unions failed to secure victory for their demands in the public debate or in legislation. Their only success lay in blocking attempts to jeopardize what they called employees' "acquired pension rights." Particularly memorable was a large-scale mobilization triggered by a Laniel government decree raising the age of retirement in certain special plans. This brought all rail and other public services to a halt during the summer of 1953 and provided an indication of working-class enthusiasm for pension plans, notwithstanding their imperfections. It also put an end to the government's projects for raising age limits and retirement age, which, as this chapter has described, were often mooted during this period because of labor shortages. In other words, there was a blocking majority capable of defending old-age insurance from attack, and this defensive role was carried out by the labor unions, left-wing parties, and the MRP. The Pinay government was overthrown under similar circumstances in December 1951 when a minor bill was proposed to fund social security out of taxation. However, there were no longer sufficiently powerful forces in the country to impose reforms and advance the development of a general pension scheme, which was slowly becoming ossified. Moreover, the decline in the power of the unions, which was very marked over this period, prevented them from imposing their views, as they had done immediately after the Liberation. Their membership had collapsed,[129] and their influence in the political system and the state had declined with the "disintegration"[130] of the labor union movement as a whole. The forces opposing social security were meanwhile gathering strength.

The temptation to favor fragmentation as a way out of the impasse. While old-age protection was evolving in the direction of minimum provision, workers were increasingly being tempted to find a remedy for the inadequacy of old-age coverage in the complementary pension plans run by companies. The CFTC and CGT-FO were the first to decide in the 1950s that it would be easier to find a way out of the impasse, and obtain improvements in the pension system, through step-by-step negotiations with employers rather than in confrontation with the state. Until 1958, the CGT maintained that "the first thing to do was to move in the direction of the General Scheme,"[131] while acknowledging that "complementary pension plans meet a vital need of workers,"[132] and that, from 1960 onwards, they were in a better position to "satisfy workers' demands as they were less subject to government supervision than social security."[133] Disillusionment with the pension system prompted the unions to opt for the lesser of two evils, and this fitted in with the pension initiatives of the big employers, who, as a later section will show, wanted to vary the right to retirement according to their labor requirements or tactical objectives. At the time of the UNIRS negotiations in 1957, Roger Mario of the CGT spoke of "the distressing situation of old people in France, which has forced those still working to look for a pension plan that provides better coverage, and this has in turn caused complementary old-age pension plans to spring up all over the country" (*Le Peuple*, 15 January 1957). Similarly, in an overview of complementary plans in his report to the Economic and Social Council (session of 10 July 1962), Mr. Mathevet (CFTC) described how workers and labor unions had fought for complementary pensions because of "the shortcomings of the social security general scheme" and its "ossification," for which the state was responsible. Mr. Lucas of the CFTC also admitted, "If it had been possible, we would have preferred to obtain an increase in contributions, and therefore in the general scheme, but at the time the employers were hostile to the idea."[134]

The state encouraged an understanding between employers and unions because it had to cope with the aging of the French population and the growing deficit in health benefits, and wanted to restore more responsibility for social protection to employers and employees. Everything was in place for a rapid breakup of the social right to retirement, and its replacement by a proliferation of complementary plans whose very existence was an impediment to a common, universal right to retirement.

The evolving public debate, insofar as it can be reconstructed from a thematic analysis of articles in *Le Monde,* reflects these transformations. The theme of pensions gradually returned to prominence and occupied first place in nearly 30 percent of articles during the period 1960–67; meanwhile, the previously predominant issue of monetary benefits lost much ground and during 1960–67 was featured in only 18 percent of articles.[135] However, the question of pensions was now taking on an entirely new form: it was no longer a matter of public retirement policy, as it had been in 1946–47; the debate was no longer about institutions and the establishment of the workers' right to retirement; and it no longer examined the legislative process through which the general retirement system was being constructed. From the late 1950s onward, the pensions debate was framed in contractual terms, and the employers and unions discussed and negotiated joint agreements on complementary pensions.[136] This shift in the debate merely reflected the increased fragmentation of the right to retirement that took place during this period. Retirement was no longer a common employment right; it had become a matter to be negotiated between the social partners, and the change led to a proliferation of arrangements for different work categories and the occupational stratification of the right to retirement. Accordingly, the labor union position of a universal and unified right fell by the wayside, although pensions were at least improved under the new agreements.

THE EMPLOYERS' BID TO RELAUNCH PENSIONS AS A WORKFORCE POLICY AND A TACTICAL INSTRUMENT

In 1948 the big employers resumed their long-standing tradition of setting up employers' retirement funds, and these automatically triggered complementary pension plans for noncadres both in companies and in industrial sectors such as food, book and cement production.

The conditions for benefiting from these plans reveal their neopaternalist origins. They were designed to ensure the employee's loyalty to the company or job, as the right to a complementary pension was always dependent on conditions of seniority and age, conditions often quite strict. Once again, pensions had been partly reintroduced as a reward for workers' docility and loyalty; it was an additional benefit that employers could vary depending on how prosperously the company was faring and on their labor requirements.

The employers made use of complementary pensions for three main purposes. First, complementary pension plans were able to stabilize the workforce. Before 1950, when wages came under state control, a pension plan was one of the few substitutes for a pay policy in which the employers had no say.[137] Then, under the 11 February 1950 Act which reintroduced free collective bargaining, benefits could be negotiated as part of company or intercompany agreements.

Second, complementary pension plans were a way of getting rid of older workers who were considered unsuitable for the work process, and a means of rejuvenating the age pyramid. It should be borne in mind that the period also saw the development of a number of contradictory trends. Employers, and more particularly those running large companies, were very reluctant to employ older workers. Industrial employers had already expressed their reluctance in this respect in 1946, even though it was a time of serious labor shortages, as Daric's examination of the period shows:

> When industrialists are asked about extending the working lives of their employees, they raise a number of objections. The most frequent of these relate to the decline in working efficiency that comes with age. They stress that the increasingly rigid organization of production, the concern to achieve the highest possible productivity at the lowest possible cost, combined with the necessity to make expensive equipment pay for itself quickly, encouraged them to look for employees in good physical health so as to be able to

> make the best possible use of them. They consider that such demands are incompatible with the employment of workers whose physical well-being declines with age. They also stress that production methods are changing so rapidly that only a young workforce can adapt to new techniques, and be trained to use them rapidly. Mass-production processes, especially work on an assembly line, discourage the employment of older workers who are not able to keep up. Some people also maintain that the risk of industrial and work-related accidents and illnesses is higher among older workers, and this increases the cost of insurance. Other arguments include the fact that younger workers can be taken on at lower rates than those commanded by older workers, and some managers argue the need to employ young staff for certain jobs involving direct contact with the public.
>
> Resistance to the employment of older workers increased as companies got bigger (because of the need for stricter collective discipline, with individuals losing their identity in an anonymous mass), and with the introduction of greater mechanization and rationalization. Where standardized production norms were the rule, that is to say where there was a predominance of specialized operations, the employment of older workers was considered difficult, and possibly quite undesirable.[138]

Employer prejudice about employing older workers was even more apparent in a survey carried out by IFOP in 1961.[139] Not one employer wanted the legal age of retirement to exceed sixty-five, and as many as 60 percent opted for sixty; in other words, retirement age was felt to be too high from the point of view of productivity. Furthermore, the low level of pensions kept older workers at work and prevented employers from "condemning them to poverty."[140] The introduction of complementary pensions resolved this dilemma by increasing them by about 50 percent.[141] As one employer in textiles said in response to the 1961 survey, "We are currently reviewing this policy of keeping staff on after retirement age. With complementary pensions, we will have fewer scruples in our dealings with the elderly."[142]

Third, complementary pensions had a tactical value for those who had introduced them—in this case, the employers. An example was the Renault agreements of 15 September 1955, which placed an obligation on the company to provide noncadres with complementary pensions; these had such an impact that they may be said to have been the basis for the UNIRS and ARRCO agreements,[143] and were clearly intended to put an end to the unrest then prevalent in the metallurgy sector of western France (Nantes and St. Nazaire) and spreading to the Paris region. In the event, they succeeded in restoring calm.[144] The complementary pension agreements also enabled employers to maintain and deepen labor union divisions throughout the period by increasing the standing of the CFTC and CGT-FO, with which agreements had been signed, and by isolating the CGT. The latter union was usually excluded from the negotiations and was only later party to the agreements; this applied to the Renault, UNIRS, and ARRCO agreements in particular.

The employers' initiative in setting up complementary pension plans therefore reflected their constant concern to make retirement an instrument of personnel management. By introducing these plans, the employers were actually striking a double blow. They not only provided themselves with an extra tool for controlling the quality and flow of the workforce, but also counteracted the development of the general scheme and, in so doing, moved from making criticism to offering a counterproposal. Their private plans corrected two fundamental errors that they believed had been committed in 1945. First, they introduced a new way of distributing power in the management of the pension funds. Employers had been in a small minority on the social security management committees, where their very presence had been contested by the CGT since 1950, but the new plans gave them an equal, if not predominant, role.[145] Second, the complementary plans restored priority to insurance, which the employers consistently preferred to pay-as-you-go. Workers' rights were guaranteed only to the extent that their contributions made them money. It was as if the employers, conscious of the impossibility of backtracking in the area of social security, had merely worked out solutions that suited their views. These formed an alternative to the development of the old-age branch of social security, which they were secretly trying to block. The employers' strategy on retirement is illustrated by its attitude towards social security contributions. At the same time as they vigorously opposed an increase in employers' contributions, which in their view was a severe handicap to the competitiveness of French industry,[146] they set up complementary pension plans[147] whose cost was often borne by the company alone and was far higher than the increase in employers' contributions. The employers' attitude can be understood only in light of the economic and political benefits they gained in return for additional social advantages, which could in a way be deducted from the expense incurred. As for the general scheme, they never got any of their money back, as it fed a system over which they had very little control, even though they saw themselves as its main sponsors.

The initiative taken by the employers in setting up complementary plans was clearly in line with their thinking, and reflected the success they had had in imposing their definition of the right to retirement. It was no longer a question of a common, universal right to retirement. That definition, which had been imposed by the labor unions at the time of the Liberation, was now reduced to a minimum right to subsistence. The right to retirement was henceforth segmented, and could be varied according to a company's economic capacity, its pay and employment policies, and various tactical considerations.

The employers were able to impose their definition of the right to retirement, because they were now back in the political arena, following their eclipse at the time of the Liberation. With the resurgence of right-wing political forces, they were once more able to count on parliamentary support, and their rehabilitation under the plan allowed them to establish closer links with the administration.[148] Their greater strength on the political and administrative scene also enabled them to give clearer expression to their reservations about a general pension plan that had been imposed on them, and over which they had little control.[149] Throughout the period, they concentrated on containing the plan, with a view to turning it into a minimum assistance scheme. The priority given to complementary pension plans reflected the fact that they wanted to redirect the system of old-age risk protection so that it tallied with their constant concern to subordinate social policy to economic imperatives and personnel management.

THE STATE CAUGHT IN A TRAP

The state, which was synonymous with the Fourth Republic for much of the period under examination, had very little capacity for autonomous action. With the breakup of the three-party government, there was a move towards a multiparty system. The Right and Center held the balance of power through complex alliances between the Christian Democrats and Socialists and, in an assembly system where Parliament held all the power, the state was extensively penetrated by a range of diverse social interests through the mediation of the party system. Divisions within the working class, the decline of the SFIO, and the Communist Party's move to the opposition ranks meant that working-class interests henceforth had less influence in the political system and the state, and that the middle classes and their interests were largely predominant both in Parliament and in the Executive that reflected it.[150] The ossification of the general pension scheme underlined the state's powerlessness to act. It was caught between a rock and a hard place: on one hand, growing opposition to the principle of national solidarity as the basis of social security (right-wing parties, employers, and traditional and new middle classes); on the other, the maintenance of a defensive majority in the Assembly large enough to save the general pension scheme from collapse. The state was paralyzed, and it accordingly restricted itself to the implementation of a policy of assistance for the elderly and minimum cash benefits: the *carte d'économiquement faible* (poverty card) and the National Solidarity Fund. These enjoyed a fairly broad, favorable consensus in the country at large, provided that the budget remained modest. The state was also caught in the health insurance trap, and handed over responsibility for improving provision for the elderly to negotiations between employers and workers. This laissez-faire policy inevitably led to a decline in national solidarity. General scheme pensions were very close to being minimum plans; they were crushed by a ceiling that was rising too slowly, squeezed by the priority given to family assistance (and later on by an increasingly expensive health insurance scheme) and weighed down by the assistance payments (from the National Solidarity Fund) that the state transferred to the general pension scheme in 1958.[151] State withdrawal from this area also resulted in the gradual segmentation of the right to retirement, as employers and workers gradually reached agreements in certain sectors and for the benefit of certain categories of worker. This gave rise to the anarchical development of private pension plans and to the reemergence of insurance companies as managers.

The many schemes that were set up[152] had few of the hoped-for guarantees of durability and presented the promoters with serious problems. In their anxiety to return much of the responsibility for the provision of the elderly to the social partners, the state encouraged the reorganization and general availability of complementary pensions. They facilitated the establishment of the UNIRS and ARRCO[153] through exemption from the insurance tax on contracts between insurance companies and pension funds that gave them the right to manage their capital (20 February 1958 act). Thus, at the very time when the government was having the greatest difficulty in funding the National Solidarity Fund—it eventually made it the responsibility of old-age insurance—it was helping to set up complementary plans; these ensured the downfall of old-age insurance, transformed it into a minimum plan, and reduced the capacity for public action in this field.

Conclusion: The Social Dynamic of Producing a Retirement Policy

This chapter has shown how the fragmentation of the right to retirement followed profound changes in the balance of power that had triggered the establishment of social security.

Divisions in the labor union movement and its declining power prevented any further extension of the right to retirement, and the unions permitted a tactical withdrawal only to preserve the rights won at the time of the Liberation. From then on, alternative forms of complementary pension drawn up by employers gradually appeared to be the only way out of the impasse created by the paralysis in public pensions policy. What the employers hoped was to reformulate the right to retirement in such a way as to subordinate it to the demands of production. The common, universal right to retirement was then cut back and topped up with a fragmentary right to retirement dependent on economic or tactical imperatives. Negotiations between the unions and employers led to national agreements, UNIRS and ARRCO, which got rid of the most blatant instances of employer largesse and led to a system that, through equal representation, gave employers far more power in the complementary schemes than they had had in the general scheme.

An occupationally based contractual pension plan was then superimposed on the general scheme. It spawned a wide range of pension plans and rights, at a pace dictated by the prosperity of the economic sector involved,[154] in a way, this made the noncadre pension plan more like the scheme that had been open to cadres since 1947. The contractual pension policy was clearly effective, as it made possible a considerable increase in retirees' replacement income, and therefore a significant improvement in their living standards. A corollary of this, however, was that it helped not only to perpetuate, but also to accentuate, inequalities in the socioprofessional status of retirees. In this sense, it can be seen as a way of dismantling part of the original plan for a single system of solidarity for all French citizens. Another interpretation is to see in the success of the complementary pension plans the decline of the exclusively bureaucratic machinery, and victory for civil society and the occupational groups that made it up; the latter then acquired more autonomous responsibility for the management of old-age pensions. Whichever reading is correct, it is certain that occupational fragmentation of the right to retirement and resulting variations were the expression of the waning of the working-class struggles over retirement, and the prevalence of reformulations that favored the middle classes and employers in different ways.

This analysis of the formation and evolution of French pension policy concludes with an attempt to summarize the outcome, and then shed light on the social dynamics underpinning the policy. The particular forms taken by pensions at any one time were the result of a complex web of disputes, negotiations, and agreements involving unions and employers—or, more precisely, different sections of those two forces. Each of the parties drew up a definition of retirement in accordance with the place it occupied in social relations and associated interests, and then tried to impose it. For the labor unions, the issue was the fixing of a right to retirement for workers; they wanted to establish rights for older workers, who would thus escape the alienation of being a labor commodity and enter a stage of remunerated disalienation. By contrast, the employers wanted to subordinate the treatment of the elderly to the imperatives of the production system, and therefore to turn retirement into a mere instrument of labor management.

This chapter has demonstrated that the development of pensions as a social wage took place within the dialectical movement of employers' and workers' struggles. Successive redefinitions reflected confrontations between these two groups and the balance of power between them. The prevalence of the formulation of retirement as a work-related social right reflected a social balance that favored Labor, whereas the predominance of the idea of retirement as a factor that contributed to personnel management and its adaptation to production imperatives reflected a balance favoring Capital. State action in the field of pensions mainly consisted of giving shape to the definition prevalent at any given time, and consequently arbitrating to a certain extent between the two. The legal forms taken by retirement can be interpreted as a function of the complex interplay of these three forces. As an earlier section has shown, the Social Insurance Act was notable for employers' initiatives in the field of retirement, and linked the level of contributions to the preexisting price of the workforce. The social security plan established a general right to retirement based on a broad system of redistribution, and reflected a balance of power that was heavily weighted in favor of the working-class movement at the time. The working class not only dominated society but also penetrated the state extensively, and succeeded in imposing many of its interests with respect to retirement policy. However, neither of these state retirement plans was a simple transcription of the dominant interests of the day; rather, they were the embodiment of social agreements that bore the marks of the state in its capacity as a unifier and agent of change.

The evolution of the retirement system in the direction of occupational segmentation reflected not only a decline in union power and the rise of the middle classes in the political system and state but also, following a brief eclipse at the time of the Liberation, the political reemergence of employers. The latter tried to hinder the development of a social security plan that, in terms of principle and organization, was too close to the labor union issue of security. To this end, both they and the middle classes took action on two fronts. First, they adopted initiatives in the field of retirement designed to promote their own definition of it. Second, they encouraged an uprising against old-age insurance that was carried out by middle-class people keen to defend their place in the hierarchy and their corporate interests, and anxious to bring about a stratification of the retirement system. The state's capacity for autonomous action had been reduced by the advent of the Fourth Republic, and the general old-age scheme was now stagnating. This in turn made it more dependent on the political system and its parties.

There were still forces in society powerful enough to defend the scheme, but they were no longer dynamic enough to guarantee its development. The state accordingly abandoned the future of old-age protection to negotiations between employers and labor unions and in so doing accepted restrictions and divisions of the general old-age pension scheme.

Public retirement policy fundamentally reflected the balance of power between the unions and the employers. Throughout the period in question, retirement as a work-related social right was triumphant, and it made further advances each time the labor union movement was in a position of power or experienced a resurgence of activity. Retirement was established as a social right at the time of the Liberation, when the working-class movement was at its height. Pensions legislation extended the common right to retirement only after 1968, when labor union activity was again on the increase.

The Boulin Act of December 1971, which raised pensions by altering the way they were calculated,[155] reflected this new union pressure. Although it was not sufficient to win total victory and obtain the extension of the right to retirement that the unions had asked for, including a lower retirement age, it was enough to obtain an improvement in the level of pensions. By contrast, the decline in the right to retirement and its fragmentation came about as a result of the waning power of the unions and the increasing influence of employers.

However, state action in the field of pensions was not simply a direct and automatic expression of current social relations; it also reflected the extent to which the state organization was open to dominant social interests. The period that this chapter has mainly examined is the Fourth Republic. In the National Assembly system, the Executive was subject to a Parliament, which held most of the power. The state of the Fourth Republic was thus one over which social forces mediated by the party system had an important hold, while its capacity for autonomous action was correspondingly limited. Accordingly, the dominant social interests made their way into the state to a very considerable extent. This chapter has described how the working class was successful in this respect between 1945 and 1947. It was extremely powerful in society at large, and was also well represented in the Executive through political parties, while enjoying a solid foundation in the administration. However, the advent of the Fifth Republic widened the gap between the party system and the state by reducing the role of Parliament; there was also a special fusion of powers between the Executive and the upper echelons of the administration. The result of these changes was a marked increase in the state's relative autonomy of action compared with the social interests expressed in society. Later sections of this book will show that the Gaullist state did not invest this new autonomy in the field of pension policy. The pension system was the concrete expression of relations among the classes. The state was restricted to the role of an economic agent that carried out a more or less broad-based redistribution of income according to whatever social class happened to be favored by the balance of social power. The state's new autonomy during this period manifested itself in the promotion of a new definition of old age as a specific status and as a way of life. Within the framework of retirement policy, the state merely provided itself with a definition of old age as a position in a system of income redistribution that had been constructed largely independently of it. It used its new autonomy by opening up a new area of intervention in old age: the way-of-life policy. This enabled it to reorganize the relationship between old age and society, and to try to impose a new definition of the final life stage as the third age—that is to say, a place in a sociopolitical system, and no longer simply a position in a system of resource transfer.

The emergence of a statelike capacity for action took two forms. One was the introduction of a new issue in the social struggle concerning the management of the elderly population—the defense of the status of old age and its social integration; the other consisted of repeated public attempts to shift the debate on old age from pensions to way of life. These changes, which took place at the level of the state, had an impact on public pension policy throughout the period. The administrative and financial reorganization of social security in 1967 was a departure from the more withdrawn posture that the state had adopted between 1948 and 1958. It is true that the change was influenced by employers' ideas on social protection,[156] but it also reflected a new public concern to limit this redistributive form of protection and explore new forms of social action. The Boulin Act of 1971, which raised the level of pensions, similarly reflected the increasing importance of the labor union movement in society, while the limited scope of the reform reflected poor penetration by the social interests of labor in a state now enjoying a certain autonomy of action.

Everything in the system of relations summarized above suggests that the elaboration of public decisions that established or extended workers' common right to retirement reflected both the power of the labor union movement in society and its capacity to pervade the state with its social interests. The latter in turn reflected the link between state organization and the arena of social relations, and the resulting degree of autonomy for the state.

Once it has been developed, any policy induces new conceptions and affects social relations. What follows is only an outline of the retroactive processes that are implemented with the establishment of a right to retirement. First, the spread of retirement profoundly changed the social construction of the reality of old age by giving it the new form of inactivity on a pension. This both endowed old age with an identity and made it identifiable. With retirement, old age moved away from poverty and the physical inability to work. A new phase in the life cycle was identified with the emergence of the new economic definition of the older worker, whereby one was considered to be too old for the labor market even before serious physical incapacity set in. The limit that the economy placed on occupational usefulness through advancing years met the workers' desire for disalienation and for a period of rest at the end of the working life; the latter aspiration grew in strength as work processes became more demanding. Old age was reconstructed as retirement, thereby simultaneously triggering an economic devaluation of the workforce and exercising the worker's right to a period of rest. This then brought about a redefinition of the cutoff point between age groups, and of the organization of the stages of life. Old age, which was now associated with retirement, began earlier on average, and qualification for entry was on the basis of formal criteria (age or length of service) and no longer according to an individual's incapacity for work.

Second, the general availability of the right to retirement transformed social relations and took over the public debate on old-age protection; this indicated the limits of what might have been seen as a union victory, and as this chapter has already had occasion to demonstrate, highlighted the ambivalences implicit in retirement.

The working-class demand for retirement was a complex one. It involved both the demand for a right to subsistence in old age, based on society's indebtedness to workers for a life of toil, and the struggle against alienation, which led to the demand for a right to a period of rest at the end of the working life. The second part of this demand meant that workers' struggles for disalienation hinged on a search for freedom from work rather than for ways of restoring its meaning. The linking of disalienation with retirement provided a setting in which all aspirations for leading a full life could be focused on retirement itself, and this was something that developed with the accelerated pace of work and growing exploitation of the workforce.

In the framework of setting up retirement institutions, however, this complex social demand of the workers was reformulated as a simple demand for cash payments. Industrial society had transferred solidarity from density of primary networks to systems of financial exchanges centered on networks of production. The demand for a reduction in the level of exploitation and for disalienation then found a response in a pension system, in a system of redistribution of resources, and in the extension of the concept of wages to social wages. This monetarization of the demand inevitably opened up a gap between supply and demand, and also allowed the supply-demand dialectic to get out of control. This was one of the causes of the crisis in the various welfare states, and will be examined in the final chapter of this book. Once the pension system had been established, it changed the way labor unions operated. They now directed their campaigns at improving the criteria on which the right to retirement was based. This chapter has described how, after the social security system was set up, labor union demands in the field of old age concentrated heavily on lowering the age of retirement and on raising the level of pensions. In the debate the problems of old age were subsumed under the question of the level of the pension and the point in the life cycle at which it should be paid. However, the pension system matured and became more widely available.[157] The final stage of life, which was increasingly structured by retirement, acquired the social content of inactivity on a pension as the level of pensions improved and retirees no longer had to carry on working full- or part-time. This change in the form of the final stage of life stimulated new aspirations and demands on the part of retirees. They were now experiencing marginality and isolation, and discovering that the solution to their problems did not lie solely in improvements to their standard of living, but was associated with the way of life that society allotted them. However, these questions were still largely underestimated in the public debate on pensions, which focused on the greater or lesser redistribution of resources to retirees without any consideration of the social content of retirement or the retiree's place in society. To a certain extent, the success of the labor unions in imposing their issue—the development of a universal right to retirement—at the time of the Liberation restricted the debate on old-age protection to the right to retirement. It also largely restricted the dynamics of old-age policies to an interplay that this chapter has already examined: that of conflicting relations between unions and employers and their regulation by the state. This development marked out the spaces into which a way-of-life policy spread, and it is this evolution that will be discussed in the next chapter.

2

Old Age and Ways of Life: The Emergence of a Policy of Social Integration of the Elderly

Economically, the elderly have generally stood on the margins of the market, while their needs were defined, and their way of life structured, by charitable organizations and by state and private bodies providing public assistance. Since the expansion of the welfare state, the latter have had the greater role to play. The aim of this chapter is to analyze the social dynamics that have dominated changes in these way-of-life policies for the elderly in France since 1945. Unlike retirement policies, which were an expression of conflictual class relations, way-of-life policies have the state as their central actor; social relations play a much lesser role.

A reconstruction of philosophies whereby the state has intervened in this field since 1945 will be followed by an attempt to give an account of changes in public management. The reasons for the state's newfound dynamism in structuring a way of life for the elderly will be analyzed, as will the conditions that prompted the development of a new public doctrine for social integration in the early 1960s. Finally, there will be an examination of the factors that, in the 1970s, led to the implementation of this doctrine, as well as to a number of dysfunctions.

The State and Ways of Life of the Elderly Since 1945; From Public Assistance to Enabling the Elderly to Carry on Living in a Social Environment

Since 1945, the state has adopted three successive arguments in determining the way of life of the elderly. In the first period, which lasted until around 1960, the state's actions conformed to the traditional pattern of public assistance, although it gradually began to implement plans targeted at the elderly. The second period (1960–69) saw the development and promotion of an alternative global model for managing the way of life; this came about as the result of a state initiative. New stated policies were superimposed on a public policy that remained largely based on public assistance, and was mainly concerned with housing. The third period, from 1970 onwards, saw the principle of coordinated and continuous public action related to the structure and way of life—its main focus was better integration of the elderly into society—implemented within the framework of the planning process, and forming part of the Sixth and Seventh Plans.

Public Assistance for the Elderly (1945–1959)

CHANGE AND NO CHANGE

Public management of the way of life of the elderly at this time consisted of a traditional range of public assistance benefits: elderly people were put into old people's homes, or they received a minimal amount of assistance in cash or in kind. At this time, the main options were set out in two pieces of legislation: the 7 August 1851 act on hospitals and hospices and the 14 July 1905 act providing mandatory assistance for the elderly, the infirm, and incurable patients without sufficient financial means. These laws were of particular significance in that social legislation of the period separated the elderly from other traditional categories of people entitled to assistance.

The elderly now acquired an autonomy of their own, and for the first time they were targeted for specific public assistance. This development reflected the spread of retirement schemes and provided a common feature that was shared by all elderly people: that of having no job but bringing in an income, i.e., a pension. This paid inactivity converted the elderly into a coherent, autonomous group who demanded special social action. They were now detached from the population of which they had previously been a part, and the result was a new form of poverty and social destitution. Just as social legislation was beginning to separate the elderly from other traditional categories of people entitled to assistance (e.g., the infirm and incurable patients), old age became more closely associated with this new destitution. This is explained by three essential characteristics of the period in question: first, the elderly had been especially affected by the ravages of war; second, the creation of the welfare state meant that public assistance played no more than a complementary role; and third, the decisive social policy was a family policy that encouraged a high birth rate.

To begin with the first point, the socioeconomic position of the elderly was particularly affected both by the structural upheavals that the war had brought about and by the country's subsequent economic recovery. Industrialization and rapid urbanization destroyed the traditional consumer networks[1] that the elderly had previously used, while the level of contributory pension provided by the old-age risk protection scheme remained low. The average state pension provided by the general scheme in 1956 was 860 francs per year, and this included benefits paid to older salaried employees; by contrast, the minimum wage during the same year was 4,200 francs, and the Fonds National de Solidarité (National Solidarity Fund) had recently set its basic limit at 2,010 francs. Furthermore, a large number of people reaching the age of sixty-five did not have a pension, did not receive salaried workers' benefits, and were not entitled to the *carte d'économiquement faible* (poverty card); a 1950 survey into the incomes of elderly people showed that 45 percent of those aged sixty-five or over fell into this category.

In a statement to the National Assembly on the reasons behind the draft poverty card legislation, the president of the Family Commission described the appalling conditions in which a large proportion of the elderly population lived:

> People living on small private incomes, and proud of their hard-earned savings, should be able to look forward to a peaceful retirement; however, their situation now borders on destitution as a result of monetary and economic upheavals. Then, there are former salaried employees not covered by social security legislation, and self-employed workers forced to stop work due to illness or age and who have the greatest difficulty in climbing out of the poverty in which they now find themselves. Apart from a few people who have become rich, and who should consequently be hit by legislation, the categories I have mentioned are the new poor who have been created by the war. The phrase *économiquement faible* (living in poverty) will now become part of everyday speech, and public and private institutions should now come forward with appropriate measures to assist them.[2]

In the second place, the setting up of social security in 1945 involved the reorganization of measures for providing public assistance. Many people thought that the new form of social protection established by the social security retirement scheme would eventually lead to the disappearance of assistance for the elderly: as these services disappeared welfare policy would then be restructured and become complementary to the social security system. The shortcomings of a system often seen as temporary would thus be camouflaged. The public assistance reform of 1953, referred to as a "patching-up exercise" *(replâtrage)*[3] by some analysts, was an attempt to coordinate the right to public assistance with the right to social security. This "patching up" was mainly concerned with a unifying of allowance conditions and a stricter interpretation of nutritional obligations. These measures were accompanied by a change in terminology, with "assistance" becoming "social aid." The aim of this change was to reflect a new concept of solidarity that underpinned the new arrangements, a concept that was barely evident in principles based more on charity.

In the third place, the underlying aim during this period was to rebuild national production. In terms of social policy, this had the effect of promoting a high birth rate and put the emphasis on family policy rather than on services for the elderly. The latter were no longer a vibrant force in the country's economic development.

The effect of these three main characteristics of the period under examination was that measures to improve the way of life of the elderly were concerned only with their most urgent needs. These measures responded to problems selectively, and corrected only those shortcomings in the social security system that were deemed to be temporary. In other words, benefits were dispensed according to a logic of state paternalism, and basic needs were treated in a piecemeal manner.

PUBLIC MEASURES IN THE MANAGEMENT OF THE DAY-TO-DAY LIVES OF THE ELDERLY

Public assistance for the poor. Examination of the most important measures determining the way of life of the elderly (including an analysis of the debate on old age as covered by the press) confirms how dominant the public assistance program was during this period.

In addition to setting up pension schemes, legislation at this time was mainly devoted to the introduction or reintroduction of minimum cash benefits for certain categories of elderly people. These allowances were noncontributory, and were intended to fill gaps in a pensions scheme that was still not universally available. A number of new laws were passed. They included the 13 September 1946 act, which introduced a temporary allowance for elderly people living in hardship (it was renewed almost every year until 1951); the 17 January 1947 act, which established an allowance for retired nonsalaried employees who did not have enough contributions to qualify them for a pension (this repeated an allowance introduced by the Vichy government for salaried employees in 1941 and confirmed by the decree of 2 February 1945 on social security); the 10 July 1952 act, which paid out a special allowance to elderly people with no other retirement income; and the 30 June 1956 act, whereby the National Solidarity Fund topped up existing old-age benefits to enable a beneficiary's income to reach a basic minimum. This latter piece of legislation was initially inspired by the principle of national solidarity for the elderly, and its achievements proved to be similar to those of traditional public assistance.

Two other measures involving benefits in kind and specifically targeted assistance were introduced at the same time as these cash benefits. These were the poverty card and an allowance compensating for rent increases: both were specifically aimed at elderly people who did not have enough money to live on.

The provisions that determined the way of life of the elderly on a day-to-day basis were rooted in the old public assistance traditions. They consisted of small benefits to cover the most pressing needs, the most important being community-based housing.

Old people's homes. Putting the impecunious elderly into homes designed for them was still the most common solution, and in 1959, this kind of public assistance on housing the elderly still accounted for 89 percent of all money spent on this group.[4]

Management of the way of life in these totalitarian (in Goffman's sense of the word) institutions was characterized by segregation, and this essentially represented society's response to impoverished elderly people. Old people's homes had been designed for the very poor, and insofar as they now had to specialize in catering to the elderly, the hospital system began to differentiate and produce institutions adapted to different health requirements and other needs.[5]

This period also saw the setting up of institutions that specialized in housing elderly people who did not fall into the previous "impoverished" group. Retirement homes eventually forged ahead of old people's homes[6] and were targeted for more government regulation; for instance, the ordinance of 18 December 1958 provided for the setting up of not only old people's homes but also public retirement homes for the exclusive use of the elderly.

Most elderly people who were allocated accommodation continued to live in old people's homes and retirement homes attached to hospitals: in 1962, 71percent of the elderly were housed in institutions of this kind (156,640 out of a total of 220,338 in receipt of accommodation).[7] However, they were the oldest (a large number had been built before 1920), the largest (a high number of establishments contained two hundred beds or more), and also the least comfortable (the beds were in dormitories).

No new legislation was introduced between 1945 and 1960 on the running of old people's homes, and although accommodation provided for the elderly became increasingly specialized as a result, it still betrayed its origins: it was a successor to the general hospital, it had been developed to fight poverty, and it was founded on a public assistance-based ideology.

Housing for the elderly at this time was a formal acknowledgment of the long-term destitution that the elderly were experiencing, and it also continued to have a repressive and moralizing effect.[8]

Although specialized housing for the elderly followed from policies enabling the elderly to be more independent, it was not matched by an increase in the amount of accommodation available. Census data even suggest a decrease in the number of elderly people housed in institutions between 1946 and 1954, although there was a gradual increase from 1962 onward.[9] This development doubtless owed much to the poor quality of elderly people's accommodation at the time; the period was also marked by a general housing crisis that was not resolved for years to come. Furthermore, the level of bed occupancy was close to 100 percent, and those on waiting lists had to wait several years. The waiting lists alone were reliable indicators of a severe accommodation shortage.[10]

A statement of one's needs in exchange for the status of needy: the poverty card. The view taken by the author is that the measures set out in the 2 August 1949 act on the poverty card were typical of the logic determining action taken by public authorities at the time. An examination of these measures reveals the kind of action in favor of the elderly that was given most prominence. The card was intended to provide evidence of the holder's financial situation; it also gave him or her access to certain exemptions and to certain benefits in kind that were fixed by regulations, although they were far from generous. These benefits mainly covered essentials such as coal, medicine, and food, gave subsidized entry to community centers providing food, offered reductions on the price of certain public amenities (such as gas, electricity, and rail transport) and provided a number of public assistance benefits including free medical treatment and legal aid.

An individual claimant's particulars were examined, and the card was then means-tested by welfare commissions.[11] By the end of 1949 there were an estimated 2 million potential recipients out of a population of 4,435,000 people aged sixty-five or over. In other words, almost one out of two elderly people was declared to be on a low income, and these figures incontrovertibly confirm the level of poverty at which the elderly were then considered to be living. The card was a success, despite the fact that it offered very limited benefits; there was also controversy in the press about the time it took for benefits to be paid and about which benefits should be included. At all events, its success was short-lived, and the number of beneficiaries fell rapidly because the financial ceiling determining access remained extremely low.

The idea of giving public assistance to those who most needed it characterized the introduction of the poverty card, and can also be discerned in the 25 May 1951 act. This legislation, which brought in a compensatory allowance for rent increases imposed on poor, elderly tenants, was part of an attempt to remedy the effects of the 1948 rent act.

Laws passed at this time in favor of the elderly incorporated many features of public assistance legislation, including the same subsidiary characteristics. Benefits were paid out only if there was evidence that the need could not be made good either by the claimant himself or herself (who also had to present proof of incapacity) or within the framework of family solidarity.[12]

Subsidiarity of assistance obliged individuals to itemize their needs in order to be registered as poor, and the process was inevitably degrading and stigmatizing. The procedure was patently unreasonable on two counts: first, there was the probing, humiliating investigation to which the claimant had to submit in order to make a claim and qualify for the marginal and dependent status of destitute; second, the benefits themselves were extremely small.[13] The dependency and the degradation occasioned by this policy were of much greater significance than the benefits received. The solutions provided by assistance measures for the elderly concealed a clear image of old age and the needs of the elderly. At the time, an assessment of these needs focused on subsistence, and the main objective of the management of way of life was therefore to make their lives less wretched. The social condition of the elderly was therefore dependent, marginal, and segregated, and no one thought of challenging it.

An examination of the measures governing the day-to-day lives of the elderly demonstrates how deeply rooted they were in public assistance; moreover, an analysis of the debate on old age, such as took place between the various social forces during this period, similarly confirmed the prevalence of a public assistance-based logic.

THE MAIN ISSUES IN THE PUBLIC DEBATE ON AGING

By completing our quantified analysis of the thematic content of relevant articles in *Le Monde* with a more qualitative analysis of labor union publications and National Assembly debates, it is possible to validate the breakdown a posteriori, compare the period in question with subsequent periods, and identify the key players.

The aims of the content analysis. A content analysis of articles in *Le Monde* that dealt with retirement, old age, and aging over the period 1945–75 provided the original data. These completed a complex system of collecting and processing information in order to piece together and interpret the recent history of the management of old age.

A systematic study of these thirty years has made it possible to follow the progress of the public debate on aging. Other information that was collected (interviews with key players, analyses of the labor union, and employers' press and government documents) facilitated a reconstruction of the positions and actions of key players and institutions. Although this in turn provided a more detailed analysis of each actor's role in the formulation of an old-age policy, it was less effective than the content analysis of *Le Monde* in that it failed to furnish a synthesized view of their approaches that would show how their views changed, what their polemical relationships were, and who was gaining the upper hand.

Through this information it was possible to follow, over a long period, the construction and deconstruction of orthodoxies related to the needs of old age and ways of meeting them. Old-age policies are not simply a corpus of political and administrative decisions; they produce a constant redefinition of the last stage of life and the way it is managed. The press, insofar as it transforms daily events into "stories" with a symbolic value,[14] provides a setting in which these social constructions are condensed. According to the analysis developed for this book, it was not a matter of querying the distortions and deformations of reality that had appeared in the press, but rather of using it as the basis for reconstructing what people thought of old age and how these ideas were changing.

The chronological study of the transformations was carried out through quantified thematic content analysis. This was complemented by a less systematic analysis of permanences, breaks in lexis, and changes of semantic field. Chronological ordering of subject areas under each of the headings permitted an a posteriori, and therefore nonarbitrary, periodization based on the same data; all of this helped identify the various issues of aging that dominated the different periods. It also enabled an identification of the cut-and-dried explanations that had previously been accepted and to observe the gradual emergence of new principles for the management of old age by pinpointing not only textual changes but also the actors and social groups that had proposed them. Finally, the data made it possible to establish, for each player concerned, a chronological profile of the themes under each heading. This information provided an opportunity to reconstruct the qualified approaches of all those taking part in the debate when they argued among themselves and when they reached agreement by incorporating elements of each other's ideas into their final positions.

Prevalence of an orthodoxy based on public assistance. The results of the thematic analysis of *Le Monde* confirmed that the approach to aging during the period 1946–59 was based on public assistance.

The results contained in the column "Issues Occurring in the Debate," which made it possible to follow the main points of the old age debate over a long period and to identify the main protagonists, confirm both the focus on public assistance old age way-of-life management and the relevance of considering the years 1946–59 as a distinct period.

A more detailed, year-by-year analysis reveals that between 1946 and 1960, press reports of matters related to aging concentrated on two main issues: the assistance policy for the elderly (which received most attention) and retirement policies. This balance of attention remained unchanged except for the years 1946 and 1947, when 50 percent of articles were devoted to retirement policies, and 1950, when both topics were covered equally and accounted for a total of one-third of all articles.

The 1946–50 period was marked by increased interest in the issue of public assistance; for example, from 1946 to 1950 it took second place (32.4 percent of articles) behind retirement policy (50 percent of articles). From 1951 to 1954, assistance policy for the elderly took the lead with 39.5 percent of articles; in joint second place, with 16 percent each, were retirement policy for older workers and workers of retirement age, and demands related to standard of living and the value of pensions.

From 1955 to 1959, public assistance policy still held center stage, accounting for over half the articles printed (56 percent). Aging as a scientific, medical, or demographic issue was a distant second place with 14 percent, and was followed by retirement policy with 8 percent.

The turning point came in 1960, and this change confirmed the periodization that has already been suggested. Public assistance policy continued to hold the lead, but only by a slender margin (27 percent of articles), and issues linked to protest—these concentrated essentially on retirement schemes and retirees' standard of living—were in second place with 20 percent. This renewed interest in protest was characteristic of the years that followed. Protest became more closely associated with the issue of social integration, and as this chapter will demonstrate, the question was covered much more generously in the press.

Concern for the life of the elderly, in terms of their moral and material well-being also figured in the debate on aging. These newer questions also acquired more importance in subsequent years. It is noteworthy that during the period 1946–59, the elderly themselves took no part in the debate on old age in the course of their daily lives.

The debate was formulated directly in terms of policies for action and involved a choice between retirement policy and public assistance policy. The reason why the elderly did not participate in the debate, and why their only role was to be on the receiving end of public action, was that old age was closely linked to the idea of poverty at this time and was only considered negatively in terms of its shortcomings. This attitude underlined the regular semantic model that equated old age with poverty. The words "poor" and "lower-income" were often used together with the word "old," and considerably more than half the articles published at the time show old age as equated with destitution.[15] The most frequently projected picture was of old age as a costly burden.

The poverty diagnosis that was applied to the condition of the elderly was logically associated with management principles focusing on financial and nonfinancial benefits, either in kind or specifically targeted. Examination of the results from the "Recommended or Implemented Measures" shows that the measures adopted in favor of the elderly during this period were essentially limited to these forms of action. They took first place in the press with 64 percent of articles, and in second place, a long way behind, came the pension system with 19 percent. Interventions in other fields, such as living environment, health, and housing were rarely or never mentioned, and they did not figure at all in the dominant model of the management of old age.

The measures most frequently recommended or implemented at this time fell into the category of traditional forms of public assistance. Urgently recommended improvements included the opening of day-care centers and resource centers,[16] and the provision of facilities for elderly people from lower-income groups to subsidize essential needs such as food and heating. Urgent recommendations were also made for the opening of drop-in centers and larger centers that would include reception rooms, a meal service, and a family placement scheme.[17]

Forms of public assistance in kind included coal and sugar vouchers, hot meals in community centers, tax exemptions, and targeted assistance (e.g., grants to compensate for rent increases), but a standard response to the social problems of old age continued to be the placing of elderly people in some kind of home.[18] Ideas of this type were not challenged during the last few years of the period under examination, except when a few isolated projects were proposed in an attempt to find alternatives to old people's homes. One such project was the Association Village-Retraite (Retirement Village Association), which was set up in March 1958.

The logic underpinning ad hoc responses to the most urgent needs of the elderly was clear. Alternative ways of dealing with the elderly simply did not exist, and criticism of social policy dealing with the problems of the elderly concentrated solely on the amount of public assistance that was handed out; it did not focus on how the system worked or on the marginal, dependent status that such a system forced upon the elderly. The factors most frequently decried by the press were the inadequacy of public commitment to matters concerning the elderly (22 percent of articles) and how much the policy cost (16 percent). This scenario about "Areas of Criticism" distinguished the period 1946–60 from the years that followed when the emphasis shifted to the way of life.

The content analysis of the key actors in the public assistance policy show that the state was the most important. The government and National Assembly did most to promote debate around old age at this time and to develop policy. Between 1946 and 1950, the only elements of the state that made any impact were the Executive and the Legislature, and 91 percent of articles published on this subject allocated the key roles to them, although this dominance dropped to 73 percent between 1951 and 1954, and to only 60 percent from 1955 to 1959. Subsequently, other actors took over responsibility for public assistance for the elderly: in the main, these were charitable organizations (from 1951 onward, they met annually to organize an old people's day and a public survey), and, to a lesser extent, local authorities and labor unions. The results of the content analysis of *Le Monde* confirm what an analysis of measures related to management of the way of life had already suggested.

In the absence of a pension scheme, the state granted limited ad hoc benefits to the most needy members of the elderly population. This approach was rarely called into question; indeed, it enjoyed consensual support, and was also the method chosen by some private charities. Labor unions had no countermodel of social action to help the elderly, and as was pointed out in the previous chapter, they campaigned in the arena of an old-age policy on the right to retirement. They believed that public assistance was a necessary evil caused by the fact that old-age benefits provided by the general scheme were too low. From then on, therefore, their approach to social action in support of the elderly went in two directions. On one hand, they made repeated attempts to redirect the idea of assistance into the field of retirement, and tried to turn charity, including public forms, into a solidarity measure. Against this backdrop, the CGT argued that the poverty card, which offered few tangible benefits, should be replaced by an increase in pensions.

On the other hand, at a time of escalating deprivation, and when the retirement system had ground to a halt, the unions came out in favor of developing a public assistance program specifically for the elderly. Far from questioning the prevailing assistance system, the text appeared word for word in the union press. The elderly were the target of the same collective concern and, although they were referred to as "old workers," they were also seen as "our dear old folks" *(nos bons vieux)* who would not reject the more traditional charitable associations. During this period the few articles that appeared in the union press concerning public assistance for the elderly approached the problem from a strictly charitable angle, and suggested methods that harked back to traditional public assistance methods such as old people's homes[19] or community housing in retirement homes.

In conclusion, an analysis of press coverage over this period shows that the orthodoxy of public assistance for the elderly prevailed, and its social construction was characterized by destitution; the social referent was the working class.

The Growth of State Initiatives and the Launching of a New Public Doctrine Promoting the Social Integration of the Elderly

The early 1960s saw the beginning of a new era in social policy for the elderly; this could be defined as the implementation of an alternative mode of action and more vigorous state interventions in the field. The state launched a number of initiatives, of which the most impressive was the Commission d'Étude des Problèmes de la Vieillesse (Study Commission on Old Age), which was set up by the prime minister in the 8 April 1960 decree.

The report of this commission (which informally took the name of its president, Pierre Laroque, a senior member of the State Council) produced a new doctrine of action for the elderly; this was the outcome of wide-ranging consultations with the main government departments concerned, and with the most representative professional, labor union, and employers' organizations. It set out to rationalize and implement a coherent approach to a range of activities that were happening in different places. The main points of its plan for a program of preventive medicine also included general principles for a new way of managing old age, and they thereby challenged the public assistance logic that had hitherto prevailed. The official nature of the commission, not to mention the illustriousness of its members, helped to ensure that this new doctrine was implemented; this was seen as the only all-embracing alternative to traditional practice, and came to be known as the "Old-Age Policy."[20]

The objective of this new policy for old age was prevention. It aimed to defer the onset of the dependency that came with aging by integrating the elderly into their living environment. "The commission strongly condemns any solution that causes the elderly to be segregated in any way. Of course, we cannot stand in the way of elderly people withdrawing from the world if that is their wish, but the commission believes that, in the interests of both the economy and the physical and psychological well-being of the elderly themselves, every effort should be made to keep them in their own economic and social environment."[21] Aging was accelerated by the departure from a familiar environment. By contrast, integration within a social milieu and the prolongation of independence could be achieved through the provision of certain facilities and adapted services. "As a matter of priority, the emphasis should be placed on integrating the elderly into society, and providing them with the means to continue leading independent lives for as long as possible. This involves the construction of adapted housing, the availability of home helps for all who need one, access to a range of social services, and ways of keeping them occupied and entertained."[22]

The new integration-based logic that underpinned the policy for managing the elderly ran directly counter to the principle of social exile that had been the basis for previous policies, and the new system of management relied essentially on small-scale local facilities. This new, open style of capillary management contrasted sharply with the totalitarian methods that had hitherto prevailed in old people's homes, and replaced investment in facilities with the principle of providing services. "The basic task of the home-care worker is to provide elderly people who are able to continue leading independent lives with effective and sufficiently flexible facilities in their own homes."[23] These facilities had to cover both social and health needs. In practice, promoting the home life of the elderly meant that the amount of time they spent in hospitals was reduced through the availability of treatment specially designed to defer some of the pathological symptoms of aging. The health component of integrating the elderly into a social environment included systematic health checkups, health education, a "health care in the home" scheme, and outpatient treatment.

These ideas showed that enabling the elderly to remain in their home surroundings, thereby prolonging their independence, required an action program with interdependent elements if the situation of the elderly was to be transformed. The Study Commission's recommendations touched on questions of pensions, employment, housing, and health and social services, information, and education, as well as administrative coordination.

At the same time, even though it was a comprehensive old-age policy, it constituted a long-term program that broke with the old ad hoc approach. "Any examination of the question of old age in France requires an analysis of the means and procedures that will ensure that proper living conditions are provided for the elderly over the next twenty years."[24]

The introduction of a preventive (and not simply curative or defensive) strategy into the new policy for old age meant that the target population changed. In the field of medicine, the move from curative to preventive treatment focused attention on the entire population, so that the health of all was monitored, and not just that of a small group of patients. Similarly, the introduction of a preventive aging policy meant that all elderly people came into consideration, not just the most destitute. "The work done by the home-help scheme, in the broadest sense, must be available not only to the most destitute and those most in need of public assistance, but also, gradually, to all members of the elderly population who might have need of these services."[25]

The introduction of new collective principles into the management of the elderly thus led to a new image of old age and its needs. Old age came to be seen as a new stage of life—this was evidenced by the coining of the term "third age"—that was almost a concomitant of the definition of the new management principles. A new, "natural" quality appeared in the new forms of action undertaken on their behalf.

The Laroque Report defined work on information and education with the aim of "eliminating" the depressing and threatening context that surrounded the concept of aging. The elderly now had to be seen as "citizens like everyone else";[26] "they contribute to the country's prosperity both as producers and as consumers."[27] As Philippe Ariès noted, the degrading aspect of old age had disappeared and was now replaced by the notion of preservation,[28] and the new, preventive policy responded to this new collective concern and defined methods of achieving this ideal.

The government had given the Study Commission the task "of examining the problems posed by the employment and living conditions of the elderly, and of proposing solutions to certain problems within the framework of an overall policy."[29] In fulfilling this task, the commission reformulated the whole debate on old age. The question of poverty among the elderly was replaced by a concern for their marginal status. However, the resulting doctrine did not simply set out the principles of an alternative mode of intervention in favor of the elderly, thereby simultaneously producing a new image of old age. It also prompted a redefinition of the state's role in managing the relationship between the elderly and society. Furthermore, it proposed an arena for new plans of action that were to operate outside the two main channels for the command of public old-age policy, namely retirement and assistance.

In the management model that was adapted during the first period, and that relied on pension plans and on subordinated action on public assistance, the state saw its role with regard to the elderly as strictly economic. Old-age policy was essentially a policy of transfers over which the state gradually lost control, since the rapid diffusion of complementary pension schemes gave employers and labor unions much more autonomy. At the same time, by turning itself into the catalyst for a new state doctrine on the elderly, the state played a part in redirecting the debate on old age. From then on, this debate was based on questions of way of life and marginality instead of pensions complemented by public assistance. For all practical purposes, the problem of old age supplanted that of retirement. The action model no longer linked a pensions policy to a subordinated public assistance scheme; instead, the pensions policy now became incorporated into a way-of-life policy, and was only one of its many elements.

The new structure of the plan of action on old age opened up new perspectives for more direct and more autonomous state management of the relationship between society and the elderly. The new needs of the elderly were now formulated in terms of integration rather than of poverty, and the advent of this new doctrine created new areas for sociopolitical, rather than simply economic, interventions by the state. The new areas for public action on old age were outside the field of retirement and its principal actors, and they therefore allowed the state to intervene more directly and independently. As an earlier section has pointed out, the early 1960s were marked by the state's reformulation of the principles of the management of old age. However, although these new principles redirected the debate on old age toward the way of life, and increased the state's opportunities for new initiatives, concrete policy decisions were not immediately forthcoming. It took almost ten years before such decisions were put into action.

Plans for the Continued Social Participation of the Elderly

It was not until the preparations for the Sixth Plan were underway that the new scheme for integrating the elderly into society was implemented as part of state policy. An "Intergroupe" (Intergroup) chaired by Nicole Questiaux with responsibility for problems pertaining to the elderly was set up on 14 November 1969. It attempted to translate the Laroque Commission's comprehensive analysis into administrative and financial realities, and its efforts produced a draft program for helping the elderly to live in their own homes. The aim of this program was to promote coordinated and sectoral health and social services that would enable the elderly to remain in their own home environments, thereby keeping them in touch with other age groups and the population as a whole.

The report stated in its introduction that prolonging normal life involved keeping the elderly in their own homes for as long as possible. This vital component of the Sixth Plan could only become a reality if there was a major improvement in facilities and social services.[30] In the event, the plan contained six "final programs," and the one that was designed to enable the elderly to stay in their own homes was one of the four social programs.[31] An innovatory aspect of the Sixth Plan was that it argued for "collective functions" to be provided by public institutions outside the market. This approach meant that problems pertaining to both facilities and the running costs of each of the programs now had to be taken into account.

The final program for enabling the elderly to carry on living in their own homes consisted of subsidies for amenities such as eating facilities, clubs, and day centers, but also included the "operational budget" *(crédits de fonctionnement);* these were valid for only two years and were designed to get the various services off the ground. The overall cost of the plan for the period 1971–76 was slightly over 1 billion French francs, but the state contributed only a quarter of this (265 million francs); local authorities provided 234 million francs, social security 461 million francs, and beneficiaries a further 112 million francs; Non-Governmental Organizations made up the balance.

When Parliament approved the general report on the Sixth Social and Economic Development Plan, the state assumed a new medium-term responsibility for coordinating and funding the social integration of the elderly. This became a practical reality following the publication of Ministry of Public Health circulars no. 1575 of 24 September 1971 and no. 5 of 1 February 1972; these effectively signaled the launching of the program, and ordered the immediate distribution of the funds.

This book takes the view that the introduction within the planning structure of these new principles for managing the way of life of the elderly heralded the birth of a new stage in state action in this field. For the first time, the state furnished itself with the financial and administrative means to promote and coordinate support services for the elderly, and these no longer came through retirement, public assistance, or placement structures.[32] These services were designed to integrate the elderly into their normal environment more effectively. The state's decision to carry out medium-term direct and ongoing action in the living environment sought to focus on and give new energy to the efforts of local authorities and social security funds; this task was handed over to Bureau RV 2, part of the government department responsible for social action. This final program gave the department direct responsibility for the social integration of the elderly for the first time. This was not subsequently challenged, as the Seventh Plan included Priority Action Program no. 15, which extended the Sixth Plan.

The main shifts in the logic underpinning state action on way of life revealed three successive forms of intervention: traditional public assistance, the text of a comprehensive model of action on way of life, and, shortly afterwards, the introduction of this into the planning system.

The following pages will attempt to throw light on the social dynamics of this change. First, there will be an analysis of the social conditions that encouraged the emergence of a new state-inspired model for the management of way of life in the early 1960s. This will be followed by a reconstruction of the interaction of social forces that incorporated this new management model into the planning system. Finally, there will be an assessment of the new social programs that were implemented under the Sixth and Seventh Plans.

The Formation and Dissemination of a Public Doctrine on the Social Integration of the Elderly (1960–1969)

A Turning Point in the Late 1950s

Signs of new dynamism in state action on the way of life of the elderly

The period 1959–60 was marked by a series of central state initiatives in matters concerning the elderly. They appeared to be part of a search for new areas of intervention based neither on what was left of the public assistance approach to social protection nor on the type of protection provided by pension schemes. An administrative circular dated January 1960 from the Ministry for Public Health and the Population[33] was sent to the prefects and directors of population and of health based in the *départements*. It followed up a report by the Inspection Générale de la Santé Publique (General Public Health Inspectorate)[34] on the organization of social action for the elderly; this had been made public at the minister's request in the *Journal Officiel* of 13 March 1960, and was clearly intended to stimulate debate on the subject. The report stressed the need for the elderly to be looked after properly in their own homes and called for the provision of home-care services, which, "although recommended by ministerial instructions following the 1953 reform to public assistance, are still few and far between." The report also commented on inadequate facilities in old people's homes and retirement homes and referred to the serious "medical neglect" that residents had to put up with; conditions in French old people's homes, the report went on, were disgraceful. The report's conclusions underlined the need to formulate an overall plan, as "arrangements in France for the well-being of elderly people with financial problems are unsatisfactory. This problem has been the subject of numerous studies, but because of its intensely human nature, no solution has been found."

The ministerial circular on social action for the elderly sought to provide and improve facilities in this area, and recalled the three avenues set out in current legislation. The circular contained three main points:

1. The importance of the home-care system in enabling the elderly to stay in their own homes; the construction of community centers providing food, and reform of housing benefits.

2. The instructions on the functioning of old people's homes and retirement homes: "the rules of the establishment should respect the freedom and the dignity of the elderly." The organization of health care in these establishments needed to be improved, for example, by increasing the number of nurses and installing a doctor's office in each one.

3. A plan for health and social facilities that sought to renovate departmental and community old people's homes, and to put extra beds in smaller establishments. Regional old-age insurance funds and the National Fund were expected to cooperate, as the state had recently allocated them a health and social services action fund under the decree of 25 September 1959.

The Study Commission was set up under the decree of 8 April 1960, a few months after the report and circular were published; its task was to examine the problems of the elderly and to propose an overall policy. The Comité National de la Vieillesse de France (National Committee for Old Age in France)[35] was set up a few months later. This was a standing advisory body made up of experts and of representatives of the different departments of the state and associations involved. The National Solidarity Fund Act of 30 June 1956 had made provision for this committee, but nothing had been done about setting it up. The first meeting took place on 11 January 1961, but the few meetings held in 1961 and 1962 did little more than reexamine the broad indications adopted by the Laroque Report.

All of these public initiatives indicated the state's new eagerness to be involved in the tasks of planning and coordinating social action for the elderly. The importance given to the home-care program and the criticism of conditions in old people's homes were new, and the state displayed its newfound dynamism in the management of the way of life of the elderly. Its efforts were on two levels. First, it stepped up its activities in the field of traditional public assistance programs and attempted to modernize the whole system. Evidence for this is to be found in new health-ministry circulars, and in the development of "open equipment funds" *(crédits d'équipement ouverts)* for "renovated" old people's homes and "welcoming" community centers.[36] Second, the state stimulated serious discussion on an old-age policy, and not just within a framework of social interests; this discussion triggered new plans of action that went beyond the traditional retirement system. It was as if, through persistent activity concerning the way of life of the elderly, the public authorities were trying to refocus the debate on retirement policies and the public assistance that was part and parcel of them. The state was in fact involved in a struggle to redefine the core issues of the old-age policy. It was also endeavoring to promote a new focus on old age and on needs that were no longer expressed in terms of retirement and the social right to a pension. In the view of the state, these needed to be set out in a way that saw old age as a stage of life, linked to the individual's way of life and social integration.

The author takes the view that the state's new dynamism in the field of old age was stimulated by the interaction of three factors. First, the rebuilding of the political and administrative system after the birth of the Gaullist state introduced a new form of voluntarism. Second, old age gradually emerged as a problem characterized by major social, political, and economic implications. Third, with the rapid expansion of complementary pension schemes, the state's ability to control retirement policies was sharply reduced. An examination of each of these three changes will be followed by an analysis of the effects they had on state action in the early 1960s.

CHANGES IN THE POLITICAL AND ADMINISTRATIVE SYSTEM

The Fourth Republic gave Parliament the powers it needed, although the Executive was already subject to them. The government's instability underlined how little autonomy the state had, compared to civil society at this time. Changes in production processes and the need to face up to membership in the European market meant that the dominant class increasingly needed help from the state as agent of development. If, as Pierre Birnbaum (1977) suggests, there was a link between the upper ranks of the administration and the major employers during the Fourth Republic, the government was unable to play its role of modernizer to the full, as it was effectively deprived of support from the Executive. This executive power was too unstable, and was subject to a parliament where widely diverging socio-economic interests (often very different from those of the major employers) fought for control. The instability and lack of credibility that beset the political apparatus prevented it from fulfilling the conditions that were necessary if the economy was to be effectively developed. During the Fourth Republic, the state seemed incapable of resolving the problem of colonial wars, and only with difficulty managed to give support to the long-term modernization of the French economy.

The transition to a Gaullist state occasioned the reconstruction of a political and administrative system that later promoted greater autonomy from social forces. This reconstruction took place through institutional reforms in 1958 and 1962 and through "Gaullist ideology" (i.e., the state placed above political parties). The result was a considerable degree of executive power that relied on the upper echelons of the administration, and was generally independent of political parties. The state's capacity for real action was used to develop voluntarist interventions at all levels of society, particularly in economic matters; the objective was to speed up the modernization and concentration of production processes, thereby enabling the state to counter foreign competition.

The state clearly operated as the agent of development during this period, handing planning departments an important role in the overall process. The national development plan, in short, the plan, became a "burning obligation," and the state allocated to itself new administrative departments where these were necessary. Major national projects were also planned, and attempts were made to exercise more effective control over key social problems. The creation of the Study Commission in 1960 and the series of initiatives that have already been examined in the field of old-age policy were further examples of the state's new capacity for action.

In the early 1960s, the large number of state interventions on the question of old age did not merely reflect the Gaullist state's new autonomy. They also flowed from the fact that old age was proving to be one of the major social problems of the period, and in the circumstances, the new voluntarism of the public authorities could not remain aloof.

OLD AGE: A PROBLEM WITH MAJOR SOCIAL, POLITICAL, AND ECONOMIC IMPLICATIONS

The changes that affected French society between 1945 and 1962 gave rise to new aspirations in relation to old age. The comprehensive insurance program that was born with the social security system in 1945, and the complementary retirement schemes that were subsequently attached to it, encouraged people to develop a more sympathetic understanding of social protection. From now on, social security was seen as a right. By contrast, public assistance was deemed degrading because people were now demanding the right to a comfortable, unrestricted, and dignified old age. Preventive medicine for elderly residents of old people's homes was now the norm. The uncomfortable surroundings of these homes, the degrading lack of privacy, and the sense of having been thrown on the "scrap heap" recalled the poorhouses of old, and increasingly justified the view that such institutions should be abolished.

Furthermore, rising household consumerism from 1959 onward led to the development of new ways of life and aspirations, and the fate awaiting most elderly people now seemed all the more unacceptable. In their daily lives, new retirees grimly contemplated the gap between real retirement (which was frequently wretched) and the retirement they had been looking forward to (a newly won entitlement to a period of rest on a pension).

The public opinion survey carried out in 1961 at the request of the Study Commission neatly captured a burgeoning awareness of these contradictory experiences. It revealed that public opinion saw the problem of old age and the housing crisis (another major concern at the time) as the most critical preoccupations of the period. The same survey also reported that 45 percent of people aged sixty or over considered their financial situation unsatisfactory, with only 25 percent claiming to be content. Poverty among the elderly became known to the public at large following long debates about the National Solidarity Fund; it was also the subject of numerous press articles and many interventions in the National Assembly. Poverty on this scale was now seen as something shocking, and was considered a scandal now that the elderly had a right to protection based on their past contribution to production.

The content analysis of *Le Monde* confirmed this shift in public perception. As has been noted elsewhere in this book, the plan of action regarding the elderly was rarely questioned between 1946 and the late 1950s. In fact, the only issues that came in for criticism were the cost of old age and the overall inadequacy of the state's response. This fact underlines the poor critical judgment brought to bear on the logic of the methods used. The debate centered on the amount of public assistance, and only rarely examined how it was distributed. Occasionally aspirations were articulated and demands formulated, and these led to skirmishes and negotiations over pensions with the labor unions.

The problems were tackled from a different angle in 1959 and 1960. These two years saw such an increase in demands and aspirations that it was not long before they appeared to be dominating the debate: 28 percent of articles between 1960 and 1967,[37] compared with 18 percent devoted to public assistance policy and 16 percent covering integration policy.

Demands pertaining to the pension scheme still held the lead, but the issue of elderly people's standard of living was catching up and now came a close second. This change underlined how much attention was now given to the elderly and their lifestyles. It was also expressed in more sympathetic responses, which stimulated questions about the fate awaiting the elderly. The elderly were no longer a pawn in the complex workings of institutions like the pension schemes and the public assistance policy that took care of them, and they now began to play a full role in the debate. Additional anxiety about their needs later emerged from criticisms of their material living conditions. This subsequently became the issue that attracted the largest amount of comment during the period 1960–66 with 38 percent of articles.[38] Old age began to be acknowledged as a social problem, and in consequence as a general target of specific political action. Poverty could no longer be analyzed by examining lower-income groups or elderly people living in penury. The elderly under consideration were the entire elderly population, not simply its poorest members.[39]

Although the material living conditions of the elderly were now perceived as a social scandal, however, it was not so much a question of the degree of destitution in absolute terms or contrasted with an earlier period; it was more that information about the traditional way of managing old age was no longer considered reliable. Moreover, the validity of the public assistance or segregation-based nature of the measures in use was more frequently questioned in the press from 1960 onward.

This problem was having a profound impact on public opinion, and the authorities did not ignore it. As one deputy disarmingly put it in the Chamber of Deputies: "Will we ever encounter an issue like the elderly, which directly affects 5 million French people, and indirectly touches their families and children and everyone who cares for them?"[40] Throughout the period 1958–62, the Chamber of Deputies was the setting for a steady stream of oral questions, interventions, and debates on bills, most of them raised by opposition parties. In October 1959, members of various political groups even created a Groupement National d'Action en Faveur de la Vieillesse (National Action Group for the Elderly), whose declared aim was "to better the financial and moral situation of former workers."

Each intervention stressed that the situation of the elderly had now reached alarming proportions, and pressed the government to act; it was felt that "recent action on behalf of the elderly was clearly inadequate."[41] Members of the parliamentary majority believed that this inadequacy was mainly due to a lack of coordination and overview of action in favor of the elderly. The state thereupon found itself with a new task, and several bills sought to establish a High Commissariat for the Elderly using the Youth Commissariat as a model. Members from all political parties stressed the urgency of the home-care service, a basic minimum income for the elderly, and improved housing. Although a much more sympathetic approach to such questions had now developed on the political scene, no political organization had so far come up with an alternative model for managing old age. There was clearly a need for measures covering a wide range of problems, but an overview of the entire issue was also required.

Labor unions had little input into the way of life of the elderly. They had hitherto concentrated their efforts on a campaign to defend and extend the right to retirement (raising pensions and lowering the retirement age) and to control the governing institutions. Indeed, two unions, FO and CFTC, saw recent agreements on complementary pensions as the culmination of their strategy to improve pension schemes; this involved sidestepping the general scheme and reaching ad hoc agreements with employers on complementary arrangements. As a result, the unions felt that they had won a major victory for working people, and one that followed in the footsteps of their 1945 achievement of setting up social security.

Although the CGT had not been in the vanguard of these policies, and had joined the institutions only after they had been set up, it devoted much column space to the development of complementary pension schemes. The three labor unions now joined forces to fight for an increase in noncontributory benefits from the National Solidarity Fund, and demanded swift action on the question of raising the old-age minimum income as a way of eliminating the scandalous misery of older workers. They believed that the state was not sufficiently involved, and criticized the ordinance of 30 December 1958 for making the social security system bear an unfair amount of financial responsibility for the fund.

In the early 1960s, old age was not only a problem that posed major social and political questions; it also had considerable economic implications. The signing of the Treaty of Rome offered new prospects of growth on a European scale, and people began to realize that the elderly could retard development in many ways. The introduction of the Study Commission's report echoed these concerns:

> Of all the countries in the world today, with the exception of East Germany (where the situation is explained by the special circumstances obtaining in that country), France has the highest proportion of elderly people.
>
> An aging population impacts on every aspect of national life, and slowly but surely, it puts a strain on the living conditions of all French people. First of all, looking after elderly people who are not in work puts an increasingly heavy burden on the shoulders of those who are employed, regardless of the origin and legal status of the income of these unemployed people—be it in the form of retirement pensions financed from contributions, public assistance paid for by state organizations, or income from capital or living allowances. It is quite clear that the unemployed live on the goods produced, and the services created, by people in work. The employed population are therefore responsible for this increase so that old people who are not in work can survive. Bearing demographic projections in mind, and assuming that the level of income guaranteed to the elderly remains constant, the amount of this increase will continue to rise until 1975. It will be only after 1975–80 that the proportion of consumers will stabilize, at least temporarily, at about 1:5. By contrast, in economic terms, population aging exerts a certain amount of influence on occupational structures, facilities and work methods—at least in sectors that employ relatively large numbers of older workers.
>
> Finally, as far as political and psychological matters were concerned, aging was expressed in terms of conservatism, adherence to old habits, lack of mobility and poor adaptation to progress in the modern world.
>
> The Study Commission was set up by the decree of 8 April 1960 to analyze the cost and consequences of population aging, and to provide guidelines for an old-age policy.[42]

Shortly before the Laroque Report was published, employers began to make nervous claims that the aging of industrial workers carried with it the risk of economic stagnation. An opinion poll by IFOP of one hundred company directors in 1961 showed that employers were prejudiced against older workers: 58 percent of employers claimed that older workers produced less; 34 percent cited problems of poor adaptability to new work techniques and methods; and 24 percent spoke of a loss of skill and accuracy. When asked to elaborate on the problems posed by older workers in industry, the employers mentioned lower production rates first, then retirement age, and finally the cost of pensions. As for employee productivity, they felt that retirement age was too high; indeed, 60 percent believed that the retirement age for men should be lowered to sixty. However, it was the level of pensions that prevented them from reducing the number of older workers as they would have liked. The directors spoke of their feelings of guilt when forcing older workers to retire, and of the pressure they were under from such workers to let them keep their jobs. The directors thus wanted something done to improve the living conditions of the elderly, so that they could avoid this difficult situation. Such ideas were aimed specifically at bringing economic imperatives to center stage at a time when the perspective of European competition was starting to take shape.

Furthermore, the directors who took part in the survey had no faith in attempts made by older workers to adapt to new tasks. Of those surveyed, 78 percent did not really believe that large-scale retraining was possible for older workers, and few of them ran such schemes, even on an empirical basis; 76 percent of those surveyed also rejected the idea of part-time work for older workers, and felt that policies for keeping older employees in work were pointless. Like the unions, though for different reasons, they believed that improving the lives of the elderly depended directly on lowering the age at which they stopped work and on raising pensions.[43] Thus, the state was receiving increasingly urgent appeals from both unions and employers to deal with the problem of old age.

The new dynamism injected into planning—it had once again become a "burning obligation"—invited more farsighted approach; it also encouraged a greater sensitivity toward forms of social and economic interdependence. Social progress was seen less as a by-product of the economy than as a factor capable of adapting society to development and technological change.[44] It was becoming increasingly clear that social reform had been designed as a tool to aid economic growth.

Seen in this light, the traditional way of providing the elderly with public assistance seemed particularly inadequate. Apart from the fact that it functioned according to the ethos of charitable institutions, themselves now the subject of some criticism, it created an image of the future that was completely out of kilter with a society in which growth and planning were becoming well established, and which operated on the basis of a philosophy of social exclusion that was becoming increasingly ill-adapted to the period. If any kind of management plan for the elderly was to be produced, much would have to be done to shape public opinion. This shaping would provide every generation with a definition of aging and of the future, something that was particularly relevant to a society where increased life expectancy made old age a part of everyone's future.

A previous section has shown that the traditional way of providing the elderly with public assistance, the main element of which was the old people's home, created a negative image of old age, and one that was associated with great poverty. One advantage of this negative image was that it promoted saving and encouraged the entire working-class population to plan ahead for old age. However, focusing on the future in this way (via the management of old age) totally contradicted both the idea of a society in which growth and planning were establishing themselves as key components and the kind of relationship with the future that this society was trying to develop. This was to be a relationship based on forecasting strategies, not merely on providence.

The negative image of old age disseminated through the traditional system of management obscured all view of the years to come; it also placed a heavy burden on the future of each person living in a social world dominated by medium- to long-range planning. This system was also setting up increasingly restrictive institutions that forced people to adopt individual strategies based on the same horizons (e.g., rationalization of educational and occupational choices, installment buying—even the virtues of saving) that formed part of the traditional public assistance model. The negative image was also opposed to the "solidarity education"[45] demanded by the new mechanisms of social policy based on collective insurance.

The state, now armed with its new voluntarism, was trying to deal with a problem that, owing to its social and political consequences and the inadequacy of traditional management in the new economic setting, was in danger of impeding the progress of French society in the long run.

A DECLINE IN THE STATE'S ABILITY TO CONTROL PENSIONS

This period was marked both by the emergence of a multidimensional problem related to old age and by a decline in the state's ability to control pensions—at the time, the main instrument in the organization of relations between society and the elderly. The state had some control over the general scheme, as it supervised the general operation and was in charge of setting contributions and fixing ceilings. However, outside the scheme, complementary pension plans, which were fixed by collective agreements and were jointly managed, were spreading rapidly. The role of the state was thus reduced to giving official approval. In this way, what the public authorities had previously blocked for lack of a coherent old-age policy had now been obtained by the elderly themselves, outside the general scheme. This was how Pierre Laroque himself saw the adoption of complementary schemes; these had started up with only a few hundred thousand cadres in 1947, but by 1957, when UNIRS (Union Nationale des Institutions de Retraites des Salariés—National Union of Employee Pensions Institutes) was established, there were 1,700,000 members, of whom 500,000 were cadres. When ARRCO (Association des Régimes de Retraite Complémentaire—Association of Complementary Pension Schemes) was founded in 1961, it became a kind of second general scheme that was largely free of public control.

The Gaullist state, with its new capacity for action and a desire to prove its autonomy, tried to redirect the debate on old age away from pensions, as this was an area in which its role was restricted to ratifying agreements based on relations between labor unions and employers.

TOWARD MORE DIRECT STATE CONTROL OVER THE ISSUE OF OLD AGE

The interaction of these three new social conditions (the emergence of the voluntarist state, the importance of the issue of old age in the public debate, and the public authorities' diminished control over pensions) produced a state with a more dynamic outlook on questions pertaining to the way of life of the elderly. The state was eager to play a more direct role in what was becoming an increasingly acute problem, and tried to cease restricting its interventions to the remote role of transferring money. It accordingly attempted to restructure its response in more sociopolitical terms; it did this by upgrading or relaunching its traditional services for the elderly and by encouraging a shift in the debate on old age away from pensions and toward way of life. This new direction succeeded in broadening the state's room to maneuver in social protection of the elderly, and as a result, made it easier for the elderly to depend more directly on society; however, it also became possible to reactivate systems of public action in a way that was more appropriate to a state eager to place itself above political parties, and at the same time increase its distance from social classes. In terms of way of life as opposed to pensions, this reformulation of the main component of old-age policy opened up new means of communication and mediation between civil society and the state. The latter no longer worked exclusively through intermediary groups representing the political and labor-union views of particular social interests; earlier sections of this book have provided examples of these interests, which were the driving force behind the retirement policy.

The Role of the Study Commission in Relation to the Problems of Old Age, and as an Instrument of Policy Change

The Study Commission played the leading role in giving a new focus to the debate on old age. The establishment of the commission enabled the state to promote a new line of attack on the problems of old age, the objective being to open up new lines of state intervention that excluded pensions and public assistance. Like any commission, it was used as a stalling device, particularly as far as the National Assembly was concerned, but its social role was not confined to such maneuvers. Everything about the Study Commission, from the way it functioned to what it actually discussed, underlined the reason for its existence: the production of a wide-ranging technocratic plan for managing old age.

A COMMISSION STANDING BACK FROM SOCIAL INTERESTS

Setting up the commission was a perfect illustration of how the Gaullist state worked. One of its constant concerns was to signal its independence from political parties and representatives of social interests, although it was quite prepared when necessary to introduce new administrative structures outside the hierarchy in order to carry out its functions as an agent of change.

The commission originated with the state. The idea was even conceived at the highest reaches of the Executive, having been the brainchild of the prime minister of the day, Michel Debré. The commission was chaired by a senior civil servant who had wide-ranging authority in the field of social protection; this came from his previous involvement in the production of the French social security plan and from subsequent high-ranking posts at the Direction Générale de la Sécurité Sociale (General Directorate of Social Security) and later the presidency of the Caisse Nationale. In the president's own words, the commission operated like a British royal commission; it had only nine members and twelve rapporteurs, and all the members had been selected for their expertise in the field. None represented social interests, and with one exception, they were all high-ranking civil servants (from the Council of State, the universities, and the Collège de France); the rapporteurs, too, were mainly recruited from leading state institutions such as the Revenue Court (Cour des Comptes) and the Council of State.

The organization of the commission placed it above specific interests and at a remove from the administrative hierarchy. The reason for this was that the senior civil servants who sat on it had no links with the government departments that provided services for the elderly. The commission's work was thus marked by a twofold independence that was essential for its task, which was to explore new arenas for action outside the traditional channels and away from the social actors that distributed the benefits. The nature of its composition and the eminence of its members ensured a significant and wide-ranging impact on the new principles.

At this time, the state was working hard on a series of major technocratic plans in a number of different fields, and the organization of the Study Commission was similar to that of other state projects. It also reflected the state's enthusiasm for increasing its autonomy from civil society. The commission's statements confirm a view propounded elsewhere in this chapter that it had been set up as a state initiative to look into new ways of intervening on behalf of the elderly outside the channels concerned with retirement.

A REVERSAL OF PERSPECTIVE

It is the view of the author that, by proposing a coordinated plan of action, the main effect of the Study Commission's report on the problems of old age was to shake up the hierarchy of interventions in the field. Up till then, the prevalent view had been that the problems of the elderly had to do with their pensions; this had also been the position of the unions. Other aspects of the policy were seen as residual, and were expected to disappear once the pension system offered sufficient protection.

The new proposals of the Laroque Commission turned this logic on its head and focused on the question of the way of life. The new "old-age policy" sought to "enable the elderly to remain in society and to avoid an abrupt change in their living conditions."[46] As has been pointed out, this principle of nonsegregation meant that an impact on the way of life of the elderly became the central element of the old-age policy. Other areas of intervention such as pension schemes and employment had to work toward that objective. In practice there was no prolongation of normal life for the elderly unless they had sufficient income and unless there was a constant process of adaptation of people to work, and of work to persons of advancing years. From this point on, wider access to the right to a period of rest and replacement earnings ceased to be the aim of state action on the elderly; it was now simply a component of the new goal: the social integration of the elderly population. By setting up the Study Commission, the state was now participating in a struggle in which the definition of old age and its management were at stake.

Old age, once it had been interpreted by the Laroque Report against a backdrop of marginalization and isolation, was no longer defined in terms of retirement and the right to a period of inactivity following a period of employment. It was now a social status linked to a stage of life.[47] The coining of the term "the third age" implied a less robust definition of retirement, favoring one that described an individual's position in the life span. By the same token, the new approach identified the way of life of the elderly as the key area for action.

NEW SUPPORT SYSTEMS FOR PUBLIC ACTION

The shift in perspectives stimulated by the Laroque Report not only led to new state actions in the field of social protection of the elderly, and new areas of intervention; it also identified new social support systems for this state action.

As the focus of social protection shifted from pensions to way-of-life policies, state interventions acquired a new basis of social and political support. This book has already shown how, as a result of their conflictual relations with employers, the unions had been a driving force behind the retirement policy, but as far as the way of life was concerned, they played a much more subdued role. This field had traditionally been the territory of private charities, professional organizations of medical and social workers, and federations of such social institutions as the Union Nationale des Bureaux d'Aide Sociale (National Union of Social Welfare Offices). These had links with people like doctors and town councillors, and complementary pension scheme funds had recently added their support; the latter were in direct contact with the elderly population and were therefore more sensitive to their changing needs. Each group developed new practical formulas at the grassroots level, based on its individual beliefs, strategies, and interests. The complementary pension-scheme institutions were particularly well placed to make innovations in the way-of-life policy: the reason for this was that their clients were retired workers fortunate enough to enjoy double social protection (both general and complementary), or else they were former cadres. Through their contact with new retirees, these organizations were already able to sense that beyond material requirements lay certain moral needs associated with the struggle against boredom, loneliness, and marginality.

Indeed, competition was such that the complementary pension institutions had to work hard to increase the number of member companies, and this forced them to anticipate the demand taking shape in a new captive market of employees. They thus promoted their own form of social action, to which they referred when presenting their services to companies. In this way many complementary pension funds, and especially those set up for cadres from 1947 onward, made way of life (and no longer simply standard of living) the basis of their social policy for the elderly.[48] They developed new social policies shortly afterwards and opened leisure and holiday clubs for retirees, and social clubs for the elderly where beneficiaries could meet. They also came up with new housing ideas that did away with the overcrowding associated with old people's homes: these included retirement villages,[49] old people's residential homes, and community centers that provided housing.

What all these activities had in common was a desire to be quite different from traditional public assistance services. The new clubs took their inspiration from the British formula and were a far remove from the traditional workhouse. Similarly, the housing schemes were very modern and comfortable, providing retirees with individual accommodation. They stood in marked contrast to the earlier old people's homes, which now served as a model of what not to do.[50] However, this departure from the traditional range of public assistance for the elderly also reflected the fact that a number of social referents had been replaced. These new services and facilities were a far cry from the appalling situations of the destitute old people for whom the old people's homes had been a kind of refuge. In fact, much of the sociability and lifestyle suggested salaried middle-class values, and that was why changes in the practices of the management agents of old age were accompanied by a "drift" *(glissement)* of the social referents.

The Study Commission report was the fruit of wide-ranging and systematic consultations carried out through interviews and questionnaires; all the aforementioned groups were questioned. It also organized what had already been achieved in different places into a coherent plan of action. These groups now saw that their work enjoyed official legitimacy; they also discovered that their work was a key link in coordinated interventions in favor of the elderly, and was admirably suited to such a program.

In the early 1960s, new social conditions prompted the state to try and take firmer control of the management of the elderly. This led to the setting up of the Study Commission and to the state claiming as its own the new definition of the main component of its old-age policy—action for an integrated way of life. The adoption of this definition made pensions, at the time an issue for which the state had eschewed responsibility, a much less central matter altogether.

This interpretation seemed to be confirmed by the welcome given to the Laroque Report by the labor unions. They made it quite clear that the debate on old age could be shifted away from an extension of the right to retirement only as long as workers' interests were protected. The unions defended their definition of the issue against that contained in the report. While maintaining the principle of nonsegregation of the elderly, Laroque also recommended that retirement age should not be lowered, and that age limits for employment should not be lowered, lest one encourage age discrimination in employment.

The unions agreed with some of the report's reforms—for example, those related to methods for calculating pensions and increasing the minimum old-age benefit. This was because they believed that low income was the major problem faced by the elderly. However, they fiercely criticized "the social regression implied by the commission's clearly articulated preference for extending the working lives of the elderly."[51] According to certain Marxist analysts, this approach was even seen as an indication that the "commission has looked for ways to reconcile employment of the elderly and capitalist interests once and for all."[52] It was a question of turning the retired population into a "reserve army of labor" that could be used as the economic situation demanded. This position reduced the debate on old age to a confrontation between, on one hand, workers fighting for their right to a period of rest at the end of their lives, and on the other, capitalists trying to transform old-age policy into an employment policy. The approach developed in the Laroque Report declined to incorporate either point of view. Here old age was not defined as a social right, and the elderly were not seen as a part of the workforce to be utilized when required. Old age was a stage of life that merited full citizenship and social integration for each individual. The retirement and employment policies proposed were subordinated to this central objective of nonsegregation and an integrated way of life for the elderly. By claiming this approach as its own, the state took charge of all aspects of old-age policy, and thus maximized its own capacity for action and signaled its autonomy from social actors and class struggle.

State Building Programs and Local Mobilizations (1962–1969)

A TECHNOCRATIC AND UTOPIAN PLAN

There is forever a yawning gap between a commission's enthusiastic statements and a government's interventions. There was no less of a shortfall between the Laroque Report's new policy for old age and what was implemented as part of state action in the period 1962–69.

In decrees passed on 11 April 1962 shortly after the report's publication, the government agreed to emergency measures to increase, improve, and unify minimum noncontributory allowances, but these fell short of the report's recommendations. The Employment Ministry pointed out that the government injection of 1 billion francs was substantial,[53] and promised that there would eventually be a detailed reform of this legislation that was in line with the commission's proposals. These measures appear to have been enough to pacify a National Assembly looking hard at the problems of a minimum income for the elderly. Ministry of Public Health circulars then followed at periodic intervals: these dealt with approaches that had previously been adopted and with existing legislation, all of which could be used to help keep the elderly in their own homes without recourse to new measures. For its part, the Employment Ministry tried to redirect the work of the social security organizations it controlled, and it recommended that top priority should be given to the home-care program and housing benefits (administrative circular of 14 September 1965), so that elderly people could enjoy as independent an existence as possible. In practice, the social action budgets of regional old-age funds (until the 1967 ordinances) and the National Fund were almost entirely devoted to investment in building projects to provide temporary and permanent housing for the elderly. This investment accounted for 64 percent of money spent by the Old-Age Fund between 1959 and 1967.[54] Money spent on individual social action (home improvements, home help, and holiday allowances) had to come from the remaining 36 percent: the home help service qualified for most with 24 percent, and holiday allowances took 7 percent.

Social action carried out by the old-age insurance scheme was therefore only marginally affected by the Laroque Report recommendations. Even in the field of housing investment, a segregation policy promoting accommodation in old people's homes and retirement homes (these received two-thirds of all housing expenditure between 1959 and 1967) was preferred to housing policies involving residential homes and community centers providing housing; this is borne out by an analysis of public assistance expenditures by the National Old-Age Insurance Fund for Salaried Workers (Caisse Nationale d'Assurance Vieillesse des Travailleurs Salariés) during this period.

The housing crisis and the size of the aging population combined to draw the Study Commission's attention to the problems of housing[55] and to the fact that the emphasis had been placed on housing investment for the elderly; however, the approaches adopted by the Old-Age Fund by no means coincided with those recommended by the commission. Laroque had mainly encouraged the construction of community centers providing housing, because he believed that these were more effective at preserving the independence of the elderly and provided an intermediate stage between community housing and private accommodation.[56] It was only in cases where a community-based solution was necessary that the commission opted for small-scale retirement homes.

Like the Old-Age Fund, neither of the two French plans covering the period 1962–69 included a social policy for old age that adhered to the commission's recommendations for social integration; in fact, they agreed with the Old-Age Fund in contributing to the development of segregated social housing. The Fourth French Plan (1961–65) called for the provision of forty thousand extra beds in private and state-run old people's homes and retirement homes, but in the event, actual spending came to just 67 percent of the initial projection. According to a Conseil Économique et Social (Social and Economic Council) analysis of the Fourth Plan's achievements with respect to social and health facilities, much effort had been put into dealing with the problems of children with behavioral problems, but there had been considerable delays in building retirement homes and community centers providing housing for the elderly. The Fifth Plan (1966–70) continued along these lines, with the same gap between budgeted projections and actual spending, and in the case of the elderly, this did not exceed 50 percent. Altogether the number of retirement homes and old people's homes rose substantially from 270,778 to 320,797 between 1962 and 1970; by contrast, there were still only 9,358 elderly people living in community centers in 1968.[57] This figure was well below the number of people in need of such housing; the following year, the Fourth Plan's Elderly Persons' Intergroup estimated that the overall requirement was for 110,000 places.

This suggests that the new global preventive and promotional model for the management of the elderly, as recommended by the Study Commission, had had no influence over the work of the public authorities; for all practical purposes, the latter were still carrying out a policy of segregated housing.

Work on helping the elderly to continue living in their own homes remained at an embryonic stage. The home-help scheme, which had been mooted in legislation back in 1954 and formally introduced by the National Old-Age Fund in 1959, covered only 36,300 elderly people in 1968. In the same year, it was estimated that there were 716 home-help services, and these were poorly distributed geographically. Again, in 1968 only 538 community centers provided food, and these catered to 34,592 elderly people. At this time, clubs were just beginning to get established: a national survey of clubs for the elderly carried out by the Ministry of Public Health and Social Security on 30 September 1972 revealed that, of the 2040 then in existence, 38 percent had been opened in 1971 and 1972. Only 34 percent had been established between 1966 and 1970; 9 percent had opened between 1961 and 1966, the remainder having been set up prior to 1961. In other words, in 1968, there were fewer than a thousand clubs for the elderly in the whole of France.

A comparison between the total measures enabling the elderly to stay in their own homes and the number of people in the population aged sixty-five or over (6,680,000 in 1968), which accounted for approximately 0.5 percent of the population, demonstrates that they were clearly inadequate during the period when preparations for the Fourth Plan were about to commence. This suggests that, by and large, the Study Commission's report was still a technocratic utopia.

This book's author takes the view that there were three main reasons for this: the social support systems that were vital for implementing these measures were inadequate; the recommended action model went far beyond the state's capacity to intervene in many areas; and a series of political and economic events meant that the Executive was not properly cognizant of the issue of aging.

Taking the first reason first, many of the commission's recommendations did not find the kind of social support that was necessary for state action. Redirection of the employment policy for older workers received no support from either employers or workers, despite the fact that it was based largely on a policy of negotiated settlements. The employers were preoccupied with making profitable investments and were not attracted by the idea of improving conditions of employment, or prolonging the career of workers whose productivity was poor; this was particularly true at a time when there was little social campaigning, and what little there was failed to focus on the subject. Workers, for their part, were more interested in achieving the right to a period of rest and in shortening the working life through lowering the retirement age; this objective also overlapped with their desire not to undermine opportunities for young people to enter the labor market. Nor was the Employment Ministry tempted to involve itself in measures whose chances of success were slim, through a lack of support from social forces. This was particularly true since as far as employment policy was concerned, the emphasis at this time was on industrial growth, mobility, and support for essential restructuring; a policy promoting better employment prospects for older workers was clearly at odds with this. The few initiatives undertaken by the Employment Ministry, such as setting up a task force on arduous work, made little headway and produced nothing. In 1968, the Inspection Générale des Affaires Sociales (General Social Affairs Inspectorate) carried out surveys in companies with a view to understanding the general problems of employing older workers. It concluded that "there had been no follow-up to the commission's suggestions for removing obstacles to the recruitment and hiring of these workers."[58] Similarly, proposals for an income policy for the elderly came into conflict with a series of social categories that defended rights that had been acquired in the field of social protection.

Recommendations related to medical and social support for the elderly found few active supporters among professionals, local authorities, and directors of social security bodies and complementary pension funds, despite the fact that it was they who had stimulated the commission's proposals in the first place. A subsequent section of this book will examine some of the Laroque Report's reorientations, but this will be preceded by a look at the obstacles that stood in their way. Examination of the very nature of the actors mobilized around this project will shed light on some of the differences between the overall old-age policy proposed by the Laroque Report and the policy that finally saw the light of day under the Sixth Plan.

The second obstacle to the implementation of the Laroque Report's recommendations was undoubtedly the state's limited capacity for intervention. As in the field of social action, there were groups that were able to give support to these ideas and put them into operation, but administrative and financial backup were in short supply. In other words, the proposals went beyond the state's scope of action. Although the Study Commission had carefully drawn up a list of objectives to be included in a state old-age policy, it had given much less thought to procedures and means for putting them into practice. Furthermore, the commission consistently rejected the notion of segregation, having abandoned the idea of setting up an administrative structure specializing in the coordination of services for the aged, such as a Commissariat for the Elderly. It relied to a large extent on the pervasive power inherent in the guidelines it set out, and assumed that these would galvanize public and private organizations alike. The authors of the report openly acknowledged that their proposals were ambitious, but they still insisted that such proposals were necessary, given the economic changes taking place. On the subject of employment, they wrote:

> The commission makes no secret of the difficulties it faces in defining and implementing this kind of employment policy; it is a policy that involves an almost revolutionary upheaval of established ideas and current practices. The commission nevertheless believes that, in view of the ever-increasing pace of economic and technological change, this policy will not only bring a satisfactory solution to the problems of old age, but will also provide social and economic mechanisms with the flexibility that these changes require. The task calls for an energetic training program to alter the way workers and employers think. Training is also essential to prepare workers for the changes they face in the future. Finally, there is a need for close collaboration between individual employers, employers' and workers' organizations, and workers themselves.[59]

It is easy to see why the commission's recommended measures could not be implemented given the state of employment offices *(bureaux de main-d'œuvre)* during the early 1960s—staff shortages (only one employment officer for every 5,268 workers in France in 1963), poor quality of personnel, antiquated premises, and the fact that their main job was to register unemployed people receiving benefits.[60]

To make matters worse, social administration was traditionally the poor relation, not only because of its low budget, but also because of its own staff problems: too few employees, inadequate training, and the absence of a powerful corps of high-level civil executives ("Grand Corps") capable of ensuring that its objectives were carried out, in the way that senior civil servants guided the fortunes of other government departments. Furthermore, social administration had the task of looking after a widely varied population; within this population, the elderly were clearly least able to organize themselves into a pressure group, while children with behavioral difficulties (and others) found devoted supporters within the powerful network of family unions. This heterogeneous clientele was catered to by a disparate network of support bodies whose disjointed work caused interventions to be fragmented. Furthermore, because these people had been absorbed by the public assistance program, they no longer had sufficient material or human resources to promote the newly recommended types of home care.

This problem was particularly relevant because the home-care scheme demanded the kind of close collaboration of the health and social services that social administration had failed to encourage, at least until the reform of 30 July 1964; this latter development took what had been divided up, and regrouped it into a *département*-based Directorate of Health and Social Action; this theoretically put an end to administrative rivalries between health-care and social service agencies.

The barriers that stood in the way of implementing state action based on the Laroque Report's recommendations derived both from difficulty in finding social bases for such action and from the inflexibility of administrative structures. There was also a third obstacle: a series of political and economic events that occurred shortly after the report's publication and that resulted in the Executive according the matter less attention. The legislative elections that took place in the autumn of 1962 provided the government with a more stable majority in the National Assembly, and simultaneously diluted the effect of political mobilization on the fate of the elderly. Moreover, the new head of government, Georges Pompidou, was less sympathetic to population problems than his predecessor had been. Finally, the stabilization program implemented in the summer of 1963 included price freezes and budget restrictions; neither measure was likely to encourage social spending.

An earlier section has shown that the new ideas set out in the Laroque

Report remained in abeyance. During the period 1962–69, the public policy for old age consisted mainly of action on segregated accommodation. The three main obstacles to the implementation of the new public ambition for an old-age policy ensured that the state's voluntarist project was short-lived. However, the fact that the new doctrine had no influence on the state's decision making does not mean that it had no effect at all. There is plenty of evidence to suggest that the main impact was of an ideological nature. As far as planning in France was concerned, some research shows that the commission's influence was not so much at the level of this or that decision, but rather at an earlier stage in the process, at an ideological and legal level.[61] The next section will attempt to establish that the new thinking made more of an impact in the way it contributed to the socialization of conditions surrounding local decision making. It was a way of producing a sociological analysis of a public commission.

UNIFYING GERONTOLOGICAL ISSUES

The new state policy for the social integration of the elderly provided the many scattered agents working on the way of life of the elderly with a common language and series of concepts. They also found in this doctrine a new rationale for their work and state legitimation for their interventions. The Laroque Report henceforth functioned as a frame of reference that gradually unified the representations and work of people who, for different reasons, were already engaged in a wide variety of initiatives.

Local authorities, members of *départements,* general councils, charity directors, complementary pension funds, and professionals in medical and social matters eagerly embraced this new measure, which served their interests so well. By making social integration of the elderly the main priority and by shifting the focus of the debate on old age from pensions to way of life, the report designated a large number of parties in the sociomedical field to be the new managers of old age, and thereby united their activities. The numerous indicators of this will be discussed in the following pages.

Conversely, the fact that the debate on old age was beginning to incorporate the way of life consigned the labor unions to a more peripheral position; in fact, the debate dealt with problems with which the union movement was quite unfamiliar. The unions focused on work, and they were therefore ill-equipped to understand what old age was all about; they saw it as the opposite of work, disalienation as opposed to alienation, and abject poverty due to the absence of a sufficiently developed right to retirement.[62]

The content analysis of articles in *Le Monde* confirms that the issues of an integration policy for the elderly and of the new agents implementing it (e.g., local authorities, complementary pension institutions, and experts) both figured during the period 1960–67. Labor unions representing both cadres and manual workers were very active in the debate on pension schemes and worked within a broad political front to defend the standard of living of the elderly. Their allies included political parties, charitable organizations, and local authorities. As a result, new agents were identified as being capable of sustaining the momentum that the state had initiated, and their various views were brought together. At the same time, however, labor union influence on the debate was on the wane.

Structure and unification of gerontological output. Gerontology established itself as a new discipline in France after the Second World War. It had three central elements. The first had a basis that combined a study of demography and economics, and was led by Alfred Sauvy and the Institut National d'Études Démographiques (National Institute of Demographic Studies); the second had a medical/hospital bias and was organized around Léon Binet and his pupil, François Bourlière; the third was more political and included general practitioners, some of whom also held political office. Falling into the latter category was Dr. Huet, a former doctor at the Nanterre old people's home who practiced medicine in Paris; he was an elected Socialist representative in the city's suburbs and had served as president of the Seine General Council. Relations among these elements was rather distant—some would say circumspect—especially between the first and the third.

This small group of specialists intervened on a variety of occasions from the mid-1950s onward.[63] The demographers focused attention on France's aging population; the hospital doctors stressed the possibilities of a branch of medicine for the elderly and the prevention of ailments associated with aging, and condemned staffing shortages in old people's homes; and the medical-political experts criticized the idea of old people's homes and asylums, recommended medical-social measures aimed at enabling the elderly to stay in their own homes, and promoted a new image of an active elderly population that participated in life on a day-to-day basis. This image also sought to free the elderly from the stigma of old age through a new activist approach that helped them to improve their quality of life; it was this that came to be known as the "third age."[64]

As a discipline, gerontology in France was still just finding its feet[65] and was still very fragmented, but it gained new momentum from the Study Commission's work on the problems of old age. This gave gerontology a degree of state acceptance and helped it to focus its ideas. Moreover, the most eminent representatives of two of its components, Alfred Sauvy and François Bourlière, were commission members. Furthermore, the contribution that the human sciences specialists (newcomers to the field of gerontology at this time, and well represented on the commission) made to this unification and consolidation of discussion on old age deserves mention. Clearly, the link that now existed between the official political project and gerontological know-how could act as a form of scientific guarantor.

The special May 1963 edition of the magazine *Esprit*, published a year after the Laroque Report and devoted to the theme "Old Age and Aging," clearly showed how gerontological ideas were being unified. All of the leading actors—demographers, hospital doctors, general practitioners, senior civil servants, and representatives of the newly formed discipline of human sciences—were represented. Their ideas were generally convergent, and explicit references to the Laroque Report were frequent. They also agreed that it was necessary to put an end to the social exile into which the elderly had been cast. Old people did not simply pose a problem of coverage. Nor could they simply be treated as a group of destitute people, since that general approach isolated them further and made their plight worse than ever. This reassessment of the elderly came about partly thanks to specialists now known as gerontologists. Old age was no longer a form of degeneration, but a new phase in an active and participatory life. The interventions of human sciences specialists in particular highlighted the existing union between their interpretation of aging and what the Laroque Report had described in more official terms. When the philosopher Michel Philibert spoke in support of a "reversal of the 'scale of ages'" and of "an old age-policy based on restoring both a doctrine for the continued spiritual growth of human beings and a wide-ranging program of continuing education,"[66] these were surely ideas that directly reflected the commission's approach to a policy for employment and social integration. The ideas of human sciences specialists on the question of old age originated largely in American gerontology, and more particularly in the theoretical current referred to by its critics as "activist."[67]

Other research[68] has examined the three tenets on which this activist theoretical approach to old age was founded. First, it recognized what the elderly had in common—age and activity—to the exclusion of all else: this approach ignored what divided them, and failed to situate the elderly in relation to the different social classes they came from. There was therefore a great danger of turning the characteristics that had their origins in the social system into natural qualities specific to old age. This in turn could lead to what might be called a "naturalization" of old age.

Second, it gave prominence to psychological and psychosociological factors, and stressed the personal characteristics that allow an individual to make a success of his/her old age. In so doing, it largely ignored the political and social conditions in which individuals adapt to old age. The result of such psychologism was a voluntarist philosophy that based the success or failure of old age on personal decision.

Third, the activist approach led to the development of the art of enjoying an agreeable old age, and this involved the active and highly skilled adaptation of attitudes and approaches as the years passed. In this way the desocialization of the elderly could be avoided as long as the rules of aging were observed. All of the specialists reached the same conclusions in *Esprit*, albeit in different ways.[69] The magazine's general conclusion also took up this issue.

Through the unification of gerontology the art of enjoying an agreeable old age was developed, based on new gerontological know-how that insisted on new normative models of behavior and legitimated political approaches.

The unification of gerontological work, an advance linked to the publication of the Laroque Report, occurred at the same time as significant structuring developments in this scientific field. There were a few embryonic signs of gerontology after the war: the Centre d'Étude et de Recherches Gérontologiques (CER—Center for Gerontology Study and Research)[70] was set up in 1949; 1954 saw the launch of the *Revue de Gérontologie d'Expression Française* (French gerontological review), and the Association Gérontologique Claude Bernard was established under François Bourlière as part of Paris's Public Assistance Department in 1955. However, despite these stirrings, no substantial developments took place until after the Study Commission reported. A number of organizations were then formed. They included the Société Française de Gérontologie (French Gerontological Society)[71] in 1961, the Association de Gérontologie (Gerontology Association) in Paris in 1963, the Centre de Gérontologie de la Caisse Nationale de Retraite des Ouvriers du Bâtiment (Gerontology Center of the National Retirement Fund for Construction Workers) in 1966, and the Fondation Nationale de Gérontologie (National Gerontology Foundation) in 1967; the latter was the idea of Pierre Laroque, and its president was François Bourlière. The task of bringing together the work of experts in gerontology and building up their specialist field coincided with the rise of a new dynamic of activities in the field of gerontology.

A new dynamic in local gerontological work. A unification of the ideas emerging in gerontology was reflected in a sharper focus of action generated within the field, and alliances between various agents aimed at encouraging gerontological activity now seemed viable. The policy adopted was one that promoted the way of life of the elderly. It concentrated on social reintegration and enabling the elderly to stay in their own homes, and in this way it conformed to the principles of the Laroque Report; the procedures recommended at this time influenced state actions at a later stage. Although innovative policy on the management of the elderly as stated and initiated by the state did not lead to public decisions, it did at least further the cause in the minds of people generally. It also paved the way for a revival in state action and encouraged the establishment of networks of agents and pressure groups that were soon helping to ensure that the way of life of the elderly became part of the planning system.

Several data sources have been used in this book to reconstruct the network of agents that influenced the revival of discussion and practices in the field, and to analyze their alliances and agreements. First, there was the content analysis of *Le Monde,* which made it possible to date changes in stated policies on old age and identify the agents of those changes. Second, a great deal of information was derived from interviews conducted with most of the people promoting these actions; they were able to throw particular light on the strategies of change adopted by the various categories of agents. And third, monographs on local work identified the groups that formed the alliances and reached agreements that initially stimulated the work.

Content analysis of *Le Monde* confirms that from the early 1960s onward, debate on old-age policy moved away from the question of public assistance and pensions towards that of a way-of-life policy focusing particularly on social integration. This question made steady progress between 1960 and 1968, and eventually occupied a central position in the debate. It was also the most popular of all the recommended changes. Previously, the most stoutly defended issues had been reform of the pension system, changes in the retirement age, and the development of public assistance; now, for the first time, the key question was social integration of the elderly, and it accounted for 41 percent of articles.

An examination of the characteristics of the agents introducing the issue into the public debate shows that statements related to these new directions were introduced in equal measure by the government and by experts. For the most part, these experts were demographers and doctors who were influenced by the new science of gerontology. On the other hand, activities that were noted in the press and inspired by these new directions were the work of local authorities and complementary pensions institutions. Certain charitable organizations and, as a later section will show, medical experts also fell into this category. In this way, the agents who worked in the field—and actually put these public plans into practice—were identified. It is true that interest in the subject as far as the press was concerned fell away, but this was counterbalanced by an expansion in the range of measures used to meet the needs of the elderly population.

During the period 1946–59, the two main elements that comprised the old-age policy were cash benefits and pension schemes; they accounted for 83 percent of articles published during this time. However, from the early 1960s onward, concern with these two issues slipped to just 50 percent. At the same time, interventions that had a direct bearing on way of life (e.g., housing, health, lifestyle, and leisure), having been virtually nonexistent in previous years (6 percent), now began to be mentioned more frequently, appearing in 28 percent of articles. As before, local authorities and complementary pension funds were usually responsible for these new interventions.

In many cases these innovators acted in an uncoordinated way, building a community center with housing and collective amenities in one area and setting up a home-help service in another. However, properly coordinated way-of-life policies were implemented in some places, and these served as pilot schemes both for other local directors and for the public authorities.

What, then, was the social dynamic that informed these achievements? And what convergent interests and alliances were involved in the setting up of new local mechanisms for the management of the elderly? This process will now be examined by looking at a specific case. The city of Grenoble has been selected because it illustrates two aspects. First, it represents one of the first local examples of the implementation of a coordinated way-of-life policy. As such, it served as a model and reference both for much other local practice and for subsequently inserting into the planning stage a program for enabling the elderly to stay in their own homes. Second, Grenoble provided a typical example of a network of agents working in the field and carrying out a new way-of-life policy. This was confirmed by other case studies and by the content analysis of *Le Monde* described above.

The network of alliances of the new managers of old age in Grenoble. This new network was formed in Grenoble in 1965, following the election of a left-wing municipal council made up of Socialists, radicals, and the PSU (Parti Socialiste Unifié). This grouping attempted to implement a dynamic social action policy that was comprehensive and opposed to segregation, worked in close contact with private associations, and sought to break free from piecemeal public assistance measures.[72] This enthusiasm for concerted action in the field of old age brought together a number of local agents; the main protagonists, apart from the local authorities, were a complementary pension fund, social workers, private associations, and specialists.

The complementary pension fund, which had been established in 1955, concentrated its efforts on the *département* of Isère. Being locally based, it had a number of strong ties with the leading political and economic figures in the region, and, like all complementary pension funds, had a strategy for extending its influence over the whole *département* through a dynamic social policy. This was its main approach when it went looking for business in local industry. The new municipal government gave it an opportunity to work cooperatively, increase the amount of work it did, and thereby extend its influence locally. There was similar acceptance of a new, promotional social action policy that resolutely turned its back on the idea of public assistance. In the case of the local authority, this change of policy was influenced by the new petty bourgeoisie, its main supporters, while the pension fund's policy came from contact with new retirees, who received double social protection and also included elements of the new petty bourgeoisie. The pension fund's functions of recognizing and providing for new needs were concretized following the fund's survey of the elderly in the *département* of Isère in 1966. This study was one of the first of its kind in France.[73]

For social workers and private associations, this alliance with the local authorities coincided with their eagerness to escape from traditional clients and modes of action. At the same time, they were aware, albeit in a rather confused manner, of the new generation of retirees that was beginning to emerge. This was a generation whose pensions allowed them to live more comfortably[74] and whose needs were more spiritual than material. An example of this was their need to combat feelings of social exile, uselessness, and boredom. This new generation provided social workers and private associations with an opportunity to rethink their activities, and throughout the period 1960–68 there was clearly a movement that operated just as effectively on behalf of new retirees as the movement that later represented fifty- to sixty-year-olds who had taken early retirement. A new population sector had been identified. Little was known about their hopes and needs, and they stood on the margins of social action. However, they were also pawns in the struggle between social organizations and professional groups keen to widen their clientele and extend their influence. The new activist approach, which identified new requirements for entertainment and the need for social integration of the elderly, legitimated and guided the interventions of these new managers of the elderly.

Two specialists from different origins, one from the medical sector and the other from human sciences, were added to the network of alliances that acted as the agent of change in Grenoble's old-age policy. The doctor was a general physician from the hospital sector, but he was relatively marginal because of his previous work (in the military) and the services that he ran (chronic illnesses and an old people's home). His life illustrated most of the factors that shaped both the career paths of those dedicated doctors who promoted the new approach to care of the elderly and provided local support, and community practice that combined gerontological and geriatric work.

Experience of medicine in old people's homes was often the starting point for gerontological militancy. This was certainly true in Grenoble. It was also the case for Dr. Huet who was one of the first to promote work on gerontology in France and who founded the Société Française de Gérontologie (French Gerontological Society) in 1961. Despite being a private practitioner from the nonhospital sector, this doctor worked in the Nanterre old people's home for thirty-five years.

There was undoubtedly a meeting between, on one hand, a humanist critique of segregation and banishment of the elderly to old people's homes, and, on the other, the discomfort of the doctors who worked there. The new doctrine of social integration for the elderly, as propounded by the Laroque Report, gave a glimpse of a new representation of old age. Old age was no longer seen as a time of decline or degradation, but rather as a period of preservation and the continuation of a normal life, thanks to preventive medicine. Doctors working in old people's homes and in chronic illness units with a high concentration of elderly patients learned two things from the new social approach to old age. First, there was a legitimate basis for a medical approach to an age group that, when reassessed according to social criteria, demonstrated that medicine could be reassessed as well.[75] Second, there was justification for extending medical practice beyond the confines of the hospital and into prevention, screening, and social reintegration.

The second type of specialist to play an important role in the Grenoble initiative was a human sciences academic. He was a national expert on social gerontology who had studied the stages of life and social gerontology in the United States, and he provided other partners in the alliance with the theoretical background for their gerontological work. He was an intellectual and a philosopher and had connections with the Christian humanist current; and he had been striving to link theoretical research and practical work for some time. Through an alliance with other agents seeking to establish gerontology in Grenoble—it was an intervention that exactly mirrored his field of expertise—he discovered how to make his academic career relevant to local life. This objective translated into the setting up of a Centre Pluridisciplinaire de Gérontologie (Multidisciplinary Gerontology Center) at the University of Grenoble. The main activity of the center was training, but it also played an important role in the unification and dissemination of operational gerontological procedures in France. In the course of interviews with many people promoting gerontological work, it was observed that few local gerontology policies were drawn up either in France or in neighboring French-speaking countries that were not associated with the center.

THE OUTCOME: THE ESTABLISHMENT OF A NETWORK DEDICATED TO DEVELOPING A WAY-OF-LIFE POLICY, AND DYSFUNCTIONS OF THE TECHNOCRATIC PLAN

What general conclusions may be drawn from the above description of the Grenoble initiative with regard to the nature of the alliances and the consequences of the policy?

The setting up of a specific dedicated network. The composition of the network of agents that took charge of the new aspects of managing the elderly, as designated by the official doctrine, indicated the emergence of a group that supported these new ideas; however, it was not a group that was directly linked either to pensions or to traditional agents in this field. As happened elsewhere, the Old-Age Fund and the main groups active in the retirement field had nothing to do with implementing the way-of-life policy; indeed, their work even formed a countermodel for the new managers. Moreover, an earlier analysis of the policy implemented by the Old-Age Fund at a national level between 1959 and 1967 revealed the minor role played by this fund in promoting a way-of-life policy and its lack of sympathy for nonsegregated accommodation. At a time when many people were trying to eliminate the social exile that elderly people experienced, the regional old-age funds were still spending two-thirds of their housing budget on institutionalized and segregated accommodation. It was only after 1973 that the Old-Age Fund's health and social budget began to include expenditure on individual programs to enable the elderly to stay in their own homes, rather than on segregated housing projects.

The composition of the new network of agents also showed that for the most part this new support group had been formed independently of traditional intermediaries of public assistance. Charitable and religious associations and *bureaux d'aide sociale* (BAS—welfare agencies) working in the same field and doing the same work as *département*-based health and social work units discovered that their activities were usually nullified by the new initiatives. Only a few of the traditional social-action providers took the opportunity to change direction and thereby maintain or extend their influence at the local level.

The support networks involved in the new way-of-life policy included many supporters who had different ideas and interests. For various reasons set out above, these agents were eager to get involved in an innovative local policy on the way of life of the elderly, and did so by setting up a complex, and not always very stable, network of alliances. The various groups that formed the support network for this revived way-of-life policy are identified below.[76]

With a few exceptions, such as Paris's thirteenth arrondissement, local authorities were involved in every case. They found that adhering to the new official doctrine of prevention and nonsegregation enabled them to supply the entire elderly population with services previously restricted to the most needy. The doctrine also gave them the opportunity to develop a more direct relationship with the elderly people for whom they were responsible, and outside the framework provided by public assistance legislation, *département*-based social housing management, and social security funds.

Linked to the political forces were professionally trained medical-social workers; these were doctors and social workers who found that the definition of the "third age" gave them a tool with which to reassess and liberate their respective professions. In this way they became the new specialists and managers of old age. Social-action associations often joined forces with the political alliances when the latter decided to turn their back on public assistance (and, in so doing, on the misery of the destitute), and renew or extend their clientele. In the same way, and for reasons outlined above, complementary pension funds were often involved in practical, grassroots work.

The technocratic project supported these agents in their attempts to establish their representative rights at the local, and in some cases even national, level. They tried to set themselves up as the new mediators of the old-age policy by highlighting the demands of the elderly population, whose new activists they wanted to be, and by disseminating the new public guidelines at grassroots level.

Although this new network of peripheral innovators had to be set up if the state project was to be implemented, it also caused the project to change direction. The very nature of the network mobilized by the project meant that the initial model for action was scaled down, and its work redirected toward social interests dominated by these new agents.

The project is scaled down. The old-age policy program that had been announced saw itself as comprehensive and preventive. Its aim was the prolonged social integration of the elderly through coordinated work on employment, retirement, and sociomedical interventions.[77]

It transpired that none of the main actors in employment and retirement policy, however, were willing to support the project. The only groups that took action worked in the field of the way of life. The result was that the recommended model began to malfunction, and action was concentrated downstream, on the way of life of the elderly. It ignored all aspects upstream concerning people's working lives, and also moved away from retirement policies. Of the pilot schemes that directly influenced subsequent government action, the experiences of Grenoble and the thirteenth arrondissement in Paris[78] are good illustrations of the fragmentary action that took place. The policy they carried out was directed exclusively at the "third age" population, and sought to prevent their isolation and marginalization. The dependency problems of old age during the "fourth age" were not dealt with. In the same way, the issues of an income policy for the elderly, and their relationship with employment, were placed outside the scope of the local action program. The overall project to develop an old-age policy had shrunk to no more than a policy to enable the elderly to stay in their own homes.

Laws aimed at prolonging the autonomy of the elderly were drawn up and adopted by Parliament; they concerned such amenities as clubs, day centers, home-help schemes, community centers providing housing and other community facilities, definitions of areas of responsibility, and coordination. They soon came to be identified with a whole range of services and equipment related to old age. In other words, the means became the end. The implementation of measures introducing services and facilities soon replaced the idea of policy, and became a substitute for the ambitious project of creating an old-age policy.

The project declined not only because of segmentation in what had been carried out locally, but also through the involvement in the project of social interests headed up by peripheral actors. As a result of this involvement and the class to which they belonged, and because of changes among the elderly population for whom they wished to become the activists, the new mediators were keen to serve as vehicles for the interests and values of the new salaried middle class.

A real change took place in the makeup of the elderly population between 1959 and 1967. The increasing number of middle-class salaried workers reflected the diversification of the production system[79] and, as the average age of the population rose, gave rise to a new group of retired workers with a new social profile. Complementary pension funds, certain private associations, social and medical workers involved in the old-age policy, and those working on the fringes were fully aware of this transformation taking place among the elderly population. In fact, all of them were in direct contact with the elderly and were trying to enable them to enjoy a degree of representation at local level.

Table 2.1. Distribution of the total working population and the male working population in the 1954, 1962, and 1968 censuses (%)

	Total working population			Male working population		
Socio-professional groups	1954	1962	1968	1954	1962	1968
Farmers	20.7	15.8	12.0	18.6	14.7	11.5
Farmworkers	6.0	4.3	2.9	7.9	5.8	4.0
Senior managers in trade and industry	12.0	10.6	9.6	11.6	10.3	9.6
Liberal professions and senior cadres	2.9	4.0	4.8	3.8	5.1	6.1
Middle-ranking cadres	5.8	7.8	9.9	5.6	7.2	9.0
White-collar workers	10.8	12.5	14.8	7.8	7.9	8.9
Blue-collar workers	33.8	36.7	37.7	40.1	44.0	46.0
Domestic staff	5.3	5.4	5.7	1.6	1.6	1.8
Other	2.7	2.9	2.6	3.0	3.4	3.1
Total	100.0	100.0	100.0	100.0	100.0	100.0

Source: 1954, 1962, and 1968 censuses, *Population active* documents INSEE.

Table 2.2. Fluctuations in the Numbers of Male Working Population Aged Fifty-five to Sixty-four by Socioprofessional Category (1954, 1962, and 1968)

	1954	1962	1968	Movement 1954–62 %	Movement 1962–68 %
Farmers	379,120	451,060	385,000	+19	-15
Farm workers	101,280	124,600	96,280	+23	-23
Senior managers in trade and industry	264,000	300,540	289,840	+14	-3.6
Industrial employees	16,180	18,300	17,680	+13	-3.4
Craft workers	106,740	124,340	124,980	+16	+0.5
Owners of fishing boats	2,900	2,540	2,060	-12	-19
Big business	28,140	30,650	32,800	+8.5	+7
Small trading	110,140	124,720	112,320	+12	-10
Senior cadres	77,400	111,900	136,640	+44	+22
Liberal professions	17,900	21,340	24,880	+19	+17
Teachers, literary and scientific professions	5,520	8,640	12,500	+57	+45
Engineers	10,420	20,180	23,380	+48	+16
Administrative cadres	43,560	61,740	75,380	+42	+22
Middle-ranking cadres	90,340	117,140	131,320	+30	+12
Primary school teachers, Health and welfare service workers	9,040	10,480	19,520	+38	+57
Technicians	17,600	31,240	36,840	+79	+17

(Table 2.2 continued)

	1954	1962	1968	Movement 1954–62 %	Movement 1962–68 %
Administrative and middle-ranking cadres	63,700	73,260	74,960	+15	+2.3
White-collar workers	118,560	140,700	158,540	+19	+13
Office workers	96,820	115,700	134,340	+19.5	+16
Sales staff	21,740	25,000	24,200	+15	-3.2
Blue-collar workers	475,820	675,640	665,640	+42	-1.5
Foremen	21,900	51,980			
(Foremen and professional workers)			280,000	+24[a]	+0.2
Professional workers	204,200	227,540			
Specialized workers	133,220	222,360	227,200	+67	+2.2
Miners	7,360	7,960	5,000	+8	-37
Fishermen	2,860	2,340	1,360	-18	-42
Apprentices	80	240			
Blue-collar workers	106,280	163,380	151,660	+54	-7.1
Domestic staff	38,080	49,060	48,400	+29	-1.3
Total aged 55-64 including other professions	1,565,940	1,999,960	1,943,780		

Source: 1954, 1962, and 1968 Censuses, *Population active* documents.
[a] In 1954, foremen in the public sector were included with professional workers.

In view of the shortage of data showing changes in this group's social composition,[80] the assessment made in this book[81] was based on the many changes that took place in the years in question, and on the basis of an analysis of transformations undergone by fifty-five- to sixty-four-year-olds between 1954 and 1962. These data explain changes in the socioprofessional composition of retirees between 1960 (when those aged fifty-five to sixty-four in the 1954 census retired) and 1972 (when nearly all of those aged fifty-five to sixty-four in 1962 were retired).[82]

A study of variations in the numbers of employees in different socioprofessional categories over the periods 1954–62 and 1962–68 (tables 2.1 and 2.2) shows that the biggest growth among wage-earning middle-class employees occurred during the former period. This means that there was a particularly large increase in the number of retirees coming from these social groups a few years later when they reached retirement, between 1959 and 1968. For example, retirements in literary and scientific professions rose 57 percent, engineering 48 percent, administrative cadres 42 percent and technology 79 percent. On the other hand, over the period that followed (1962–68), the increases were more moderate (literary and scientific professions: 45 percent; engineering: 16 percent; executive administration: 22 percent; and technology: 17 percent). Overall, between these two periods, growth among senior cadres and liberal professions went from 44 percent to 22 percent and middle-ranking cadres from 30 percent to 12 percent. A study, not of changes in numbers, but of developments in the internal social structure of the elderly population confirms this. However, the slow fall in the number of agricultural workers in the upper age brackets partly conceals the increase among the new salaried middle classes within the elderly population. (See table 2.3.) As soon as employees in these categories retired, they formed an important group among new retirees because they enjoyed better social protection and had more money. Their previous occupations had enabled them to retain a larger number of skills and possessions, and they had hopes and aspirations for the future that reflected their former positions in the production process. This new type of retiree brought new characteristics to old age such as good health, relative financial comfort, dynamism, and sociability. The traditional stereotype of old age as a time of poverty, isolation, and illness was no more.

The enormous increase in the number of middle-class retired workers did not go unnoticed by groups and organizations specializing in public assistance. For them, assistance was a completely new issue, and the preventive measures set out in the Laroque Report had targeted the whole of the elderly population for assistance, not just the most needy.

The task of replacing services and facilities for the elderly was carried

Table 2.3. Shifts in the Socioprofessional Structure of Male Working Population Aged Fifty-five to Sixty-four between 1954 and 1968

	1954	1962	1968
Farmers	24.2	22.6	19.8
Farm workers	6.5	6.2	5.0
Senior managers in trade and industry	16.9	15.0	14.9
Liberal professions	1.1	1.1	1.3
Teachers, literary and scientific professions	0.4	0.4	0.6
Engineers	0.7	1.0	1.2
Senior administrative cadres	2.7	3.1	3.9
Senior cadres	3.8	4.5	5.7
Primary school teachers, medical and social service workers	0.6	0.6	1
Technicians	1.1	1.6	1.9
Middle-ranking administrative cadres	4.1	3.7	3.9
Middle-ranking cadres	5.8	5.9	6.8
White-collar workers	7.6	7.0	8.2
Foremen, skilled workers	14.4	14.0	14.4
Specialized workers	8.5	11.1	11.7
Miners, sailors, and fishermen	0.7	0.5	0.3
Blue-collar workers	6.8	8.2	7.8
Workmen	30.4	33.8	34.2
Domestic staff	2.4	2.5	2.5
Other categories	1.4	1.5	1.7
Total male working population aged 55–64	1,565,940	1,999,960	1,943,780

out by peripheral workers, and their efforts were clearly influenced by the Laroque Report. These new services and social facilities were part of the work of local gerontology groups and they were gradually codified; they also reflected the shift *(glissement)* of social referents in the old-age policy. The referents were no longer elderly members of the working class, but new middle-class retirees; to take one example, the new professionally run clubs for people now referred to as the "third age" replaced the traditional open center previously patronized by elderly members of the working class. The contrast between these two formulas was extremely clear, and had been established by a national representative of the St. Vincent de Paul Groups during a UNIOPSS colloquium in 1970. The meeting had brought together all the various actors in the field of gerontology, and was a high point in their codification work. Everything in table 2.4, including the less elaborate—and more personal and selective—forms of sociability points to a shift in the social referents of action being undertaken on behalf of the elderly.

The new activist approach to aging bore signs of its social provenance. The new standards introduced by this activist approach judged a successful old age by the degree of participation in society and the vitality of the individuals as they got older. These standards also turned the social practices of the new salaried middle classes—who were the most skillful at converting the capital that they had saved during their working lives into retirement activities and sociability—into a model for an active and sociable old age.[83]

CONCLUSION

This book's author takes the position that the period 1962–67 was characterized by the meeting of, on one hand, the technocratic project initiated by a voluntarist state seeking new channels of more direct intervention on behalf of the elderly, and on the other, a range of local political agents, associations, and professionals who found that they had a common interest, albeit for different reasons, in promoting an alternative plan of action for the management of old age. There followed a detailed process of hammering out a unified approach to the subject and a considerable amount of gerontological work. A network of new managers of old age was then set up, and this established the state's new ambition to establish an old-age policy, although it simultaneously encouraged malfunction within the initial project. On one hand, the original plan was restricted to fragmentary action dealing with the way of life; on the other, it was reinjected with the interests, opinions, and problems of the new salaried middle classes, who subsequently developed the new solutions adopted in favor of the elderly.

Getting Things Moving: Writing the Way-of-Life Policy into the Planning System

The Revival of Study Commissions and Other Think Tanks

The events of 1968 were immediately followed by signs of renewed government action on a way-of-life policy for the elderly. This revival of interest initially took the form of numerous centrally organized conferences and working groups and the publication of their reports. The aim was to inject a new impetus into the doctrine set out in the Laroque Report, and to collate and disseminate related ideas and innovations. In June 1969, the new State Secretariat for Welfare, which was attached to the Ministry for Health and Social Security, organized a major "consultation on the problems facing social action in favor of the elderly."[84] The meeting was attended by 140 individuals representing leading agents in the field of gerontology at the local level; an earlier section has already identified them as officials of complementary pension and mutual insurance funds, members of charitable organizations, representatives of BAS (*bureaux d'aide sociale*—welfare agencies), politicians, gerontologists, senior civil servants, trade unionists, and journalists. Over the five days of the conference, the participants evaluated experiments and achievements since the Study Commission's report. Then, at the end of 1969, the annual report of the General Inspectorate of Social Affairs took as its theme "the social problems of the elderly" and highlighted the limitations of state action that had been undertaken in line with the 1962 recommendations. In November 1969, an Intergroup dealing with the "problems related to the elderly" was set up as part of the preparations for the Fourth Plan. The president of the Intergroup was Nicole Questiaux, one of the Study Commission's rapporteurs.

Finally, in March 1970, a task force was set up under the minister for public health, Robert Boulin; it was charged with providing practical solutions to the "medical aspects of old age."[85] Although this Intergroup was smaller than the Dienesch Colloquium[86] and was more medically based, the members were virtually the same. This phase of intellectual activity was followed by measures designed to put the results into action. In July 1971, Parliament adopted the Sixth Plan, one of whose priorities was the final program to enable the elderly to carry on living in their own homes. The 16 July 1971 act extended the housing allowance to people aged sixty-five and over, thereby creating a private accommodation policy that complemented that of enabling the elderly to stay at home.

A Way-of-Life Policy Versus an Extension of the Social Right to Retirement

This revival in the state's centralized actions on the way of life came at a time of general political crisis and of intensified social struggle; both of these developments had been spurred on by the events of May 1968. More specifically, from 1969 onward, the issue of retirement figured in union demands with increasing emphasis; the CGT and CFDT joined forces after the autumn of 1970, and they worked throughout 1971 on a common plan of action. All of this suggests that the state's renewed interest in the way of life had been inspired by a wish to respond to the labor union campaign to improve pensions and lower the retirement age; at all events, the parties to the debate fought hard to impose their own definition of the old-age policy.[87]

The state responded to the united campaign on retirement age and levels of pension by opening up a new front: the way of life of the elderly. In fact, the state attempted to defuse the conflict by transposing the question of old age to a terrain that was already largely marked out and encoded by the state's official approach. As has been pointed out, the unions possessed no alternative model. The plans for integration that formed part of the official action on way of life allowed the state to hold its ground on retirement age. The Sixth Plan, which made a priority of the elderly, was adopted in July 1971 and included a final program to enable the elderly to stay in their own homes. This was followed on 31 December 1971 by the Boulin Law, which made only minor concessions to union demands. As far as retirement age was concerned, it followed the recommendations of the Sixth Plan in abandoning plans for a lower retirement age across the board, as this was held to infringe on the right to work after the age of sixty. It also ran counter to the aim of social integration and of enabling elderly people to live normal lives. In the new model for state action, these objectives were of prime importance. The Law of the Sixth Plan pertaining to the "the problems of the third age" gives a perfect illustration of how a counterforce was later used by the program to enable the elderly to stay in their own homes:

> The Sixth Plan shall pursue three main courses of action with respect to the elderly. The first concerns retirement age.
>
> On this matter, the solution involving *a lowering of the retirement age across the board cannot be countenanced.* The consequences of such an

approach would be serious, both from a psychological and an economic and financial point of view.

From a psychological point of view, it is undesirable that the entire population aged sixty or over should be made unemployed. As long as the state of health and the professional capacities of the persons concerned permit them to continue in employment after the age of sixty, the right to rest should not be systematically invoked to the detriment of the right to work.

From an economic point of view, the current de facto situation that is making employment difficult for older workers underlines the problems of adaptation. Essentially, the only solution is to be found in appropriate in-house staff policies and ongoing training. Lowering the retirement age would only obscure matters and ensure that the same mistakes were repeated. This in turn would lead to more and more workers being unemployed, and affect economic growth accordingly.

From a financial point of view, the cost of all types of benefit—long-term unemployment, preretirement or early retirement and sickness benefits—accentuated the imbalance already predicted for the social security schemes. This instability could have become intolerable and caused the financial resources of those concerned to be prematurely reduced.

On the other hand, it is necessary to soften *the blow when people move from employment into retirement* by adapting to individual conditions when the situation is irreversible. In this respect, the *reform on disability legislation will* allow the workers affected to anticipate the consequences of premature unemployment by giving them an early pension. However, the processes used to implement this measure must ensure that it does not become an easy way of systematically removing older workers from the production process. Conversely, steps will also be taken to make sure that pension plans contain the appropriate clauses to meet the needs of those who can, and wish to, remain at work.

The Sixth Plan's second course of action will involve a special commitment to an annual and substantial review of a minimum income for the elderly.

Third, the Sixth Plan will promote a series of actions in the fields of health, welfare, and housing services. In the spirit of the preceding paragraphs, these actions will, wherever possible, enable the elderly to remain in familiar surroundings and in contact with other age groups and the population as a whole.

It says much about relations at that time among the social partners (to which the Sixth Plan's "third age" action program was dedicated) that the document opens with a long rejection of the directions favored by the unions; this is followed by an analysis of the content of the positive action that was to be carried out.

This new stage in the development of a way-of-life policy confirms the interpretation of events at the turn of the 1960s that this book has suggested. In its new voluntarist guise, the state had to take the initiative of

Table 2.4. From the Traditional Day Center to the Ideal Club

The traditional day center was a place where elderly people in the community could meet over a drink. It provided opportunities for relaxation, conversation, and meeting friends.	*The ideal club is an enlarged and more effective version of such a meeting place for elderly people who come from different backgrounds, and who relax by taking part in cultural and craft-based activities.*
The average age of people using the center's facilities was high (seventy-five to eighty-five years of age).	*Elderly people become club members as soon as they retire, and take over certain responsibilities.*
Because of a shortage of premises and voluntary workers, meetings could only take place monthly, semimonthly, or weekly. Day centers were closed during the summer.	*The club meets weekly at the beginning, but soon opens daily in response to demand from members. Facilities on different days include shelter and various activities; the club is open all year round.*
Meetings brought large numbers of elderly people together—as many as the premises could hold.	*The number of elderly people in attendance depends on the activities. Ideally, there should be no more than about forty present at any one time.*
Adults and young people who were members of charitable organizations managed and supervised the centers, ran the activities, and carried out day-to-day duties. They met once every three months to make key decisions.	*All responsibilities and day-to-day tasks are shared among the elderly themselves, and among more able adults and young people. Ongoing, nondirective entertainment ensures that the club is dynamic and lively. A monthly meeting provides coordination.*
Meetings were organized around a drink. Entertainment was of a passive nature, and did not go further than conversation, information on social issues, games, songs, parties, and outings.	*Tea is optional and self-service. It is simply a break between workshop activities (crafts, DIY, ladies' handicraft) and group activities (visits to exhibitions and museums, conferences, discussions, recreational activities, and games). Interclub meetings are also planned.*

Source: *Personnes âgées. Valeurs sociales,* proceedings of a colloquium organized by the Comité National d'Entente pour la Journée des Vieillards (Paris: CLEIRPPA, 1971), pp. 165–66.

reorganizing the old-age policy so as to find new, direct, and autonomous channels of action that were not mediated either by the pension system or by agents representing social classes and fighting one another at the grassroots level. However, the new situation called for more than repeated statements of intent; it demanded that something be done.

Putting the Measures into Practice

As with so much social policy, the measures were implemented through work on planning. An analysis of this process is set out below.

The establishment of new state measures promoting the well-being of the elderly came about as a result of close cooperation between two departments of the state: the DAS (Direction de l'Action Sociale—Social Action Directorate) and the Social Affairs Service of the Commissariat du Plan. The work of both depended on agents who had patiently built up local gerontology services outside the state system, and had incorporated into public programs certain instruments used by professionals at the grassroots level. The initiative came from the new State Secretariat for Social Action and Rehabilitation. This was soon taken over by the Commissariat du Plan which, on 14 November 1969, set up the Intergroupe Personnes Agées (Elderly Persons' Intergroup) as part of the preparations for the Sixth Plan.[88]

On 23–27 June 1969, the State Secretariat organized a major consultative conference on social action issues facing the elderly. The meeting was sponsored by the public authorities and was attended by a large number of local gerontology activists with a view to "evaluating what had been achieved since the Laroque Report" and "setting out the general directions that the work of the Sixth Plan will take from the forthcoming autumn onwards."[89] It announced the government's new intention of strengthening its position in, and influence over, the way-of-life policy. It also revealed the strategy for change chosen by a State Secretariat of modest financial and staffing means and its administration—the Directorate of Social Action—for new action on the part of state policy concerned with the elderly. This strategy was to rely on a network of people who had worked on the project outside the state structure, reintroducing and combining the formulas and instruments they had developed in the field. Within the state structure, it also sought to forge close links with the Commissariat Général du Plan. This relaunch of government action was clearly focusing on a way-of-life policy. The conference made no reference to employment for the elderly or to their financial resources; the focus was exclusively on welfare policy.[90] Circumscribing the issue in this way followed the guidelines suggested by the local gerontological program, while at the same time respecting administrative compartmentalization.

The support role played by peripheral innovators. A process that Robert Castel has described in the field of mental-health policy may also be found in the role played by agents involved in local gerontology work as the new state program for the elderly neared completion. Castel showed that tools had been developed by professionals and adopted by the public authorities for both the "therapeutic seclusion" policy (which had been promoted by the 1838 legislation) and the "psychiatric sectorization" policy (which had been official policy since 1960). The same went for the idea of "therapeutic seclusion" as developed by the Pinel School, which formed the basis of a policy for placing individuals in confined spaces.* Similarly, sectorization—which at first had appeared to be utopian, and then became the method used by progressive professionals fighting against the traditional asylum—became the inspiration for the new community-based policy.[91] However, a distinction needs to be drawn between the mental-health policy and the old-age policy. Although professionals working in the field of old age were agents of change, this was true only in the final stage of the process. The first initiative was taken by the voluntarist state when in 1969 it appointed an administrative commission to set out the new principles of action on the elderly. This action, as has been explained, both encouraged and unified the work of professionals.

It is equally true that, during the period under examination, a strong alliance grew up between peripheral innovators and modernizers in the central social administration.[92] The innovators hoped that the state program, "which has only just got under way,"[93] would enable the experiments, whose very future was threatened by their success, to survive.

Faced with upheaval in such traditional social services as assistance and community housing, the modernizers saw the alliance as an opportunity to introduce a new plan of action into social administration. This was based on preventive and promotional (i.e., confidence-building) action, and had impact not only on the individual but also on the environment in which he or she lived. This gave social administration a chance to extend its clientele to include the entire elderly population, not just its more marginal members.

---

*"Isolement thérapeutique" has been translated as "therapeutic *seclusion*" rather than the more obvious "therapeutic isolation" on the grounds that "seclusion" is much more commonly used in English in the context of such leading figures as Cullen, Tuke, Esquirol, and Pinel. *Trans.*

In his introductory paper to the conference, the director of Mme Dienesch's cabinet recalled that "social action should not solely provide the most needy members of the population with assistance. The aim of social action should be to improve common living conditions, and to encourage contact between individuals and different social groups. This aim of improving the living environment is, in a way, the noble function of social action, and is the function that should be developed in the future."[94] For certain modernizers in the Directorate of Social Action, the issue consisted in reassessing and boosting this administrative body by giving it the new task of coordinating a services policy.

There was close cooperation between peripheral and civil-servant innovators throughout the period when the new action model was being set up. This coalition was in evidence during both phases: the first was the consultation period within the State Secretariat, when senior civil servants and representatives of local innovation initiatives worked together as corapporteurs on the various issues under discussion; the second was the preparatory period leading up to the Sixth Plan, when the same local innovators were also members of the Elderly Persons' Intergroup chaired by Nicole Questiaux. Her experience as a rapporteur for the Study Commission symbolically marked the community of planners' aim of implementing the Laroque Report's theoretical directives at a grassroots level.

The Intergroup expressly based its proposals on the results of gerontological work carried out in the thirteenth arrondissement of Paris and in Grenoble.[95] It adopted the full range of services and facilities that had been put in place for these experiments, and retained their modus operandi. The Intergroup even took its inspiration from norms related to the theoretical needs of the elderly (in terms of services and facilities) that had been brought to light by the two experiments.

The administrative circular of 24 September 1971 on the policy for health and social facilities contained ministerial instructions that later controlled the application of the program to enable the elderly to carry on living in their own homes; they also scrupulously observed the codification carried out by peripheral agents. As a result, the range of small-scale way-of-life initiatives included community centers that provided club facilities; these brought together the idea of self-management as developed by Grenoble and the ideas for entertainment promoted by the thirteenth arrondissement experiment.[96] The idea of the day center, which was borrowed from the Paris experiment, was referred to in the administrative circular, but it subsequently encountered many setbacks.

The organizational side relied on the principles that had been given prominence in the two experiments, sectorization and coordination.[97] The sectoral contract formula that was adopted as part of the program's implementation sought to translate these principles into administrative practice. However, by incorporating the types of facility that had been developed by peripheral innovators, the administration integrated those needs and aspirations of the new clientele that local actors had tried to take into account. The social content was also integrated as a result of this functional definition. The new ideology of an active, participative third age had the new salaried middle classes as its social referent, and was therefore able to infiltrate state policy in a subtle manner. It has been demonstrated elsewhere[98] how the new institutional setting assigned to the elderly (as part of the program to enable them to stay in their own homes, and described in precise terms in the administrative circular of 24 September 1971) had the new salaried middle classes as its referent. The old people's home *(hospice)* effectively disappeared.[99] It was replaced by clubs and community centers that provided housing, both of them facilities that broke with the traditional public assistance practice.

The clubs and the entertainment that they provided were even used to improve the image of centers that provided food, and which still had strong connotations with soup kitchens: "Organizations involved in providing social services should make every effort to improve the image of these centers by stressing the entertainment activities, as this will encourage the adoption of the community center-club formula. Changing the name from 'community center providing food' *(foyer-restaurant)* to 'community center providing club facilities' *(foyer-club)* will not only mean more appealing terminology but also a real change in how these services are used."[100] Finally, community centers that incorporated accommodation in housing estates produced the formula that came the closest to independent housing, and was least reminiscent of the lack of privacy associated with the old people's homes. The new range of facilities designed to enable the elderly to stay in their own homes was now a far cry from the traditional services that the working class had previously received.

Cooperation between the Directorate of Social Action and the Commissariat Général du Plan. Social policy analysts have often commented on the weak position occupied by social administration in the hierarchy of the major administrations. Over the period in question, the weakness of the State Secretariat for Welfare and its administration can be measured by the limited range of measures that it was able to promote in favor of the elderly. Consultation on assistance issues had already restricted its ambitions to dealing with matters that came strictly within its competence, as questions pertaining to elderly people's money and employment were now separate. As a result, the only measures advanced by the State Secretariat dealt with information for the elderly, and instructions contained no reference to the specific means necessary for financing them. The administrative circulars of 24 September 1969 and 9 October 1970 set up the Comités Départementaux d'Information aux Personnes Âgées (CIDPA—*département*-based committees providing elderly people with information) whose role was at best uneven, depending on the *département*, and was sometimes very limited.

Lacking the power to promote any real coordinated action on behalf of the elderly, the State Secretariat was restricted to disseminating the new approach to old age through study group meetings and information structures. Several factors led the State Secretariat for Welfare and its administration, the Directorate of Social Action, to try and find a reliable ally in the plan's Social Affairs Service. This phenomenon was not unique to the elderly, and there are accounts pertaining to other sectors.[101]

First, sectoral administrations, and particularly the weakest ones, were tempted to see the plan as a way of breaking away from uneven, bilateral dialogue with the Ministry of Finance. Second, the preoccupations of the modernizing directorate civil servants coincided with those of the planners; indeed, they were often the same men that had led the debate first at the DAS and then at the Commissariat Général du Plan. They came from the same "community of planners"[102] that had developed the ambitious project of global preventive and promotional action, and had attempted to impose it by coordinating the actions of the state through social planning. In developing this new orientation, the DAS saw an opportunity to reassess its actions by abandoning the idea of simply applying assistance legislation to the groups in need for which it was responsible; instead, it assumed the much more fulfilling role of coordinating the state's numerous interventions with respect to each of the target groups. Further evidence of this is to be found in changes in the kind of activity undertaken by Bureau RV2,[103] when it took over responsibility for managing the final program for the elderly.

This general orientation was particularly well established at the directorate at this time, as it had recently taken on new members of staff who already held these views; one of these was René Lenoir, who became director in September 1970. These new staff members brought a new dynamism, and strengthened links with the modernizers.

The plan revealed that the directorate's willingness to coordinate gave it legitimate grounds for intruding into the "reserved sectors" of other, more powerful social administrations such as the Directorate of Social Security. These administrations guarded their monopolies jealously, and all they asked of the plan was integration of the political project that they had set up internally so that they could obtain the funds necessary to put them into practice.

Elsewhere, the community of planners' global project found support at the highest levels of the Executive. The Chaban-Delmas Government elected in July 1969 revived both social issues and the social integration policy through the way of life as part of the "Nouvelle Société" (New Society) Project. This was headed up by Jacques Delors, who had created the plan's Social Affairs Service and introduced into France the idea of social indicators.

There were two main reasons why these convergences took shape in a program[104] for the elderly within the framework of the Sixth Plan. First, political assent combined with the political urgency that had been produced by the union campaign on pensions; second, French demographic projections gave new weight to the budgetary argument.

The community of planners had clearly identified an ideologically and politically favorable climate for action on behalf of the elderly. By setting up an Elderly Persons' Intergroup, they sought to launch a global intervention project whose main principles had already been set out in an advisory report *(rapport d'orientation),* and which enjoyed support from a network of dynamic agents at the grassroots level. With regard to the elderly, they hoped to go beyond the segmentation of state actions and link up interventions in employment, social benefits, and assistance. However, the favorable circumstances that made the elderly the target group under the Sixth Plan led to segmentary action that did not go far beyond what the Directorate of Social Action had achieved.

According to the Laroque Report, and in terms that were taken up in the introduction to the Intergroup's report, the aim of the project for global preventive action was to "prolong normal life for as long as possible and, within this objective, to approach the two main tasks head on: meet the current needs of the elderly population, and work with those now in employment to help prepare them for a more agreeable old age." In other words, the project made two commitments: to review the minimum guarantee for the elderly, and to prevent the loss of complete autonomy (e.g., being put in an old people's home) through a policy for helping them to live in their own homes.

Although old-age policies for action upstream continued to figure among the Intergroup's concerns—a whole chapter of its report is devoted to "employment and aging"—they were nevertheless abandoned. All that survived of this thinking in the Sixth Plan's general report was the statement that lowering the age of retirement across the board was unacceptable, and a few vague concluding sentences about detailed studies that should be carried out.

The outcome: segmentary action to enable the elderly to stay in their own homes. What can the explanation be for this decrease in the amount of work if the old-age policy was actually in the process of being implemented?

It has already been pointed out that the coalition of peripheral innovators, which had been built up and mobilized outside the state but around the state project, had already led to dysfunction at the level of local practice. Why, then, did the coalition now adopt segmentary action when a state program was in the process of being set up?

Within the state structure, there were several reasons for scaling down the action and reformulating it into a simple policy for helping the elderly to carry on living in their own homes. There was the weakness of the administrations supporting it within the structure of the state,[105] and there was the fact that they were unable to broaden the basis of the coalition of modernizers by recruiting the most powerful government departments such as the General Directorates of Health and of Social Security, and even departments within the Ministry of Labor, Employment, and the Population. The "pedagogy of interdependences" that some analysts identified as one of the functions of the plan's consultation phase[106] did not materialize in the case of old age. The joining together of forces, which had enabled an old-age policy to come to fruition within the state system, had also restricted it to action on making it possible for the elderly to live in their own homes. The planners, who wanted to see facilities replaced by community-based functions, were prepared to see the overall project cut back provided that a policy of a variety of services and small-scale facilities was implemented and replaced large-scale facilities, such as housing. The Intergroup's tactical adoption of the procedure for rationalizing budgetary choices within the own-home policy canceled out the reticence of the Budget Directorate. The latter had been tempted by the prospect of financial gain to be derived from this kind of reconversion, especially if account were taken of demographic projections and the effect that they would have on housing demand.[107] There is no doubt that money played an important part in the ultimate adoption of a final program to stabilize the number of people aged sixty-five to seventy-four living in institutions; one hundred thousand elderly people were thus saved from having to do so while the plan was in operation.

In trying to give the project financial credibility by rationalizing budgetary choices, the Intergroup adopted a formulation that was couched in language familiar to the directorate bureaucracy. This enabled the directorate to take over the program. The logic behind sharing social fields, so beloved of social administrations, is well known. The concept of a target group of third-age citizens, identified by a system of special allowances enabling them to stay in their own homes (although "in the interests of efficiency and distinctiveness, we are keeping actions on housing separate"),[108] led to the curtailment of this work. It coincided precisely with the field of expertise of one of the directorate sections, which was thus able to claim responsibility. Meanwhile, the directorate-plan alliance, which initially gave support to the project, had been reducing its scope and placing it more directly under directorate control.

The political urgency of state interventions concerning old age responded to the growing union pension campaign, and also contributed to a reduction in the project's overall scope. Something had to be done without delay about the issue of the way of life—something that would undermine the grassroots mobilization for a lower retirement age. In order to justify the Sixth Plan's choice not to lower it across the board, the government defended social integration of the elderly and their right to work. This argument would have carried little weight or credibility if the state had not started to make it one of the administration's new tasks. The program to enable the elderly to stay in their own homes provided an opportunity to launch a social-integration policy immediately, but the aims of the public authorities now ran up against the coalition of peripheral innovators and civil service modernizers.

Given the political urgency, the state naturally chose to rely on the only groups in society that could take charge of the movement it was trying to initiate. The state later integrated into its program the new institutional measures that the coalition had created at the grassroots, and simultaneously incorporated approaches that they traditionally took. All three groups were happy that the program had been adopted, and in fact it marked the end of the segregated housing formulas. It was now clear that the state public assistance policy, which was still the only state action that supported the way-of-life policy despite numerous challenges, was now going to be abandoned. By taking over management of the program, the administration assumed direct responsibility for ensuring the day-to-day social integration of the elderly, and for the first time promised continued financial incentives to this end. As a result, the forces that had brought the social-integration policy into being could now do no more than enable elderly people to stay in their own homes.

It is important to stress that this interpretation—which sees a wide-ranging state project for an old-age policy slipping into a segmentary way-of-life program—is very different from an analysis that blames a cynical and manipulative state for the gap between its approach to integration and the eventual implementation. The latter view interprets the drift towards the social referent of the public program's "new middle classes" as part of the state's plan to keep more effective control over the dominated classes and to please the new, up-and-coming middle classes.

Contrary to this, we believe there was a complex two-way relationship between the state and civil society, whereby an innovative technocratic project encouraged the emergence of a network of peripheral innovators, who have in turn supported the innovative strategy of certain sections of the state. In return, they increasingly absorbed privileged representatives of the coalition of modernizers that existed within the state. The grassroots solutions provided by these new mediators were incorporated into the new state program. As these mediators were working for a union between the administration and society, the state simultaneously integrated the interests and viewpoints of which these new mediators, by their very nature, were the bearers in the same way that it had subscribed to the approaches that they traditionally adopted.

Assessment of State Programs for Social Integration of the Elderly

Setting up the Final Program to Enable the Elderly to Stay in their Own Homes (1972–1976)

As demonstrated earlier, the final program was the result of a compartmentalization of the comprehensive policy recommended by the Laroque Report. This section will show that it was further segmented in the course of its implementation, and ultimately became a collection of unconnected actions that actually increased its beneficiaries' dependency.

A modest project. The aim of the final program was to act on the need to prolong the normal lives of the elderly and allow them to remain in their own homes. To do this, the program tried to step up efforts in relation to facilities.

The program aimed to pay for the facilities and running costs of 332 sectors, each serving the needs of around three hundred elderly people. This demonstrates how modest the program was. Setting up 332 sectors in four years came to little more than one new sector per *département* per year, and altogether 99,600 elderly people were to be covered, or just over 1 percent of the population aged sixty-five and over. The implementation of the program meant almost one hundred thousand elderly people aged sixty-five to seventy-four not having to be placed in some kind of home. It should be remembered that the idea of helping the elderly to continue living in their own homes had not hitherto been seen as realistic. The idea had raised anxieties in the minds of retirement home directors, who felt that they had been ignored when the plan's priorities were being drawn up. As a result, they had had to be reassured by using an age limit in calculating objectives. The state only contributed a quarter of the necessary money, with local authorities, social security, and users themselves making up the balance.

The program was clearly both innovative and experimental. The state's contribution came to 265 million francs over the five years that the plan was in operation, and over half of this was used on "operational budgets" *(crédits de fonctionnement)* granted for a fixed two-year period. Another illustration of the modest funding is the fact that the state's five-year contribution was well below what the National Old-Age Insurance Fund paid to the Social Action Fund in 1974 (515 million francs), and much less than public-assistance expenditure on housing for the elderly in the same year (1,393 billion francs).

Unachieved objectives. The final program's statistical objectives were modest, but they were still not achieved under the Sixth Plan.

The total number of sectors was attained and even passed. On 31 December 1975, the report on the implementation of the Sixth Plan stated that 378 sectors were functioning partly or fully; however, fewer than half the state funds had been taken up (128 million francs out of a total credit of 265 million francs), and even less than that had actually been spent.[109] This meant that even if there had been payments in 1976, implementation of the final program was incomplete. The shortfall between the number of sectors set up and the money spent shows how limited state-initiated actions on funding were. In fact, it was mostly smaller-scale C and D sectors[110] that were set up: of the 378 sectors, 118 were type D and 117 were type C. Taking into account the limited nature (both in terms of funding and duration) of the operational budgets *(crédits de fonctionnement)* that were added to the equipment budgets *(crédits d'équipement)* this program simply caused the funds to be distributed. An examination of the results of each of the program's actions confirms this first general impression.[111]

Of the technical measures aimed at encouraging the elderly to stay in their own homes, only home-care help, clubs, and *community centers that provided food* were really effective when the final program came to be implemented.[112] By contrast, the home-care service and the day-center scheme, both of which required a new form of cooperation between the health and welfare administrations, hardly existed at all. Similarly, the achievements of the housing policy, which formed the basis of the policy for enabling the elderly to continue living in their own homes, were equally modest. Apart from the individual housing benefit introduced in July 1971, the construction of community centers incorporating housing provided barely half of the fifty-five thousand places that the Elderly Persons' Intergroup had called for.

An examination of the extent to which the final program's objectives were achieved during the life of the Sixth Plan shows that they fell below 20 percent on several counts. Similarly, the overall indicator of the program's achievements—stabilizing the number of people aged sixty-five to seventy-four in old people's homes, thus saving around one hundred thousand of them from being institutionalized—was not achieved either. A study in 1975 by the Ministry of Health's Studies and Plan Division showed that the number of people aged sixty-five to seventy-four living in retirement homes or old people's homes had increased significantly between 1972 and 1974.[113]

A study of the distribution of public-assistance expenditure among the elderly reaches similar conclusions. In 1974, funds had not yet been transferred from housing to help the elderly to stay in their own homes. Total spending on public assistance on the elderly came to almost 1.6 billion francs that year, and nearly all of it (90 percent) went for housing; only a very small proportion was spent on actions designed to enable the elderly to stay in their own homes.[114] Even though the unitary cost of helping the elderly to carry on living at home was three times less than placing them in special accommodations, and the home-help/residential care costs ratio rose slightly between 1968 and 1974 from 9.2 percent to 11 percent, attempts to effect this transfer were still unsuccessful.

The main obstacles to implementing the program. Implementing the program had little to do with the ambitions of its promoters, but this was because the introduction of the program ran up against a number of obstacles, one of which was clearly the absence of a coherent legal and financial framework at the center.

The aim of the final program was to coordinate and expand the work so far carried out by the state, social security offices, and local groups.[115] However, this combined exercise never happened. The Old-Age Fund was jealous of its autonomy and systematically refused to subsidize action that was associated with the setting up of sectors by the finalized program. In the wake of an open dispute with Bureau RV2, the body that had responsibility for creation of the final program and partly supervised the social action of social security organizations, a decree was issued on 31 January 1974, confirming the autonomy of the Old-Age Fund with regard to the final program. Following an earlier decree published in March 1973, which obliged the CNAVTS to play a part in the final program (and which was accordingly the subject of an appeal to the Council of State on a charge of abuse of power), the January 1974 decree determined only the vague principle that these actions should have priority with regard to funding.

As a result, there was no coordination between social security and state credits. The CNAVTS made a considerable effort with respect to the home-help service, but operated its own schemes to help the elderly carry on living in their own homes, and did not link up with sectors involved in the final program. Furthermore, four years passed before agreement was reached with CNAVTS on funding facilities for thirteen day centers (1974). Funds for running the program also remained a problem as the Caisse Nationale d'Assurance Maladie (National Health-Insurance Fund) belatedly (1977) operated from a very narrow interpretation of the medical care to be provided.

These disagreements between the DAS and social security about setting up the final program confirm the above interpretations of the process of drawing up an integration policy. This policy seemed very much like an attempt to open up new and more direct areas of intervention regarding old age that were outside the realm of retirement and the forces controlling it.

The reason for the fierce antagonism among the parties involved in the field of pensions and those concentrating on the way-of-life policy is that the latter wanted to force the former to play a subsidiary role in the implementation of their innovative policy.

The CNAVTS contribution largely depended on the success of the final program.[116] The excessively small budget was only going to be enough if other regular funders contributed more. For local groups, the Old-Age Fund's more reserved position meant that ways of funding operations to enable the elderly to stay in their own homes were numerous and complex. Many therefore hesitated before launching actions based on such precarious funding. For those that did experiment, the complexity of the funding circuit and the diversity of national decision-making organizations (including the State Secretariat of Social Action, the Ministry of Health Directorates, the National Insurance Funds for Sickness and Old Age, and complementary pension plans) made it virtually impossible to maintain any coherence in the definition of action at the local level, because each funding and decision-making body had its own criteria and regulatory practices.[117]

The Directorate of Social Action, which managed the final program, was unable to establish links with the Old-Age Fund or identify any political determination in the Ministry of Health. Accordingly, it failed in its role as program coordinator. From this point onward, the lack of central coherence could only lead to fragmented action on the periphery. It was the same for all the actions that required coordinated funding covering both health and social work. These actions could not succeed because the necessary legal and financial measures had not been carried out. Achievements such as the home-care service and day centers were outside the competence of the Directorate of Social Action; they came within the scope of the health or social security directorates, neither of which had a well-defined role within the program. They demanded the introduction of new formulas that had nothing to do with daily costs or medical consultations, but which provided funding for prevention and other nonmedical work. Formulas of this sort could be implemented only rarely and on a step-by-step basis, and even then it was often thanks to their promoters' personal influence.

Elsewhere, the Ministry of Housing carried out its policy for providing homes for the elderly (it was, after all, the basis of the policy for helping the elderly to remain in their own homes) without much conviction and without consulting other administrations concerned.

As a result, without any central coordination or legal and financial framework, the final program had to make do with fragmented funding and dispersed responsibility; this made real achievement in the field almost impossible. These obstacles discouraged many local authorities and *département*-based health and welfare directorates, and they adopted a cautious attitude toward a program that not only changed the way their administration functioned but also seemed incoherent and difficult to apply. The lack of central determination and coherence was highlighted and increased by gaps at local level with regard to promotion and coordination.

The community of planners drew up a strategy for local change by appointing "final program leaders" who stood outside the administrative hierarchy and whose role was to promote the program by informing and training local agents. However, this classic strategy for change did not in fact come into being. Despite plans to hire twenty-two club leaders in 1972 and another twenty-three in 1973, only fourteen were actually on the job when the program came to a close on 31 December 1975; further issues were their uneven distribution and their ambiguous status in relation to DDASSs (Directions Départementales des Affaires Sanitaires et Sociales—Departmental Directorates for Health and Social Affairs). Club leaders were mostly retired people (twelve out of fourteen), and their jobs were part-time, poorly paid, and very isolated. Furthermore, their marginal status locally did not usually allow them to perform the jobs they had been hired to do—which was to inform and train. For their part, the departmental directorates, feeling that they had been bypassed when the program was being drawn up, did not put much energy into the program; DDASS inspectors devoted only 10 to 15 percent of their time to the program over and above their supervision and welfare work.[118]

From that point on, consultation among agents at the grassroots level was often avoided, and the relatively innovative project was often misunderstood by promoters at the local level who had been inadequately trained. The result of these lacunae was an element of empiricism in the development of services and the absence of links between them. The policy for helping the elderly to continue living in their own homes developed at a rhythm determined by goodwill and local strategies.

This powerful local trend involving the disarticulation of action could be resisted only by the central administrative body responsible for carrying out the program. This organization, Bureau RV2, had always been poorly staffed, employing no more than two civil administrators and two or three assistants. Its clear lack of administrative support stopped it from taking part in the verification and assessment of actions that were in progress, and even prevented it from keeping up to date with initiatives that had funding. There was no real follow-up from the sectors, or any check made of what was happening at the local level. To use the dichotomy proposed by Theodore Lowi,[119] the logic behind the program was therefore of a distributive, rather than a redistributive, nature, because the latter involved arbitration among conflicting social interests. The administration responsible dispensed the funds provided by the regional prefects. As there was no guidance for the distribution of credits in the final program, they were handed out according to the promoters' dynamism or political interests rather than according to the region's particular needs with regard to the elderly.

Distorted action. The wide-ranging preventive measures included in the Sixth Plan aimed to prolong the normal life of elderly people, and was intended to defer the need for segregated housing. It never saw the light of day.

As has been explained, only a few services and facilities were developed by the program, but as it was scaled down, the whole action became distorted. What had been intended as an integrated package of interventions was reduced to little more than a series of compartmentalized and isolated facilities. The objective of mobilizing and promoting the elderly was now out of the question, and gave way to a public-assistance scheme that had hardly changed and was still based on segregation and dependence. Unlike the new directions developed in the Laroque Report—these were taken up in the Sixth Plan and sought to "reach a broader section of the population than relied on public assistance, possibly by asking for a means-tested contribution from those affected"[120]—most services had in fact been available only on a means-tested basis. This mainly applied to home helpers, the home-care service, and assistance with vacation and housing expenditure.[121]

An examination of the social characteristics of people who benefited from the various facilities and services enabling the elderly to stay in their own homes points to a similarity between these actions and the traditional public-assistance measures.

The impact made by the final program. Careful study in a particular locality of the interface between the elderly population and new local measures allowing them to stay in their own homes shows that new, restricted services and facilities were made available to the most disadvantaged sections of an elderly population that had become a captive clientele. The elderly found themselves segregated into specific sectors. In other words, the main effect of the new measures was to increase beneficiaries' dependence and, in a sense, legalize their marginality. Uncoordinated and compartmentalized actions were unable to bring beneficiaries back into normal social life. The new measures naturally gave beneficiaries access to certain benefits such as vacations, recreational activities, and home-based services that they had been unable to afford on the open market, but the price was increased segregation and subjugation. This is supported by the conclusion that the same study reached on third-age clubs, the most typical facility provided under the new measures and one theoretically accessible to all the elderly in a given district.

First, an analysis of the social composition of third-age club members, compared with that of the potential clientele, established that the most needy of the elderly (former manual workers and domestic staff) were overrepresented, and that cadres were underrepresented. In other words, clubs had been designed as new instruments for integrating and mobilizing the entire elderly population, but they were apparently still performing their traditional function of catering to the most disadvantaged. Except in terms of age, the social profile was basically not different from that in neighboring old people's homes. Second, a qualitative study of the organization of services provided by clubs highlighted the importance of supervision, organization, and the popularity of certain activities.

The combined effect of the layout of the clubs, the activities offered, and the rules governing access to them meant that a line was drawn between third-age activities that were allowed and those they were not. Daily outings, card games, television, reading, handicrafts, conversation, and afternoon tea (usually provided at around four o'clock) were among the permitted activities, while club rules barred smoking and all political debate on the premises and obliged members to dress appropriately, with overalls and slippers specifically prohibited; noisy behavior was also banned. Furthermore, the sale of any handicraft objects made in the club was forbidden. The overall impression to be derived from this notion of permitted and proscribed activities is of a lifestyle based on sociability and leisure time to the exclusion of all other activities.

This examination of the way clubs were run, their guiding spirit, and other measures recalled the practices and representations of the new middle class. For example, internal rules governing social behavior and dress were influenced by middle-class values, although this did not apply to the layout, which took the form of small, private, enclosed rooms; these were in direct contrast to the large, noisy, smoke-filled rooms in popular cafés where working-class activities took place. From that time on, clubs were places where middle-class retirement practice was imposed on elderly people with working-class backgrounds.

As a result, the effect of local measures to enable the elderly to stay in their own homes had less to do with their autonomy and integration than with increasing the dependency of the most disadvantaged, and of further isolating them inside a system of restricted activities. Further examination reveals that the new social-integration policy consisted of the traditional public-assistance program with a few modifications. It allowed for the setting up of new third-age facilities and services, but these were juxtaposed and had no link either with each other or with the health and housing sectors. At the same time, such new agents as club leaders, home-care workers, caseworkers, and leaders of community centers providing food were taking up their positions as managers of old age. However, the interests of the elderly were not promoted. Instead there was a fragmented, noncomprehensive approach to beneficiaries' psychological needs, and these were in turn broken down into a large number of abstract needs to which an uncoordinated system of services and facilities responded. The model of bureaucratized assistance was not far off.[122] A shift away from a traditional "custodial" policy to a type of capillary management based on a wide range of local facilities may not have fundamentally changed the nature of the care provided, but it certainly extended it.

Whereas attempts to provide community housing for the elderly had never managed to provide accommodation for more than 5 percent of the population aged sixty-five or over, the new network of localized facilities for helping the elderly to remain in their own homes affected 25 to 30 percent of elderly people living in a given area, although some of the measures went only part way.[123] As the facilities introduced under the new legislation still resembled public-assistance measures, the effect was to extend the dependence of the elderly population in proportion to the increase in the care they received.

The policy for helping the elderly to remain in their own homes had been originally designed to preserve their autonomy and to stabilize expenditure, but in fact it increased the level of dependency and therefore the cost as well. The policy produced a rise in the number of elderly men receiving assistance, but the impact needs to be assessed in terms that go beyond its direct effects on the activities of beneficiary groups.

This program appears to have been an important instrument of change in the way people thought about old age. It hastened the transformation of the cultural model of old age by introducing the activist representation of old age on which it was based at a grassroots level. By encouraging the development of new forms of cooperation among local partners, the program often brought about a change in the local management of old age by introducing the notion of services instead of housing. This clearly gave a new impetus to local authorities, which, with or without state funds, were working extremely hard in the field of old age.

Priority Action Program no. 15 (1976–1980): Stagnation

The "Programme d'Action Prioritaire" (PAP—Priority Action Program) designed to "encourage the practice of elderly people continuing to live in their own homes" was one of twenty-five such programs set up under the Seventh Plan. However, it did little to reverse the serious trends described above related to the effects of the final program.

Apart from a more flexible definition of services in the sector—this aimed to establish the importance of operational issues over facilities—and the availability of substantially more money, the PAP was more or less a copy of the final program. Indeed, an examination of its implementation shows that it produced the same results as the Sixth Plan. The large number of sectors set up was in stark contrast to the tiny amount of money spent, and it was therefore predictable that Seventh Plan and the final program should both result in waste and the provision of public assistance.

Altogether 460 sectors were set up (20 more than had been planned) at a cost of 388 million francs, or less than 20 percent of what had been budgeted.[124] The program continued to be very modest, was again experimental, and like its predecessor, the Sixth Plan, it provided for the setting up of barely one gerontology sector per *département* per year. There were a number of indicators that the state was becoming less dynamic in this field.

The first sign of the state's disengagement was that the planning stage of the Seventh Plan contained no specific structure designed to set up a social system for the elderly of the type proposed by the Sixth Plan's Intergroup. There was confirmation of this in the three innovative principles introduced in the Seventh Plan's Priority Action Program.

In the first place, PAP 15 was notable for an easing of its regulatory framework. The definition of the new range of services designed for the gerontological sectors was much more wide-ranging than it had been under the Sixth Plan. Only two services were compulsory for the new sectors: better living conditions and social/cultural activities. The very vagueness of the latter service gave free rein to any form of local initiative. In addition to these compulsory services, three other services or facilities had to be selected from an impressive list.[125] By providing an à la carte definition of this sort, the new program did not produce a set plan of action for the elderly, and as a result of the crisis in local funding, local authorities often had to weigh the possibilities set out in the PAP and choose those third-age services and facilities that cost least and had the biggest impact. The unprecedented success of third-age clubs was doubtless due to the fact that they took these two concerns into account.

In the second place, the PAP was innovative in that it provided funds for training local managers. This seems to have been an attempt to avoid earlier mistakes by redirecting managers' policies through an intensified approach to the work and a systematic presentation of the main principles, rather than through increased material commitment by the state.

The policy for enabling the elderly to continue living in their own homes became a more administrative matter under the Seventh Plan. The DDASS took more direct control, and this accentuated the trend toward breaking schemes down into numerous administrative areas and reinforcing the distributive nature of the program. This, as far as the administration was concerned, was because success was measured in terms of the speed at which grants were used.

The general trend in every field at this time was toward the development of qualitative orientations, thereby allowing for innovation in the field of living environment without a proportionate rise in costs. The new action program on behalf of the elderly fitted this perspective perfectly.

It is significant that the services such as home-care service—they were the most necessary if the elderly were to be able to stay in their own homes, but also the most costly, as they required new funding formulas—were rarely selected by PAP 15 sectors. They were also optional, and services that were difficult to set up were ignored in favor of programs that were easier to run, more flexible, and less costly. For this reason, interventions that sought "to bring the generations closer together" were more frequently adopted than the home-care service, which was chosen by less than 10 percent of the sectors. After home help, third-age cultural and physical activities, and information, the most popular optional services were those that had a high profile, made a major symbolic impact, and did not cost much.

During the period 1976–80, the program was interpreted from a Malthusian standpoint. This was partly linked to the economic circumstances of the time and a slowdown in economic growth; however, it was also associated with the discovery that enabling the elderly to carry on living in their own homes led to an increase in the overall cost of old age rather than to a decrease in the cost of putting the elderly in homes. In this context, the policy of enabling people to continue living in their own homes was associated both with a strong temptation to achieve financial reform and with the expectation of making money.

As a result, the National Sickness Insurance Fund (the French expression "sickness insurance" is equivalent to "health insurance") took steps to slow down the introduction of services or benefits that it funded itself. Examples included an unwillingness of the CRAMs (Caisses Régionales d'Assurance Maladie—Regional Sickness Insurance Funds) to accept fixed-price treatment in the context of setting up the home-care service, the delay centrally in putting these services on a legal footing (this did not happen until 1978), and the eighty-day limit (subsequently deemed unfair) on elderly people staying in short-term homes. The decision to terminate the day-center experiment was also evidence of the incremental approach that henceforth governed the implementation of PAPs. Action designed to help the elderly to remain in their own homes was increasingly aimed at an elderly population that was open to ideas; it inspired these people with ideas of self-management and activism, and moved away from the concept of old age beset with problems.

Priority was given to interventions that had a high symbolic value and whose costs were easy to keep under control. Although the Seventh Plan program worked hard to change public opinion,[126] it also stressed the increasing number of individualized, proactive services; these were turning a growing proportion of the elderly population into a group in receipt of benefits and covered by a network of specialized services and facilities.

As only symptoms and representations were touched upon, and in the absence of a resolute policy for preventing the disappearance of social participation and autonomy, the threat posed by the marginalization of the elderly was not eliminated. Instead, new demands were developed and directed at the state, which was in turn in danger of being trapped in a budgetary crisis and a separate crisis of legitimation. At the same time, an ever-widening gap was beginning to appear between the increasingly extended and dependent expectations of the state and compartmentalized responses that were unable to resolve the vicious circle of aspirations and dissatisfaction.

Conclusion: Social Dynamic in the Production of a Way-of-Life Policy for the Elderly

This book has reconstructed the history of the management of way of life of the elderly since 1945 and provided an analysis of the play of social and political forces that produced a policy for enabling the elderly to continue living in society. Both throw light on the social logic governing the production of a way-of-life policy that broadly reflected the state's variable capacity for autonomous action.

An earlier section has shown how the development of an innovative way-of-life policy, which sought to achieve social integration of the elderly, coincided with the final stages of the building of a Gaullist state with highly integrated powers and a capacity for independent action with regard to social agents. The policy emerged after a period during the Fourth Republic when the state had, by contrast, been heavily infiltrated by social interests and had played only a subsidiary role in the day-to-day management of the way of life. Its purpose was to fill gaps in the retirement system by giving assistance to the most needy—in other words, those who had fallen through the safety net of the new pension plan. As a result, management of the way of life appeared to play second fiddle to pension policies. As far as the elderly were concerned, the new capacity for action that the state enjoyed in the early 1960s was expressed in a new ambition to restructure the relationship between the elderly and society. In particular, this led to the setting up of the Study Commission on Old Age.

This state initiative was an attempt to redefine the central issue of the old-age policy in terms that would increase the state's own capacity to intervene. It formulated a new interpretation of old age in terms of marginality and isolation, and in this way shifted the focal point of the old-age debate away from improvements in the right to retire and toward the promotion of an integrated way of life.

The new definition also corresponded to a redefinition of the state's role in managing relations between the elderly and society, and designated new areas for state action that were no longer restricted to the abstract economic role of vectors of money transfers or subsidiary public assistance. The state developed closer links with those who came under its jurisdiction, and henceforth intervened on a more sociopolitical plane. It was now able to stretch beyond the simple regulation of employer/union relations, where it had been restricted to pensions.

By adopting marginality and isolation as the new definition of the problems of old age, the state took on more direct responsibility for this sector of the population and assumed the role of defender and organizer of the social status of the elderly. This kind of response enabled the state to expand its representative role; as far as the elderly were concerned, it simultaneously developed more direct control over society above and beyond social forces and the institutions (e.g., pension plans) that were largely the concrete expression of those forces.

The new state plan of action, which targeted the entire elderly population and aimed at sustained social integration, meant that the elderly, who had previously been seen only in terms of their poverty, now enjoyed a new political citizenship. The emergence of an old-age policy, and therefore of a public identity reserved for the elderly, coincided with the formation of a new category of citizens in France henceforth known as the "third age."[127] They had new rights to social integration and to continued participation in society. The new policy was also accompanied by the introduction of a new, direct relationship between the elderly and the state. The new rights granted to the elderly reflected their particular stage of life; they also constituted senior citizens' rights, and were quite different from the right to retirement, which was an entitlement to inactivity following a period of employment—not a civic right, but one based on work.

The state's efforts to promote a new model for the management of old age contained a clear attempt to impose a new definition of old age as the "third age" and not simply "retirement"; it also sought to extend its own capacity for direct action beyond the realm of pensions, and set itself above the social forces controlling it. In return for recognizing this new category of citizens, the state was able to extend its scope for representation and increase its legitimacy.

The emergence of a way-of-life policy thus appeared to be an expression of the state's relative autonomy in relation to civil society. Each time the political-administrative system tried to mark out or defend its autonomy, a new sense of dynamism appeared in the old-age policy with regard to the way of life. This was the situation in the early 1960s, when a highly autonomous state tried to develop plans of action, other than pension plans, that could more directly restructure the relationship between the elderly and society. The same thing happened in the early 1970s, when the policy for enabling the elderly to stay in their own homes was set in place. In so doing, the state tried to strengthen its own definition of the old-age policy as a way-of-life policy, so as to preserve its scope for direct, independent interventions concerning old age. At the same time, the unions launched an attack on pensions and again raised the issue of "improving the social right to retirement," thus jeopardizing both the state's capacity to act in this field and the legitimation that it derived from it. By contrast, as soon as the gap between the state and social classes closed, and when the state became more influenced by social interests and saw its voluntarism reduced, the way-of-life policy stagnated. This book has demonstrated that this was equally true during the time of the Fourth Republic and in the Seventh Plan's Priority Action Program.

The state's own capacity for action lay at the very heart of the formation of the way-of-life policy. An analysis of the development of this policy shows that it was influenced by the coalitions and conflicts that developed among the different sectors of the state, and by alliances with social-support networks that this political orientation had succeeded in promoting or discovering in society. For these reasons, it was still the state, through its internal functioning or through the footholds that it managed to establish in society, that was the central figure in this policy.

It has already been pointed out how the nature of intermediary groups standing on the border between the administrative system and civil society played a very important role in the formation of way-of-life policies. They breathed life into the state's project and at the same time moved it in a new direction. The social dynamic of way-of-life policies depended critically on the dialectic of the relationship between the state and these intermediary groups. It also hinged on departments of the state and social-support networks renewing their alliances through action.

Clearly, the way-of-life policy could not be seen as an expression of class struggle. On the contrary, it reflected the way in which the state impacted on society.

A longitudinal analysis of the debate on old age demonstrates that the unions campaigned only around retirement issues. There was no popular countermodel for managing the way of life, and it is important to remember that the union response to the alternative management approach proposed by the Laroque Report was to resuscitate arguments for an improved right to retirement. The way-of-life policy was not fully developed outside social relationships, but as part of a movement opposed to the retirement policy and the social forces that controlled it. On acquiring its own capacity for action, the state tried to develop or reconstruct areas where more direct intervention on the relationship between old age and society was possible, and which would encourage the formation of a way-of-life policy. State action of this type was accentuated whenever union campaigns against pension plans forced the state, now able to act on its own, to assert its autonomy by consolidating its definition of old age and its main field of action. However, it had a tendency to relax when developments in the balance of forces between the classes distanced the labor unions from the struggle for the right to retirement. This was what happened in the final period. Subsequent sections will show how the unions concentrated on defending jobs, with retirement one element in their struggle to maintain employment. The issue of defining the old-age policy as the way of life seemed to be less fundamental for a state no longer threatened in its arena for intervention. As a consequence, the way-of-life policy stagnated.

It should not be forgotten that once a policy has been developed, it affects the social relationships that brought it into being in the first place. In the light of the above analyses of the impact of the way-of-life policy, there was a clear danger that its stagnation could lead to crisis. The new social-integration policy grew out the autonomy of a Gaullist state that was increasing its legitimacy and capacity for representation by granting the elderly population new citizenship and new rights. For this reason, the new policy succeeded only in increasing the number of elderly people who came under its jurisdiction and in focusing all demands concerning old age on the state. This could only lead to a deepening of the crisis in the welfare state by encouraging a process of delegitimizing the system, and it compounded the financial crisis that had been brought about mainly by the pension plans.

3

Old Age and Employment: A Sharp Rise in the Adoption of Early-Exit Schemes

The definition of policies for old age that has been adopted in this book—a series of public interventions structuring the relationships between old age and society—is now followed by an examination of a third fundamental dimension of these policies: the dimension that takes account of the employment of older members of the population. It is true that this dimension is often far removed from an administrative conception of policies for old age, as these usually come to little more than social actions and policies focusing on retirement; it is nonetheless a key instrument in the structuring of relationships between old age and society. In fact, the age cutoff points and classifications based on the organization of production needs, and the age-based employment policy that flows from them, represent the fundamental elements of a social definition of old age for every society in every period. It follows that older workers' levels and modes of participation in the production process are a basic component in any discussion of old age and its management, together with the establishment of a social right to retirement and the definition of a specific way of life.

This chapter aims to restructure the discussions of this third dimension and the space occupied by the relevant parties in dispute; the purpose is to reconstruct the social dynamic that lies at the heart of the implementation of employment policies for older workers.

Our study will start with an examination of the successive philosophies that the state followed when intervening in the employment of older workers after 1945; this will be followed by an analysis of the play of social forces that, within the framework of unemployment insurance, presided over the implementation of measures dealing with early exit, and subsequently led to their being taken up by so many people. The widespread use of a form of early exit now called "preretirement" *(préretraite)* elevated it to the status of a societal phenomenon; the concluding section will attempt to identify the implications of this. The steep rise in the popularity of preretirement schemes has effectively led to a reorganization of the life course and to a social redefinition of old age. It has also opened up a crisis for the whole old-age policy, which now finds itself corrupted by the fact that the employment dimension has acquired a newfound importance.

The State, Old Age, and Employment after 1945

From 1945 onward, the state dealt with relations between old age and employment in three successive ways. In the first period, which extended until the end of the 1950s, employment policies were mainly aimed at mobilizing older workers and providing them with incentives to remain on the job longer. In the second period, which ran approximately from 1963 to 1972, employment policy covering older workers diversified: measures for enabling older workers to remain in employment complemented a policy of social assistance that was conditional on early exit; it also sought to introduce more flexibility into the management of older workers so as to facilitate changes in, and the merging trends of, French industry. Finally, during the third period, which continued into the 1980s, employment policies moved toward the systematic removal of older workers from the labor force through the widespread introduction of early exit schemes.

The content of these major periods will be examined in turn, and in this way the main characteristics of the last period will be highlighted. It will thereafter be accorded the fullest attention.

Incentives to Remain Longer in Employment

During the period immediately following the Second World War, state interventions in the relationship between old age and employment sought to encourage older workers to remain on the job longer.

These measures were based on economic, demographic, and financial considerations, as the effort needed for national reconstruction demanded the mobilization of all able-bodied workers. Demographically, France had an aging population, and its inhabitants of working age were few in number. This situation was to remain unchanged for over ten years because of the arrival on the labor market of working-age members of small birth cohorts; meanwhile, both an accelerated birthrate and an increase in the number of elderly people as a percentage of the overall population were placing a further burden on the labor force.[1] Accordingly, the financial threats that this burden posed to the stability of the new social security old-age scheme compounded the shortage of workers, and to such an extent that it was necessary to call on the reserve labor force that comprised the elderly population. This situation was in turn exacerbated by the fact that the government's family policy was opposed to the employment of women, another natural pool of labor widely used in time of war. In its role as industrializing agent, the state encouraged older people to carry on working;[2] it also tried to develop a rational system of using older members of the labor force by promoting the introduction of appropriate retraining and job-search procedures. However, the public authorities ran up against opposition from both employers and the labor unions in their attempts to push these measures through.

Employers were keen to maximize the productive capacity of their plants, and wanted to use workers only when they were at their most efficient. They therefore chose to take advantage of employees' new pension entitlements in order to get rid of unprofitable staff.[3] The unions, for their part, actively defended their recently won right to retirement and even tried to extend it by putting in a claim for a lower qualifying age.[4]

The Fourth Republic enjoyed little independence from political and social forces, and faced with this opposition it opted for a persuasive approach as opposed to constrictive legal measures. Significantly, the administrative means necessary to implement an employment policy were still very limited.

In the late 1940s and throughout the 1950s, there was a plethora of government statements, meetings, and study seminars organized by the public authorities; these stressed the dangers posed by population aging and the need to make more rational use of older workers.[5] However, these warnings and recommendations failed to elicit any legal measures. As far as older people were concerned, the pension system constituted the main instrument of public employment policy throughout this period. In practice, the method of calculating the social security retirement pension was a powerful incentive for people to stay at work until a relatively advanced age: it provided only 20 percent of average salary of the last ten years of employment at the age of sixty, as opposed to 40 percent at sixty-five, and thereby made sixty-five the effective age at which the pension was paid out. In fact, with its system of raising the rate of pension by four points per year deferred beyond the age of sixty-five, the scheme encouraged payout to take place at an even later date.

One explanation for the stagnation of pensions in the general scheme—it was a phenomenon of critical importance during this period—is doubtless to be found in the beneficial effects that this stagnation had on prolonging the working life at a time of full employment. It is something of a paradox that the right to retirement, a victory that had been achieved by the working class at the time of the Liberation, was partly converted into an incentive to remain at work.

Selective Preretirement Schemes Introduced and Controlled by the State

By setting up the FNE (Fonds National de l'Emploi—National Employment Fund) under the 18 December 1963 act, the state introduced a new approach to the employment of older people. An agreement signed by the state and employers, which also covered certain occupational sectors and/or localities, enabled older workers to cease employment earlier; the machinery for this was the provision of a special allowance that permitted dismissed workers aged over sixty to take early exit. Accordingly, having encouraged people to stay at work, the state then sought to introduce more flexibility into the employment of older workers but kept the initiative strictly under its control. Cash benefits were granted only by agreement with the state, and these enabled the Labor Inspectorate (Inspection du Travail) to lay down certain conditions in the course of negotiations. This new legislation heralded a second period in the public management of the relationship between old age and employment. Early exit was now an option for workers aged over sixty, but it was exceptional and came under the control of the public authorities. The device was used mainly in the textiles, shipbuilding, and coal-mining industries, and in certain regions.[6] In a period of substantial growth, it was important for the state to help in the restructuring and merging of the country's productive resources, and it achieved this by giving financial assistance to encourage workers to retire.

This measure was an excellent illustration of the philosophy underlying state policy in the early days of the Fifth Republic. The state now enjoyed considerable internal homogeneity; this was exemplified by increased executive power and in the development of a technocracy and a public-service ideology. The state therefore discovered it had more independence for action, compared to social interests. For the most part, it made use of this independence by promoting the restructuring of French capitalism so as to make it competitive within Europe and by pursuing a policy that, although conforming to the interests of the big employers, was implemented without their involvement and never received their approval.

The use made of the FNE preretirement allowances demonstrated that this formula was soon seen by all social actors as a convenient palliative to a sectorial crisis. In fact, from the outset the FNE had had an extended mission, which was to promote the geographical and occupational mobility of employees who had been laid off, or were threatened with layoffs. To achieve this aim, the scheme offered not only special preretirement allowances but also a wide range of interventions that included relocation expenses, training grants, and a sliding scale of unemployment allowances. All of these financial measures were spurned by employers, except for the preretirement schemes that constituted the basis of the FNE's interventions.[7] Preretirement schemes were supported both by employers, who saw them as a solution that caused less social conflict than dismissal, and by the labor unions, which considered them to be a first step toward a lowering of retirement age to sixty. Faced with widespread agreement on these measures among social forces, the state took advantage of its financial control and eventually limited the extent to which these forces were able to develop. The disputes in the Nantes–St. Nazaire shipyard in 1965 were an excellent illustration of this balance of forces. Management had made considerable use of the preretirement solution in frequent downsizing. As a result, in 1965 over one-third of the workers earmarked for dismissal were over the age of sixty. The labor unions—the CGT, CFDT, FO and CGC—thereupon launched a fierce joint campaign, involving strikes and then major demonstrations in Nantes and Paris in response to a management lockout; the objective was to achieve early retirement of all steelworkers at the Nantes yard. The unions believed that retraining procedures for dismissed workers under the age of sixty were illusory. It was their view that the only way of avoiding massive regional unemployment in engineering was by reducing the total labor force through extending the early exit from workforce of aging workers. The minister of labor, Gilbert Grandval, rejected this extension of early exit; he preferred to move toward a job-creation policy in the *région* and would grant it only through the agency of the FNE to older workers who had been dismissed. It was already possible in this dispute to discern certain strategies and areas for compromise that would lead to a steep rise in early exit in the forthcoming period.

At this time the state was opposed to the systematic shedding of older workers, and accordingly developed its strategy under two headings. On one hand, it attempted to encourage companies to improve work conditions of their older staff. On the other, the state's aggressive social policy with respect to the aging population's way of life and social-integration issues enabled it to turn down persistent union demands for a lower retirement age. Between 1961 and 1970, the average retirement age rose from 63.7 to 64.5 years. This mainly reflected the effects of a pension system the funding base of which had increased, and which therefore gave more encouragement to people to stay at work until the age of sixty-five. However, it also illustrated the state's ability at this time to resist a conflict of interest between employers and unions on the question of people leaving the labor market.

Toward the Provision of Compensation for all Dismissed Older Workers

By contrast, the employment policy for older workers during the third period was characterized by the spread of early exit. Attempts to retrain or find new jobs for workers approaching retirement age were unusual, and activity was concentrated on better compensation for unemployment, which had risen in the wake of the economic crisis. However, "good compensation" simply encouraged companies in difficulty, and those needing to reduce the labor force, to get rid of large numbers of older employees, and they did so on the grounds that they were more expensive and often lacked the necessary skills to meet new requirements of the production system. This immediately gave rise both to an extension of procedures for excluding older workers and to an exponential rise in the number of retirees.

The National Interoccupational Agreement of 27 March 1972 introduced guaranteed income for unemployed people aged sixty and over within the framework of unemployment insurance. It constituted the starting point for this new philosophy.[8] Early exit, whether selective or specific to a company, region, or sector, now ceased to be the exception and was extended to a whole age band. This agreement was followed by the 5 July 1972 act, which set the state's financial involvement in these new measures. The 1972 agreement was finally liberalized by an amendment dated 13 June 1977: this extended guaranteed income *(garantie de ressources)* to workers retiring voluntarily after their sixtieth birthday.[9] A guaranteed income in the event of layoff (*garantie de ressources licenciement*—GRL) was therefore established to run in tandem with another guaranteed income scheme for workers who had resigned (*garantie de ressources démission*—GRD). This extension of the agreement of 27 March 1972 never led to any legislation: it remained a matter for collective agreements to take up, and its validity, which was limited to two years, was extended on two occasions, in May 1979 and in February 1981. The abolition of guaranteed income by the Socialist government in May 1982, following the publication of the ordinance lowering retirement age, did not halt an extension to early exit measures. On the contrary, it accompanied a marked increase in measures aimed at fifty-five- to fifty-nine-year-olds; the most prominent of these were preretirement solidarity contracts. For a period of two years

(1982–83), these contracts gave employees aged fifty-five to fifty-nine the option of voluntarily stopping work on 70 percent of gross salary, on condition that the employer made a contractual commitment to replace each one. Meanwhile, the preretirement scheme funded by the FNE for workers dismissed on economic grounds survived, and took care of such employees from the age of fifty-six years, two months. The move to make early exit available to everyone was still very much in evidence.

The passage from the second to the third period of the public employment policy for older workers represented a quantitative change, but also one of scale. Two important qualitative transformations took place. First, there was a shift in how the system was controlled: whereas, during the second period, it had been introduced and controlled by the state, during the third period it was based much more directly on agreements and accords among social partners. Second, the nature of the preretirement policy changed as its influence became more broadly based. Preretirement was no longer a selective solution to problems posed by pockets of unemployment and industrial restructuring, and a more humane policy aimed at alleviating the distress of older workers who had lost their jobs. Now that the labor market was shrinking, it became an important means of accelerating early exit. The employment policy, or, more accurately, the unemployment compensation policy for older workers, acted as the main regulator of early exit, thereby taking over a task traditionally fulfilled by pension plans. This inevitably caused the mechanisms covering pension and unemployment to be confused, and caused the whole purpose of the pension system to be abused. At the same time, the pattern of life was reshaped, and, as a result, a new definition of old age was developed.

In the pages that follow, this author will attempt to reconstruct the play of social forces that presided over the emergence of the third period of the older workers' employment policy that was pursued after 1945. This final period will be scrutinized with particular care, as it clearly represents the point at which a new philosophy underpinning durable and wide-ranging public practice was institutionalized. My line of inquiry is to look at the configurations of social relations that formed the matrix of public decisions on each of the basic dimensions of a policy for old age. This perspective involves identifying significant cuts when the policy-making process is opening new avenues. This chapter will seek to demonstrate that neither the first period, which concentrated more on stated policies than on decision making, nor the second period, which was characterized by an employment policy that was still limited and selective, was as relevant as the last period in developing an analysis of the social dynamic that extended the scope of an employment policy to older workers.

This investigation will therefore concentrate on 1969–84, a period dominated by a dramatic increase in the number of preretirement schemes. First, it will explain the "invention" of guaranteed income for aging unemployed workers that followed a long prologue of successive offensives and counteroffensives on the subject of pensions and the way of life of the elderly. Second, there will be an analysis of how this measure was so widely adopted; it spread particularly quickly after the period 1975–77 when employment-related issues began to be clarified in response to economic developments, and following the emergence of new political relations. Finally, there will be an examination of the system's astonishing rise and the social changes it brought about.

Social Forces and Career-End Employment: The Prologue (1968–1972): Offensives and Counteroffensives on Specific Issues

The Interoccupational Agreement on the guaranteed-income scheme for aging unemployed workers of 27 March 1972 was confirmed by the 5 July 1972 act. The decision-making process that led up to this may be interpreted as the result of a series of decisions and counterdecisions on the definition of the issue of policies for old age. It was a relative success for the employers' counteroffensive. What triggered this process was an offensive by the labor union centers, the CGT and the CFDT, on the question of pensions. This offensive formed part of the social campaigning that intensified from 1968 onward, and stimulated counteroffensives on the part of other leading agents, that is, the state and the employers. Each of the three parties attempted to ensure that its own definition of the issue, and its own rationality, prevailed.

The unions developed their campaign under the banner of the *social entitlement to retirement;* the public authorities responded for the most part with pronouncements about the "way of life of the elderly." The employers sought to counter salary claims by diverting the discussion toward the whole question of employing older workers; the definition of the issue as they saw it was that pensions should be seen as *an instrument for regulating employment*.

In order to reconstruct the process that led to the establishment of the guaranteed-income scheme, the next section will pull together the rational positions put forward by the three main parties. It will then examine how matters developed as far as specific issues were concerned, and finally look for the significance of the agreement that flowed from these confrontations.

Labor Unions and an Extension to the Social Entitlement to Retirement

Most of the following analysis of the labor unions is devoted to the behavior and strategies of the two union centers, the CGT and the CFDT. These organizations fought for an extension to the social entitlement to retirement during this period, and often did so on a joint basis. The FO and the CGC adopted very different positions; these will be referred to briefly insofar as employers used their differences of opinion in order to impose their own positions.

The question of lowering retirement age and raising the level of pensions had been a recurrent item in union demands since social security was set up in 1945, but the May 1968 movement demonstrably gave these claims fresh momentum. In fact, they crystallized the rejection of conditions that constrained employment rights, which was precisely where the campaign to lower retirement age was rooted. Moreover, by leading on to the Grenelle Agreements, which were designed to achieve a better distribution of the benefits of economic growth, May 1968 helped to highlight exactly how far behind pensions had really fallen.

Pensions became one of the more important components of social struggle for the first time after 1968. They were defended independently by each of the labor union confederations until 1970, when, as working relations between the CGT and the CFDT grew closer, the issue became a priority objective for joint action.

The main events that marked the intensification of the union campaign on pensions were as follows:

• May and June 1968: Organization of a national conference of CGT Retired Members (8–9 May) and setting up of the Union Confédérale des Retraités CGT (Confederal Union of CGT Retired Members) (June). Efforts also made by CGT and CFDT to establish an organization for members who had retired from the private sector.

• March 1970: Major meetings of CGT retirees. Demand for guaranteed minimum of 750 francs. Memorandum sent to the prime minister.

• September 1970: Closer working relationship between CGT and CFDT, agreement on priority objectives, including pensions.

• November 1970: The CGT and CFDT call for union-employer-government negotiations on pensions.

• February-March 1971: Planning of joint campaign and publication of joint document by the two union centers.

• 29 March 1971: (1) The confederations appeal to the entire movement involved in the joint campaign: they recommend company-level initiatives (stoppages, sending demands and petitions to management) and meetings of employed and retired people in large cities; (2) letters sent to the prime minister and to the president of the CNPF (Conseil National du Patronat Français—the French Employers' Association) calling for tripartite negotiations on problems pertaining to pensions.

• 1 April 1971: Joint CGT-CFDT press conference.

• April 1971: FO, CFTC, and CGC agree to discussions proposed by the CNPF on early exit for those incapable of work or laid off.

• 24-27 May 1971: National day of action in support of pensions; united campaign on pensions is brought to a close by demonstrations and stoppages throughout France.

• 27 May 1971: CGT and CFDT organize a march through Paris from the Opéra to the Palais Royal; over thirty thousand employed and retired workers call for retirement age to be lowered. Main slogans: "Retirement in an armchair, not in a coffin," "Increase our pensions," and "I'm sixty-three years old: I've had enough."

• 8 June 1971: Agreement among the FO, CGC, and CFTC to initiate discussions on early exit for older workers who have been laid off.

• 10 July 1971: Organization of joint campaign involving the sending of postcards to the prime minister and the CNPF: "If I live to be sixty, I want to be able to put my feet up." Two million postcards sent by October.

• November–December 1971: Union campaign relaunched. Delegations to CNPF and the prime minister asking for negotiations on pensions not received.

• 19 November 1971: CNPF writes to all labor unions, inviting them to start negotiations within the context of collective agreements on guaranteed income for aging unemployed workers.

• 2 December 1971: National day of action on pensions to coincide with a debate in the National Assembly on the draft of the Boulin Law on pensions.

• 6 December 1971: Union-employer negotiations open on the situation of older workers who have been laid off.

• 27 March 1972: National Interoccupational Agreement signed on a guaranteed income for aging unemployed workers.

What were the main objectives of the CGT and the CFDT in their united campaign on the problem of pensions?

Their joint platform of demands of 4 March 1971 contained four main points:

1. revaluation of pensions and minimum allowances;[10]
2. right to full pension at sixty;

3. adjustments to conditions of employment that might cause workers to be worn out prematurely;

4. improvements to the living conditions of retired people, particularly through the development of facilities for the elderly.

Unions were aware of the need for a global approach to the problem. They wanted the fruits of economic growth to be shared out in a way that favored older staff, and a more equitable place given to the old-age allowance in the distribution of national revenue. For the CFDT, General Secretary Edmond Maire stated at the 1 April 1971 press conference that the union's action "had aimed to change political priorities, and that his union was ready to discuss it with state and employers' representatives." On behalf of the CGT, Jean Dubois thought that "the country had to make the political choices necessary to lay the groundwork for a real policy for old age." Throughout the campaign, the unions called for tripartite union-employers-government negotiations on "all of the problems currently posed by pensions."

However, the union struggle focused mainly on the question of retirement age and the level of the pension. It sought to bring down the age of entitlement to a full pension and to have pensions revalued; the campaign also took up the question of threshold, and generally concentrated on the first two objectives set out in the joint platform. By contrast, in the public debate, they omitted to mention activity upstream (such as employment policies facilitating the adaptation of the work of older workers) and downstream (e.g., actions designed to improve the living conditions of the elderly, including the introduction of the necessary community facilities and services). This concentration within the union debate on the question of the pensions threshold was linked to the fact that pensions were able to reconcile several objectives that union action took on board at this time. The campaign for an extension to retirement entitlement (i.e., triggered earlier and at a higher rate) provided an arena where at least four essential union issues in the period could emerge.

First, because of a shift in strategy, the campaign for a reduction in working hours began to refocus on retirement age. Second, the rise in unemployment among older employees and the arrival on the labor market of large numbers of young workers turned the lowering of the retirement age into a convenient palliative to these employment problems. Third, at a time when the standard of living of working people was rising generally, the failure of the general scheme to keep pace with rising costs encouraged unions to mount a spirited defense of the income levels of retired people. And finally, in a period marked by an upturn in social struggles, the labor unions based their organizational strength on the issue of retirees. Their demand for an extension to pension entitlement enabled them to mobilize around common objectives together with the working population.

These four questions, which turned the "extension of the social entitlement to a pension" into the main thrust of the union campaign on pensions, will now be examined one by one. There will then be an analysis of the consequences, limitations, and misunderstandings that may have been caused by concentrating the social campaign on this question.

Lowering retirement age and the campaign against exploitation. The demand for the age of entitlement to a full pension to be lowered to sixty was certainly the issue that had the greatest impact on public opinion during the union pensions campaign of 1971, and the concern that was best remembered and most widely shared. It also directly formed part of the struggle for a reduction in working hours, and as such was a traditional area for union action.

The CGT and CFDT wanted workers to be able to stop working at the age of sixty on a full pension, if they so desired. The unions believed that it was a simple matter of equity: as a CGT representative pointed out at the joint union press conference on 1 April 1971, pensionable age had not been changed in twenty-five years, whereas production, productivity, and capitalist profits had risen substantially.[11] Lowering the retirement age was to compensate for what the unions claimed were ever-worsening conditions at work; it was also designed to enable the most underprivileged workers, who had started work while very young and whose life expectancy was very short, "not to pay into pension schemes any longer and derive no benefit in return."[12]

The difficulties that the unions encountered throughout the earlier part of their campaign to reduce working hours and improve conditions of employment revealed one of the reasons why their offensive shifted towards a lowering of retirement age in late 1968.

The long period of intensive capitalist accumulation and the vastly increased productivity that France had recently achieved encouraged the unions to step up pressure for a wide-ranging reduction in working hours. The purpose was to limit the extent to which workers could be exploited. "Increasingly exhausting work (even if the effects have been attenuated by union action and mechanical advances), mind-destroying work rates, the breakdown and distribution of tasks and the resulting nervous pressure, travel time that prolongs the working day, teamwork and shift work, and the entitlement to rest periods, leisure time and cultural activities—all of these must lead to a reduction in working time."[13]

As a result of their actions aimed at limiting the working week and year, the unions ran up against stiff resistance from employers, who mainly feared that such measures would increase payroll costs.

The unions concluded that their efforts had met with only limited success in this direction: in fact, between 1964 and 1969, the working week dropped from 45.9 to 45.1 hours, a reduction of only forty-eight minutes. They also considered that their victories—improved working conditions arising out of various disputes—were largely illusory, and that any gain they had made had been won back by employers through higher work-rates and the development of shift work.

Realizing that they had not been able to reduce in any important or lasting way the extent to which employees were being exploited at work, the unions concentrated their efforts on shortening the working life so as to allow workers to escape sooner from exhausting and alienating conditions of employment. They were encouraged in this by the fact that lowering the retirement age was a working-class gain that could not in any way be taken away by employers.

The unions therefore chose to focus on the consequences of alienation (i.e., working hours and conditions of employment) rather than on its causes. Initially they wanted to "limit the damage that [had] unfortunately been done."[14] Given the situation at that time, following a shift in strategy, the aim to lower retirement age was exactly where the battle against exploitation was going to be fought.

Employment problems and lowering the retirement age. The demand for a lowering of retirement age was not just part of the struggle for a reduction in working hours; indeed, once the union campaign got under way in 1968, it absorbed many other concerns related to employment, despite their lesser importance. The backdrop against which the union action was played out consisted of the increased vulnerability of older workers to unemployment[15] and the arrival on the labor market of the numerous early representatives of the postwar baby boom. The unions saw a lower retirement age as a well-timed palliative to this two-pronged challenge. On one hand, retirement at sixty meant a way of rewarding workers prematurely worn out by intensive work; on the other, it was also a way of "giving the mass of young men and women the prospect of finding a job more easily at a time when they [formed] a significant proportion of the unemployed population."[16] Therefore, the union demand for retirement at sixty simultaneously and ambiguously expressed a wish to enjoy the right to an earlier respite and the "need to give way to young people."[17] By adopting this latter position, the CGT and the CFDT were subscribing to the principle of unequal distribution of work between generations. Far from questioning the scheme of social organization—according to which, in our society, old age is a form of social unproductiveness—the unions actually supported it by opting for this particular policy. The union position was more favorable to young people than to older workers, whose removal from the labor force was now considered legitimate. It also carried the seeds of the huge shift toward the preretirement formula; this took place in the period that followed, and at a time when the economic crisis was intensifying the struggle for work to be distributed between generations.

Raising the incomes of retirees. The union demand for retirement age to be lowered was linked to an equally frequent claim that pensions should be revalued. A broad right to retire meant not only a chance to stop work earlier, but also an opportunity to lead a reasonable life.

Widespread social mobilization at this time enabled the unions to launch vigorous attacks concerning the issue of pensions. Furthermore, the recent social security ordinances of 1967 had reduced much of the union movement's capacity to manage the pension scheme; this encouraged the labor unions to take up a more critical position on the question as a whole.

"France is no longer in a state of underdevelopment, but that is where she has abandoned her old people." This statement, made by the Parliamentary Group on Problems of the Third Age in 1972, neatly summed up labor union feeling in late 1968 about retired people's incomes. Despite the sustained growth that France had been enjoying, retirees still formed an island of poverty. Pensions had not risen in proportion to salaries, and of the six Common Market countries, France was where the elderly had benefited least from economic expansion.[18] Efforts made by the French government were markedly less energetic than those made by governments in other countries. The unions claimed that, according to EEC figures, France occupied the bottom position, spending only 39 percent of social expenditure on the elderly compared with over 50 percent in Germany and Luxembourg.[19] They argued forcefully, on the basis of these comparisons, that public resources had to be increased substantially.

The Old-Age Fund for wage earners was still based largely on public assistance and dealt with the question of retirement in terms of subsistence; for example, almost a third of all pensioners (900,000 out of 3 million) received benefits from the National Solidarity Fund. In a piece headlined "Refus d'assistance à personne en danger" (Person in danger refused public assistance) in the October 1968 issue of its journal, the CFDT stigmatized "a society that leaves its old people by the wayside." The CGT newspaper *Le Peuple* of 1–15 April 1969 ran an article entitled "Relèvement immédiat des retraites et des pensions" (Immediate lengthening of retirement and raising of pensions) in which the union noted that "the misery in which elderly people currently live is a scandal that should not be allowed to continue." In a joint letter dated 29 March 1971 addressed to the prime minister, the two union confederations called for retirement age to be lowered; they also demanded an increase in pensions and allowances that "improvements over the last few years have not brought up to the level that the 1961 Laroque Report recommended for immediate and urgent introduction." The unions went on to say that "for their living expenses, several million elderly people have less money than is needed for certain basic needs that cannot be reduced any further." The two union centers called for "real national solidarity" in support of older workers. They argued that "it was unacceptable, in a modern country like ours where so much wealth is produced, that the people who have spent their lives producing this wealth should enjoy such low esteem, despite the fact that they have wholeheartedly deserved the gratitude of the whole nation."[20] The unions also stated that a real policy for old age had to start off with proper retirement schemes, and they fiercely criticized government action that placed social action in favor of the elderly above increases in their incomes.[21] "No matter how important the social aspect is, it must not be allowed to blur the fundamental problem, which remains that of satisfying the most pressing needs of elderly people, specifically through an immediate rise in allowances, annuities, and pensions."[22]

The plan to improve the general pensions scheme, which the government announced as part of its preparations for the Sixth Plan, was quite inadequate from the union standpoint. It did not provide for a revaluation of the level of pensions, which remained at 40 percent of average salary over the final ten years at the age of sixty-five; instead, the government proposed an increase in minimum allowances bringing them to no more than 50 percent of SMIC (*Salaire Minimum Interprofessionnel de Croissance*—Guaranteed Minimum Wage) in 1975.

The unions gave top priority to improving the social entitlement to retirement. In view of the appalling failure of the General Pension Scheme to keep pace with the cost of living, they also campaigned for an increase in the level of pensions and linked this closely to the objective of lowering the retirement age. However, their insistence on the social entitlement to retirement led them to underestimate the problems posed by the way of life of the elderly, which, as has been noted, had been largely abandoned by the government.

Retirees: a new organizational issue. In the late 1960s, most older people had retired, and were therefore on the margins of employment and labor-union activity. Apart from those who had retired from public-sector employment, they constituted a predominantly unorganized group of people unaware of what class actions they could undertake and often, therefore, of who wielded political power. Moreover, it was a group whose numerical importance was growing rapidly, as the 1968 census returns had demonstrated. For all of these reasons, the issue of retirees could no longer be ignored by labor unions seeking to gather strength in a period of intense social mobilization. By the late 1960s, the unions were setting up pensioners' associations as part of an attempt to organize retired and employed people on a class basis. The CGT in particular devoted many column inches in its publications around this time to bringing retired people together. In 1969 the union organized a national conference of retirees, and set up a Union Confédérale des Retraités (Confederal Union of Retired) under the slogan *Même en retraite on peut agir* (Even in retirement, you can get things done).

Clearly, this attempt to reinforce union organization in favor of retired people was closely linked to work that various government departments were involved in at the time, and was aimed at producing a policy of social action on issues affecting elderly people.

Through their promotion of organizations of retired people, the CGT and the CFDT hoped to counter what they saw as ideological offensives by the public authorities in this area. They were eager to reaffirm the common class interests of employed and retired people, and to lead the latter into battle alongside the former. However, the only chance that such a plan had to succeed was to develop a campaign involving slogans that unified and mobilized the two groups. The focus on the question of threshold demonstrated how vital this was. For one thing, as far as retirement itself was concerned, lowering the age at which workers were entitled to retire was the keynote that most effectively mobilized employed people anxious to see their working lives shortened. For another, the fact that pensions failed to keep up with rising prices made them easily the most popular issue with retired people and the population at large.

It is worth noting that the decision to run a united campaign around the question of retired people—it had already been announced by the two major union confederations in the autumn of 1970—intensified the extent to which the debate concentrated on retirement age and the level of pension. Technically, it limited action to the issues on which the two union centers agreed; objectives related to interventions upstream (adapting conditions of employment) and downstream (planning the lives of retirees) were based on specific CFDT sensitivities.[23]

The limitations of union mobilization. The considerable popularity enjoyed by the demand for a lowering of retirement age[24] prompted large-scale mobilization of employed people around this theme, together with numerous class actions that united retirees and the employed. The CGT and the CFDT succeeded in creating a major groundswell of opinion on these matters, and their decision to concentrate the debate on retirement age and the level of pensions clearly made a considerable strategic impact. The union campaign forced the public authorities and employers to come up with answers, and in so doing, triggered the development of a policy for old age and pension reform. It therefore helped to advance the cause of the elderly, but focusing the union campaign in this way put the unions themselves at cross-purposes, and this had repercussions on the policy for old age at a later stage.

It has already been established that the ambivalence of the union demand for a lowering of retirement age—focused both on attempts to limit the exploitation of workers and on a solution to unemployment when it occurred after a long period at work—left scope for the employers to develop their counterattack. The fusion of retirement and employment matters had already emerged in the positions that the unions adopted, and this situation later became more acute following the employers' initiative on guaranteed income. Furthermore, the union line on retirement as a period of rest that compensated for job alienation[25] did little to support the right of workers to choose whether to take early exit; this was a principle to which the CGT and the CFDT had always previously subscribed. As there had been no careful examination of ways in which workers could stop work when they wanted to, entitlement to a pension was in danger of being turned into an obligation to stop work; this inevitably replaced an obligation to remain at work—the situation that had obtained before the right to retirement was won. The older generation would then have won the right to retirement, but at the price of a reduced right to work, and their life options would also have been restricted as a result. The scant interest that the unions showed in the question of employed people's independence of choice heralded certain changes of direction, which in turn led to the setting up of preretirement schemes; these schemes were based precisely on such a substitution. The unions' lack of vigilance with regard to the "social death" aspect of retirement partly explains why their campaign had not found more active support among the public. It also exposed some disagreement between the actions of the CGT and CFDT and those of the other unions (FO, CGC, and CFTC); the latter were keen to protect employees' choice when it came to exit from work. This interunion rift was used by employers when attempting to impose their own interpretation of retirement.

By focusing on the issue of threshold, the unions' position on pensions distracted them from problems downstream, such as life in retirement, or else encouraged them to reduce the problem simply to one of income; in this way they failed to appreciate the dangers of social exclusion and marginalization that can result from stopping work. The limited success of the unions' retiree associations was probably not unconnected with this. As a result, a whole series of questions on what life in retirement was like remained unanswered. It has been noted above that this was exactly where action by the public authorities was developing.

Employers and the Regulation of Employment through Retirement

The rationality of employers and the labor unions. Employers are forever looking for maximum flexibility from the labor force, and therefore see older employees as a marginal resource to face labor-market flexibility as far as production needs are concerned.

During the critical 1969–76 period, several factors combined to make the dismissal of older workers an attractive solution. Older workers were seen as less profitable members of staff, and employers believed that their productivity declined as they got older, although their salaries tended to rise through seniority. The practice of setting age limits when hiring new employees, and the higher rate of unemployment among workers aged over fifty (in 1970, 40 percent of all job seekers were over fifty), reflected employers' reticence with regard to older workers. For employers, dismissing them was a less expensive solution, at least in the short term, than redesigning jobs or introducing redeployment procedures. This was particularly true given that the state, whether in the shape of the National Employment Fund or through unemployment benefits, bore some of the cost of the operation. Moreover, if job cuts were unavoidable, laying off older workers stimulated much less social unrest than the sacking of younger employees because, as an earlier section described, this approach was broadly accepted by the unions, if not actually recommended by them.

Getting rid of older workers was therefore an important personnel management tool whenever there was a need to lower the labor force's age profile, rebalance the age pyramid, or encourage internal promotion.

All of these reasons encouraged employers to take a favorable view of early exit for older workers, and union and employer positions converged in that both parties agreed, albeit for different reasons, on a policy for bringing forward the age of exit from work.

However, they disagreed on the fundamental question of exactly how this policy was to be interpreted. Whereas the unions demanded a lowering of the retirement age across the board, arguing for the social entitlement to retirement and even its extension, the employers preferred to see retirement as a component in their employment policy. They wanted to be able to get rid of older staff if compelled to do so by economic events, or if new quantitative or qualitative labor force needs were imposed by changes in, or the unavoidable reorganization of, production methods. Employers did not take to the idea of a wide-ranging, definitive legal measure for bringing retirement age down, as that would have affected the flexibility of the labor market; it would also have deprived them of a tool that provided conjunctural regulation over this market. They preferred to negotiate specific conditions in the framework of collective agreements.

The development of company preretirement schemes. The dramatic spread of company agreements from 1968 onward introduced career-end leave, gradual retirement, and early exit schemes;[26] these admirably illustrated the employers' tactics as well as their need to respond to the union counterattack that formed part of the campaign to lower the retirement age. The employers' first line of defense was clearly the establishment of "in-house preretirement schemes": these had undeniable advantages for employees, and the unions usually saw them as progressive: "Before the employment problem became really serious, we made a number of advances and achieved a number of successes. A number of company-level and sectoral agreements were signed that gradually reduced the working hours for employees approaching the age of exit from work."[27]

Employers saw early exit agreements as an opportunity for introducing substantial flexibility into labor force management. Much depended on the situation in which an individual company found itself and on its labor force needs, but employers were able to achieve employee mobility by using measures already in place and by invoking certain criteria, such as seniority and relevant occupational categories. However, this employers' strategy was counterbalanced by the equally pressing need to keep in check the social charges levied on companies.

Demographic and economic arguments related to the cost of lowering the retirement age. National preretirement agreements were signed at the company and sectoral level when circumstances allowed, but the CNPF still sought to counter union claims in the general area of pensions by stressing the high cost of the measures they were demanding. Union preretirement claims were described as unrealistic and incompatible with the development of demographic and economic stability in France. The CNPF published its first paper on the cost of lowering retirement age in February 1970;[28] it marked the beginning of a wide-ranging and confused battle of statistics that never developed into a proper debate among the parties. The main aim was to discredit union demands in the public eye by demonstrating that they did not take overall economic stability into account. First, as the employers' argument ran, the unions ignored the possibility that the ratio between employed and unemployed people could be seriously affected if the retirement age were brought down. Given the way this ratio had developed in the past, the realistic alternative, according to the CNPF (Confédération Nationale du Patronat Français—National Confederation of French Employers), was as follows: if retirement age were to be lowered across the board, either pensions would have to be reduced, or the living standard of employed people would have to be cut as a result of a rise in pension contributions. Second, lowering the pension threshold, another union demand, would eventually place an intolerable financial burden on the country as a whole. Here the employers' association won support from government experts who estimated that the reforms demanded by the unions "would cost almost as much as the entire social security budget for 1975." In other words, financial and economic arguments were intertwined, and social progress could be financed only by growth. Lowering the retirement age would cause deductions levied on companies to be raised, the employers argued, and this would weaken their investment capacity and slow down their rate of expansion. Furthermore, any diminution of national growth that flowed from this arrangement would lead to difficulties, not only in funding social expenditure but also in maintaining the standard of living and rates of employment. There would therefore be a serious danger of a recession, which would in turn ultimately lead to an increase in unemployment.

Initially, the CNPF tried to take the sting out of the union demand for an extension to retirement entitlement by presenting demographic and economic arguments. Later, in March 1971, the employers sought to recapture the initiative by offering to meet the unions for discussions limited to early exit for older employees who had been laid off. At the same time, the CNPF claimed that it was not competent to negotiate over union demands for a lowering of retirement age and passed this matter over to the government on the grounds that "it posed a problem relating to the general stability of the French economy, and decisions were therefore a matter for the government and Parliament."[29]

The counteroffensive and the reasons for its success. Following the claim for an across-the-board entitlement to a full pension at sixty, and the demand for tripartite global negotiations on retirement issues, the CNPF selectively shifted the debate into the arena of employment for older workers—and, more specifically, better compensation for older workers who were unemployed. In practice, improved guaranteed income for older workers gave employers more latitude for laying off employees approaching their sixtieth birthdays.

The unions were not taken in, and accused the employers' association of trying "to sack workers they no longer needed and, while claiming to be using an 'à la carte retirement' scheme, of carrying out 'à la carte dismissals' when individual employers felt so inclined."[30]

Despite impressive mobilizations between March and December 1971, however, the unions failed to check the employers' counteroffensive. In June 1971 this took the form of bilateral employer-union meetings to prepare for negotiations, which eventually opened on 6 December 1971 with all the unions present.

There appear to be three reasons for the success of the employers' counteroffensive:

1. To an extent, it benefited from government support; this, together with the role that the state played in this dispute, will be examined in detail later on.

2. The employers were able to home in on interunion disagreements related to retirement policy.

3. Although the employers' proposal did not amount to a concession to the unions' demands in any way,[31] it met some of their demands in part, and this virtually obliged them to agree to negotiations.

Taking advantage of interunion disharmony. Force Ouvrière (FO) and the Confédération Générale des Cadres (CGC) did not participate in the CGT/CFDT campaign. They held similar positions on pensions, but, as has been pointed out, they stressed that there should still be an option to take retirement, and that this might even be extended; they basically felt that the CGT and CFDT positions with respect to independent employee choice were unsatisfactory. They also argued that the reform to lower the retirement age as articulated in the joint CGT-CFDT campaign was not financially viable "either for companies that were restructuring or for workers."[32] They took a positive view of the draft pension reform that had been drawn up in the spring of 1971 by Robert Boulin, the minister for health and social security: this proposal laid the emphasis on raising the level of pensions and on injecting flexibility into the scheme for those incapable of work. There were therefore grounds for expecting that entitlement would be broadened to include the right of every individual aged sixty to sixty-five either to opt for retirement or to carry on working. In May 1971, referring to the government's plan, the CGC stated that "the process for improving pensions [was] underway."[33] However, the FO and the CGC felt that in view of the massive financial commitment, a project of this kind could only move forward step by step. They therefore kept up the pressure with a view to solving a uniquely acute and urgent human problem—that posed by aging unemployed workers who could not find jobs, and who had to wait until they were sixty-five before they qualified for the full pension.

In fact, it was a demand that the FO had made previously with support from the CGC; the first sign that the claim was making any headway came in an undertaking to negotiate within the framework of national job security agreements that had been signed with the employers in February 1969. Throughout 1970 and 1971, both the FO and the CGC frequently repeated their demand for discussions on the setting up of a broad-based scheme of guaranteed income for workers aged sixty to sixty-five who were out of a job.

Availing itself of a well-tested tactic, the CNPF then took over the FO/CGC demands, using them to turn the preretirement negotiations into a counterattack against claims made by the other unions. The moment chosen by the CNPF for officially agreeing to negotiations on this issue neatly demonstrated the employers' wish to use it as a way of recapturing the initiative. It was a contest in which the unions had previously been on the offensive. On 4 June 1971, shortly after the massive CGT/CFDT action of 24–27 May, the CNPF president wrote to the general secretary of the FO, suggesting a preliminary of exchange of views on guaranteed income for aging unemployed workers.

A successful diversionary maneuver. The employers' proposal to open negotiations was a source of keen embarrassment to the CGT and the CFDT. On one hand, they realized that by agreeing to negotiations on guaranteed income for aging unemployed workers, there was a strong possibility of losing sight of the overall problem of pensions, and a danger of tripartite discussions on the question being compromised for a long time to come.[34] On the other hand, the unions could not refuse to take part: they could scarcely stand aloof from a humanitarian measure that would give guaranteed income to aging unemployed workers who were running out of entitlement to benefits and had no hope of finding work. At the same time, they could see that the agreement, whether they liked it or not, provided some workers with an opportunity to take early exit. What the unions were being offered, for all its imperfections, was a small step along the road to achieving the aims they had originally adopted when launching their mass campaign. Furthermore, there was a need for labor unions to be able to point to concrete results after all the effort that had gone into the mobilizations on pensions; they also needed to demonstrate that the Boulin Law—it had been passed by the National Assembly only a few days before negotiations started on guaranteed income—had made only small concessions to their claims, i.e., no lowering of the retirement age and only a delayed increase of the level of pensions. So far, union action had achieved very limited tangible results, although in a more general way, the unions had forced the public authorities to come up with answers in areas other than those where they had concentrated their efforts. Furthermore, as the last chapter has demonstrated, they had been the driving force behind the establishment of a new policy dealing with the way of life of the elderly. In these circumstances, the signing of an agreement on guaranteed income was an opportunity to make at least some headway.

For all the reasons set out above, the CGT and the CFDT had to agree to negotiate an agreement in the full knowledge that it meant that the debate was drifting the employers' way, and that their claims for an extension of the right to retirement were unlikely to make rapid progress.

The agreement of 27 March 1972 provided workers with unambiguous guarantees, but it was nonetheless firmly rooted in an employer-oriented philosophy. The reason was that it gave employers more flexibility in the management of the older members of the labor force, because they and they alone could now use dismissal to bring forward the date when these employees ceased work. In this way they were able to get rid of older employees as necessary, and they did not need to have recourse to expensive "in-house preretirement schemes";[35] nor were they obliged to abide by the Labor Inspectorate's control and approval procedures, a step that involved the use of FNE money.

The State: Toward an Employment Policy Subordinated to a Way-of-Life Policy for the Elderly

A way-of-life policy and an employment policy. As the last chapter made clear, the state's main response to the social struggles developing around pensions was to establish a new way-of-life policy. The principles of this new policy had been enunciated by the Laroque Commission back in 1962, but it was not until the spring of 1969 that the plan of action designed to enable the elderly to remain socially integrated was relaunched. It began to be implemented with the adoption in July 1971 of a program whereby opportunities for the elderly to carry on living at home became one of the two social priorities of the Sixth Plan.[36] The way-of-life policy was now the issue that structured public initiatives. The pensions policy was presented as complementary to action on facilities for the elderly and their way of life, but the employment policy was designed in such a way that it was subordinated to the new priority objective of social integration. It therefore had to anticipate any sign of premature rejection or social exile of older workers. Clear guidance on the employment of older workers formed part of the new public policy for the integration of the elderly, but it was at odds with both the union position (which called for a broadening of the entitlement to retirement) and the employers' viewpoint (which demanded maximized flexibility in their handling of the labor force).

Under the Sixth Plan, the "community of planners" had given concrete shape to the new way-of-life policy by means of a final program. They were now fully aware that if they treated the consequences of the rejection of the elderly without attacking the causes, a sharp rise in demands and costs was the likely outcome, because palliatives simply reinforced the exclusion procedures upstream. For that reason, the planners simultaneously drew up new guidelines on the employment of older workers.

Double justification for rejecting a lowering of the retirement age. The approach adopted by the Sixth Plan was not to lower the retirement age across the board, but rather to enable older people to find work. Two arguments were used to justify this: a social argument based on a concern to preserve the status of the elderly population, and an economic argument designed not to threaten the scheme's future stability.

Preserving the status of the aging population. Any prolonged social integration of the elderly would be undermined if, as soon as workers reached the age of fifty, their contribution to the country's economic activity was deemed less productive, and if they were then driven with increasing frequency into forced unemployment. In other words, rejection from the production system was at cross-purposes with the project of social integration. The authors of the General Inspectorate of Social Affairs Report noted that "withdrawing from the production process a worker who has the strength and will to produce is to implant or accelerate in that person the process of aging"; meanwhile, members of the Intergroup underlined "their firm conviction that employment, as long as that is what the individual wants, remains a link with other people and a factor of personal equilibrium."[37]

However, companies were increasingly withdrawing workers from the production cycle as they got older; this tactic was especially pernicious in that it condemned individuals with increased life expectancy to premature unemployment. It was therefore right to defend the "right of older workers to employment" and their "dignity as producers";[38] otherwise, they were not free to choose whether to take retirement, and did not have an opportunity to adapt to it.

Not compromising the future of the economic system. A lowering of the retirement age, like any improvements in older workers' unemployment benefits, encouraged companies to resolve staffing and employment problems by getting rid of them.

These measures therefore, which were conjunctural difficulties or a matter of inadequate vocational training and retraining, were made irreversible charges on the state. More generally, the measures now meant that the country's productivity was being left to an ever-decreasing group of active population, and it was this productivity that had to come up with the substitution salary on which older workers in forced unemployment depended. "If, as part of a company plan, the departure of older workers can assist in the restructuring process, it is difficult to see how the country can simply rely on an ever-shrinking group to do all the work. The country needs also older members of the labor force to contribute to the social charges which are crippling a working population that is far too small."[39]

It was the government's view that the systematic dismissal of older workers was not beneficial to companies in either the relatively short term or the longer term, particularly in a country where population aging was already pronounced and likely to accelerate. Such a policy "partly absolves companies from improving conditions of employment, equipment, and premises, and from rationalizing production methods in such a way that productivity can be improved."[40] This approach may have appeared attractive to employers in the short range. It was also undoubtedly "an easy way out"[41] that served two employers' goals: on one hand, they wanted to shed older workers whom they considered to be less productive, and less adaptable to technological change; on the other, it was a vehicle to lower their payroll costs.

The policy of keeping older workers in employment; the significance of, and obstacles to, implementing this policy. These two complementary arguments formed the basis of the government's approach to supporting an employment policy for older workers. This was a policy that stressed the importance of work adaptation as employees got older, and of keeping them in employment; as such, it was closer to a way-of-life policy, and one that sought to prolong normal life and social integration. Accordingly, the state had the task of making arrangements for every phase of its citizens' lives, thereby ensuring that old age was something other than a crisis period involving a high degree of welfare dependence.

In this way, the state became the defender of older workers' right to employment, and it refused to support empirical reactions in society where it was felt that the elderly were jeopardizing the future of the economic system. The state also opposed any systematic measures for getting rid of older workers, in the fear that such measures would make the French economy increasingly inflexible and endanger its development and competitiveness.

The orientations that the state expressed in these choices were also the ones it employed in its autonomous role as an agent of change. It was clear that the approaches that formed part of the Sixth Plan, and which pertained to career-end employment and retirement age, did not figure either in union claims or in employers' expectations or practices.

By agreement with the Commission de l'Emploi (Employment Commission), the Intergroupe Personnes Âgées (Elderly Persons' Intergroup) did not support a lowering of the retirement age, which was what the unions had demanded. On the contrary, it called for the removal of age limits, both for employees remaining in their jobs and for employers hiring staff, and recommended an ongoing policy to redesign jobs and update skills as workers got older. This policy did not meet with the approval of the unions; they saw it as "a way of putting a check" on the move to lower the retirement age, and of intensifying the exploitation of workers by keeping them at work for as long as possible.

These approaches to employment did not meet employers' aspirations either: the recommendations earmarked financial assistance for the vocational integration of older workers, whereas the employers felt that the money could have been better spent on increasing their unemployment coverage. Underlying these ideas was the view that when all was said and done, no form of protectionism had ever been known to assist in the integration of a protected sector of the population. For that reason, the recommendations did not support any change in the unemployment compensation scheme that involved specific measures for the protection of older workers; this was despite the fact that, as an earlier section has pointed out, this was where the CNPF counteroffensive had been concentrating its fire since late 1970. Furthermore, the way in which employers were dismissing older workers attracted government disapproval. The 1970 Report of the General Inspectorate of Social Affairs, on which some of the Commission du Plan's ideas were based, contained a fierce indictment of company employment policies.[42] The aim of these criticisms was simply to try and persuade company bosses to adopt a more rational system of personnel management. Accordingly, the Report of the General Inspectorate concluded its chapter on employment by stating that, although "in the near future, a number of statutory prohibitions (e.g., pertaining to age limits, age-related dismissal, and retirement against the employee's wishes) will have to be introduced to oblige companies to make the effort of imagination that some have already made, an information exercise is just as necessary. That will be less expensive and more beneficial than the dismissals that have taken place in certain occupational sectors."[43]

In this context it is worth pointing out that, as in many other fields at this time, the state was operating an employment policy that, although contrary to employers' short-term wishes and interests, was extremely favorable to them in the long term.

A number of measures were introduced during this period by the Ministry of Labor with a view to promoting "a policy for adapting work to the real abilities of workers in the final years of their working lives, thereby facilitating the gradual transition from full employment to full unemployment."[44] Specifically, a decision was made to set up a new unit that issued information and documentation on the redesign of jobs; it was located in the Direction Générale du Travail et de l'Emploi (General Directorate of Labor and Employment) and was charged with producing and disseminating studies to enable "employers and employee representatives to find the most suitable solutions to each concrete situation." Similarly, the AFPA[45] was asked to adapt its training and further training methods for older workers aged over sixty, while the Agence pour l'Emploi (Employment Agency) was invited to upgrade its information on suitable job openings.

Not much use was made of these new structures and directives, and there was little follow-up. The point has already been made that as far as work on the way of life was concerned, the state had been able to construct a network that carried forward its administrative actions; however, the same could not be said of the employment policy that it had approved with a view to prolonging its actions upstream associated with way of life. The partners in this policy were not the ones that the state had mobilized in connection with its action to improve the way of life.

A policy for keeping older workers in employment could be implemented only if it managed to ally itself with certain sections of its natural support groups—in other words, employers and employees. However, it has been pointed out that employers were more interested in getting rid of older workers than in adjusting working conditions, and efforts made by the Ministry of Labor to disseminate information fell far short of modifying these attitudes.[46] By contrast, having been unable to make lasting changes in working conditions, the unions were anxious to free older workers from them as soon as possible. They were therefore extremely suspicious of a policy that, it seemed to them, intensified the exploitation of workers by trying to prolong their working lives. Quite simply, the state was unable to find any forces in society that would provide support for its actions.

The state was not able to impose the employment policy that it had approved, which sought to preserve both the social status of the elderly and major components of economic and financial stability. Moreover, the policy was clearly defended with less wholehearted conviction by the Ministry of Labor (whose main concern was settling the most serious disputes brought about by short-term economic trends, and whose initiatives involved reaching a consensus among different social agents) than by the Commissariat du Plan (which, because of its structural position, was more concerned with economic and financial stability in the longer term).

Toward a compromise: retreating to a policy for compensating aging unemployed workers. The state failed to turn the way-of-life policy into a pivotal feature of the policy for old age; indeed, it did not even manage to win the day on its definition of an older workers' employment policy secondary to the way-of-life policy.[47] Thereafter, the state adopted a more defensive strategy and steadfastly refused to lower the retirement age; in return, it made limited concessions to employees with respect to levels of pensions, and supported the employers' strategy of regaining the initiative by proposing an extension of unemployment coverage for older workers who had been laid off.

The 31 December 1971 act focused on improving the old-age pension under the general scheme, but responded only halfheartedly to union demands that pensions should be revalued "to an extent that is compatible with our demographic perspectives and economic capacity."[48] By making a minor concession on the level of pensions,[49] the act enabled the government to reject an amendment on age conditions, except for an element of flexibility in the scheme covering those incapable of work. This refusal to lower the retirement age supported the right of older workers to make up their own minds about stopping work. An earlier section described how union rationality had led the labor-union centers to underestimate this aspect, and as their campaign proceeded, this undoubtedly deprived them of backing from certain elements of public opinion. The government's limited concessions in extending the right to retirement were not enough, however, to weaken the popular movement arguing for a lower retirement age, and in May 1971 the government came out in support of the employers' counteroffensive that focused on unemployed older workers. As a result, the state rejected the ideas contained in the Sixth Plan and committed itself to a policy of raising unemployment coverage for older workers. Those responsible for the employment policy were clearly alarmed to see figures for job seekers continually inflated by an ever-increasing number of aging unemployed people for whom the normal measures for absorbing unemployment were quite inappropriate.[50] On the surface, the introduction of a guaranteed income scheme for unemployed older workers seemed to be an attractive solution, as it should have been able to respond to diverse, even contradictory, demands. For one thing, it was a social measure in that it put an end to the climate of job insecurity that had been increasingly pervading the final years of employment, and it also had the virtue of no longer counting beneficiaries of this particular scheme as job seekers.[51] For another, it was a tactical solution in that it destabilized the union campaign on retirement age and created a diversion by offering negotiations that, for reasons set out above, could not be rejected. In other words, it was a procapitalist solution in the sense that it directly met the employers' need to make older members of the labor force more malleable.

The joint agreement signed on 27 March 1972 gave concrete form to the success of the employers' counteroffensive. However, it was not without benefits to the other parties. The point has already been made that for the unions, it was a fallback solution; despite the fact that the issue was a difficult one to negotiate,[52] the joint agreement had produced concrete results that provided a basis for relaunching the campaign at a later stage. For the government, on the other hand, it was a way of legally lowering the retirement age for a particular category of workers, but it did not involve direct responsibility, as the whole matter was dealt with by collective agreements.

There is ample evidence to suggest that during this period, the state was seeking to retain a degree of latitude so that it could continue its attempts to promote an employment policy for older workers; this was linked to the way-of-life policy, and its principles were contrary to those governing the guaranteed-income scheme. In 1972, older workers' right to work and freedom of choice were still sources of concern for the government. This desire to preserve the right to work was initially designed to block the unions, which in early 1972 had demanded the direct involvement of the public authorities through an extension of special allowances *(allocations spéciales)* under the FNE (Fonds National de l'Emploi—National Employment Fund) early-exit scheme; they preferred this to the guaranteed-income project within the joint UNEDIC (Union Nationale pour l'Emploi dans l'Industrie et le Commerce—National Union for Employment in Industry and Commerce) framework. The government's concern was also to be seen in the limitations attached to guaranteed income by the draft legislation adopted on 5 July 1972, which gave form to the joint agreement of 27 March. Under Article 4, it was the Ministry of Labor's responsibility to ensure that the measure supporting older workers was not used by employers to get rid of their older staff too hastily.

Statements made by Joseph Fontanet, then minister of labor, employment, and the population, in the course of a National Assembly debate on the bill on guaranteed income[53] clearly reflected the government's resolve to promote an older workers' employment policy that tallied with the project to improve elderly people's way of life:

> The government's third concern has been, and continues to be, to avoid encouraging companies to dismiss their older employees systematically when those workers would prefer to remain in their jobs until normal retirement age. In addition to the measures that I have already mentioned, the public

> authorities must continue with their efforts down a second, complementary route that leads to an improvement in the employment conditions in their final years at work. In fact, there is much anxiety about the opposition I have already referred to between, on one hand, advances in public health that prolong the amount of time most of our contemporaries remain in possession of their physical and intellectual faculties and, on the other, the growing trend in our industrial society to reject job seekers from the labor market at a younger and younger age. It is clear that, if nothing is done to halt such a development, it will eventually lead, as was underlined in an important report in 1961 by a committee appointed by the government of the day to draw up proposals for a policy for old age, to extreme economic, social, and moral difficulties. It is therefore essential to study the best arrangements within the framework of a third-age employment policy, so that people can avoid the brutal transition from full employment (often unsuitable for workers as they get older) to a time of no employment at all; the absence of any preparation or transitional stage often turns a change of this sort into a traumatizing break with the past. With this end in mind, your committee proposes the setting up of a foundation to look into all the questions posed by the employment of people approaching the end of their working lives. This plan incorporates the government's intentions, and has its support. During the negotiations that accompanied the implementation of the 27 March 1972 agreement, the government suggested that the "social partners" carry out joint discussions and action in certain fields. The main aim would be to explore the possibilities of part-time work, to produce studies into the redesign of career-end jobs, to publicize successful examples, and lastly, in collaboration with UNEDIC, to set up experiments in job placements for workers who have been unemployed for a certain period of time. It might therefore be preferable to make the proposed foundation a tripartite body based on a joint initiative of the state and the "social partners," and vest it with all moral and practical advantages so that it can involve these diverse parties in resolving one of the great human and social problems of our time.

As far as funding was concerned, the government's contribution, which was made before the agreement came into force, was limited to paying for the public-assistance allowances; the explicit aim of this was to block any upward movement in the number of layoffs.

The public authorities were anxious to restrict the new measures adopted for older workers who had lost their jobs. Just the same, guaranteed income still carried within it the seeds of developments that contradicted government principles with regard to remaining at work, flexible retirement age, and protecting the social status of old age.

The potential of a contradictory development. The guaranteed-income formula was designed to mitigate the effects of dismissal by giving a much higher income to older people who had lost their jobs; employers were also less likely to think twice before firing them. Henceforth, there was a danger that efforts to head off dismissals and provide retraining would take second place, particularly as trends were already developing in that direction. Companies found that the introduction of this measure enabled them to lower the labor force's age profile and off-load staff, and they were soon tempted to use it to speed up work rates and thereby raise productivity.

The resulting pressure on workers was to have two effects. First, the problems encountered by older workers were passed on to the next youngest age group: this meant that workers aged between fifty and sixty were soon confronted by problems comparable to those which the guaranteed income had attempted to address, particularly as the guarantee was holding up progress in the retraining of older workers. Second, faster work rates inevitably resurrected demands for the retirement age to be lowered.

The new measure had been designed both to channel this claim and deflect it; it was now helping to revive the claim, and was even exacerbating contradictions that it had been able to cover up as a result of internal ambiguities. On the surface, it was an incomplete response that did no more than improve income guarantees for aging unemployed workers; in fact, it was an appalling mishmash that directly called into question what the state was trying to construct elsewhere as a policy for the social integration of the elderly.

Guaranteed income established a link between the end of work and entitlement to the allowance. Under the new formula, aging unemployed workers were removed once and for all from the labor market, creating a drop in the number of older workers with the right to a job. This development established an idea of what retirement was all about: a period of social exile and social unproductiveness that was entered into willy-nilly, possibly as a result of being laid off. At the same time, exclusion from employment, and the sense of personal devaluation that went with it, now occurred at an earlier and earlier stage in life.[54] One of the consequences of these developments was that age was gradually converted into an important, and almost natural, criterion on which to base the distribution of work. All that was needed was a recession, which would mean the possibility of the scenario set out in this book—the massive rejection of older workers as socially unproductive—being translated into fact. And that is exactly what happened.

An analysis of the period 1968–72 reveals confrontation over the social construction of the old-age problems among three parties, each with an individual personality and a clear definition of the issue. As far as employment went, there were two policies in a state of permanent tension. One was the policy of keeping older employees at work. This was the direct expression of the policy for improving way of life that was then being promoted by the state, and was not part of employer or labor-union thinking. The other, a policy to compensate aging unemployed workers, contradicted the above principles. It also underlined the state's task of assisting the restructuring and concentration of companies and its obligation to support a diversionary tactic by the employers; this formed part of a strategy of countering the union demands for a lowering of retirement age.

In practice, the agreement represented by the collective agreement of March 1972, and given form by the 5 July 1972 act, was a victory for the employers: they had imposed their own definition of the issue, they had won the day as far as their perspective of the problems of old age was concerned, and had ensured that the negotiations focused on their home terrain—the regulation of employment. However, their success was limited, since, although the new measure gave employers the exclusive right to send their employees into early retirement simply by dismissing them, the public authorities retained a certain amount of control over the way it was used, and the unions were still mobilized to fight for an extension to the right to retirement.

In the final phase, the issues became gradually simplified in the minds of the various parties involved; this affected the balance between the contradictory tensions reflected in the 1972 agreement, and released the full potential for drifting that the measure contained. The effect was that an important tool for the management of old age and retirement was ripe for development.

1973–1981: Gradual Clarification of the Issues surrounding the Question of Employment

The prologue we have presented above, in which the actors all fiercely defended their own positions and interests, was followed by further debate that gradually became less oppositional. The issues that the state and the unions tried to impose vanished, and confrontation centered on the question of employment and how to regulate it. An earlier section has shown how this question was initially central to the employers' views. From 1973 onwards, the older workers' employment policy evolved on the basis of a dynamic that this section will characterize as the result of finding a common ground for the respective negotiation objectives, a concept developed in game theory by G. Adam and J.-D. Reynaud,[55] who coined it for the purposes of an analysis of professional relationship.

Two stages may be distinguished in this progressive transformation of the issues: the first occurred prior to the critical period of 1975–77, when the issues were undermined by uncertainty and met considerable resistance; the second came later when everything was clarified by the regulation of the employment issue.

As far as employment policies were concerned, this simplification of the issues triggered an unrestricted extension of the guaranteed-income scheme, and in turn led to the dismissal of large numbers of older workers. This development contradicted and destroyed the way-of-life policy that was being implemented by the state at the time, and threw it into crisis.

The next section will show how the unions and the state gradually modified the issues. There will follow an analysis of the outcome of this modification process, which took the form of a fresh debate among the three parties and the new agreements that flowed from the employment issue.

The Labor Unions: From a Campaign to Reduce Exploitation to the Defense of Jobs

The main objective of the union campaign on pensions was a reduction of labor force exploitation through a broader right to retirement. The campaign began to crumble in 1974. The slowdown in growth and the deterioration in employment prospects encouraged the unions to put the issue of employment protection at the top of their agendas as a matter of urgency. The meaning of the demand for a lower retirement age was now redefined by the way in which the issues "drifted." It was no longer a demand for an extension to the right to retirement, but rather a campaign aimed at defending jobs and bolstering protection for older workers, particularly those in danger of becoming unemployed.

In 1973 the positions of the CGT and the CFDT were still unchanged. On 25 June 1973, a supplementary clause was added to the National Interoccupational Agreement of 27 March 1972 extending conditions of scheme membership and entitlement along the lines of the claims made by the union in 1972;[56] in other words, the unions' tactics had remained the same. On this occasion, however, the CGT and CFDT renewed their demand for broad-based negotiations on retirement issues, but argued that the agreement was restricted to the issue of employment and left the overall problem untouched. The unions believed that they were slowly getting closer to achieving their aim. They thought that by going into the mechanics of the reforms on an ad hoc basis (e.g., interoccupational agreements on guaranteed income and company-level early-exit schemes),[57] the employers and the government were narrowing the scope of their demographic and economic arguments and making the lowering of retirement age an increasingly unrealistic prospect. As time went by, they found it more and more difficult to turn down tripartite negotiations on this issue, and numerous early-exit schemes were introduced in companies between 1973 and 1974.[58]

In late 1974, the two union confederations planned "joint action on pensions with a view to confronting the crisis in employment." The demand for the right to retire at sixty ceased to be part of a social campaign against workers exploitation, and instead became a means of defending jobs. A slogan that made its appearance at around this time, *Mieux vaut payer des retraités que des chômeurs* (Better to pay pensioners than the unemployed), was a good illustration of the way in which the issues had evolved. From now on, lowering the retirement age became something of a palliative to the job crisis: "The gravity of the crisis in employment makes the question of early exit more timely than ever. If our claims were met, as many as 300,000-400,000 new jobs could be created."[59]

New demands then appeared, underlining how the issues had been allowed to "drift"; they included proposals for the hiring of young workers to replace preretirees, and a limitation on drawing retirement pension and earning a salary concurrently. In 1975 the unions had not yet condemned the concurrent drawing of pension and pay, but they still believed that priority should be given to finding jobs for the unemployed. All of these ideas now began to develop quite rapidly. The unions stepped up their pressure on the question of lowering the retirement age through national days of action, strikes, and stoppages throughout 1975, and particularly during the autumn when the Chirac government was preparing its relaunch plan, which included a plan to improve pensions. However, this pressure was not as broadly based as it had previously been, and their new pensions campaign achieved little.

The 31 December 1975 act set the retirement age at sixty, but restricted it to manual workers and working mothers. This represented a total success for the CNPF, which had argued that only manual workers should benefit. Promises made at Provins by the then prime minister, Pierre Messmer, and other undertakings announced during the presidential election of 1974 by the new president of the Republic, focused on the introduction of "à la carte" retirement; this was to be achieved through a staged increase in the level of pension at sixty for all workers. However, for the government, the 31 December 1975 act was more of a prevarication than an agreement of the type available under the Boulin Law. Qualifying conditions were so strict[60] that although the government talked about 3 million potential recipients, only 2,141 applications were considered during 1976. Following their unsuccessful pension campaign, the unions found themselves obliged to adopt a defensive position on jobs. As growth slowed down, employers restructured so as to achieve maximum profitability and prioritized competitiveness through numerous layoffs and factory closures. The labor unions' response was relatively muted. They found it difficult to produce a countermodel of growth and progress with which to challenge the plan that the ruling classes had developed, and their actions suggested that they were trying to shore up an industrial structure that was already falling apart. The unions now had their backs to the wall as they battled against the most immediate and harmful consequences of these restructuring exercises, and they often found themselves having to settle for the lesser of two evils: either preretirement (instead of unemployment) or defense of youth employment (as opposed to the right of older workers to have jobs). A later section shows how the signing of the 13 June 1977 agreement—extending the 1972 guaranteed-income system to older workers who had resigned—was a perfect illustration of this relationship of forces; it also demonstrated that the debate around the question of employment was now completely harmonious.

The State: A Drop in the Number of Actions Enabling Older Workers to Stay on in Employment, and Withdrawal from the Arena of Early Exit

From 1974 onward, the state began to see its margin of autonomy whittled away as the Gaullist state with its voluntarist tendencies turned into a Giscardian state inclined towards economic neoliberalism. As a result, the way-of-life policy, which was linked to the state's independent capacity for action, lost much of its dynamism. It survived after 1975 mainly thanks to the support it had found among the public at large. The Seventh Plan incorporated a Priority Action Program that was a follow-up to the project designed to enable older people to carry on living in their own homes; it had featured in the Sixth Plan but, as an earlier section of this book pointed out, the evidence suggested that the public were now much less solidly behind the idea. As support for a way-of-life policy fell away, the determination of the public authorities to subordinate decisions on jobs for older workers also weakened. The government was no longer promoting the principle of an employment policy that prepared conditions for good social integration of the elderly upstream, and it therefore no longer intervened to defend the right of older workers to have a job. Resistance to a downward "drift" in the age of early exit was now fading, and although the public authorities were still defending "à la carte" retirement in the Provins Program and in the National Assembly in 1973,[61] by the autumn of 1975 the Chirac government had committed itself to the principle of retirement at sixty on full pension, according to a timetable yet to be determined.[62]

What had previously been denounced as a dangerous option, both for the social status of old age and for the efficient running of the economy, was now one of the government's objectives for the near future.

Henceforth, there was relative unanimity among unions, employers, and the government that retirement should become a tool to be used in implementing employment policy. Consultations carried out by the prime minister, Jacques Chirac, that had been designed to "tinker with the right to retirement" reflected this new consensus, since the prime minister's view was that there was agreement among the three parties on "the principle of retirement on full pension at sixty, an entitlement that is currently not granted until sixty-five."[63]

However, the principle was not protected in law, except with respect to manual workers and working mothers who were covered by the 31 December 1975 act, and under very restrictive conditions that have been referred to elsewhere. The state had once again rejected the lowering of retirement age, but this was not part of a social-integration policy enabling the elderly to stay at work. This time it was more a question of a fallback to the employers' position, which was fiercely hostile to a lowering of the retirement age across the board but was in favor of lowering it for certain categories of workers, such as specified manual workers who were considered too old and unproductive long before they reached sixty. The CNPF's hand was also to be seen in the restriction on concurrent drawing of pension and salary; this, too, was covered by the act. The employers' association did not want newly retired workers to be able to draw their pensions while they still had a job, and the new legislation therefore had at least some impact on employment. All of the government's measures clearly showed how the state had changed tack during this period. The great, broad-based ambition to reshape relations between old age and society, which had been embodied in the innovatory way-of-life policy, was no more. The state's room for autonomy was restricted, and its actions demonstrated how susceptible it was to employers' concerns. This situation was further accentuated by the developing economic crisis, which gave prominence to issues of economic management and downgraded questions that had to do with ways of changing society. Priority was no longer given to the integration of excluded members of society or to the foundation of a "new society"; the most important issues were the reestablishment of economic stability and the growth of company profit margins. In these circumstances the state was no longer concerned with keeping older employees in work; in fact, the unemployment situation was so acute that the government was prepared to support any system that would help the working population adapt to the slackening growth of the economy. As a result, there was a double modification in the position of the public authorities. First, they jettisoned all attempts to define the employment of older workers in such a way that it could be linked to the way-of-life policy, and they agreed that the latter should be formulated as a function of company imperatives. Second, they began to withdraw gradually from this arena, leaving all initiatives to agreements negotiated between employers' associations and labor unions. This gradual retreat by the state from an employment policy for older workers was clearly illustrated by the way that control of the new arrangements for early exit was transferred. The state had previously exercised complete control over early-exit procedures through the FNE during the period 1963–72. Subsequently, however, between 1972 and 1979, it enjoyed only limited control; it was now shared with UNEDIC, a joint body that took over responsibility for some of the funding. The state lost even this influence after 1979, when, following the introduction of guaranteed income, the FNE was incorporated into the unemployment-insurance scheme. Thereafter, government action in this field was confined to formulating recommendations requested by the social partners. These recommendations were a clear illustration of the double modification that the state's policies had undergone during the period 1975–81. When the National Interoccupational Agreement of June 1977 was renewed for a second time, the Ministry of Labor recommended that the social partners should extend the preretirement formula to workers under the age of sixty who had resigned. It was plain that the country was as far from a policy for keeping people in jobs as it was possible to be. In this way, the government was expressing a maximalist position as far as early exit was concerned. However, this approach was put aside by the CNPF, which refused to raise the number of people covered by the agreement unless the government gave a separate and precise financial commitment. It is important to bear in mind here that the state's disengagement affected its control over the measure itself and the financial arrangements. The role played by the state in financing this measure was minute[64] because, as a subsequent section will show, the rapid rise in the number of beneficiaries was having a deleterious effect on the financial stability of the unemployment-insurance scheme, which was itself responsible for most of the expenditure.

The 13 June 1977 Agreement: The Production of a New Social Dynamic Underpinning an Employment Policy for Older Workers

The National Interoccupational Agreement of March 1972 was extended by the introduction of a supplementary clause signed on 13 June 1977 by all the "social partners." Signed for a period of two years and renewable, the additional clause extended guaranteed income to employees aged sixty to sixty-five who had resigned voluntarily; hitherto it had been restricted to older workers who had been laid off. Under this agreement, therefore, early exit, which had previously been limited to workers who had been dismissed, was now opened up to a whole new age group. The new agreement established a new balance of forces, and was proof that there now existed a different employment policy dynamic in support of older workers—and one that was going to cause a steep rise in the number of preretirement schemes. This dynamic survived until 1981 and even beyond, following extensions granted by the Socialist government in promoting "early exit solidarity contracts." The employment issue had completely clarified the whole debate and was the only matter on which the various social agents henceforth disagreed. Furthermore, not a single voice was raised on the subject any more, and this put a brake on the development of early exit. As has been noted, the state abandoned its already scant interest in promoting a policy for keeping people at work, although this would have conformed to the integration policy that it had itself initiated. The state also disliked acting as "project manager" for employment and retirement matters. In fact, it did nothing that might encourage any concretization of the perspectives agreed to by the signatories to the 1972 agreement; the aim of this, it will be recalled, had been to "examine, at the earliest opportunity, all of the problems relating to the definition of an employment policy for older workers." As far as early exit was concerned, and in line with promises made in 1973 and 1974, the state also refused to get involved in the "à la carte" early-exit policy. Indeed, the only two reforms to the pension scheme carried out between 1975 and 1982 were minute adjustments related to claimant categories.[65] Against such a backdrop, the fixing of the final retirement age began to be established less and less on legally based pension schemes and was increasingly established within the contract-based framework of unemployment insurance. Furthermore, the public authorities no longer acted as a brake on this downward "drift" in the age of exit from work, which is what they had done in the previous period. As the economic recession deepened, they became more and more aware of the opportunities presented by early exit, both as a method of downsizing the labor force and as a means of reducing the number of registered unemployed. The public authorities accordingly allowed the "social partners" to get on with negotiating, and for the most part left employment policy and retirement arrangements for older workers to be determined by the dynamic of their relationships. In this way, issues were gradually simplified in the course of confrontations between mutually hostile employers and labor unions.

The unions' pensions offensive now collapsed into a defensive position on employment. This came about during a period of economic crisis when, as far as older workers were concerned, more importance was being attached to economic power, and therefore to the employer as the organizer of production. By contrast, the employers themselves maintained their negotiating stance and continued to fight for their original objective: a definition of an employment policy for older workers as a function of the imperatives of company personnel policies. From now on, employers and labor unions confronted one another on the same terrain, that of employment, and an opportunity for this arose in negotiations between the two parties that took place under the 1977 agreement. The CNPF sought a conjunctural solution within the extension to the 1972 agreement; the reason was that it wanted to be better placed to adapt the labor force qualitatively and quantitatively to the restructuring and reorganizational exercises that had been forced on companies by the manner in which the crisis was being managed. The employers' association rejected broader-based negotiations on employment, preferring to facilitate the dismissal of older workers through measures that gave companies maximum flexibility, i.e., short-term selective measures. The CNPF envisaged an agreement lasting for one year. The employers' association therefore agreed to discuss a formula—one for extending preretirement to workers who had gone voluntarily—which the FO and the CGC had been asking for since 1973. As far as the CGT and the CFDT were concerned, the focus of these negotiations was no longer an extension to the right to retirement but the defense of jobs. Indeed, one of the main planks of their bargaining position was the replacement of workers taking voluntary preretirement with new, younger workers.

This indicated that because of pressure caused by the economic crisis, the unions had made up their minds. In other words, they were prepared to sacrifice older workers' right to work, and to defend that of young workers instead. From now on—and this was no trivial contradiction—the union struggle on the employment front was shaped by the departure of older workers, and there were procedures in place for them to stop work and receive guaranteed income. What the unions failed to head off were the dismissals that companies were able to get away with after the older workers had gone. Whereas the employers saw the signing of the agreement as an additional conjunctural means of cutting jobs, the unions wanted to use it to free up jobs for other age groups. However, in a climate in which the balance of forces was tipped in favor of the employers, the views of the CFDT and the CGT on replacing departed workers fell on stony ground. Indeed, there was now agreement between the two parties that produced a relative consensus, and they agreed on earlier and more wide-ranging job losses, although their objectives were different. The supplementary clause of 1977 radically changed the nature of the 1972 agreement. This had been designed to improve the compensation given to older workers if they were laid off; it partly responded to social concerns, but by the same token—and this was outside the scope of the agreement—it also encouraged ways of dismissing the beneficiaries. In fact, the signing of the supplementary clause of 1977 responded less to social concerns than to economic necessity, as the preamble made extremely clear:

> With the aim of contributing to an improvement in the employment situation at the present time, the signatory parties have agreed to offer employees on a temporary basis the opportunity to put in voluntary requests for the guaranteed-income scheme provided for in the Agreement of 27 March 1972 as amended. The signatory parties expect that freeing up jobs in this way will make it possible for a large number of job seekers to be taken on.

What this meant was that guaranteed income, which had previously been available to older employees, now became an explicit means of excluding them from the labor market, and even had the avowed aim of freeing up jobs. Closer study of this joint agreement shows that it was in many ways a triumph of employer ideology. The 1977 agreement was actually presented as the reverse of an extension of the right to retirement, the objective that had been sought by the unions. An examination of some of the agreement's features, including the mechanism for unemployment insurance and the fact that its period of validity was limited to two years, reveals that, in the words of a CNPF spokesperson, it was "an antiretirement-at-sixty agreement." It permitted companies to do exactly as they liked, which was to implement a flexible policy for getting rid of older workers. Analysis of management strategies on early exit[66] highlights how advantageous this new measure was to employers. In practice, by making them more appealing or more coercive,[67] they were able to base early-exit packages for older workers on staffing and restructuring needs. Companies found that these measures gave them the flexibility they needed, and at very little cost, although they later upset the balance of labor-force age profiles and caused problems for career paths. However, few managers bothered themselves about that in the early days. It is true that in some respects the agreement might have appeared to limit management control over departures, as, unlike the 1972 agreement, the 1977 supplementary clause allowed workers to decide when to leave and offered guaranteed income to employees who resigned. In this sense the FO and the CGC thought the clause was an important step toward the drafting of a measure providing "à la carte'" retirement, while the CGT and the CFDT saw it as "a new and important stage in the broadening of entitlement to retirement at sixty." At all events, whatever the victory bulletins proclaimed, the unions could not ignore the huge range of practices used in certain companies and industrial sectors to solicit and obtain the tacit agreement of older workers to be dismissed.[68] There can be no doubt that they were used to achieve a large number of "negotiated resignations."[69] The dividing line between dismissal and leaving a job voluntarily continued to be very unclear.[70] The agreement provided opportunities for stopping work; however, by permitting the use of various forms of economic and moral pressure that persuasively stressed the attractions of early exit, it paradoxically gave more encouragement to forced departures than to voluntary ones.

The extension of guaranteed income to older workers who had resigned marked an important stage in the growing influence that this conjunctural employment measure had in the process of definitive exit from work. The law had moved into an arena previously regulated by retirement mechanisms, and it had abused the rules. Stopping work no longer had much to do with exercising one's right to retirement and free time; it was more a function of a mechanism for ejecting workers from the labor market; moreover, it was determined by companies and their staffing needs. It would be wrong to see the appearance of this new measure, and its subsequent widespread use, as the sole mechanical effect of the deepening crisis and of the general decline of employment. On the contrary, as this book has demonstrated, it was the outcome of a particular social dynamic that enabled the employers to ensure that their definition of old age and retirement—a function of the labor market and of its demands—was the one that prevailed.[71]

The extreme ambivalence of the preretirement solution made it possible to find a simultaneous resolution to three urgent and radically different problems:

1. lowering the retirement age;
2. unemployment among older workers;
3. the flexible shedding of staff as required by employers.

It also enabled the formula to evolve at great speed, as the gradual disengagement of the state and the increased overlap with economic power encouraged government to abandon its global aim of integrating the elderly in favor of more limited and selective facilities and services. The definition of an employment policy for older workers was therefore left to negotiated relations between employers and labor unions. The economic crisis caused relations between employers and unions to change in two ways: first, union priorities switched to defending jobs, and this led to an agreement between the two parties to get rid of older workers; second, because of the urgency of the situation, the social debate concentrated on questions of economic management, giving ammunition to the employers' preference for an employment policy that provided companies with a flexible approach to off-loading older workers. This new balance of forces between the employers and the unions was to continue, and its survival was underlined by subsequent renewals of the 1977 agreement in March 1979 and March 1981. These renewals even marked an acceleration in the process of shedding older workers. Qualifying conditions were now even easier than before,[72] and as a later section will show, the number of recipients grew rapidly. Preretirement schemes were extraordinarily popular and became more widely used as the employment situation deteriorated. Employers and unions agreed to make age a basic criterion in the distribution of work, and there were very considerable dangers of escalation inherent in such a solution. When the act was extended for the second time, the CGT and the CFDT proposed that guaranteed income should become a permanent feature; this shows how far this kind of distribution had permeated, and slowly dominated, their way of thinking.[73] There were further developments and new extensions after the Socialists came to power. Later, in 1984, only budgetary considerations prompted the introduction of initiatives designed to control how far the measures could be extended.

The Implications of the Widespread Adoption of Preretirement Schemes

The above sections have highlighted the configurations of the state's social relations and types of action that underpinned the elaboration and development of preretirement as a new measure enabling employees to stop work before normal retirement age. This chapter will attempt to assess the main consequences of the social dynamic of the employment policy then in force.

First, this social dynamic stimulated the widespread adoption of these preretirement schemes, which now supplanted normal retirement and became the main pathway for stopping work. Second, such a transformation in turn involved a major reshaping of life patterns, and led to a new social definition of old age to be outlined in this section. Finally, there will be an examination of the considerable contradictions that these employment measures introduced into the policy for old age and the major crisis that resulted.

The Widespread Adoption of Preretirement Schemes: A Statistical Analysis

After guaranteed income was first made available to older unemployed workers in 1972, the rise in the number of employees taking early exit within the framework of UNEDIC was consistent with the aforementioned analysis of a social dynamic that had dominated decisions in this field. The issue of employment clarified the debate among social forces from 1977 onwards. As a result, the guaranteed-income scheme was extended at a rate never since equaled. In its first five years of existence, the numerical index of guaranteed-income beneficiaries rose from 100 to 305: there were hardly more than 100,000 claimants. In the next five years, from 1977 onward, there was a steep rise in claims; there were more than 300,000 beneficiaries in 1981, and over the whole period the progressive increase jumped from 305 to 850. (See table 3.1.) This rise could not be attributed to a change in the number of people in that age group; in fact, there was a major drop in their numbers during this period due to the passage of the small birth cohorts of 1915–19 at this age bracket from 100 in 1972 to 61 in 1981.

This astounding spread of preretirement schemes continued well into the 1980s; there was even a further acceleration after 1981, when the number of preretirees more than doubled between 1981 and 1983, the progressive increase moving from 850 to 1889. (See table 3.1.) There were two quite different reasons for this acceleration. One somewhat mechanically reflected the arrival of new full birth cohorts in the sixty to sixty-four age group; these doubled in number between 1980 and 1985. The other was the impact of the political decision to extend early exit arrangements to the age group immediately below fifty-five- to fifty-nine-year-olds. The increase in the number of employees taking early exit may have been impressive, but it is still no easier to distinguish the major changes that were taking place in the diffusion of these measures.

What was revolutionary about this increase in the number of claimants was the fact that early exit was becoming the main transition mode from work to retirement. An early indication of the growing impact that guaranteed income was having on early exit was the increase in the number of people qualifying as a proportion of potential beneficiaries (i.e., wage earners making contributions to the unemployment fund and aged between sixty and sixty-five).

Table 3.2 shows how rapidly this measure spread after 1977. For instance, in 1975 only one person in eight relied on guaranteed income (12.8 percent), while in 1978 this ratio had gone up to over one in three (36.6 percent); from 1981 onward, over one in two potential beneficiaries were covered. Other data show that from 1981 onward, wage earners aged between sixty and sixty-five on guaranteed income actually outnumbered those at work (293,562 as against 287,496). If those who were excluded from the labor market but were seeking work are added to guaranteed-income beneficiaries, the figure was increased by 33,422 individuals aged sixty to sixty-four. There were therefore 326,984 older wage earners relying on UNEDIC

Table 3.1. Beneficiaries under Various Preretirement Arrangements, 1968–88 (as of 31 December each year)

Year	1963 FNE Act (1)	Guaranteed income dismissal (GRL) (2)	Guaranteed income resignation (GRD) (3)	Subtotal 1+2+3 programs covering 60- to 64-year-olds (4)	National Employment Fund (AS-FNE) (5)	Solidarity contracts pre-retirement (ACS) (6)	Solidarity contracts gradual preretirement (ACC) (7)	Subtotal 5+6+7 programs covering 55- to 59-year-olds (8)	Progression basis of 100 in 1972	Grand total
1968	11,333			11,333						11,433
1969	13,868			13,868						13,868
1970	13,405			13,405						13,405
1971	13,992			13,992						13,992
1972	14,151	23,186		37,337					100	37,337
1973	11,921	40,984		52,905						52,905
1974	9,423	54,924		64,347					172	64,347
1975	7,393	76,827		84,220						84,220
1976	5,942	91,412		97,354						97,354
1977	4,753	99,571	9,598	113,922					305	113,922
1978	3,629	99,983	43,441	147,563						147,563
1979	1,975	93,754	62,891	158,610						158,610
1980	1,221	118,029	95,538	214,788						214,788
1981	642	154,893	138,027	293,562	23,792			23,792	850	317,354
1982	53	201,831	197,472	399,356	53,207	61,701	146	115,054		514,410
1983	2	204,531	229,551	434,084	86,456	183,448	1,199	271,103	1889	705,187
1984	1	188,849	220,790	409,640	121,750	150,545	1,432	273,903		683,543
1985		159,800	190,582	350,382	155,493	107,622	2,805	265,920		616,302
1986		126,840	162,254	289,094	175,000	62,680	5,370	243,050		532,144
1987		88,920	137,980	226,900	184,670	21,740	8,080	214,490		441,390
1988		84,800	135,100	219,900	186,230	18,510	8,510	213,250		433,150

Source: UNEDIC, *Bulletin de liaison,* appendix VIII, no. 92–206, 1987

Table 3.2. Population Claiming Guaranteed Income, in Thousands

	End July 1972	End July 1975	End July 1978	End July 1981	End July 1982
Guaranteed-income claimants in thousands	14.1	68.1	136.7	275.7	399.7
Proportion of the total population aged between 60 years and 65 years and 3 months, in %	0.5	2.7	7.4	12.4	14.0
Claimants as a proportion of the of the population	2.2	12.8	36.6	50.2	56.7

Table 3.3. Distribution of the Population Aged between Sixty and Sixty-Four on 1 January 1981

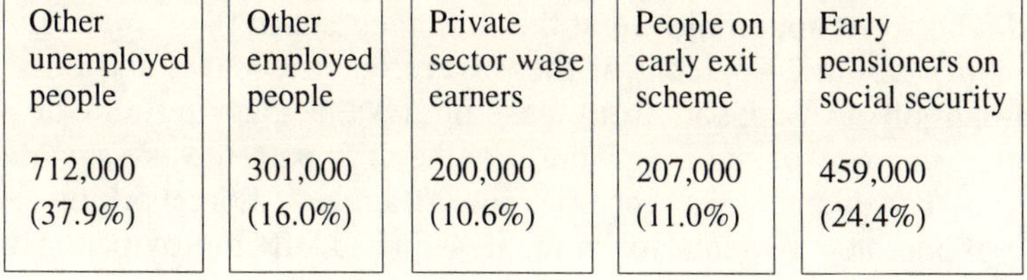

Source: A. M. Guillemard, *Le déclin du social* (Paris: PUF, 1986), p. 174.

as opposed to 287,496 people employed.[74] By this time, work had become a minority activity for those aged between sixty and sixty-four.

This is wholly credible if existing statistics are used to make an approximate reconstruction of the 1981 employment situation among French people aged between sixty and sixty-four (see table 3.3).[75] At that time, only 26.6 percent of this age group were still at work (see columns 2 and 3 in table 3.3), and significantly, 24.4 percent were drawing pension from social security (column 5). Even in 1981, there were slightly more people who had taken early exit than qualified for guaranteed income. Could this mean that with the reforms brought in during the 1970s, early retirement had more influence on how people stopped work than the new measures introduced as part of the unemployment insurance scheme?

The answer is no, and there are two reasons for this. The first is that the development of early retirement was greatly hindered by the astonishing success of preretirement scheme, the latter being financially more attractive for those who qualified. This is borne out by an analysis of the comparative growth in the number of people on guaranteed income and taking early retirement in the period 1975–81 (see table 3.4 below). The numerical index of workers taking earlier retirement only rose from 100 to 126 between 1975 and 1981, as compared with an increase of 100 to 395 for those qualifying for early exit schemes. There was even a drop in the number of wage earners who took early retirement after 1977; this was largely due to the passage of the small birth cohorts of 1915–19, and to a lesser extent to the introduction of the guaranteed-income scheme for resignees; the latter offered a more attractive financial package.

The second reason is that an analysis of workers who took early exit shows that, strictly speaking, it was not usually a matter of *stopping work*. Pensions for those incapable of work represented the bulk of early pensions paid out every year, varying between 60 percent and 90 percent from one year to the next. The General Inspectorate of Social Affairs has shown from its own surveys that with the exception of workers who had moved from the disability scheme to old-age insurance, applicants for incapacity pension were mostly women (63.3 percent), many of whom had large families and who were not employed at the time they put in their applications (58 percent). Some 24 percent of them were on sick leave, and only 11 percent had jobs.[76] It appears from these figures that early retirement was only a marginal way of stopping work. For the most part, it was a system of granting a "complementary" income, set off against short working lives and only moderate payments, to claimants who had left employment a long time before.

The exploding number of guaranteed-income beneficiaries signaled a revolution. This scheme, soon the major early-exit pathway, was reshaping

Table 3.4. Comparative Increases in the Number of People on Guaranteed Income and in Those of the Same Age Receiving Early-Retirement Pensions from Social Security

		1975	1977	1979	1981
People drawing guaranteed income (layoff and resignation schemes)[a]	Numbers	76,827	109,200	160,250	303,805
	base (1975)	100	142	208.5	395
People drawing early retirement pension (aged 60–64)[b]	numbers	367,988	479,514	437,415	464,155
	base (1975)	100	130	119	126
Total population of the same age	numbers	2,622,954	2,194,522	1,751,289	1,878,909
	base (1975)	100	83.7	66.8	71.6

Source: UNEDIC and CNAVTS.

[a] Numbers at 31 December.

[b] Numbers at 1 July. These were mostly people on full pension. The number of those on a reduced pension had been accelerating since 1972, when a new definition of incapacity was introduced. This increase was to continue. In 1979, people on reduced early pensions represented about 12 percent of all those on early exit and aged sixty to sixty-five (*Source:* CNAVTS).

the process of definitive exit. A new phase of life, called preretirement *(préretraite),* was now occurring for most wage earners in the private sector between the time they stopped working and the time they started receiving an old-age pension. The Unemployment Compensation Fund, whose duty was to compensate wage earners for short periods of joblessness, was assuming responsibility for covering jobless aging workers for as long as five years or more. It was being changed into as sort of old-age fund.

To glimpse the guaranteed-income scheme impact on definitive exit, we need but notice that, by 1981, a minority of sixty- to sixty-four-year-olds in the private sector still had jobs. The Unemployment Compensation Fund had grown so much that it was taking the place of the Old-Age Fund in providing the means of definitive exit from the labor market. According to a 1981 Ministry of Labor survey about definitive exit in the private sector (see table 3.5) a minority—less than 18 percent—of departures from the labor force involved entering retirement at sixty-five. Moreover, taking early retirement (at that time possible at sixty) with full or reduced pensions accounted for only 14.5 percent of departures. In contrast, nearly two-thirds (60.2 percent) of these definitive cases were "preretirees" managed by Unemployment Compensation. A small percentage (7.6 percent) had given up their jobs under company-sponsored programs.

The most important of these company- or industry-wide programs (which have nothing to do with the Unemployment Fund) was the 1977 iron and steel agreement, part of a plan for "restructuring" this industry in France. This agreement, renewed since then, provides that workers doing hard labor can stop working as early as fifty, and the others as early as fifty-five, while receiving 75 percent of former wages. To give an idea of its impact, it covered nearly thirty thousand wage earners from mid-1979 until the end of 1981, half of whom stopped working before fifty-five.

The full impact of preretirement via unemployment compensation as a means of regulating definitive exit cannot be assessed without counting the mass of jobless fifty-five- to fifty-nine-year-olds, who, in fact, formed a "precategory" of preretirees.

To conclude, the above examination shows that preretirement had become extremely common in France, and that it was beginning to be applied to younger and younger age groups. Numbers rose dramatically and appeared to be rising even more rapidly between 1979 and 1984.

It follows that there was an increasing number of fifty-five- to sixty-five-year-olds who had left the labor market for good, and that they lived on replacement incomes provided for under the unemployment insurance scheme until they qualified for pensioner status.

For most people, a new phase was now being constructed between stopping work and retirement. It was managed by the unemployment

Table 3.5. Definitive Exit by Pathway, 1981

Pathway	Men (%)	Women (%)	Total (%)
1. Retirees at 65 with full pensions	17.3	18.4	17.7
2. Early retirees			
With full pensions:			
a. Disabled	8.8	6.8	8.1
b. World War II prisoners and veterans	2.2	0.3	1.5
c. Working mothers, manual workers, and women who had worked for 37.5 years	1.9	2.7	2.2
With reduced pensions	2.7	2.6	2.7
3. Preretirees under:			
a. The special National Employment Fund Program (AS-FNE)	15.6	12.8	14.7
b. The 1972 guaranteed-income dismissal scheme (GRL)	17.1	16.9	17.1
c. The 1977 guaranteed-income resignation scheme (GRD)	26.7	32.1	28.4
d. Company-sponsored gradual retirement programs	7.7	7.4	7.6
Total	100.0	100.0	100.0

Note: These statistics cover wage earners in the private sector who, at the age of fifty-five or over, went on retirement, early retirement, or preretirement between 1 January 1981 and 31 October 1981.

Source: Ministry of Labor Survey (cited in G. Magnier, "Les sorties de la vie active en 1981," *Bulletin mensuel du travail,* no. 95 (October 1982).

Table 3.6. Changes during 1962–78 in the Age at which 50 Percent of Males are Still Employed

Year	Age
1962	65.5
1968	65.0
1975	62.7
1976	62.3
1977	61.6
1978	60.9

Source: Michel Lévy, "L'âge de la retraite s'abaisse," *Population et Société*, no. 117 (October 1978).

insurance scheme and was therefore partly transforming itself into another form of old-age insurance. The rise in preretirement schemes upset the entire pattern of the life course, and, by setting new upper and lower age-group limits, also produced a new social definition of old age.

Lowering the Age of Definitive Exit

With the coming to power of the Socialists in May 1981, two sorts of measures were adopted to lower the definitive exit age. For one thing, the normal retirement age was lowered from sixty-five to sixty, a decision that somewhat restored the Old-Age Fund its power to regulate definitive exit, at least of sixty- to sixty-four-year-olds. For another, preretirement was shifted toward fifty-five to fifty-nine-year-olds, increasing numbers of whom would now go, first, on preretirement under unemployment compensation and then, at age sixty, on retirement.

Lowering the retirement age. Following a 26 March 1982 decree and a concomitant 4 February 1983 agreement (which made adjustments in the supplementary pension funds), wage earners could receive a full pension at the age of sixty if they had contributed to the Social Security Old-Age Fund for at least 37.5 years. This decree, which went into effect on 1 April 1983, covered both the private and public sectors. This decision to lower the retirement age affected the prevailing definitive exit arrangements.

It should be kept in mind, however, that many wage earners taking retirement before age sixty-five had already stopped working because of the guaranteed-income schemes. Lowering the retirement age did not, therefore, fully restore the Old-Age Fund as the regulator of definitive exit. What it did do, above all, was replace one arrangement with another; and it did this, initially, in order to limit early-exit costs. Thanks to this reform, wage earners who have contributed for 37.5 years to the Old-Age Fund are no longer covered by preretirement arrangements under Unemployment Compensation. Instead, they now depend on the Old-Age Fund, which provides pensions at a lesser percentage of former wages than the guaranteed-income schemes. Consequently, these now useless schemes have been left to run out. Nonetheless, doing away with them has not put an end to preretirement, for it has been shifted forward in the life span, under arrangements covering fifty-five- to fifty-nine-year-olds, as we shall see.

As a result of the retirement age reform, the Old-Age Fund has been able to take up from the Unemployment Compensation Fund responsibility for the age sixty to sixty-four stretch of the life span. Although this reform especially helped the Unemployment Compensation Fund solve its financial problems caused by the guaranteed-income schemes, public opinion took it to be a sign that the government had finally yielded to labor unions, which had, for a long time, been demanding a lower full-pension retirement age. This popular reform brought about a new legal situation that differed from the contractual agreements underlying the guaranteed-income schemes, which, tied to the business cycle, were of limited validity. Moreover, those in previously ineligible categories, such as public-sector employees, could now retire earlier.

Extending preretirement to fifty-five- to fifty-nine-year-olds: Solidarity contracts. In order to halt unemployment, the government, besides lowering the retirement age, set up in early 1982 a new preretirement program valid for two years. These so-called solidarity contracts *(contrats de solidarité)* were an attempt to regain control over definitive exit. During former president Giscard d'Estaing's term, early withdrawal had been more or less left up to employer and union organizations, and arrangements had come out of labor-management compromises. Now the state would systematically cover a large part of preretirement cost under solidarity contracts to be signed between it and firms. Public authorities thus became a full party to preretirement agreements with the objective of stimulating hirings. To this end, three sorts of measures were proposed, only one of which would have a significant impact.

1. *Government aid for shortening the workweek*
2. *Solidarity preretirement resignation contracts*
3. *Solidarity gradual preretirement*

Of these three formulas, only the preretirement one was widely successful. The number of beneficiaries exceeded all expectations. During the first two years, nearly 200,000 older workers took this pathway out of the labor force (column 6, table 3.1), whereas its potential had been estimated at 50,000 a year! The gradual preretirement formula (column 7) was not much of a success, having 1,199 beneficiaries during the same period. Its conditions were not attractive, because the beneficiary, by working half-time, received only 10 percent more than the full-time "preretiree" and accumulated half as many Social Security retirement points. Gradual preretirement was not very attractive to employers either, because it forced them to reorganize work.

In late 1984 the total number of fifty-five to fifty-nine-year-old preretirees reached 273,903 (table 3.1). Afterward, it decreased as solidarity preretirement resignation contracts ran out. In late 1984, there were also about 150,000 ordinary jobless persons in this age group, whose employment rate had fallen to 63 percent for men and 39 percent for women. From 1982 to 1984, a period when solidarity contracts were being signed, the employment rate for men in this age group dropped from 76 percent to 62 percent.

Preretirement and Changes in the Stages of Life

The stages of life are constantly in the process of being socially redefined. What is more, the number of phases, ways of moving from one phase to the next, and specific functions allocated to each phase vary as a function of social transformations. However, this is not an appropriate moment to examine all the factors that determine those occasions when the pattern of life is recast. We certainly live substantially longer than people did a hundred years ago; as Louis Roussel and Alain Girard have reminded us,[77] this change in life expectancy has led both to an increase in the number of stages in the life course and to a reinterpretation of what the pattern of the life course actually means. This section will attempt more specifically to identify the role that preretirement schemes have played in the social redefinition of the last stages of life. By crystallizing certain definitions and helping to make them better known, political measures play a significant role in the social construction/deconstruction process of old age at any one time.

The following analysis of the relationship between the policy of freeing up the labor force and changes in the last stages of life will highlight an aspect of social policy that is often ignored; social policy provides a social and cultural redefinition as it redistributes goods and services, and the symbolic aspects are of no less importance than the impact that it has socioeconomically.

This author has already observed that the wider acceptance of retirement divided the life course in a new way and gave a new form to old age. The emergence of an innovative way-of-life policy dismissed the image of an impoverished and feeble old age and substituted a new activist picture of the third age. Which changes in life course, and which new definitions of old age, were linked to the widespread diffusion of conjunctural employment measures designed to free up an aging labor force?

Three major changes in the last stage of the life course, which naturally affect social representations of old age, may be attributed to this diffusion of employment measures. When preretirement became the most common way of stopping work, it speeded up the timetable for definitive exit. It also turned retirement into a period that included no work at all, and thereby made the transition into unemployment much more sudden, brutal, and inevitable.

Major acceleration in the timetable for definitive exit from the labor market. The background to the campaign to bring down retirement age contained many elements, such as wage levels, flexibility and maturation of pension schemes, and the state of industrial relations. The major role played by preretirement schemes in the decision of workers to stop work in the late 1970s and early 1980s also did much to lower the age at which people stopped working for good.

A long-term analysis of changes in labor participation rates of workers as they got older provides a good indication of this (see table 5 in the appendix). From 1974 onward, there was a rapid reduction in the labor participation rate of workers aged between sixty and sixty-four. Between 1954 and 1974, the male participation rate dropped by 11 percent, but the trend accelerated thereafter: between 1974 and 1984, over a period only half as long, the rate fell by almost 50 percent, and after 1977 the working population (i.e., individuals actually working or unemployed) represented under half the number of people in that age band.

As for workers in the fifty-five to fifty-nine age group, their participation rate remained high,[78] but in an observable trend that took place during the period 1977–84, the age of exit from work dropped back to fifty-five. During this time, the male participation rate fell by 18 percent; this was particularly pronounced after 1981, illustrating the impact that the preretire-πment system had as it began to encroach on this age group.

There were similar developments among women, but the effect was narrowly focused. An important exception emerged among fifty-five- to fifty-nine-year-olds whose participation rates remained relatively stable, the drop in participation rates of older workers being counterbalanced by the increase in the number of women having entered the labor market overall. This more recent phenomenon was more spectacular among workers under forty years old, but was still quite impressive in the slighter older age groups.

An analysis of changes in participation rates for every age group between 1975 and 1978 confirms observations made over five-year periods. The analysis demonstrates that from 1976 onward, the fall in participation rates of sixty- to sixty-one-year-olds was greater than that for sixty-five- to sixty-six-year-olds.[79] It also highlights a clear rise in the incidence of early exit. This development was easily observable in the light of the age variations that corresponded to 50 percent of employed males. This age may also be fixed globally as that at which half of the age group has withdrawn from the labor market; as table 3.6 shows, it was dropping fast.

The early-exit trend became particularly pronounced in France and the Netherlands. As the table comparing the evolution of unemployment activity rates shows, this trend has continued uninterrupted until today. In 1995 hardly one out of three men in the fifty-five to sixty-four age group were still part of the labor market in France (38 percent) and 40 percent in Holland. Fewer than one out of two were in the same situation in Germany and Spain (See table 6 in the appendix).

Dissociation between work and retirement. The widespread adoption of unemployment measures for older workers not only made retirement longer and set new limits on old age; it also transformed the social content of this period of life. Retirement became a period without employment, and this change was linked to the issues surrounding the introduction of preretirement; an important factor in this respect was the fact that these measures were designed within the framework of unemployment insurance, and therefore imposed their inherent logic of separating benefits from employment. This disjunction broke both with the principles on which retirement was constructed and with the practices and representations of retirement as it had been previously understood. These principles, such as they were formulated in 1945 by the Social Security Act, stated that retirement was a pension entitlement based on age and period of employment, and was not subject to any conditions relating to ceasing work.

The principles were incorporated into common representations of retirement of the type that emerge from various surveys. These surveys suggested a growing wish to retire early,[80] but these expectations must not be misunderstood. Close examination of the same surveys reveals that workers were less interested in stopping work early than in bringing pensionable age forward. In a survey carried out by the polling organization SOFRES in 1975, 89 percent of the men questioned wanted to retire at sixty or earlier, but 48 percent said that it was better not to stop working completely at retirement age and that it was preferable to be in some form of employment.[81] Retirement was not associated in people's minds with doing nothing. What it meant was entitlement to a pension, and therefore a guarantee that retirement was possible on a replacement income—if that was what the individual wanted. Under the rules governing unemployment insurance, guaranteed income subordinated replacement-income entitlement to an obligation to stop work, and all work during the period of preretirement consequently became illegal. It also separated the right to work and the right to retirement for a very considerable period of time.[82] The consensus that greeted the success of this measure also ensured that a new representation of retirement—as an age at which work was illegal—gained rapid currency.

The new dichotomy that arose between employment and retirement could also be seen at the level of general social practices. As has been pointed out earlier, participation rates dropped between the ages of fifty-five and sixty, and collapsed after sixty. It was not unusual for salary and pension to be drawn concurrently for a transitional period lasting a few years, and this greater flexibility was expressed by a wider distribution of participation rates according to age. The final life phase therefore focused on unemployment. It was as if older workers, many of whom were no more than fifty-five years old, had been somehow branded as serving no public use. The rise in the number of unemployed workers aged fifty-five to fifty-nine referred to above provided eloquent testimony of this. Older workers had become the main target for job cuts because their right to employment was no longer recognized, and they now found themselves categorized as socially unproductive, as people who were no longer "doing their bit," and therefore having to be dependent on their more active peers for subsistence allowances. Moreover, they now swelled the ranks of those who lived on the margins of society because they had to be supported.

The brutal, inevitable transition into unemployment. The extensive distribution of preretirement schemes not only hastened entry into old age, but also, by reducing the extent to which workers could plan early exit in advance and make their own decisions, profoundly changed how people stopped work. They now approached old age, not freely exercising their right to retirement, but as a result of being laid off or dismissed. The social definition of old age was no longer formulated in terms of an entitlement to retirement or to a specific way of life, but as a function of the labor market and of the importance of keeping staffing levels in check. It was clear that the new social definition of old age, which had become widely disseminated as a result of preretirement schemes, bore the mark of the social dynamic by which the preretirement schemes had been imposed. As this book has demonstrated, the balance of social forces that presided over their implementation was dominated by employers who, aided by favorable circumstances, were able to ensure that their views on the employment of older workers prevailed. The new social construction of old age that was imposed thereafter reflected the balance that had produced it in the first place, and bore a striking resemblance to employers' viewpoints and their definition of age.

Early exit was not simply a way of allowing workers to retire sooner; it had more to do with rejection and with a disenfranchisement in which the right to work was no longer recognized, despite the fact that society picked up the bill by paying out large sums in replacement earnings. In fact, older workers no longer had any scope for choice between retirement and employment, as they were denied the right to work. Acceptance of a limitation on the right to work called into question the very basis of the right to retire, and turned those who did have that entitlement into persons in receipt of public assistance.[83] The massive increase in the number of preretirement schemes went hand in hand with a reduction in employees' autonomy and in the expunging of their capacity for choice. The schemes even placed a period of unemployment between leaving employment for good and the paying out of the pension; previously, these two events had followed one another without a break. This period without work took various forms, as it was subject to fluctuations both in the rules governing unemployment insurance and in the balance of forces that obtained at the time when these rules were being negotiated.

Unemployment could last up to ten years; an individual's status was frequently transitory, and even relatively precarious, as a result.[84] Many people first drew unemployment insurance and then took preretirement through the guaranteed-income scheme before finally qualifying for their pensions.

The new stage that came between employment and retirement was in no way transitional. The journey into unemployment was much more sudden and unpredictable than the old system of slipping into retirement; that, after all, had been a change that was easily anticipated, and appropriate arrangements could be made with equal facility. Stopping work for good was much more abrupt, and this showed up in the narrower range of participation rates among older workers.

Dismissal, layoffs, and health were now the main reasons for ceasing employment. The existence of a resignation-linked guaranteed income, and the rapid increase in the number of people receiving it, might give the impression that many had decided for themselves when they wanted to leave, but closer examination shows that opportunities for choice were theoretical rather than real. Early exit was not really an option; much more often it was a matter of choosing the lesser of two evils. Faced with ill health or with work that was getting more and more arduous as the years passed, many felt that resignation—maybe a resignation that had been "negotiated" with the employer—was an honorable and financially satisfactory solution.

The survey I carried out on a sample of ASSEDIC (Association pour l'Emploi dans l'Industrie et le Commerce—Association for Employment in Industry and Commerce) beneficiaries aged fifty-five to sixty-five in Lyon underlines that options regarding preretirement schemes were very limited, even for resignees.[85] In answer to the question, "What was your main reason for leaving?" only a small minority spoke in terms of a positive life plan; most said that they wanted to be able to lead their own lives at last, and talked of their weariness with jobs, which they found uninteresting or in which they considered the atmosphere to be degrading. That was why there were a lot fewer volunteering for early exit than resigning.

There were other, more imaginative people whose values transcended the work ethic; these individuals had resigned because they had been able to choose their date of departure and had therefore been able to express their individuality, but they represented no more than 10 percent of the beneficiaries questioned. The ambiguity of the administrative category of resignation became more apparent when the reasons for resignation were analyzed (see table 3.7, column 5, total percentage). In fact, only a quarter

Table 3.7. Main Reasons for Going on Preretirement

Status ASSEDIC	1 Economic situation of the firm—Layoffs	2 Firm's restructuring	3 Fatigue-Hard work	4 Health problem	5 Positive life plans	
GRL*	89	2	2	3	5	100%
GRD**	8	16	16	35	25	100%
Total %	71	5	5	10	10	
Total numbers	236	17	16	33	31	333

Chi_:188,318 signif. 05

*GRL = Unemployment compensations or guaranteed income dismissal.
**GRD = Guaranteed income resignation.
Source: Survey by questionnaire ASSEDIC-Lyon 1980 conducted by the author.

of them could be considered to be real volunteers for retirement; this underlined the crisis in the value attached to work, and the enhanced value attached to free time, a phenomenon that Joffre Dumazedier has analyzed in much detail.[86] The most common reason given by this group for stopping work was health problems (35 percent).[87] Next came reasons associated with harsh working conditions and fatigue, together with dissatisfaction with the way in which the job was changed (16 percent). Resignation was therefore more often the result of constraints (e.g., state of health or changes in working conditions) than of the development of a positive life plan.

The drive to promote early exit went hand in hand with a considerable reduction in the amount of say that individual workers had in determining details; the time of departure and other conditions were also being continually adjusted. Thereafter, the margin of choice open to employees was more theoretical than real, and greater dissemination of preretirement schemes led to the brutal and wide-ranging removal of an expanding age group from the labor market.

Emergence of a new social definition of old age. The last life phase had previously been the time when people exercised their right to a period of rest and leisure pursuits; now, as a result of the development of "unemployment" measures for older workers, it had become a time when the right to work was denied.[88] There was also a striking contrast between the importance that retirement had acquired in life, in terms of both time and of the purely negative nature of its new social definition; the latter could be summed up as relating to nonworkers or nonlegitimate workers. The eminently sensible view that was disseminated of old age as an active and participative third age was now succeeded by a negative definition of the end of the life course.

The image of old age as an active, participative third age had been developed during the preceding period, but it patently concealed the disenfranchisement in which older workers now found themselves. The new dignity acquired by retirement[89] was simply a euphemism for voluntary retirement, which in turn was usually nothing more than exclusion and enforced leisure time. It is illuminating to recall that the word most frequently used to describe this new condition was "preretirement"; as a result, this situation was directly linked to retirement and was associated with all its new positive aspects (e.g., free time and recreational activities). All references to unemployment and the ban on working were erased.[90]

By making age a major discriminatory factor in the distribution of work, measures for freeing up the aging labor force produced a new model for the organization of age groups. As a result, phases of life were more clear-cut, the transitions from one to the next were more controlled, and life choices were less open. The distribution of functions among different age groups also became urgent and brutal, and there was now greater specialization and more segregation. For example, the period of youth was lasting longer and was specializing more specifically in training; adulthood was shorter and was given over to production; and old age, which was starting earlier and earlier, had no functions at all apart from unemployment. Old age now belonged to a new "postwork" sequence of life that lasted almost a quarter of a century.

Conclusion: Toward a Crisis in the Policy for Old Age

The new representation of old age gained currency at the same time as the cost of employment measures rose; it also directly contradicted the new status of an active and socially integrated third age that the innovative way-of-life policy was trying to promote. This latter policy sought to put an end to the exile that old age had become, but the employment policy that succeeded it produced little more than social exile and handouts.

Following further extensions to the "early exit" policy for older workers, French policy for old age boasted two contradictory dimensions: on one hand, in the context of the way-of-life policy, it aimed at better social integration of the elderly and a prolongation of normal life; on the other, under the employment policy, it caused marginalization by cruelly curtailing their status as workers. The antagonism between these two dimensions prompted a crisis in the policy for old age. Once it was accepted within the framework of the employment policy that there was a division into two camps governed by age—and as soon as it was acknowledged that everyone beyond a certain age (which was being pitched lower and lower) was socially unproductive and welfare-dependent—it became superfluous to argue later on against a form of segregation that had already been consolidated. As a result, the "early exit" policy for older workers devastated the way-of-life policy that the state had been simultaneously promoting.

The employment dimension was now a decisively important tool in the management of old age, and it both invaded and perverted the purpose of the entire policy for old age. Guaranteed income had been designed to sidetrack union claims for an improved right to retirement, a demand once considered unrealistic and expensive; however, guaranteed income was now seen as more costly after all, and also more harmful to the future of the policy for old age than an extension of the right to retirement.

Guaranteed income replaced the pension schemes for the fifty to sixty-five age group, but it did them few favors. The social protection it offered was more expensive; furthermore, it was inequitable and even irresponsible insofar as it was based on criteria inappropriate to unemployment. Moreover, guaranteed income not only introduced an initial, precarious stage of retirement; it also reduced employees' right to work and their ability to decide on retirement arrangements for themselves, and represented the payment of a number of benefits, including the cushion of income guaranteed by preretirement schemes, which the unions now supported.

The guaranteed-income system therefore accentuated the contradictions that had given rise to its inception in the first place. It made reform of retirement policies more difficult. It also jeopardized the future of a policy dedicated to improving the way of life of the elderly, which not only aimed at providing access to new goods and services, but also sought to carry out a review of the social status of old age.

4

The Elaboration of Policies for Old Age, and the Crisis that Ensued: Clues for an Interpretation

This book has so far examined, with respect to each of the three fundamental dimensions of intervention on old age, the social dynamic that has governed the development of associated political decisions. It has also made it possible to assess the social impact that these decisions have had. Accordingly, this is an appropriate moment to pull the strands of the investigation together. This chapter will include a summary of work on old-age policy and then set out some interpretation hints. These will be based on two fundamental questions:

1. What do this book's sociohistorical analyses of the three dimensions of old-age policy tell us about the formation of social policies, and more specifically about figures of the state on which these policies are based?
2. What do they tell us about the current crisis in the welfare state?

The State, Old Age, and Society: The Process of Forming a Public Policy

The previous chapters have examined an old-age policy and its decomposition into basic components, and sought to reach an understanding of the configurations of the underlying social relations. The policy will now be reassembled, and this chapter will analyze the decision-making process of the state on old-age issues. The aim is to achieve such an interpretative reconstruction. The starting point of this study was old-age policies that were differentiated according to their fundamental dimensions; the finishing point is the state and the way it reaches decisions.

In other words, this chapter will identify the factors that determine state action in the field of old-age policy. The analysis will make it possible to circumscribe the state's forms of dependence and independence, and to understand the dialectic of these forms. It will also highlight those moments when the state's decision-making procedures illustrate two characteristics. One is that it is controlled by certain social forces; the other is its relative capacity for evading social relations, and instead influencing them and turning itself into an important social force within society. The analytical method to be adopted in this chapter is set out below.

There has so far been a longitudinal analysis of the social dynamic whereby each of the three main dimensions of an old-age policy was produced. There now follows a cross-sectional analysis of the way in which interventions on the various dimensions of old-age policy combine within the state during every period, and then give way to what might be called the *methods of state management of old age*. This phrase refers to the way in which there is a coming together of public actions within the state that pertain to the three essential dimensions of management: retirement, way of life, and employment. These dimensions have been isolated for the sake of this analysis. It must be clearly understood that referring to the method of management in no way implies that it is characterized by any form of coherence. This analysis is solely concerned with how public actions, however discordant or harmonious they may be, are combined. Earlier research has suggested that the ways in which public interventions are structured changed substantially after 1945. This chapter will therefore present a periodization of the methods of state management of old age; these result from the points of inflexion that are observed in the way the three dimensions of intervention combine within the state. It should be stressed that these successive methods of state management could not be identified a priori, and that such an identification is in fact one of the outcomes of this research. This is not to confuse the intentions of senior officials and the policies they have followed; nor is this looking upon the state as an independent, homogeneous, and rational agent. This should certainly not be postulated as the basis for an analysis of state interventions. A concise reconstruction of successive philosophies, whereby the state has operated with respect to old age, is here referred to as methods of state management of old age, and will constitute the dependent variable. There will also be an examination of the factors determining these philosophies in the configurations of relations that develop between state and society in every period. The hypothesis underpinning this analysis is that at any one time, the methods of state management of old age reflect the link—which is in perpetual tension and transformation—between the arena of the state and that of social relations. A close examination of the play of social forces that has produced public decisions for each dimension of old-age policy will make it possible to identify the extent to which the orientations of state action, embodied in the method of state management, tally with the views of a given social force (and which social force), or on the contrary, whether they indicate that the state has some autonomous capacity for influencing society. In addition to making state actions in the field of old age intelligible, this study will contribute to a better understanding of those interventions between state and society that lie at the heart of social policy. It will also turn the spotlight on the conditions in which the state is controlled by social forces or, alternatively, escapes from them and functions according to its own rules.

The Three Successive Methods of State Management of Old Age

From 1945 to the early 1960s, the main issue on which the state intervened in relations between old age and society was pensions policy; it was this that structured all public actions in the field. The way-of-life policy for the elderly was reduced to the provision of public assistance and was massively subordinated to pensions. During this period, assistance benefits were reorganized so as to make them complementary to the pensions system. Either through the provision of social housing or through newly introduced assistance in cash or in kind,[1] they were designed to respond to more serious levels of poverty, and they filled the gaps left by the new, developing pensions system. Finally, demographers led by Alfred Sauvy called urgently for a prolongation of the working life to be accompanied by an employment policy for older workers. The purpose was to compensate for the shortage of employees, a situation that remained acute until 1948, but no public policy of this type was ever implemented. The pensions measures adopted in 1945, which were partly intended to bring down the age of retirement, were a substitute for policy in this field. Public interventions in employment were therefore very limited, and during this period consisted largely of the pensions policy.

It is instructive to distinguish two periods in state action during the period 1945–60. The first, which was brief, followed close on the heels of the Liberation and coincided with the time when the public authorities were introducing the right of workers to retirement in the shape of the General Social Security Scheme. It was characterized by intensive public activity that polarized all state action on the relations between old age and society. The second period, which fell after the beginning of 1947, was much less dynamic. Retirement was still the state's main instrument, but public mobilization around this issue was more subdued. The institutions that had been set up continued to operate, but their output was declining, and the retirement dynamic placed itself outside the public arena; the institutions now relied increasingly on employer-employee relations to develop complementary pension plans that the public authorities would then ratify. At about this time, old-age insurance was slowly becoming a minimum scheme that topped up the FNE allowance of 1956 for the worst off. The public-pensions policy was not only cut back and forced to operate more like a welfare scheme, it also became corporatist. The principle of a wide-ranging national solidarity scheme covering workers against all risks was beginning to erode. The right of all workers to retirement was succeeded by individual schemes of social protection, and even pensions legislation divided employment up into narrow occupational groups. Not only were there small plans covering such sectors as mining, railways, electricity, and gas, but new autonomous ones were also set up for the independent professions, such as craft workers, industrial and commercial professions, the liberal professions, and agriculture. During this second stage of the first period, pension policies were no longer a structuring issue of state action on old age. Some of the initiative no longer lay with the public authorities, and they reverted to settlements negotiated among the social classes. Elsewhere, the balance in state action between public-pensions policy and old-age welfare policy was restored.

State management of old age underwent new transformations in the early 1960s, and the three fundamental issues of public action were once again organized into a hierarchy. About this time, the state attempted to redefine its role in the management of relations between old age and society and gave support to a definition of a new way-of-life policy, whereby it became the defender and organizer of the social status of old age in society. It also redefined its political priorities in this arena. Henceforth, action on way of life was directed toward better social integration and became the structural issue of state interventions in this field. This was what was meant by the newly coined phrase "old-age policy." Retirement and employment policies for older workers were now subordinated to actions related to the way-of-life issue, and the central objective was that the elderly should be enabled to remain socially integrated. During this period, public attention was increasingly drawn to the interdependence of the three dimensions of the old-age policy. Furthermore, public authorities had a newfound ambition to coordinate all of their interventions in action relating to the way of life. Initiatives related to retirement age, the level of pensions, and measures enabling older workers to remain employed were later brought together, and they supported what became the central action of promoting an integrated way of life for a new category of citizens belonging to the "third age."

This project dominated state action on old age throughout the period 1960–75; it found expression in major political decisions, particularly from the late 1960s onward, although it also existed alongside initiatives at other levels of public action. The setting up of the Fonds National pour l'Emploi (National Employment Fund) in 1963 coincided with the introduction of special allowances for dismissed employees over the age of sixty, and this naturally flew in the face of moves being advocated at the time to keep older workers employed. The availability of these allowances was based on another component of public action. This was the role of the state as a modernizing economic agent whose task it was to encourage a restructuring of the French production system; it sought to achieve this by setting up mechanisms designed to facilitate redeployment programs, and in this case by reducing the number of job seekers. This public intervention was exceptional (there were only 18,717 preretirees between 1964 and 1966) and strictly controlled, and it did not challenge the prevalence of a policy for integrating the elderly through the way of life. The integration policy focused on all the public measures in this field that were carried out under the Sixth Plan, but it declined in importance after 1975.

Between 1975 and 1981, the bipolarity of the method of state management of old age became more and more marked. For one thing, public interventions in support of an integrated way of life for the elderly were nothing more than a policy designed to enable them to carry on living at home: although it reappeared unchanged in the Seventh Plan, it reflected the spirit of change that now informed the implementation of social policies at a time of economic crisis. Priority was now given to interventions that made a powerful symbolic impact and whose costs were easily controlled; meanwhile, the movement that structured action on the way of life was losing its impetus. For another thing, given the economic crisis and the effect it was having on employment, the management of jobs for older workers was ceasing to be the insignificant issue in the context of old age that it had once been. The state was gradually abandoning its role as defender of the right of older workers to have jobs, and was instead accepting—and subsequently encouraging—an acceleration in the incidence of early exit within the framework of unemployment insurance; in this way it raised the whole question of older people having a right to work at all. During this period, action on jobs did not simply play a subsidiary intervention by comparison with the way of life; it even began to contradict it directly. The method of state management of old age then exploded into a series of contradictory interventions, as the exclusion ideology took over the philosophy of integration. The method of management could no longer be defined by a hierarchy of ideas, but by a tension between two antagonistic sets of actions. State interventions were divided into two parts: one was an "early exit" policy for older workers, which, although now largely in the hands of the "social partners," was receiving increasing support from the public authorities; the other was a way-of-life policy for the elderly, which was being torn asunder by action on employment. In these circumstances, public interventions on the way-of-life issue could only try and fight off the marginality and segregation that the early-exit policy was producing and consolidating earlier in the life course. The retirement policy also found itself absorbed, and abused, by unemployment mechanisms; these were transforming the right to a pension into an obligation to stop work and a ban on taking employment, and were turning the right to retirement into enforced leisure.

Linkages between the State and Civil Society Based on Types of Public Management of Aging

What is the explanation for these successive methods of public management of old age? What factors make it possible to appreciate the differentiated ways in which public interventions observed during a given period are structured and organized into a hierarchy? Why, during the initial period, did pensions constitute the state's priority area of intervention in relations between old age and society, and what lay behind the prevalence of the way-of-life policy, a tool that was becoming the structuring issue of state action? The purpose of all these questions is to identify the social determinants of public action in the matter of old age. What is also at issue is the need to throw light on the relations of autonomy and independence that the state established in social policy with various social forces during the period under examination. With respect to the issues of the old-age policy, this book has put forward a careful analysis of the dynamic of social forces governing the formation of decisions. Periods in state initiatives have been identified as a function of the particular way in which decisions on these three issues were structured, and there are empirical analyses for each of the issues. These can now be used to establish how state initiatives that have been dominant in each of these periods reflect the ideas of a given social force or, on the contrary, express a certain capacity for autonomous action on the part of the state.

Research makes it possible to establish the following general proposition: *the way in which public interventions are organized on the different issues in each period corresponds to the dominant linkage between the state and society in each period.*

The priority accorded to retirement policy in public interventions on old age in 1945 and 1946 was a response to the power that the unions wielded in society, and to the fact that the state laid itself open to their social interests. After the profound upheavals caused by the war, the state had to rebuild, restore its authority, and reestablish national cohesion. Its autonomous capacity for action on societal issues was now reduced. In fact, it could only achieve its objectives at all by relying on the social forces that were dominant in society and in the political arena; in practice, this meant the working class and in particular, the ways in which it expressed its will politically and through labor unions. Working-class interests penetrated deep into the state through the tripartism that held sway in the Constituent Assemblies, where working-class representation was predominant. In a way, public policy ratified the prevalence of working-class interests in both society and the state by promoting the introduction of a workers' social right to retirement, and, in so doing, by linking its action to labor-union ideology. However, as has been pointed out, the retirement policy that was finally adopted was not a simple transcription of working-class interests: it was a social agreement that bore the stamp of the many components of state action. Of course, state action is not simply a reflection of class relations or the expression of a form of social domination; the state also has a unifying role, and within its synchronic dimension, it is an agent of change. After the deprivations of war, old-age insurance and, more broadly, social security allowed a redefinition and reactivation of the social link that brought French citizens together and united them with their government. The introduction of a social right to security and retirement was obviously an expression of the political and economic clout that the working class then enjoyed, but it also affirmed the working class's reintegration into the nation by restoring the representation and legitimacy of the state as a national state. In exchange for the construction of a distributive social state, the working class agreed to incorporate its actions within the framework of capitalist relations of production and a liberal democratic system. Consensus was thereby reestablished; the country reunified, and by setting itself up as the redistributor of resources, the sate managed to combine its roles of unifier and agent of transformation in society. In fact, by ensuring that everyone was involved in France's reconstruction, it even ensured the country's economic development. The apparatus of social protection that had been put in place in 1945 later became one of the fundamental elements in relaunching the capitalist economy.

The second stage of the initial period saw a limited mobilization by the state around the issue of pensions. With the setting up of complementary pensions, some of the state's responsibilities passed into the arena of social relations; at the same time, public-pensions policy split into a variety of actions and shifted in the direction of minimum protection. This new method of state management of old age mirrored a decline in union power and a dilution of the unions' definition of pensions as a universal social right for workers. It also underlined the limited autonomous capacity of the Fourth

Republic, an institution heavily reliant on the political system and political parties. The era of largely majority *tripartisme,* which had provided public interventions with a stable social base, was followed by a period of multiparty instability dominated mainly by moderate center parties and the SFIO (Section Française de l'Internationale Ouvrière—French Section of the Workers' International). The action of the French state, described as a "go-between" in Alain Touraine's system of categories,[2] depended significantly on the social relations that governed society. Changes in public interventions in the field of old age during this second stage reflected the way in which relations between the state and civil society were evolving. They were partly an expression of a working-class retreat, and partly reflected the prevalence of a large number of social interests emanating from a range of groups, mainly new and traditional middle-class strata. The state had become a client state that was dismantling the right to retirement under pressure from these groups, and introducing minute welfare payments for all who did not want to pay the price of solidarity.

The state was now relatively dependent on a wide range of social interests, and its method of public management was no longer so strictly organized into a hierarchy; it was also speaking less and less with one voice. If, in spite of all these reverses, there was evidence during this second stage that retirement still played an important role in public policy, this was more due to the influence of institutional mechanisms set up in 1945 than to any priority accorded to pensions. The resuscitation of a public-assistance policy during this time also indicated a decline in the role of the state (i.e., a welfare state providing social security) and the revival of a more traditional statelike image, which, through the passing of public-assistance laws, maintained social order and public security. The work of Michel Foucault has shown the close linkage between social order and power, and the inescapable exclusions induced by the so-called technologies of social order.

The method of state management during the second period was characterized by the predominance of way-of-life interventions. It was also notable for repeated attempts to organize action on other issues in the old-age policy; these conformed to moves to ensure social integration and were linked to the way-of-life policy. The introduction of this new logic of public action on old age should be seen as a function of the changes in relations between the state and society that followed the setting up of the Fifth Republic and the construction of a Gaullist state. The new institutions gave the state more independence from political parties. Now, better insulated from organized social interests, the state enjoyed a new autonomous capacity for action, thanks to a special kind of cooperation that existed between the administration and the government. The new, looser link between state and social interests and the state's reduced involvement in society stimulated new aspirations on the part of public authorities to influence and shape society, and to structure it as a function of statelike collective objectives. In the context of old-age policy, the priority given to the new objective of integrating the elderly population through action on both its general living conditions and the individual's way of life was a direct expression of this new situation. The state turned its autonomous capacity for action to good account in an attempt to tackle the central issue of the old-age policy, and at the same time redefine its own role in the management of relations between old age and society.

In fact, by turning itself into the promoter of a policy for integrating the elderly, the state sought to change its approach to society and thereby reestablish a hold over it. The state also built new direct routes of social intervention; at the same time, it retreated from the arena of protection and control, where it had been hemmed in by both action on welfare and macroeconomic intervention and where it had been pinned by pension issues. Instead, the state undertook activities that were societal in outlook; it also intervened directly in the arena of values and norms with a view to defining a new social status of old age that later formed the core of its new political doctrine. By reformulating the central issue of the old-age policy as a means of integrating the elderly through their way of life, the state was not simply creating an arena for new and more immediate interventions in society; it was also engaging in a strategy for off-loading the traditional representative structures that linked it to society. In particular, and on its own initiative, it bypassed the bureaucratic/corporatist links that were the only channels of representation on relations between old age and society: one of these was related to retirement and involved the "social partners" and the social security administration, while the other focused on public-assistance policy, which brought together networks of "notables" (political personalities) and the social administration. This expansion of the state's autonomous capacity for action was illustrated by the way it sought to distance itself from society—by sidestepping traditional intermediary organizations that were too closely linked to a rigidified, clientelist system of representation, and that had been rejected by the Gaullist state. Instead, it embraced new, energetic forces and furnished them with a new principle for aggregating their interests around the statelike objectives that it now sought to impose.

In this way, the state made itself the driving force behind civil society. The aim was to encourage the setting up of new mediators between the administrative system and society, and it proposed to use them as a basis for resuscitating public action in favor of the elderly. This book has already examined the complex two-way movements that led to the meeting of the Laroque Commission's technocratic project and peripheral innovators; this dynamic survived until it was implemented under the Sixth Plan. This book has also commented on the fact that throughout the period, the new social agents were consulted about, and involved in, the definition of orientations and the setting up of means through committees and meetings. This new approach to public action signaled the emergence of a new form of administrative regulation: the state no longer solely intervened through rules and the law, or through macroeconomic regulation, but by influencing, consulting, and mobilizing the decision makers. There was further evidence for this in the importance accorded to planning in the introduction of the way-of-life policy, as shown by the choice of the "sectoral contract" formula for local implementation. However, this approach was not specific to the old-age policy. It extended to all public authority interventions during the period, and the example of concerted planning, possibly the most explicit intervention, highlighted how widespread this new form of regulation had become. Passing power to a method of public management of old age controlled by action on the way of life may be seen as a consequence of the state becoming less involved in society. In fact, the state actively used this type of action in an attempt to reform its linkage to society fundamentally; the corollary was the setting up of specific administrative procedures designed to mobilize a new network of allies and mediators. In the framework of the old-age policy, a new pattern of exchanges was established between the administration and the environment. This structure was no longer based either on relations between the state and discordant class links, or between the administration and traditional networks of "notables." It was founded on the identification of new intermediary agents, such as elected, professional people who both gave support to the public project and fertilized it with new demands formulated by society. It functioned according to a mutual movement of legitimation. By formulating a project to integrate the elderly, the state became the promoter of a new social status for older people. Old age was recognized as a special experience that could not be allowed to deteriorate into poverty or marginality, and enabled the elderly as members of the "third age" to enjoy a full social life by conferring upon them new rights to social integration. Creation of the new social status was therefore a measure that was first and foremost political, and was located in the dialectic of representation and representativeness; in return, the state could expect its representative capacity and legitimacy to increase. The involvement of the new social networks that the state helped to identify, mobilize, and unify was one of the first ways in which it and its actions were legitimated. At the same time, in their alliance with the administration's modernizers, the new mediators found support for their struggle over their representative position locally and even nationally, and drew their legitimacy from the fact that they now worked closely with the administration.

The organization of a public old-age policy into two contradictory issues during the last period reflected a move towards a new kind of linkage between social interests and the state. The state's autonomy declined with the end of the Gaullist period and the rise of the Giscardian republic; meanwhile, the great ambition that the state would reshape society, which had galvanized social planning during the Gaullist period, gradually lost impetus, and with it went the project of a global old-age policy founded on a way-of-life policy. The latter now lost all of its dynamism and simply wasted away, ending up as little more than a few measures designed to enable the elderly to continue living in their own homes. However, it found a new lease of life under the Seventh Plan after slowly gathering support in society and within the administration, and forming an additional "bureaucratic" ring. No attempts were made to extend or correct its dysfunctions, and this identical prolongation under PAP 15 marked the decline of a vast public project. Those involved confined themselves to continuing with the least expensive actions, and no work was done on plugging gaps in the intervention network, despite the fact that this was the only type of measure that could effectively enable older people to stay on in their homes,[3] let alone keep them socially integrated.[4] The management approach prevailed over any ideas about integration. An earlier section has shown that the impact of the policy to enable the elderly to carry on living in their own homes had been largely symbolic. However, it had provided support for a new, positive, and activist image of old age (the diffusion of which was now more essential than ever before), and it did so at a time when the new unemployment policy for older workers, which was developing in tandem, was given the euphemistic title of "voluntary retirement."

The collapse of the high-profile public ambition to keep the elderly socially integrated through a series of coordinated actions around the way-of-life issue led to the abandonment of an earlier government plan to promote an employment policy for older workers; this had aimed to prepare earlier in the life course the conditions in which the elderly could enjoy good social integration. The state refrained from calling a halt to the employers' policy of freeing up the aging labor force; indeed, it even agreed that this policy should be followed up in union-employer agreements, despite the fact that the policy ran counter to its initial plans. Moreover, it was accepted that steps should be taken towards developing an economically neoliberal and less interventionist state—one that handed a larger share of economic power over to companies whose aspirations the state would, in a general way, support and complement. In the debate on old age, this greater latitude enjoyed by companies gave more clout to those with economic power, and their aim, as has been shown, was to subordinate action on old age to any demands that the labor market might make. It follows that more importance was accorded generally to the issue of employment in all old-age policies. This new trend in the organization of relations between old age and society was no longer concerned with promoting an integrated way of life, but instead sought to ensure that the elderly had as favorable an effect as possible on the system of production and the job market. The impact of this trend spread as the economic crisis deepened. In the new climate, social preoccupations that had previously been significant in the matter of reintegrating *exclus* (people on the social margins), and founding a "new society," no longer figured on the agenda. The emphasis now shifted to questions of economic management, and more attention was consequently paid to interests propounded by employers as organizers of production. In these circumstances, employers found it much easier to ensure that the old-age policy was reduced to an older workers' employment policy that obeyed the needs of the production system: in the period under examination, this meant companies shedding older employees in a flexible and controlled manner.

Employers' opinions had particular influence on society and the state at this time, because the circumstances of the economic crisis simplified the issues over which unions and employers were at odds. The unions gave increasing priority to defending jobs, while the campaign against alienation, including the demand for a lowering of retirement age, was downgraded to one of secondary importance. This produced a degree of consensus between the unions and the employers for developing an unemployment policy for older workers: indeed, neither the agents representing class interests nor the public authorities any longer impeded the rapid progress that this policy was making. An earlier section has shown that it was making spectacular advances. Early-exit packages for older workers continued to proliferate, and older workers' right to work was crushed; meanwhile, employment measures reflected the precarious nature of the pension plans that had been provided for an entire age group declared to be socially unproductive. The result was that the public old-age policy collapsed. The employment policy then in force led to massive numbers of older workers being laid off, marginalized, and made reliant on public funds at an ever-earlier stage in their lives. Moreover, the policy contradicted and even rendered superfluous the action carried out on behalf of the elderly against segregation and for better integration. Indeed, the spectacular revival of the issue of employment in the public management of old age showed how much the state's relationship with society had changed. The state gradually abandoned hope of systematically achieving the economic and social interventions and planning that had characterized the Gaullist period, and instead adopted an economically neoliberal position; it gave substance to this by allowing companies much greater freedom to develop policy, and it acquiesced in their ideas. Arising out of this position, and because of constraints linked to the economic crisis, the state also became more open to employers' interests. For instance, the public authorities first approved, and later even encouraged, new employment measures for older workers that conformed in every way to employers' wishes. Their requirement was to shed staff in a controlled manner, and this had to be based on conjunctural measures that had been negotiated as part of a collective agreement and could be reviewed and modified in line with production imperatives. Public old-age policy thereafter developed in a contradictory manner. What it achieved in the employment field destroyed what it wanted as far as way of life was concerned, and this action on employment effectively stymied any effort to define the social status of old age except by reference to the labor market and its demands. Whereas the way-of-life policy had enabled members of the "third age" to enjoy social integration and had given them a new form of citizenship, the employment policy now stripped them of their entire identity and, by rationing their right to work, effectively cast them out of society. This conversion to an "economy manager" state, which concerned itself with the unemployment policy of older workers, also called into question the two-way principle of legitimation whereby the "driving force of civil society" state of the previous period had been able to broaden its ability to represent. Cracks were beginning to appear, demonstrating how the old-age policy was heading for a profound crisis.

The carefully directed attempt to analyze the social determinants of public action on old age led at once to an initial, empirically based regularity. Any variation in the structure of public interventions on old age appeared to be complemented by a coherent and concomitant variation in the nature of relations binding social forces and state organization.

The directions that state action took on relations between old age and society seemed to be a function of specific forms of linkage between the state and civil society. Therefore, depending on how much the state involved itself in society, and on the type of coalescing that took place between society and the various expressions of social interests, the method of state management of old age gave priority either to pensions, or to action on the way of life, or to action on employment. Otherwise it continued to develop in response to contradictory interventions. From a methodological standpoint, such a scenario opens up a series of more systematic propositions relating to the general dynamic of state action in the field of old age. The propositions themselves are arranged according to two fundamental dimensions that distinguish between the state and social relations, so that their forms of interpenetration can be disclosed.

The aim of this approach is to circumscribe certain periods when the state carried out actions concerning old-age policy. First, there were occasions when the state functioned as an institution that expressed current social relations and introduced into the decision-making process the various elements of a society's dynamic. Second, there were times when it managed to extract itself from the control of society and the social forces dominating it; the aim here was to develop a capacity for action on society as a function of appropriate collective objectives. Research shows that when the state had little autonomy in terms of social relations, it kowtowed to those social forces that dominated society and were able to ensure that their interests prevailed within the state. In this way, when the working class dominated society and penetrated deep into the state through labor union and political representation, the state adopted a high profile in introducing a pension policy. In other words, it intervened in the economic sphere in order to reinforce its role as redistributor of revenue.

Against that, when captains of industry recaptured their dominant roles in society, and when the circumstances of the crisis supported the view that their interests should be taken into account, public intervention in the field of old age attached more importance to an employment policy for older workers and, as this book has demonstrated, directly subjected action on old age to the imperatives of the production system. Here the state continued to intervene in the economic arena; however, it no longer emphasized its role as redistributor and promoter of consumption, but rather its role as mobilizer of revenue and its work in support of the production system. It also promoted a policy of freeing up the conditions in which older members of the labor force were managed.

It follows that the more the state found itself deprived of its autonomy with regard to society, the more prominence it gave to its economic functions; it then intervened on the dialectical issue that dealt with the production/redistribution of revenue, and favored one or the other of these poles, depending on the nature of the social interests that had acquired influence.

The more the state could aspire to a certain autonomy of action, the more likely it was that it would promote its political functions and intervene directly in relations between older citizens and the state in the hope of organizing them afresh. This book has demonstrated how the fundamental aim of action on the way of life of the elderly was to create an arena in which relations between older people and the state could be regulated. In terms of old age, therefore, the state's autonomy was expressed by giving priority to action on the way-of-life issue. We have seen how this intervention gave the state direct access to the elderly, over and above its economic role as regulator of production and redistributor of consumer goods. More than anything else, it established new relations between older citizens and the state. Here the state abandoned the economic plane of actions supporting production and the arenas of redistribution and associated interests.

Instead, it intervened at a societal level and represented its own interests as a political-administrative apparatus seeking above all to develop its representative capacity and legitimacy; the purpose was to maintain and defend its relative autonomy vis-à-vis society. This autonomy was under permanent threat and was always characterized by tension between the importance of social interests and the state's organizational work in formulating its own aims. As far as promoting a policy of an integrated way of life was concerned, the limits to the state's capacity for autonomy had been established; in fact, a condition of the development of this policy was the successful emergence of new social networks that supported public action but did not modify this action to suit the interests they represented.

By way of conclusion, the results of an empirical study of the orientations of public intervention in the field of old age over nearly forty years, and the extent to which they did or did not tally with the orientations of particular social forces, prompt a number of theoretical comments about the state and about the social determinants of public policies. What this research suggests is that there is no such thing as an essence of the state, in the sense that action by the state might be interpreted either as the pure, autonomous dynamic of an administrative apparatus or as the expression of a form of social domination. On one hand, public action has not been seen as monolithic; on the contrary, it has appeared pluralistic, and even contradictory, thereby advancing the case of multiple causality. On the other hand, the state's main interventions in the field of old age have at different times alternately reflected the interests of labor (retirement in 1945), the interests of those who wield economic power (preretirement policies), and even the capacity for autonomous action of a state apparatus and its technocracy (the policy of integrating the elderly through way of life). The foregoing observations pose serious questions about analyses of social policy that reduce policies to little more than a reflection of class struggle and the expression of a form of domination of, or resistance to, that struggle. It is not the sole function of public interventions to establish or reestablish the economic, political, and ideological conditions for domination by capital, or to be the "crutch" of capital.[5] The state cannot be seen as a docile instrument that serves the interests of monopolistic groups. In other words, the arena of the state cannot be totally dissolved in the arena of social relations. It has been pointed out that the state could, in certain circumstances, avoid social determinism and instead act on the basis of objectives more appropriate to a state. However, just as social policies do not totally or directly express the arena of social relations, so their significance should not be reduced to the operational mechanisms of a bureaucratic apparatus. This is also true of a bureaucratic apparatus. One cannot explain social policies through the management methods of the bureaucratic system such as the alliances and internal conflicts of competence among ministry departments and between central and peripheral administrations, and by the client relations binding the administration and its environment. Attention has been drawn to the joint presence of these two dimensions in state action, that is to say, in action that can never be identified with either of these poles. Public interventions reflect the way in which the arena of the state and the arena of social relations are linked in a situation of perpetual tension and change. Everything about the kind of state action in the field of old age that this book has examined accords with Alain Touraine's views on the subject: "The State is not above society. Nor is it a simple tool for unifying social practice in the service of the ruling class. The State is the arena and agent for communication between levels of social reality, it is permanently located within a form of social domination, and it never gets confused with it."[6] Such a viewpoint emphasizes the shifting and complex nature of the relations that permanently bind state and society.

Research has called into question the analysis that sees state/society relations in terms of disjunction and exteriority, and to which the only alternative is autonomy/fusion. On the contrary, it is necessary to think of them in terms of constant interpenetration, because orientations of public policies are a function of the mediation systems that enable social interests to retain a hold over the state. This research has clearly shown that, even when the organization of the state enjoys sufficient autonomy from society to have influence over it, the state can only implement a policy of social integration of the elderly through way of life (and a policy that conforms with the interests of the state apparatus) on the basis of mediating social support that it is able to find in society. Therefore, even when the state's hold over social forces is weak, its interventions need to be clarified by new forms of linkage between the administrative system and its social environment.

These observations must surely provide a more accurate definition of the notion of the state's relative autonomy, given that the definition still found in sociology literature is often vague. More generally, one may ask if the research strategy adopted in this book—a patient, long-term study of the accords and disjunctions between public action on old age and the orientations of each of the social forces—might, if replicated in a number of areas of investigation, be used to examine effectively the question of the state and its dependence on, or margin of autonomy from, French society.

Two Systems of Action that Form the Basis of the Old-Age Policy

The sociohistorical analysis of the formation of old-age policies that has been developed throughout this book demonstrates that the forms of interpenetration between state and society that have prevailed in this field can be broadly characterized by opposing two systems of action that are distinct and based on two differentiated forms of aggregation between state and society.

This book has produced two radically different matrices of policies for old age. The first presents the main protagonists of industrial society. The system of action is organized around the confrontational and complex nature of the disputes, negotiations, and agreements that take place between the organized interests of the two main oppositional forces in our society—the producers and the organizers of production. Each of these parties has been seen to have a competing definition of the old-age policy and of the issues involved in it, and the definition has been linked to the interests and rationality that the party in question wanted to promote. On one hand, employers as organizers of production were continuously trying to define the actions governing relations between old age and society, and ensuring that they conformed to the imperatives of the production system. Their main objective was to subordinate interventions on old age to the exigencies of labor-force management appropriate to each conjuncture (e.g., a flexible or fixed labor force, control of labor-force movements and quality of staff). In such circumstances, the old-age policy was circumscribed by the limitations of an employment policy. The definition of the old-age policy supported by the labor-union movement was a pension policy that constructed and expanded workers' social right both to retirement and to an escape from alienation during the final stage of their lives; the unions hoped to achieve this through a system of social protection incorporating earnings replacement. This book has described their ongoing and exclusive struggles on this question, and in this context the state acted as arbiter. The state also set out the social agreements between the opposing forces, and these reflected the extent to which the state was involved in society and the greater or lesser extent to which it was open to influence from either of the agents representing social classes.[7] What emerged from this social dynamic were pensions and employment policies: here the state intervened essentially as a regulator, and depending on the dimension relating to the dialectic of redistribution/production, it mainly concentrated on the economic issue.

The second system of action, which was the basis of the formation of way-of-life policies for the elderly, was a different matter altogether. The traditional forces of industrial society were no longer central. Instead, the system was organized around alliances and tensions that united or opposed certain administrative departments and mediating agents, and these in turn functioned as intermediaries between society and the state. They included municipal representatives, complementary pension institutions, professional groups specializing in social and medical questions, and private-sector associations working in social matters. Here we have a scenario in which state/society interpenetrations were no longer expressed in terms of class interests, but in terms of relations between the administration and "notables." The word "notable" is here used in the sense defined by Pierre Grémion, that is to say, agents defined less by their social status than by their skills as specialist representatives negotiating with the state. The dynamic of this issue of the old-age policy was no longer located in the antagonism between agents representing social class, but in the dialectic of relations between the administration and society. This dynamic was shaped by the revival of groups that stood at the point where society and the administrative system met, and that simultaneously played the roles of social "intercessors" (enabling their constituents to lead full social lives through their actions) and of supporters of administrative action. In fact, the way-of-life policy turned into action on integration only because new mediators succeeded in replacing others that had occupied positions of power in the framework of welfare policy. The intermediary organizations, which served to disseminate traditional social assistance policies, included BAS (*bureaux d'aide sociale*—welfare agencies), social security organizations, charitable bodies, and *département*-level offices dealing with health and social matters. However, their legitimacy was destabilized by the new directions for public action drawn up by the Laroque Committee. At the same time, peripheral innovators combined to produce a new form of peri-bureaucratic support, and they slowly began to speak for the modernizing coalition that was developing simultaneously in the state.

Within the context of this system of action, the state prioritized its political, rather than its economic, function and intervened initially within the dialectic of relations of representation/representativeness. This book has already pointed out how, when the state enjoyed autonomy of action, it played an active part in the redefinition of the mediating groups that anchored it in society. The state then became both the detector and the driving force behind its future systems of dissemination.

By way of conclusion to this short study of the relations enjoyed by the state, old age, and society, the question arises of the extent to which the comments formulated above may be applied more widely. Has this reconstruction of the methods of public management of old age and their social determinants helped to uncover more general philosophies of state action in the field of social welfare? The answer appears to be in the affirmative. The successive images of the state that have been highlighted in this book reflect other studies in social policy. Everything suggests three successive images of the social state in its relations with modern French society. The first image is that of the protector state of the immediate postwar period, which was closely linked to class relations and boasted a vast redistribution machinery. This is followed in the 1960s by the second image of a state as the driving force of civil society; it also promoted new social interventions that it sought to present as comprehensive actions, and gave itself the task of integrating the individuals concerned through action on facilities and their framework and way of life. These new social orientations, which were often referred to as "social planning," began to be implemented in rather the same way as old age had been dealt with. First, committees of experts set up by the state put forth their ideas in weighty reports: apart from the Laroque Report, there was the Bloch Lainé Report on the Handicapped (1967) and the Dupont-Fauville Report on Childhood and Families in Need (1971); the Bianco-Lamy Report, which was published later, also dealt with childhood. Later this work of dissemination was taken over by Commissariat du Plan committees that had played a vital role in setting them up in the first place. These projects developed in the context of a state that aspired to autonomy and that, in social and other matters, tried to develop more direct action on society above and beyond traditional forms of political and social mediation and also outside the well-established channels of public intervention. In practice, they represented attempts to reform a welfare state whose centralized and rigid regulation had proved completely unyielding to new demands that had arisen out of the new tensions, which had in turn been brought about by economic growth. This led to new exclusions and new fractures that could be dealt with through a reorientation of social action.[8] As this book has shown, the state subsequently undertook this reorientation by mobilizing the decision makers. Some writers have even described this new public strategy as *marketing de la loi* (marketing of the law) and, by analogy with the niche identification in the definition and launching process of a new commercial product.[9] This mobilizing of society was part of a major shift in ideas that was taking place at the time; it aimed at a rethinking of relations between the state and society, arguing that representative systems should be modernized and the idea of active citizenship relaunched. The new ideas attracted widespread attention, especially from the Jean Moulin Club. The validity of the image of the state as a driving force clearly went way beyond the boundaries of social policy, as it was described in similar terms in books by contemporary writers studying decentralization policies (Pierre Grémion) and planning (Lucien Nizard). These works all agreed on this image of the mobilizing state, and as this book has established using different formulations, they also believed that it was a failure as far as the way-of-life policy was concerned.

The third representation of the state in the field of social policy is often represented as that of the "manager State,"[10] which accompanied the return of economic neoliberalism and strongly characterized the period 1975–81. The philosophy of rationalizing and linking actions overturned the policy of social integration. This new action model was the expression of a new form of fusion between state and society whereby the state was more directly linked to society's economic activities. The needs of the production system became the imperatives of social policy; meanwhile, social welfare vanished under the weight of economic demands and lost its autonomy. As for the elderly, the fight against unemployment took priority over attempts to integrate them socially, and the right to retirement was once more a tool used in regulating employment. Increased flexibility was introduced to assist companies and make ways of leaving employment more rigid; this simultaneously undermined old-age policy and propelled it into a state of crisis.

The Crisis in Policies for Old Age

Throughout this book, emphasis has been placed on the contradictory nature of public actions in support of the elderly, and attention drawn to the emergence of a crisis in the policies affecting them. This has been interpreted as the beginning of a critical phase in the system of managing relations between old age and society. The new phase was caused by the incompatibility of decisions that both called into question whether this system should remain in force and ran the risk of bringing about its collapse. This is an appropriate moment to take a closer look at the dimensions of this crisis and to provide an interpretation. This will make it possible to outline a circular process whereby the aforementioned mechanisms for producing public decisions have affected relations between old age and society, causing a readjustment in the social relations and issues that form the basis of public interventions.

Any attempt to make sense of the crisis affecting old-age policies is a major intellectual undertaking in the sense that it might throw light on the (currently inescapable) debate on the crisis in the welfare state. In practice, the welfare state is largely a "welfare-for-the-elderly state." It should not be forgotten, either, that pensions are not just the main component of social expenditure in industrialized countries;[11] they also progressed structurally farther than any other benefit between 1960 and 1980.[12] It follows that expenditure on old age is a highly sensitive aspect of the crisis in the welfare state. It is decisive, too, not only for an understanding of current difficulties and their origins, but also for an appreciation of future prospects. The pace at which this expenditure has grown of its own accord is partly linked to long-term commitments already included in this expenditure, but it is particularly disquieting because both demographic and economic changes will, in time, accelerate this development.

Generally speaking, the difficulties faced by our system of social protection are usually perceived in terms of the financial impasse in which social protection finds itself. This impasse has been associated with the following developments: first, the accelerated growth that social expenditure underwent after the late 1950s was possible because of massive economic growth, and even provided a stimulus for this economic growth; second, from the late 1970s onward, a major slowdown in the rate of economic growth underlined, and made more visible, the break between movements in GDP and social expenditure;[13] third, social expenditure continued to rise, and even accelerated, mainly as a result of the social effects of the crisis (i.e., unemployment), and this came about at a time when the rate of growth was falling; and finally, compulsory contributions went up from 35.6 percent in 1970 to 42.6 percent in 1980, and in 1985 climbed as high as 45 percent because only social contributions rose, while the proportion of taxes remained stable.

Although it is very difficult to advance hypotheses about the tolerance threshold at which the level of these contributions can be fixed, most observers believed that one way or another, France had reached a point beyond which the country was in danger of running into serious trouble. Therefore, although economic and social progress had been able to develop in close harmony, their respective objectives now seemed to be coming into conflict. Furthermore, economic facts were forcing a reexamination of social policies; indeed, the cost of these policies could not continue to rise at the same rate without causing serious financial instability of a type that could threaten the very existence of all systems of protection and disrupt the entire national economy. Depending on how optimistic or pessimistic the prognoses were, there was likely to be a fallback on the distributor state, followed by either a slimming down of social welfare or the surreptitious encroachment of rampant social statism.

The analysis of the crisis in the old-age policy set out below will not take sides directly in the political debate, but information contained in the analysis may be able to throw light on it.

The most widely disseminated analysis mainly examines the financial limitations to the survival of the systems of social protection. However, this author takes the view that the upheaval in the system of management of old age was much more serious and profound: leaving financial considerations to one side, the very political and sociocultural base was itself beginning to crumble. The collapse of social welfare, as far as old age was concerned, was not simply an arithmetical calculation of the declining ratio between older employed and unemployed people, or a development brought about by a major slowdown in growth and a rise in unemployment. It was also associated with a kind of interference in the relationship between old age and society, caused by the contradictory nature of all the measures adopted; these measures sowed doubts about the aims of pensions, which had hitherto been synonymous with social progress, and deprived aging of all meaning. Old age was now seen less as a specific experience than as something that characterized a superfluous section of the labor force.

The Financial Crisis in the Redistributive State

Demographic danger: demographic development and the cost of financing action on old age. The cost of financing action on old age more than doubled between the mid-1960s and the mid-1970s, moving from 5 percent to 10 percent of the GDP between 1960 and 1980; in 1985 it rose to 11.5 percent of the GDP.

This rapid development was not unique to France; it affected all industrialized countries. With 10 percent of the GDP devoted to expenditure on old age, France's position was average for European countries as a whole.

The rise in expenditure on old age in the period 1965–85 is usually seen as the result of population aging and improvements to social benefits for the elderly. Public opinion also expressed particular anxiety about the steadily increasing cost borne by people still at work and caused by the increase in the proportion of older people,[14] and people were aware that demographic prognoses suggested that this trend would continue.[15] The level of protection for the elderly set in the mid-1980s was not considered excessive by most social parties. The real question was "Will it survive?" because the transfers of resources to older members of the population was absorbing an ever-increasing share of the GDP, and was therefore in keen competition with other social transfers and the income of employed people. Over half the expenditure on old age went for pensions, but spending on social action came to scarcely more than 4 percent of the total: the debate on the solvency of pension systems was a paradigm of one financial aspect of the crisis in old-age policies.

The arguments used in this debate are set out below, with a view to underlining the shortcomings of a strictly demographic interpretation of the crisis facing policies for old age.[16]

The much asked question "Who will pay for our pensions?" was an anxious expression of public concern about the decline in the funding arrangements of pension systems. The chronic and growing deficits that these plans had incurred gave grounds for fears that they could actually implode.[17]

In pay-as-you-go plans like the French pension system, solvency is a simple arithmetical ratio of contributors to pensioners: when population aging causes the number of aging unemployed workers to rise,[18] the balance of this ratio is disturbed.

The contributor-per-beneficiary ratio subsequently deteriorated in all the main pension plans. For instance, whereas the general scheme had 3.6 contributors for every pension in 1973, this ratio had dropped to 2.5:1 by 1981. In only eight years, the fall in the contributor:beneficiary coefficient was proportionately over four times greater than it had been during the previous seventeen years.[19]

In financial terms, France was therefore entering a critical phase as far as pension plans were concerned. Moreover, the problems were to increase enormously in the long term because of relentless population aging in France, although this prognosis was unreliable in some respects, as it was based on changes in fertility and mortality rates and on external migrations. The (60+ age group):(20–59 age group)[20] ratio will rise by almost 50 percent between 1980 and 2020, assuming constant fertility and mortality rates. Therefore, during those forty years, France will have to choose between the following alternatives, assuming a constant retirement age: "Either almost double the contribution rate to maintain the current level of benefits, or reduce pensions by almost half if contributions are frozen."[21]

Faced with such a dilemma, it is scarcely surprising that contributors were becoming anxious about the future effectiveness of the ever-increasing deductions being taken from their pay envelopes and handed over to pensioners; they were also beginning to wonder exactly how long the younger generations would agree to make contributions for pensioners such as they themselves would eventually become. People of pensionable age shied away from a root-and-branch reexamination of pensions systems: for one thing, given the eroding right of older people to have jobs, pensions represented their main source of income; for another, because of their antiredistributive effect,[22] pension plans already maintained a large number of people on the margin of minimum income.

As far as increased expenditure on pensions was concerned, the long-term impact of population aging also led to an increase in general expenditure on social protection. In fact, the ratio of older to younger unemployed people caused further increases in social expenditure because, as figures showed, there was three times more social expenditure on the former than on the latter. It should be said that before the problem of pensions becomes even more acute, France will have to confront the question of the financial burden represented by the arrival of frailer elderly people of the "fourth age" (older than the "third age" group), and by the necessary changes in the health and social systems that that will bring about. The number of people aged eighty-five and over will double between the mid-1980s and the year 2000.

A rise in the proportion of older people in the population has often been felt to be a factor in the decline of a country's dynamic creativeness, the reason being the numerous repercussions that it is said to have on economic and social life. However, this is not always the case: for example, Japan has undergone extremely rapid population aging during the second half of the twentieth century, yet has demonstrated that high levels of competitiveness and employment can be compatible with a pronounced demographic shift of this type, as long as appropriate policies, particularly related to employment and continuous training, are set in place.

However alarming these indications may be, it is important to establish how relatively important the impact of the demographic factor is on increases in expenditure on the elderly.

Both retrospective and prospective studies have established that demography is not the main factor in raising expenditure on old age. They show that this factor is still small compared with the decisive role played by changes in legislation and by economic shifts. There are two kinds of economic development. First, pressure on employment leads partly to an increase in the number of aging unemployed people, and this number rises much more quickly than the figure for older people as a whole; this pressure also brings about a reduction in the participation rate of people of working age (i.e., the contributors). The workers (i.e., contributors):older nonworking people (i.e., beneficiaries) ratio is therefore declining much more quickly than the adults:elderly ratio. Second, the slowdown in growth makes it more difficult to support an increase in the cost of funding benefits for the elderly, as this is placed in direct competition with maintaining or increasing the pay of employed workers.

This book has demonstrated that increases in the cost of pensions between 1962 and 1973 (+172 percent) were attributable less to population aging (the percentage of the population aged sixty-five and over rose from 11.8 percent to 14 percent, and anyway, population aging was compensated for by an expansion in women's employment) than to improvements in the cover provided by pension plans.[23] Forecasts showed that population aging alone would only have a limited impact on long-term increases in expenditure on the elderly.

It was estimated that expenditure on old age would rise perceptibly, but in moderation, as a result of population aging; the reason was that, other things being equal, the funding of action on old age as a proportion of GDP will go up by only two points between 1980 and 2020 (10 percent to 12 percent).[24] On the other hand, projections based on current hypotheses, and involving different parameters linked to economic development (e.g., participation rates and the level of improvements to pensions), suggest for the year 2020 a margin of 13.8 to 17.1 percent of the GDP for expenditure on old age.[25]

The economic crisis and unemployment have compromised everything. The impact of the economic crisis on the stability of pension plans is clear from a comparison between the periods 1960–73 and 1974–82.

The ratio between older employed and unemployed workers rose by 20 percent in nine years, that is to say twice as quickly as in 1960–73, when the annual rate of increase remained below 1 percent. However, the period 1974–82 was marked by a reverse in this demographic trend with the arrival of the small birth cohorts of 1915–19. Then, the cost of funding, which ought to have come down because of demographic factors, actually went up because of a reduction in the number of employed people of all ages. It is important to bear in mind that the impact on social expenditure of any downward variation in participation rates is doubled, because it leads simultaneously to the creation of a claimant and the disappearance of a contributor. The worsening during the mid-1980s of the active-per-inactive aging worker ratio, which underpins the stability of pension plans, could no longer be attributed to demographic movements; it was mainly caused by increased unemployment.

However, the effects of the economic situation on the financial crisis that occurred in the 1980s and in later years, and that affected policies for old age, went far beyond what emerged from a statistical analysis of the decline in the contributor:pension ratio. What happened was that underemployment, linked to economic difficulties, ran unemployment and retirement together, and this had serious consequences for expenditure on the elderly. The pension system was made to contribute to the fight against unemployment, and as the following paragraphs show, unemployment insurance was simultaneously hijacked and turned into old-age insurance. It follows that there was now much more scope for crisis in policies for old age: indeed, old-age policy already extended to the system for compensating unemployment and was beginning to affect the whole of social expenditure.

This chapter has shown how underemployment stimulated the emergence of a growing consensus among the social agents on wide-ranging policies for encouraging older workers to retire. As a result, retirement age fell on average by over five years in the space of a decade. Unemployment insurance had to take over responsibility for people who, although theoretically of working age, were unemployed because of this change. When retirement age was lowered in 1982, old-age insurance had to cover the cost of measures that encouraged workers to retire; until then, most of this cost had fallen on unemployment insurance. Increased underemployment, which led to a rapid extension of this formula, together with a return to a normal demographic conjuncture following the arrival of the small birth cohorts of 1915–19,[26] soon transformed unemployment insurance into a substitute for old-age insurance.

In 1984, over half of the funds in the unemployment compensation scheme were given over to providing benefits for the "definitively unemployed."[27] Spending of this sort, used to encourage workers to retire, rose very rapidly, and after 1973 it rose more quickly than expenditure on compensation for total unemployment.[28] In 1977 it represented only a small proportion of UNEDIC expenditure (2.5 billion francs); in 1982, however, compensation for preretirees and beneficiaries aged fifty-five to fifty-nine already accounted for almost 45 percent of UNEDIC's entire spending (34 billion francs out of 74 billion);[29] it reached 50 percent of total expenditure (48 billion francs out of 95 billion) in 1983.

This redirecting of unemployment compensation toward members of the population without jobs was partly responsible for UNEDIC's financial difficulties. The unemployment insurance system had been designed to pay out benefits for quite short periods of time (under six months on average); it now found itself responsible for a growing number of the "definitively unemployed" who qualified for particularly expensive benefits over long periods (up to ten years).[30]

Opportunities for early exit were now restricted, as only FNE special allowances were available, and they were worth much less than before—as were benefits compensating long-term, unemployed older workers. Irrespective of how the preretirement formula developed subsequently, the share given over to early exit was going to remain substantial in the future because of delays in expenditure linked to long-term underlying commitments.[31]

The preretirement policy in force substantially, and over a long period of time, accentuated the financial crisis that faced a state intent on redistributing in favor of the elderly. However, this fundamental factor in the increased funding of the elderly in French society was in no way the mechanical and unavoidable product of population aging or of a slowdown in growth. It flowed from a very precise political orientation, against a backdrop of economic arguments that forced a redefinition of the distribution of employment, leading to a form of redistribution based solely on the criterion of age. In so doing, it simultaneously undermined the right to work after the age of fifty-five, thereby seriously destabilizing the ratio between older employed and unemployed people. With the passing of time, it is by no means certain that employed people will agree to continue to pay for this distribution of social contributions which, when combined with the rising cost of pensions, can only exacerbate competition for distributed resources.[32] The financial impasse for which pensions were heading was quite easy to calculate, but it was much more difficult to appreciate the total economic impact of measures that had been designed to encourage workers to retire. This was particularly true of their effect on employment, which appeared to have met expectations.[33] In the future, some will find this financial charge intolerable, as they will be getting nothing in return.

A crisis in the economy or in the old-age policy? In the light of the above examination of the factors that had contributed, and continued to contribute, to an unprecedented increase in expenditure on the elderly, there is a temptation to conclude that the financial crisis, of which this expenditure itself formed part, was mainly due to a slowdown in economic growth and to the employment policies it had encouraged. Furthermore, the role of the demographic factor was more limited and had an effect only in the long term. It might therefore have been tempting to say that there was no real crisis in the policies for old age, but only in the economic environment of which they were part, and that policies for old age were in crisis only because retirement had been turned into a device for solving the unemployment problem.

By removing an increasing proportion of older workers from the labor market, the number of aging unemployed had been unnecessarily increased, and this seriously disturbed the stable ratio between the older employed and unemployed, a phenomenon that was itself likely to go into decline simply as a result of demographic changes. The result was an excessive charge on employed people that could only increase and lead to a financial impasse for benefit systems designed for older workers.

Inevitably, there would be less security in old age at the end of this chain unless growth picked up; eventually a healthier labor market would have to make compulsory contributions for the aging unemployed more acceptable, and make it possible for fifty-five- to fifty-nine-year-olds to remain on the labor market.

This line of argument makes development of the economy the prime determining factor in questions then being asked about the organization of benefits for the elderly, and takes a hardheaded look at the crisis in the distributor state.

Research shows that the end of growth has played the role not so much of prime determinant as that of a factor that has shown up dysfunctions in the system of social protection. If that is true, the financial impasse, the extent of which was outlined above, is just a symptom of a more profound social crisis destabilizing the consensus on resource transfer systems for the elderly. Furthermore, the crisis in policies for old age is not confined to problems in their demographic and economic environment; it represents a crisis in the entire method of public management of old age, in its legitimacy, and in its capacity to ensure well-being and respond to people's developing expectations. This author takes the position that it is largely because pensions have proved incapable of constructing a new perspective for old age, after the traditional aims of retirement were abandoned, that old-age policies are now seen as too expensive and in crisis. The approach presented in this book so far takes into account only the demographic and economic repercussions on the stability of the social resource transfers system, itself considered to be a pure dependent variable and invariant in itself. The next stage is an examination of how this system has changed internally, and an analysis of all the social, political, and cultural dimensions of the crisis in old-age policies.

The Social Dimensions of the Crisis in Policies for Old Age

In this section the Habermas[34] classification of trends in the crisis will be used, and three interactive aspects of the crisis in policies for old age will be analytically distinguished. At a political level, old-age policies appear to be facing a crisis of rationality, and yet another crisis of legitimation of the action that has been carried out. These crises had a tendency to invade the sociocultural system, thereby causing a further crisis in the social model of old age; in the conceptualization adopted by this study, such a phenomenon might be described as a "crisis of motivation."

CONTRADICTIONS IN PUBLIC ACTION: A CRISIS OF RATIONALITY

This book contains a full analysis of the production of public decisions on old age and of their impact. It has uncovered a host of incoherent and increasingly contradictory measures that are only distantly related to what one might call the synthetic dimension when speaking of "old-age policy." In this sense, there is no old-age policy to be found anywhere. At best there have been occasional fleeting glimpses of a somewhat optimistic ambition.

The more public interventions there were, the less they were linked together, and administrative action was marked by a lack of rationality. This book has shown that this shortcoming culminated in the development of preretirement systems. The state then committed itself to an employment policy that contradicted its way-of-life policy and perverted the purpose of the pensions system. Furthermore, it no longer managed to make the imperatives of contradictory regulations compatible; it received these from society, and consequently got involved in irrational decisions, first carrying out one action and then its opposite—promoting the social integration of the elderly, and then brutally banishing older workers from the workplace.[35] Such a statement would be a commonplace if the root cause of the breakup of these actions could be found in the malfunctioning of administrative machinery, or if the failure had taken place at the level of implementation, either because the project was beyond the capacity of administrative organization or because financial resources were insufficient to achieve these ambitions.[36] What this book has developed is not of the same order, although dysfunctions and perverse effects are undeniably produced within the administrative machine, and they create gaps between the advertised objectives and the effects of the measures that are finally adopted. This research shows that the source of the incoherence of public actions on old age lies outside the administrative apparatus, and suggests that it might originate at the very heart of the social dynamic whereby public interventions in this field are actually produced. Contradictions in the old-age policy need to be understood in the light of the innumerable systems that generate public action, and in the context of the diverse social philosophies that state action obeys.

Accordingly, the crisis in the protector state is not simply the result of the economic crisis, but is associated with the development of the protector state itself. When a form of interpenetration between social forces and state organization brings into being a specific system for protecting the elderly, the system of action that has generated it has a tendency to become quite isolated; there is then codified play between the affected social actors and the state, and this leads to a simplification of needs that are once and for all identified with the benefits being provided. Attempts to introduce administrative regulation, which would intervene in order to make the protector apparatus more open to new demands, are mostly resolved by the setting up of a new system of agents; these are different from their predecessors, and they usually add their interventions to those previously developed, but there is no real coordination or linkage of the decisions made. The decision-making system itself fragments, because each new bureaucratic/corporatist link that is constructed soon functions as an isolated system. It becomes increasingly difficult thereafter to make the various public interventions compatible, and the protector apparatus simultaneously diversifies and falls apart.[37]

This perspective may be used to reinterpret the history of the old-age policy that has been set out in this book. It will then be possible to throw light on the complicated chain of events whereby old-age policies now face not only a crisis of rationality but also one of legitimacy.

Act 1: a triumph for the retirement logic. As we have seen, actions related to retirement form part of the dynamic of class relations and their regulation by the state. They have become well established within the framework of the newly formed, modern welfare state, an institution that represents the implementation of a social agreement between opposing classes. This agreement was based on the principle that social and economic progress rely on one another—that by meeting certain social aspirations, the economic conditions for constant development can be simultaneously produced because each agent representing a social class necessarily discovers advantages in a non-zero-sum game. Through a kind of alchemy that is difficult to explain, social progress was soon entirely assimilated into the development of the welfare state, and needs were totally identified with the systems of specific benefits that it offered. The great egalitarian systems of protection against major risks (e.g., health, old age, and workplace accidents) that made up the welfare state were driven by this recognition of universal social rights, and they tended to ignore the origins and development of needs. These were simply placed in an egalitarian, unitary, top-down process, where the needs were met, and individual money transfers established a relationship between the protected individual and the protector state. Of course, there was no question that the setting up of these large institutions of social protection was anything other than essential. However, it must be accepted that it has led to the foreclosure of systems of action that once operated at the very heart of social policy. These systems of action were turned into isolated systems that had their own way of functioning but were not alive to how the environment was changing and how people's aspirations were evolving. In particular, collective-bargaining strategies became codified by the characteristics of the institutions that had been set up. The result, as the example of pensions showed, was that neither the employers nor the labor unions challenged the welfare-state system. On the contrary, their actions and counteractions took place within the framework of the new institutions; these, in turn, became a basic objective of their campaigns, with all agents trying to control them and modify the definitions of the newly instituted rights to suit their interests. An earlier section showed how labor-union struggles to improve protection for the elderly were resolved mainly by actions around pensions, seeking to lower the age of entitlement and raise the level of benefits. However, it must be conceded that the unions paid little attention to the question of way of life. A sociological examination of the administration has revealed how difficult these isolated systems found it to restructure themselves around new issues.[38] The problem of old age was given much prominence by the welfare state, and was posed in terms of replacement income. However, this essentially economic response, expressed in financial benefits, took into account only some of the aspirations contained in the call for retirement. Retirement was also, and perhaps principally, a nonmonetary matter. This book has frequently emphasized how it was linked to a desire to escape alienation. The end of one's working life marks the end of exploitation, and behind the various expectations associated with retiring lay a powerful yearning to be done with the world of work. Leaving forever the places where one has been systematically controlled, and curtailing the revenue paid to provide capitalists with their profits, should mark the beginning of a free and fairer life. Retirement is also the time when one can make up for a life that has been taken away; it is a time for recreational activities and continuous holidays, and for long-overdue self-realization; it is a time for being something other than a cipher on the payroll, or the object of exchange on a market governed by the law of supply and demand. The welfare state's response to this latent request for a change in employees' rights failed to keep pace with demand and was expressed in terms of egalitarian redistribution. This shows very clearly how in the case of the welfare state, a whole series of complex aspirations could be channeled into pressure to provide cash benefits; these benefits frequently failed to keep up with these basic needs, and this brought about increased demands, which in turn inexorably led to considerable extra spending on the part of the state. This almost mechanical self-expansion of the welfare state, whose method of intervention was basically economic and monetary, was undoubtedly one of the major factors in the crisis that it faced by the mid-1980s. The corollary of this movement was a weakening of solidarity links among individuals not qualifying for benefits from the protector state, and there were even fewer alternative ways of meeting these needs. There had been a gradual shift from societal solidarity to state solidarity, and a devolution to the state of all aspirations that could not be satisfied on the labor market. What with an omnipresent state that talked only to employers, labor unions that assumed responsibility for everything, and a society that had now disintegrated, there were no formalized systems of dissemination that were capable of giving expression to, and taking account of, the developments taking place in society.

By turning certain needs into universal rights and setting up a system of specific benefits to meet those needs, the welfare state simplified these needs, which were assimilated to the benefits offered: health needs were reduced to access to medical care, and the needs of the elderly to the availability of sufficient replacement income. There was a tendency for this system not only to express much more complex demands in money terms, but also to ignore every development associated with that demand. The consequences of this situation were twofold:

1. Given that these needs could not be met in any other way, the demands remained irrevocably attached to the welfare state's supply channels; the demands all converged on these channels, thereby causing increased social

expenditure (since the responses were essentially monetary) and an extra charge on the state.

2. In view of the discordance between developing aspirations and responses contained in social policies—the latter were in favor of a system of providing a fixed satisfaction of needs—the growth of the welfare state could not avoid attracting more dissatisfaction and less confidence in its benevolence.

Act 2: an attempt at social planning. Attempts at social planning in the 1960s may be seen as efforts to extract the welfare state from its contradictory development. As far as the elderly were concerned, these attempts found concrete form in a reorganization of the supply of facilities around two objectives: the removal of the monetary focus, and coordination. Cash benefits were complemented by benefits in the form of services and facilities that no longer aimed simply at a better standard of living, but at a transformation of the environment and way of life of the elderly. These new forms of social protection sought closer identification with the qualitative demands of the elderly (e.g., the struggle against isolation, marginalization, and the loss of autonomy), and by situating themselves between ordinary replacement income from pensions and complete institutionalization, they tried to create new ways in which needs could be met. They should also have made it possible for expenditure on social protection to be rationalized, by making sure that minor social problems of poor adaptation requiring straightforward, open solutions were not dealt with by cumbersome forms of institutionalization. This attempt at rationalizing supply also hinged on the design of a coherent old-age policy by abruptly substituting a coordinated series of interventions around the central objective of promoting an integrated way of life. The great modernizing ambition of the state to reshape the condition of old age was founded on a new global model of action and was capable of sidestepping the older population's loss of autonomy through coordinated action on income, employment, and way of life—as recommended in the Laroque Report.

However, this chapter has shown that it was in fact resolved mainly by the setting up of a new system of participants. This was situated on the margin of the system that had previously presided over pensions, and it brought together other administrative departments and peripheral innovators to promote a program of local community facilities and services for the elderly. This short-lived attempt to produce a concise old-age policy came to an end with the emergence of an additional system of action in the field of old age; a series of new interventions on way of life were added to existing interventions, although there was no way of linking them. Mechanisms for paying out replacement income and measures for providing social assistance and secure accommodation were now combined with activities designed to revive the idea of older people being able to stay on in their own homes; these aimed to limit any loss of autonomy, but were not able to attack the root causes of marginality. That would have involved intervention earlier in the life course, where the potential of individuals was established, and where research has shown that the problems of old age were built up,[39] and more broadly, action on work organization, the relations of production, and the distribution of working hours, training, and recreational activities throughout life. It should not be forgotten that in 1972, in the very early days of the way-of-life policy, the granting of guaranteed income to older workers marked a separation between actions on way-of-life and employment issues. As a result, new interventions were juxtaposed with old, and each one continued as a reflection of the social relations of which it was the expression, but the state was unable to supply evidence of any ability to coordinate and harmonize. In any examination of this attempt at social planning, it should be stated from the outset that redeploying part of the protector state into a policy of services based on social reintegration had only a limited impact on the structure of public-sector funding. The share of social action given over to expenditure on old age remained one of the smallest by comparison with all cash benefits.[40] In other words, this policy did not meet expectations or succeed in removing the money element from relations between supply and demand. Also, an assessment of the policy to enable the elderly to carry on living in their own homes demonstrates how limited the impact had been. It enabled beneficiaries to qualify for certain nonfinancial values, such as holidays, recreational activities, and some domiciliary services, which they had been unable to acquire on the open market, but it largely failed in its objective of prolonging their autonomy and independence. For the most part, it was a wide-ranging form of social assistance that had hardly ever been brought up to date, and was targeted at people who were increasingly welfare-dependent and marginalized. As a result, far from alleviating social demand, this attempt at redeploying social expenditure not only increased it but caused it to fall even more heavily on the state.

Everything was now ready for a crisis in the legitimacy of public action, the main components of which will be examined in due course. The attempt to rationalize social policies, which had been part of social planning, did not therefore lead to any extra rationality in public action; on the contrary, it opened the way for a process of delegitimation.

The final act: the philosophy underlying employment precipitates the collapse of the system of social protection. With the introduction of a wide-ranging "unemployment" policy for older workers, public actions in the field of old age were no longer simply heterogeneous and based on distinct, closed systems of action. They were now contradictory. The preretirement policy widened the gap between employed adults and those who were designated as old by the production system at an increasingly earlier stage and were now condemned to live on the resources transferred to them by the employed. Ever-increasing aging populations were being excluded from the labor market and becoming welfare-dependent, and the crisis of rationality in public actions was almost at its height. The employment policy in force not only transformed the right to retirement into an instrument for regulating employment; it also directly contradicted public integration programs that were running concurrently. It therefore led to the complete disintegration of public action on the elderly, and this action could now be seen for what it was—dismembered and in tatters. As far as employment was concerned, the new economic imperative of regulating the labor market encouraged public authorities to carry out certain actions that contradicted the objective of maintaining older people's autonomy and their social integration; the latter was at the heart of the way-of-life policy and, as this chapter has shown, it was from this that the public authorities drew much of their legitimacy. Therefore, the crisis affecting the rationality of public action immediately turned into a crisis of legitimacy. The policy to integrate the elderly through the way of life lost its credibility. It was subsequently reduced to dealing with segregation, which had already been consolidated earlier in the life course, and revealed its inability to offer second-class citizens anything more than kind words. The solution that it proposed appeared all the more derisory as the banishment of the elderly was now accentuated, and had even been brought forward as a result of other public measures.

The state was now increasingly committed to contradictory actions that highlighted an inability to reconcile its various roles and exercise its regulatory and unifying functions. This crisis in the rationality of public actions revealed two more trends in the crisis of old-age policies. First, it added to the financial problems of a welfare state anxious to pay out social-protection benefits so as to repair the damage caused by prior social-protection measures. The financial crisis of old-age policies, which has been analyzed above, was partly exacerbated by this contradictory logic in public action. Second, as this section has shown, the lack of rationality eroded confidence in the legitimacy of the system of social protection that was now up and running.

INCREASED DOUBTS ABOUT PUBLIC ACTION: THE CRISIS OF LEGITIMACY

A number of questions about the legitimacy of public actions in favor of the elderly began to surface at the same time as attempts began to be made at social planning. In practice, social planning meant that the state not only provided protection against the major risks but also took responsibility for the integration of groups under threat. The exercise of this new role led to a change in the way public action was conducted; this in turn caused more emphasis to be placed on the relationship between individuals and the state and gave the public authorities more say in the daily lives of older people. The state no longer confined itself to a remote, abstract manipulation of major economic aggregates in the framework of policy governing the transfer of social resources. Instead, it now intervened at the level of forms of local solidarity and substituted for the latter in order to ensure that older people once again managed to lead full and active lives. The introduction of a new institutional measure for keeping the elderly in their own homes had a corollary: it hastened the disappearance of what remained of local solidarity and neighborhood support and replaced volunteers with new professionals who had training in medical and social services.

From that point, public programs took over responsibility for older people's daily needs for social and other activities, and the elderly were offered the new model of active, participative behavior in addition to the network of services. As a result, there was an inexorable increase in demand for public intervention in all areas affecting the daily lives of the elderly. All expectations then focused on a state that was increasingly paying for everything. The protector state was faced with a demand and cost spiral, but it could no longer simply guarantee its citizens equal access to security; it also had to ensure that each individual had unlimited access to a certain number of benefits. The question of limiting state action was now more acute, and particularly so, as research has shown,[41] because these new benefits did not even provide the beneficiaries with the autonomy they needed; in fact, they accentuated dependence, thereby further intensifying demand for benefits. As a result, a huge chasm opened up between two options. On one hand, expectations of the state continued to rise as the state extended its role into all aspects of the day-to-day lives of older people. On the other, the state was providing fixed and juxtaposed means of satisfying these needs, but these were growing increasingly remote from demand, which was expanding and diversifying. In this way the very introduction of a system of social protection inspired expectations that outstripped the institutional powers of the public authorities to respond. The impending crisis of legitimacy flowed directly from a growing gap between expectations aroused by the system of social protection and the responses that it was able to provide.[42] This gap undermined belief in the legitimacy of public actions of social protection, and public opinion felt that a withdrawal of legitimization was justified. It also became clear that this extension of mechanisms of social protection was not unambiguously a source of social progress, equality, and freedom: it could also be a source of reduced autonomy and more deep-seated social dislocation. This new distrust of public action was later reinforced by the widespread introduction of preretirement schemes, and the pension model accordingly lost focus. It is true that no one questioned entitlement to a pension, but there was widespread skepticism about the aims of pension plans that were being imposed on, rather chosen by, younger and younger people. Some even began to suspect that the development of social-protection elements in pension plans was not entirely synonymous with social progress; it was felt in some quarters that this could lead to increased social rigidity, limitations on freedom of choice, and a decreased right to a job for older people.

As far as pensions were concerned, the lack of legitimacy scarring public action had cumulative effects on the level of confidence enjoyed by this type of benefit. As Denis Kessler has pointed out, pay-as-you-go plans constitute an intergenerational contract that only public authorities can guarantee.[43] They alone could oblige future generations to pay their contributions, and thereby make them acknowledge the obligation of the present generation to the generations that followed. Eroded confidence in the state's capacity to resolve social problems threw suspicion on its ability to guarantee the intergenerational contract implied by pension plans. Consequently, nascent doubts about the beneficial nature of pensions were accentuated by suspicions about the reliability of the intergenerational contract of which the state was guarantor. Some anxious questions, amplified by press coverage of the future solvency of pension plans, required urgent answers. It was not so much a matter of a financial impasse, or that the state's redistributive capacity had discovered its limitations. It was more a question of systems of social protection for the elderly having insufficient legitimacy. They no longer stimulated the same consensus, and instead allowed the spotlight to be turned on their financial power, and it was this that raised doubts about their future.

This querying of the legitimacy of systems of social protection for the elderly reflected a more profound crisis; in this case, it was a crisis of the social model of old age. The significance and the social status of the elderly in modern society—or, to put it in more general terms, the social organization of life patterns—were becoming problematic. The sociocultural system was unable to provide the underlying meaning necessary if the legitimacy of resource transfer systems for the elderly was to be established, and for this reason belief in these systems was shaken.

THE CRISIS IN THE SOCIAL MODEL OF OLD AGE

By the mid-1980s, the crisis concerning the significance of old age was very marked. The reason was that due to the rapid advance made by preretirement schemes under pressure from underemployment, the political system could see its needs with regard to retirement rising substantially, the sociocultural foundations of retirement weakening, and the resources of meaning necessary to motivate action drying up.

The shortfall in meaning regarding old age has been produced along two main fracture lines, which this section will now examine. In the first place, the importance acquired by the "unemployment" policy for older workers upset the traditional aims of pensions, but it was not able to resuscitate the meaning of the last phase of life. In the second place, consensus on the organization of age groups and the division of life into phases on which the whole concept of retirement was based was destabilizing at a time when the development of preretirement was pushing this division into age groups to the limit.

An earlier section has demonstrated how wide-ranging policies aimed at reducing the number of older people in the labor force profoundly transformed the organization of age groups in French society. Indeed, they brought about a major change in life patterns and a redefinition of old age. Today these developments seem to be producing a new crisis in the social meaning of old age. Successive social constructions of old age have reflected the play of social forces, the definitions that these social forces were able to impose, and the political measures that the relations between them brought into being. They then collapsed, and, in so doing, blurred the social significance of this stage of life. It is our view that expectations and aspirations were by then farther and farther removed from the social status that pensioners now had. There was tension between, on one hand, the images that individuals had of themselves, and, on the other, the social definitions to which they were subjected and which had multiplied in the confusion and ambivalence engendered by the preretirement scheme.

The new model of organizing age groups turned a large number of people over fifty into workers who were about to be made unemployed and deemed socially unproductive, but it was only able to prevail because it was based on an increasingly positive representation of retirement and on certain aspirations that it was simultaneously cultivating. The need for an employment policy—that, too, was an easy way out—succeeded in giving it the virtuous appearance of a generous social policy. This was a society that specialized ages as far as it could, using the "third age" to promote a happy face of retirement spent on permanent vacation; it also concentrated many of its aspirations on leisure time in this final phase of life and saw the expansion of this phase as the concretization of its increasingly lively expectations of free time and an opportunity to live one's own life. Surely bringing forward the moment of retirement age and stopping work was a way of responding to society's expectations![44] Paradoxically, however, it was just when the model of retirement seemed to be triumphing that doubts began to creep in about the relevance of this model and the model of the "third age." Significantly, the last life phase is marked by a dual contradictory movement: a prolongation of this period of life and a contraction of its meaning.

When the working class won the right to retirement, it enabled older workers to enjoy a modest degree of happiness at the end of their lives before they died. However, it did not respond to the expectations of generations who, just as they were entering their prime, were propelled into a period of life-after-work that was almost as long as their ancestors' entire working lives had been in the early twentieth century.[45] Retirement, an end to alienation, and half-baked integration based on third-age facilities were not sufficient to give any meaning to the average of twenty-five to thirty years that they still had to live.

Morphological transformations of the final life phase (e.g., bringing forward the point of stopping work for good, and recognition that there are no jobs during this final phase of life) prompted new expectations among the groups concerned. For one thing, they discredited the traditional images of retirement; for another, they shattered the structure of community "third age" services that had proved incapable of responding to their aspirations of active citizenship, and the new nonwork tasks that younger pensioners looked forward to. The time taken from work should really represent entry into a new time of life and access to freely chosen activities. It could even encourage the development of other ways of life that do not accord the same primacy to the values of work and instead give prominence to social life and time for oneself. Henri Mendras identified a move in this direction when he described the "third age" as a "new class of recreational activity" that concerned itself with affairs of the city, and "[applied] to nonmarket activities the energy and skills that they previously used in the production of market goods and services."[46] However, research into the way of life of preretirees shows that this prognosis was highly optimistic.[47]

Few preretirees have developed innovative models of behavior. For members of this group, past behavior is more likely to survive than behavior that challenges old ideas: for example, only 15 percent of preretirees in the sample had found new activities after stopping work, and only 9 percent belonged to an old people's association; for 10 percent, this new behavior was simply a way of adopting pensioner status by becoming users of "third-age" facilities and services (e.g., "third age" clubs and universities, holiday services, and sporting and recreational activities). Activities taken up later on were mainly of a traditional recreational variety and included reading, gardening, conferences, concerts, trips, and craft and sporting activities. This list shows retirees and preretirees to be astonishingly similar, although new participative practices in life-after-work remained an extremely minority model: for example, only 2 percent of those questioned had been involved in nonmarket, social, cultural, or political activities since they had stopped work. The small amount of time that workers on preretirement schemes devoted to socially useful work contrasted with the frequency of recreational activities in the home. It was therefore rare for postwork ways of life to escape the production/consumption option and be replaced by a context of new social roles for the third age. The latter could not be simply reduced to consumption, but instead outlined other forms of integration and extraprofessional social contributions. In these circumstances, it was hard to see preretirees as a pioneering group prefiguring new values of free time and self-development; nor could they be seen as the makers of a countermodel for a production-based society in which free work had a place beside market work.

More optimistic readings of the preretirement phenomenon failed to appreciate the close bonds that linked the demand for free time and the individual's aspirations to have more control over his or her time and way of life.[48] The paradox about the preretirement system was that it had moved away from free time during the final phase of life and at the same time radically reduced opportunities for self-determination and choice.[49] Above all, this new free time was enforced, and was unavoidably spent without employment and with imposed recreational activities. The movement to get rid of older people had become more brutal, and it was even starting earlier. Life choices in this final life phase had also diminished. There was increasing misunderstanding about the identity and social status of the elderly, and the model of a two-tiered society encouraged the view that older workers, who were automatically branded as second-class citizens and could no longer be "frontliners," had easy decisions to make: in other words, they had opted for being rather than having, and for the convivial ethic rather than the production ethic. Freed from the onus of working, older workers could go in for voluntary work or do just as they liked, and rebuild structures of local solidarity that could take the pressure off an overburdened welfare state. However, that would be to ignore the fact that there was not much room for options under this model. It has already been pointed out that when employees stopped work, they were usually no longer exercising older workers' right to retirement; they were stopping work because they were seen as superfluous to the labor force. The decision reflected the system of production and its needs, and the system of production was increasingly determining the shape of individuals' lives and their social capacity. On that basis, a selection was made between those defined as productive and those classified by their age as socially unproductive and forced to live on benefits paid for by adults of working age; the latter also swelled the numbers of people who, because they were a charge on the public purse, were also on the margins of society. In fact, individual life courses were even more strictly organized around the issue of work. The prework period, which was devoted to training, was getting longer, and postadolescence was being attached to adolescence, a period equally removed from the sphere of production. At the other end of life, there were glimpses of a "life-after-work" which started for some at fifty, and for many at fifty-five; this was more often enforced than wished for, and had no assigned social function other than unemployment.

In a social context where people were mainly judged according to how useful they were to the production process, life after work was stripped of all social value. It could not be recognized as a private experience; nor could it be endowed with any specific social content. There was therefore a dissociation between two extremes: on one hand, the expectations of a group of people for whom retirement represented the moment of free self-expression and who had agreed to defer until that point their aspirations for leading their own lives; on the other hand, social responses formulated more distinctly and brutally than before in terms of banishment and of being condemned to the world of nonproductive people, nonreciprocity, and subsistence allowances. What it amounted to was an even vaguer identification of older people who were, properly speaking, neither unemployed nor often really retired, and who increasingly refused to refer to themselves as the "third age." The dire straits in which some preretirees found themselves[50] might in some ways have formed a new picture of contemporary ills, in the sense defined by Alain Touraine as interior emptiness and external tumult: "The emptiness of someone who no longer has any personal and collective identity, and who is simply a target for commercial, political, and administrative undertakings; the tumult of so many signals, initiative-crushing instructions, and information stripped of all communication."[51]

Although the notion of the "third age" incorporated a move toward recognizing old age as a particular experience, such as leisure time, and the way of life was defined from the top down, the policy of getting rid of older workers banished all possibility of a cultural model of old age by establishing the employment issue as the fundamental organizing principle of life patterns. The elderly were now defined as a superfluous labor force, and were therefore a group of outsiders for whom the country had no use. In this context, there was no longer any collective identity possible for those who had entered the postwork phase; at the same time, their distress was not even audible to a society that continued to build up retirement as the main antidote to alienated work and could only see it as a practical way of meeting aspirations for free time. More than ever before, the worlds of work and nonwork formed a system, and it was therefore pointless to imagine, even if the former remained marked by harsh conditions and alienation, that the latter could be a time for freedom and creativity. One may well ask whether, when an entire society finds a consensus to share work out mainly according to the criterion of age, and when the state increasingly draws its legitimacy from redistributing work, all social models of old age do not inevitably fall away and old age itself is not reduced to banishment and dependence. Such a conclusion would mean that all the social efforts at recognition and reintegration of the elderly developing elsewhere were completely in vain.

The blurring of the social meaning of old age, which was brought about by the prevalence of ideas pertaining to employment and had resisted all attempts to recognize old age as a particular experience, was further accentuated by growing doubts about the relevance of the division and segregation of ages. It was precisely this that hastened the development of preretirement schemes. This chapter has pointed out that the extension of "unemployment" policies pushed the model of organizing the course of life to the extreme. This was the model on which retirement was based, and according to which youth was given over to education and training, adulthood to production, and old age to nonwork. The social conditions that gave birth to this ternary model of life, and thereby ensured the legitimacy of retirement, were undergoing major changes. The history of retirement, which was reconstructed in the first chapter of this book, has demonstrated how closely linked retirement was to the history of industrial society. Retirement was seen to have been built on competition between the dissimilar needs of companies and their organized employees, the companies having emerged from a process in which work was intensified and Taylorian schemes of production developed. In time, the emergence of postindustrial society, the introduction of new technology, and the decline of Taylorism shook the consensus that was the basis of the ternary organization of life and increased confusion about the aims of retirement. It would appear that this solution does not respond to certain new needs that companies have when managing the labor force (e.g., continuous training needs and the rigidity of the employment-for-life schema on which retirement is based); nor does it quite conform to the new job-security needs of employees, who find at earlier and earlier stages in their careers that their knowledge is obsolescent and that their employment prospects have become more precarious. Evidence for the temporal strategy on which the pension transfer is based—it meant agreeing to defer compensation for work alienation through granting entitlement to a period of rest—is therefore mainly concentrated in the latter stages of one's life, and is not imposed with the same force on employed people. These developments came to pass when the cost of the strategy of delaying the "right to idleness" was about to be made more problematic by the demographic and economic developments described above.

There is no question that the place of the elderly in society, the organization of the course of life, and the solidarity of relations between generations have been badly shaken. The entire cultural foundation on which the systems of protection for the elderly used to be based is in the process of breaking up. Relations between the elderly and society are in chaos, and even the contours of old age and retirement are growing indistinct. It is not a minor paradox of this research that old-age policies, which have been playing a fundamental role in the construction of old age as a coherent and autonomous social category, are now seen to be precipitating the decline of the very people they were designed to assist. Models of retirement and old age in our sociocultural system are collapsing. It may be that the profound crisis in motivation that is currently taking hold of old age and retirement—leaving to one side the ravages it will cause in human and social terms in the near future—will eventually trace the possible contours of a new consensus on the organization of life patterns. This would move in the direction of despecializing ages, and for each age group would create a better balance of training time, employment, and free time. Instead of very early, definitive retirement, there would then develop a form of temporary midlife retirement based on a new social right to work; such a move would encourage a start to be made on new vocational and social activities.

For the moment, that is simply utopian, although it might at least stimulate new ideas. What we still have is a society fragmented into age groups with conflicting interests and differentiated forms of social treatment.

THE SOCIALIST PERIOD: THE CONTRADICTIONS REMAIN

On coming to power in May 1981, the political Left set up a Ministry of National Solidarity and, for the first time in France, a State Secretariat for the Elderly. Did these moves reorient this contradictory development of public actions, leading both to an increase in the cost of these policies and to considerable confusion about what they actually meant? Was the country seeing the beginnings of a social model for organizing age groups (in addition to the model triggered by the movement to dualize society) that operated mainly at the expense of elderly people, who were automatically, and at an earlier and earlier age, welfare-dependent and marginalized?

The new ruling elite included many who had denounced the risks of the social fabric collapsing, a phenomenon that had been encouraged by the previous government's neoliberal economic policy. This had confined itself to expanding guaranteed income in order to rationalize a system now considered to be the natural, but fatal, way of getting rid of large numbers of older workers.[52] However, an examination of public action on old age during the late 1970s and early 1980s does not reveal a reverse in the contradictory trends whose harsh and destructuring nature is described above. However, it is the position of this author that the Left adopted an increasingly piecemeal approach and supported a more pronounced incorporation by the state in all of the measures carried out in this field. As a result the contradictions remained, and they penetrated the state even more deeply. The Socialist government's main option on coming to power was to reactivate the welfare-state model. Rather than go down the undoubtedly long, perilous road of cooperatively drawing up new forms of solidarity that might reduce segregation, the government relaunched the egalitarian and unifying model of retirement and started to look into a reform of retirement age.

It was as if there were a hypothesis that the upheavals and fractures associated with the crisis could be erased if a fresh impulse were given to the social-protection measures that existed prior to the crisis. However, by constructing a system of egalitarian social protection against risks through a broadening of workers' right to retirement, no account was taken either of the inability to reduce the inequalities that showed up in the mechanisms for the transfer of resources, or of the new kinds of rejection that developed with the crisis. It follows that because the origins of contemporary social dislocations were not tackled, a return to the unifying project could only increase the financial charge on the welfare state, and would not be able to regroup society.

The new dynamic that the Socialist government gave to the right to retire would appear to confirm the relevance of the model of forming social policies described above and its ability to take modern developments into account. In fact, as soon as power was achieved by political forces that had the support of the long-estranged labor unions, the union aim of broadening the right to retirement and pension was backed by state action. Moreover, the retirement policy based its rights on the employment policy. An earlier section has shown how a guaranteed-income scheme for workers over sixty formed part of the employers' strategy and subjected the management of old age to production imperatives; it was now on its way to extinction, and reappeared in the labor-union approach as an egalitarian right to retirement at sixty. Does this mean that public policy had a tendency to lose employment measures in considering retirement, so as to restore rights to older workers by allowing them to decide for themselves when they wanted to stop work? As has been pointed out, this freedom is something that these employment measures did much to reduce. Reform of the retirement age certainly made things slightly more equitable.[53] In particular, it put an end to the precariousness and the disenfranchisement that guaranteed income imposed in many ways. For example, it identified certain categories excluded from entitlement to guaranteed income for resignees (mainly nontenured state employees) and allowed them to stop work at sixty, but it did not restore free choice to manual workers. That change was achieved mainly by relaunching the right to work for older employees; without it, there could not have been any real options about taking retirement. Little was done in this respect. In a climate where the main issue was the struggle for employment, and where there was an implicit consensus among social agents that the distribution of jobs should be determined by the criterion of age, there was overwhelming pressure to off-load jobs among older workers. The measures adopted, together with a lowering of retirement age, were therefore exactly the opposite of a prolongation of the right to a job for these workers. Initially this was covered in regulations governing concurrent drawing of pension and pay, which were instituted at the same time as retirement age was lowered. Later there were new employment measures consisting of solidarity contracts, and particularly the resignation/preretirement contract, which was more immediately successful. In this way the preretirement system was not so much done away with as applied to younger people, and at a level at which it had more impact on employment. Recourse to early exit continued to rise steeply, and there was further specialization of ages, although it was now dressed up as fictitious intergenerational solidarity, which in turn resembled unequal competition on the labor market between young and old. By committing itself to lowering the retirement age, the Socialist government was clearly indicating that it wanted to respond to what were perceived as powerful social aspirations, and it tried to broaden the gains made by the working class at the time of the Liberation. However, it was driven to reify the union demand and underestimated the shifts in priorities that had inevitably taken place as a result of a worsening employment situation and a new political landscape.

After the Socialists won the election, bringing the retirement age down to sixty ceased to be a central labor union concern. There were three main reasons for this. First, it was because the unions had put the defense of jobs at the top of their agendas, and the very success of guaranteed income had substantially reduced the numbers of employees in the sixty-to-sixty-five age group.[54] In these circumstances, lowering the retirement age had very little impact on employment levels. What the CGT and the CFDT wanted, as far as retirement was concerned, was that the opportunity to retire much earlier (at fifty-five or even before) be extended to people who wanted it and who had been employed for many years; the intention was that the measure should have a greater impact on employment.

The second reason was that the period of employment was, in the new political context, once again a more negotiable issue, and the struggle for a reduction in exploitation was less likely to turn into a claim for a lowering in retirement age, as it had in the 1970s.[55] The third reason was that the unions were aware that as a result of economic pressure, the right to retirement had turned into an obligation to cease work. Accordingly, they realized that the retirement model no longer aroused the same degree of unanimity among the workers affected.[56] They therefore called for a measure that gave more flexibility and guaranteed more freedom of choice than simply a lowering of the retirement age, and they sought to reconcile two fairly incompatible objectives of cutting jobs through retirement and preserving employees' autonomy in deciding when to go.

The Socialist government relaunched the idea of a social right to retirement partly to establish its social objectives and partly to embrace once more the principles of solidarity that had been expressed back in 1945, and to which the unions had always been very attached. However, this reform seemed to be ill-timed compared with the social demands that had grown out of the crisis and the unions' central concerns. The government did not resist the great temptation to carry on using retirement as a way of accepting unemployment and treating it as a social issue; this was all the more remarkable, as has been pointed out, given the heavy pressure placed on the government by union organizations on this matter. New employment measures for the fifty-five to fifty-nine age group, were therefore introduced together with preretirement solidarity contracts. The key novelty of the latter, compared with earlier measures that had been drawn up by the "social partners" within the joint framework of UNEDIC, was that they represented a state initiative that, as state-enterprise contracts, bore some of the financial responsibility and thereby made a more direct commitment than before to the unemployment policy for older workers. Elsewhere, the policy for integrating the elderly through way of life was also enjoying a revival. The range of social services and facilities available to the elderly was improved and complemented (a more efficient home-help scheme and the introduction of a home-care service), local coordination of these services was strengthened (through the appointment of coordinators and the introduction of a *département*-based plan for the elderly), and structures for consulting with the elderly were put in place in central and outlying areas (*département*-based and national committees for pensioners and the elderly).[57]

However, for all its dynamism, this renewed action on way of life was still an intervention on old age that was irrevocably located later in the life course. It was a field of action that reflected the sphere of competence of the new State Secretariat for the Elderly. It is significant that this new department of the Executive did not deal either with the reform of retirement age, which was piloted through by the cabinet of the minister for national solidarity, or with employment measures for older workers, which were drawn up at the level of the cabinet of the prime minister within the framework of the plan to fight for jobs. Although it had been given the task of watching over the plight of the elderly, the State Secretariat had no control over the main instruments that most immediately defined this role and fixed essential solidarity links between the generations, such as solidarity contracts and the lowering of retirement age. These measures precipitated the marginalization of the elderly, making them a welfare "burden." They also accentuated a segregation of age groups, which the State Secretariat worked hard to eliminate through the provision of facilities and medical and social services. The relaunch of the integration policy failed to have any influence on the mechanisms that were turning old age in France into a form of social unproductiveness, in which the elderly lived on social benefits paid for by the active population. The new policy could operate only on the basis of a massive increase in the consumption of social services; this in turn raised dependence on specific areas of consumption, but it never restored to these groups, which had been socially defined as elderly, the opportunity to determine their own ways of life and forms of social participation.

What the Mauroy government achieved in services and facilities for the elderly was, as with retirement, another aspect of the reactivated welfare state and of redistribution mechanisms. The increase in social-protection benefits was powerless to define a new role for the elderly, a group now under attack as "welfare-dependent" and "on the margins." It did not create any new forms of solidarity or citizenship; instead it triggered an unending rise in social expenditure that the policy of rigor introduced in the summer of 1982 doggedly attempted to channel.

In conclusion, when the political Left came to power in May 1982, it did not fundamentally change government action on old age. Public interventions in this domain were still fragmented and contradictory: they were partial responses to problems of different orders (employment, retirement, and social services) and were not part of a comprehensive approach. The old-age policy was nowhere to be found; at best it represented a series of fragmented and circumstantial actions. As has been stressed, the collapse of interventions was accompanied by a compartmentalization of, and an increase in, the number of decision-making centers in the state. Because of the way the competencies were distributed, the new State Secretariat with responsibility for the elderly did not have the task of managing retirement or dealing with questions related to the employment of older workers. Its work was therefore reduced to a "policy for the old" that could supply older beneficiaries with tangible benefits, but was still unable to find a solution for the main problems posed by old age. These were formed much earlier in the life course, and found their source in training and employment policies, in the definition of forms of social solidarity, and in the organization of working lives and recreational activities. Lowering the retirement age and raising the age of entitlement to employment measures to fifty-five marked a new step in the movement to segregate age groups and could only reinforce the crisis in the significance of old age at the time.

The period following May 1981 was characterized by the simultaneous, although not coordinated or convergent, reactivation of the three dimensions of the old-age policy. The state relaunched a way-of-life policy, undertook to broaden the right to retirement, and gave a new dynamic to the employment policy, over which it now had more comprehensive and direct control. As a result, not only did the contradictions in old-age policy continue; they also penetrated the state more deeply than ever before. At the same time, the direct consequence of relaunching these three policies was that the welfare state was destabilized even more sharply; this was associated with a top-down reactivation of social benefits, although their underlying redistributive philosophy was recast to reflect the new social fractures that were in most urgent need of attention.

Conclusion

Throughout this book, and in its analysis of the history of social protection for the elderly, it has been possible to throw light on the mechanisms that explain the current crisis in social policy. In addition to providing a corpus of information, the book traces some of the routes that the welfare state can take to escape from its current impasse. If, as has been demonstrated, old-age policies express a link between state and society, what new link between these two structures can produce new forms of social action capable of overcoming the problems of exclusion, fragmentation, and dependence that are so widespread among the elderly?

The view taken by this author is that recourse to one or another of the three scenarios most frequently referred to in those days did not make achievement of this objective possible. The conservative scenario, which advocated the dismantling of the welfare state in favor of total individual responsibility, would have introduced conditions that would once again bring about increased financial and moral poverty among the elderly. They are a group not normally capable of adapting to the laws of a society in struggle, focusing on production, and searching for efficiency. As matters stand, a scenario involving a relaunch of the tripartite social contract among employers, the union, and the state, as advocated especially by Ian Gough,[58] could only strengthen the mechanisms for social closures of demand, as well as its rigidification and monetarization, which have been described in this book and which have been largely brought about by the failure of social policies. The third scenario, put forward by Pierre Rosanvallon,[59] sees the revival of local, informal systems of solidarity as a possible way of replacing state solidarity, the latter being overprotective and in crisis. This author takes the view that such an approach demands too much of local dynamism and innovation, qualities that research into preretirement was unable to unearth.

Furthermore, this book adopts the position that the necessary passage from pure state solidarity (which prevails today) to societal solidarity (which does not yet exist) can only take place with the emergence of new kinds of relationships between state and society.

Such a transformation suggests that the state is no longer the only body that is active in defining and implementing a policy; nor is it the remote, centralizing guardian engrossed in a multiplicity of tasks, as it is over way-of-life and "third-age" policies. A double movement needs to be set up between it and society, both at the level of the information and consideration appropriate for the drafting of policies, and at the level of their implementation through a system of decentralized dissemination. This two-way movement can only be introduced if the state sees itself as the agent that crystallizes aspirations and remobilizes society, a body every one of whose components is influenced by social forces that themselves will no longer be simply organized agencies representing social classes but also representatives of various groups and sectors of society.

Only in this way will it be possible to end both the current impasse in social policy and the contemporary phenomenon involving the dissociation and rapid fragmentation of society. The latter is linked both to the crisis and to styles of implementing social policy that have accentuated these fractures.

With regard to old age, the repairing of social dislocations first involves trying to reverse the movement to specialize age groups; this specialization turns a growing section of the population into second-class citizens who are welfare-dependent and marginal. However, the reversal of this development can be achieved only on the basis of three types of simultaneous orientation, which themselves presuppose the new forms of relations between society and the state described above.

First, we have to commit ourselves to a different conception of social policies from the one that converted them into social-protection benefits with egalitarian and unifying foundations. Compensation for the aging unemployed and retirement pensions certainly act as fundamental systems of horizontal redistribution, but they also produce rigidities and limitations on life choices, particularly when they are the only responses to a series of new social problems. More stimulating social interventions need to be developed alongside the social-protection benefits that provide essential coverages. Some of the colossal sums devoted to preretirement schemes could certainly have been more profitably used on measures to set up local community facilities.

Second, the end of the all-protecting state has to be accompanied by the state's total withdrawal from social policy. Otherwise there will inevitably be a return to the good intentions of the integration policy, which provided the model of the "third age" from the top down, together with the means for achieving the collective promotion of older people. This denationalization of the elderly required a system of solidarity that was capable of taking account of a wide range of real social demands and aspirations. The argument pertaining to the usefulness for beneficiaries should prevail over ideas about stimulating overall demand.

Third, other forms of relations between the elderly and society need to flow from policies that no longer concentrate on a later stage of life, thereby reinforcing older people's dependence and segregation at a time when the policies are giving them care. Instead, these policies should operate at an earlier stage in the life course and work on the development of each person's potential to run his or her own life and choose his or her time to retire. Instead of responding to the increasingly pressing demands for employees to be able to live their own lives by prolonging the period of retirement, would it not have been better to draw up a policy for changing work and the ways work was distributed over the course of life? The policy for aging needed to be replaced by an old-age policy. Ideally, the declining influence of the social definition of old age that has been described above would promote other ways of managing relations between old age and society; such a method of management would not have confined itself to the elderly and would also have taken account of the entire course of life.

The issue dominating the next few years is whether we plunge deeper into a society marked by segregation and—sadly, the possibility cannot be excluded—a battle between age groups. The alternative is a new political will, closely allied to the aspirations and actions of numerous social forces, that will facilitate the development of an orderly progression of life, where an alternation of activities at every age, and the banishment of the elderly would be replaced by the harmonious blending of the stages of life.

Appendix: Demographic and Economic Data on Aging

Table 1. Evolution of the Share of Different Social Program Expenditure OECD Countries Income, 1960–1981

Country	Education (%)		Health (%)		Pensions (%)		Unemployment benefits (%)	
	1960	1981	1960	1981	1960	1981	1960	1981
Canada	24.8	28.8	19.8	6.0	23.1	21.4	12.4	10.7
France	–	19.3	18.7	22.0	44.0	40.3	1.5	6.4
Germany	11.7	16.5	15.1	20.6	47.8	39.7	0.5	4.4
Italy	22.0	22.0	19.0	20.6	32.7	45.4	1.2	2.4
Japan	50.0	28.6	16.3	26.9	17.5	27.4	3.8	2.3
U.K.	26.6	24.5	24.5	22.8	29.5	31.2	1.4	5.9
U.S.A.	33.0	26.4	11.9	20.2	38.5	35.6	5.5	2.4
Average of the above countries	28.0	23.7	17.9	22.7	33.3	34.4	3.8	4.9

Source: OECD. Social Programs expenditure from *Social Expenditure, 1960–1990,* 1985, p. 25.

Table 2. France: Changes in the Structure of Social Benefits, 1960–1994, as a Percentage of Total

	1960	1970	1975	1980	1994
Health (sickness and disability)	33.1	35.9	36.8	35.5	34.0
Old Age Death Survival*	33.7	39.8	42.4	42.7	43.6
Unemployment	1.2	2.0	4.0	7.0	8.1
Family Maternity	31.0	21.2	16.5	14.6	12.7
Other	1.0	1.1	0.3	0.2	1.6
Total	100	100	100	100	100

Source: Compte de la protection sociale—Collection de l'INSEE—Série C n° 82, December 1979 and updated.

* Pensions, capital benefit on death, reversion pension.

Table 3. Share of Different Social Programs Expenditures in 1989, within EC Countries

Country	Old age and survival	Health	Employment and unemployment	Family and materinity	Other
Italy	59.6	33.8	1.7	4.8	0.0
Greece	58.3	28.0	3.2	1.9	8.6
Luxemburg	47.4	40.1	0.8	10.9	0.8
Spain	46.7	36.0	14.7	1.8	0.8
France	44.6	34.8	6.6	10.2	3.7
Belgium	43.4	35.0	11.5	9.0	1.1
U.K.*	43.4	32.7	6.2	11.1	6.5
Germany	42.5	39.4	6.3	8.0	3.8
Portugal	40.4	46.2	3.0	6.9	3.5
Denmark	36.4	31.2	14.6	12.2	5.8
Netherlands	34.5	46.8	9.6	5.5	3.7
Ireland	32.1	34.8	15.1	12.4	5.5
Total Europe	45.9	36.2	6.6	7.9	3.3

Source: Eurostat.
* 1988 figures.

Table 4.1. Changes in Life Expectancy (in Years) at Different Ages by Gender

	at birth		at 65		at 85
	M	F	M	F	F
1850	37.0	–	9.7	–	–
1900	45.3	48.7	10.5	11.5	3.7
1935	55.9	61.6	11.1	13.1	4.0
1947	61.9	67.4	12.1	14.4	4.2
1959	33.7	39.8	42.4	42.7	43.6
1964	67.5	74.4	12.7	15.9	4.6
1968	68.0	75.5	12.7	16.5	4.9
1975	70.0	78	13.0	17.0	4.9
1985	71.3	79.4	–	–	–
1990	72.7	80.9	–	–	–

Source: INSEE.

Table 4.2. Changes in Life Expectancy (in Years) at 60 by Gender

	1938	1949	1968	1971	1979	1982	1993
M	13.9	15.3	15.9	16.2	17.0	17.6	19.4
F	16.5	18.1	20.4	20.9	22.0	22.7	24.6

Source: INSEE.

Table 5.1. Changes in Activity Rates among Older People, 1954–1984

Males

Years

	1954	Oct. 62	Mar. 63	Oct. 64	Mar. 65	Oct. 66	Mar. 67	Mar. 68
55–59 years	82.0	85.8	84.2	84.5	82.5	83.5	82.4	83.9
60–64 years	68.0	70.4	67.3	70.3	66.0	67.3	60.4	65.9
65–69 years	49.5	37.6	36.9	36.2	31.9	33.1	28.4	28.9
70–74 years	33.5	23.4	22.3	18.2	21.0	16.5	14.5	14.2
75–75+ years	18.0	9.8	10.3	9.7	10.2	9.5	7.9	6.8

	1969	70	71	72	73	74	75	76
55–59 years	84.2	82.5	82.0	82.0	82.3	82.0	82.9	82.5
60–64 years	66.8	65.2	64.7	63.4	61.8	60.4	54.4	50.3
65–69 years	28.3	24.9	25.3	24.9	22.8	21.6	19.3	18.2
70–74 years	14.1	12.0	11.0	9.5	8.5	8.2	8.2	7.7
75–75+ years	5.9	5.5	4.3	4.4	3.7	3.4	3.6	2.8

	1977	78	79	80	81	82	83	84
55–59 years	83.5	82.1	82.0	80.9	79.8	75.6	71.0	68.1
60–64 years	47.6	43.6	43.7	46.9	42.4	39.9	33.6	31.1
65–69 years	16.7	16.0	13.6	11.9	10.7	11.1	10.0	10.0
70–74 years	6.6	6.5	5.2	4.8	4.9	5.5	5.4	5.7
75–75+ years	2.9	2.9	2.1	2.3	2.0	2.6	2.3	2.2

Note: Activity rates are the proportion of economically active people taking part in the census (claiming to be employed or seeking work) of the total.

Sources: INSEE, Recensement et enquête emploi (Census and employment survey), detailed series.

Table 5.2. Changes in Activity Rates among Older People, 1954–1984

Females

Years

	1954	Oct. 62	Mar. 63	Oct. 64	Mar. 65	Oct. 66	Mar. 67	Mar. 68
55–59 years	41.8	44.0	42.1	44.5	44.2	45.3	42.9	45.7
60–64 years	33.3	35.2	31.2	34.5	30.9	34.5	29.9	35.3
65–69 years	19.6	19.1	16.1	16.7	16.8	17.2	15.0	14.8
70–74 years	12.0	9.8	8.9	11.0	7.9	9.4	6.7	6.8
75–75+ years	6.0	3.5	3.1	3.6	3.9	3.6	3.2	2.8

	1969	70	71	72	73	74	75	76
55–59 years	47.2	45.8	44.5	45.0	42.9	43.6	43.3	44.2
60–64 years	33.8	33.7	32.7	32.7	32.5	31.2	29.3	27.1
65–69 years	14.9	14.0	12.5	12.9	11.8	11.4	10.6	10.5
70–74 years	7.4	7.0	6.0	5.5	4.7	4.0	3.7	3.5
75–75+ years	2.8	2.4	2.1	1.9	2.0	1.7	1.8	1.6

	1977	78	79	80	81	82	83	84
55–59 years	45.8	45.3	45.8	46.8	46.5	46.0	43.6	42.9
60–64 years	27.2	23.9	23.9	27.1	24.9	23.3	20.6	19.0
65–69 years	9.2	8.7	7.8	6.0	5.4	4.9	4.6	5.9
70–74 years	3.1	2.8	3.2	2.2	2.3	2.4	2.7	2.6
75–75+ years	1.5	1.4	1.3	1.3	1.2	1.2	0.9	1.0

Note: Activity rates are the proportion of economically active people taking part in the census (claiming to be employed or seeking work) of the total.

Sources: INSEE, Recensement et enquête emploi (Census and employment survey), detailed series.

Table 6. Employment Activity Rates from 1971 to 1997 of Men from Fifty-Five to Sixty-Five Years Old among Eleven Countries

	1971	1975	1980	1985	1987	1989	1991
United States	77.3	71.4	68.8	64.4	64.5	64.3	63.9
France	73.0	67.1	65.3	46.7	43.9	43.3	42.0
Germany*	77.1	66.7	64.1	53.6	54.1	51.7	49.9
Netherlands	79.3	69.9	61.0	44.2	44.7	44.2	41.8
Sweden	82.8	80.7	77.5	73.2	73.4	73.9	73.7
U.K.	82.9	82.0	73.9	59.4	58.1	61.6	61.5
Ireland	82.4	76.1	72.2	64.7	62.7	59.9	60.2
Portugal	82.1	77.1	74.8	64.9	62.1	63.9	66.5
Spain	82.7	76.7	71.5	59.1	57.0	56.7	56.2
Canada	78.8	76.3	72.7	64.3	61.9	61.9	57.3
Japan	85.3	83.2	82.2	78.9	78.2	79.2	82.0

	1993	1995	1996	1997	Var. in percentage points
United States	63.1	63.6	64.7	65.5	-15.3
France	40.3	38.7	38.6	38.4	-47.4
Germany*	48.0	48.0	48.0	47.3	-38.7
Netherlands	40.5	41.0	40.7	43.0	-45.8
Sweden	65.9	64.4	66.0	64.7	-22.0
U.K.	55.9	56.0	57.0	58.6	-29.3
Ireland	59.1	59.1	58.7	57.8	-30.0
Portugal	59.9	59.1	58.5	58.2	-29.1
Spain	51.6	48.0	49.9	50.5	-39.0
Canada	55.0	54.0	54.7	56.1	-29.0
Japan	82.1	80.8	80.6	80.9	-5.16

Source: OCDE-OECD. Labor force statistics.

Table 7. Retrospective-Prospective Changes in Age Structure of the Population in France over Two and a Half Centuries

Age	1780	1861	1901	1936	1954	1962
0–19	44.0	35.8	34.6	30.2	30.8	32.3
20–59	48.9	53.1	52.9	55.1	52.9	49.7
60 and over	7.1	11.1	12.5	14.7	16.3	18.0
Total number over 60			<5.0	6.159	6.976	8.352
Total French population (in millions)*			40.9	41.9	42.8	46.4

Age	1968	1975	1982	1990	2000	2010
0–19	32.3	30.7	28.7	27.8	26.0	23.0
20–59	48.9	50.4	52.8	53.2	55.0	53.0
60 and over	18.8	18.9	18.5	19.0	20.0	24.0
Total number over 60	9.334	9.965	10.0	10.4	10.8	13.1
Total French population (in millions)*	49.6	52.6	54.3	55.0	55.9	55.3

Source: INSEE.

* Estimates based on a hypothetical fertility rate of 1–8, a stable mortality rate, and an absence of external migrations.

Table 8. Total French Population by Age Group: Retrospective and Prospective Changes, 1962–2020

	1962		1968		1975	
Age	Nos. in millions	%	Nos. in millions	%	Nos. in millions	%
0–19	15.1	32.3	16.0	32.3	16.2	30.7
20–59	23.1	49.7	24.3	48.9	26.6	50.4
60–64	2.6	6.0	2.7	6.0	2.6	5.4
65 and over including:	5.6	12.0	6.5	12.8	7.2	13.5
65–74	3.5	7.5	4.1	8.0	4.4	8.2
75 and over	2.1	4.5	2.4	4.8	2.8	5.3
Total French population	46.4		49.6			52.6

	1982		1993		2020	
Age	Nos. in millions	%	Nos. in millions	%	Nos. in millions	%
0–19	15.6	28.7	15.4	26.8	12.7	23.0
20–59	28.6	52.8	30.7	30.8	29.3	53.0
60–64	2.5	4.7	2.6	3.0	3.6	6.5
65 and over including:	7.5	13.8	8.1	8.3	9.7	17.5
65–74	3.9	7.2	4.8	8.2		
75 and over	3.6	6.6	3.3	6.3		
Total French population	54.3		57.5		55.3	100.0

Source: INSEE.

Table 9. Old-Age Social Expenditures as a Share of Gross Domestic Product, Percentage, 1962–1980

	1962	1974	1980
Old-age expenditures / GDP	5.07%	7.98%	9.70%
Total social expenditures / GDP	17.0%	24.0%	27.3%

Table 10. Evolution in the Numbers of Retirement and Nursing Homes, Public and Private Sectors, 1939–1972

	1939	1946–47	1949–50	1953–54	1956	1958
Retirement and nursing homes, number of beds:						
Public sector	145,052	131,500	142,897	147,892	155,000	174,000
Index	110	100	109	112	118	132

	1960	1962	1964	1966	1968	1970	1972
Retirement and nursing homes, number of beds:							
Public sector	180,000	198,478	209,000	217,382	227,581		252,938
Index	137	151	159	165	173		192
Private sector	67,000	72,300			84,000		90,357
Total	247,100	270,778			299,428	320,797	339,954

Sources: Statistics from the Ministry of Public Health and Population (MSPP), in *Bulletin d'information du MSPP* and *Annuaire statistique de la France*

Notes

Introduction

1. On this point, our concerns recall certain orientations of symbolic interactionism as formulated for an analysis of social policy by Carroll Estes and Beverly Edmonds. These two writers base their views particularly on the negotiation paradigm developed by Anselm Strauss in his *Negotiations: Varieties, Contexts, Processes and Social Order* (San Francisco: Jossey-Bass, 1978). Cf. "Symbolic Interactions and Social Policy Analysis," *Symbolic Interaction* 4, no. 1 (Spring 1981): 75–86.

2. For the purpose of this research, the following journals were systematically perused for information on specified trade unions: *Syndicalisme Hebdo* (CFTC, later the CFDT), *Le Peuple* (CGT), *FO Hebdo* (CGT-FO), *Le Creuset* (CGC), and *Patronat, Notes et Arguments* (CNPF). Meaning of acronyms throughout the book can be found in the glossary.

Chapter 1. Old Age and Retirement

1. Association des Régimes de Retraite Complémentaires (Association of Complementary Pension Plans).

2. Named after Robert Boulin, then minister of public health and social security.

3. See Francis Netter, "Les retraites en France avant le XXe siècle," *Droit social* 26, no. 6 (June 1963): 358–73.

4. Civil servants' pensions were primarily an extension of part of their salaries, and were based on age and service; they were seen as a reward for public service.

5. The negative representation of old age as a lonely, destitute stage of life caused by improvidence was perpetuated by old people's homes, and was one of the instruments used by the middle class in an intensive moralizing campaign aimed at the working class in the nineteenth and early twentieth centuries. The existence of old people's homes urged the working class to lead ordered lives; it also taught them to be provident by building up capital through work and saving for their old age, by giving their children a good upbringing, thereby imbuing them with a sense of family, and by giving them decent living conditions through hard work. According to the liberal bourgeois thinking of the day, by fulfilling these objectives, the working class was securing for itself the best possible retirement pension.

In a society in which a reduction in the uncertainties of life depended on property, old people's homes were a way of counterdemonstrating the virtues of work and saving. It may be that their main function was not so much the discipline they imposed inside as the moralizing effect they had outside. On this subject, see the interesting appendix that Carmen

Bernard has devoted to the history of old people's homes in *Les vieux vont mourir à Nanterre* (Paris: Ed. du Sagittaire, 1978), 196–251.

6. Chamber of Deputies, 2d Sitting, 25 June 1901, *Journal officiel*, Parliamentary debates of 26 June 1901, p. 1568, quoted in Henri Hatzfeld: *Du paupérisme à la Sécurité sociale, 1850–1940* (Paris: Armand Colin, 1971), 88.

7. The breakdown is as follows:

Approved mutual benefit societies	43,764 beneficiaries
Free mutual benefit societies	19,606 beneficiaries
National Retirement Fund	243,000 beneficiaries

Source: Francis Netter, "Les retraites en France au cours de la période 1895–1945," *Droit social*, July–August 1965, 452.

8. Calculations for this are based on figures supplied by ibid., 368. The same work contains a detailed description of the pension schemes that developed during the nineteenth century for workers in private industry (pp. 365–69).

9. According to Imbert, *Les retraites des travailleurs* (Paris: Alcan, 1905), the average pension was less than fifty centimes a day.

10. Antoine Prost was deploring this deficiency as long ago as 1964 in "Jalons pour une histoire des retraites et des retraités," *Revue d'Histoire moderne et contemporaine* 11 (1964): 280. Graebner's painstaking work in the United States may have been the first attempt at such a project: William Graebner, *A History of Retirement: The Meaning and Function of an American Institution, 1885–1978* (New Haven: Yale University Press, 1980).

11. This view is supported by the work of Henri Hatzfeld, Rolande Trempé, Peter N. Stearns, and William Graebner.

12. J. Lefort, *Les caisses de retraites ouvrières* (Paris: A. Fontemoing, 1905), 1:240, quoted by Hatzfeld, *Du paupérisme à la Sécurité sociale*, 205.

13. Prost, "Jalons pour une histoire des retraites et des retraités."

14. Peter N. Stearns, *Old Age in European Society* (New York: Holmes and Meier, 1976), 46. "Retirement was completely alien to working-class culture."

15. Response from trade unions representing masons in Roanne (east central France) to the 1901 government survey of professional organizations seeking opinions on workers' pension funds, quoted by Hatzfeld, *Du paupérisme à la Sécurité sociale*, 231.

16. Cf. Rolande Trempé, *Les mineurs de Carmaux, 1848–1914* (Paris: Éditions Ouvrières, 1971); and idem, "The Struggles of French Miners for the Creation of Retirement Funds in the Nineteenth Century," in *Old Age and the Welfare State,* ed. Anne-Marie Guillemard (London: Sage, 1983), 101–15.

17. The first Congress of French Workers held in Paris in 1876 adopted a resolution on the organization of pension funds: "The cost of insurance, and particularly disability and old age insurance, shall be raised from taxes on capital, income, and inheritance. In other cases, the cost of insurance shall fall on workers' wages even when the employer pays contributions." Quoted by Guy Perrin, "La naissance de l'assurance sociale, institution centenaire," *Prévenir*, March 1982, 16.

18. Paul Lafargue, *Le droit à la paresse* (Paris: Maspero, 1975).

19. Quoted by Trempé, "The Struggle of French Miners," 103.

20. Denis Poulot, *Le sublime* (Paris: Maspero, 1980).

21. For detailed descriptions of the setting up of social benefit funds as an instrument of personnel management, see Hatzfeld's chapters on the policies of railway and mining company employers.

22. Statistics produced by the chief engineer of the St-Étienne Coal Mines for 1901, quoted by Rolande Trempé, clearly show the extent of this mobility. Of the average total workforce, 56 percent were recruited during that year; the figures for Rives-de-Gier and Firminy were 64 percent and 70 percent respectively. In Trempé, "The Struggle of French Miners."

23. Quoted by Rolande Trempé in *Les mineurs de Carmaux,* 585.

24. Graebner, *History of Retirement*, 121–34.

25. Ibid., 53. The author's detailed analyses of this issue cover mainly the printing, railway, and iron and steel sectors: see pp. 18–53.

26. Peter N. Stearns, *Lives of Labor. Work in a Maturing Industrial Society* (London: Croom Helm, 1975).

27. Ronald Melchers, "La vieillesse ouvrière, 1836–1914. Les origines de la retraite ouvrière" (doctoral diss., University of Aix-Marseille II, Laboratoire d'Économie et de Sociologie du Travail, 1984).

28. Trempé, *Les mineurs de Carmaux*, 604.

29. François Ewald, "Formation de la notion d'accident du travail," *Sociologie du travail* 1 (1981): 13. Ewald also applies this approach to the formation of old age as a social risk. François Ewald, "Old Age as a Risk: The Establishment of Retirement Pension Schemes in France," in *Old Age and the Welfare State*, ed. Guillemard, 115–26.

30. In addition to company bankruptcies that swallowed up workers' savings, there were many examples of employers having discretionary powers over pension funds. The funds could be used for purposes quite unrelated to pensions, and workers nearing retirement age could be deprived of their rights through dismissal.

31. See in particular Trempé, "The Struggle of French Miners," 101–14.

32. Alain Touraine, *La Conscience ouvrière* (Paris: Le Seuil, 1966).

33. In 1906, 68 percent of industrial workers were employed in companies with a maximum workforce of ten; in other words, the industrial scene was still dominated by small enterprises. By 1926, this figure had fallen to 40 percent, and companies employing over one hundred people had risen over the same period from 25 percent to 37 percent.

34. Cf. Melchers, "La vieillesse ouvrière, 1836–1914," 429–43.

35. It proved abortive only because a legal ruling put an end to the principle of obligation, and permitted only part of the law to be applied. As a result, the number of workers insured, which should have exceeded 7 million, having reached 3.5 million in 1913, barely managed to stay at around 1.6 million until the Law on Social Insurance was passed in 1930. Then, retirees under the 1910 law accounted for scarcely 20 percent of the elderly population. Francis Netter has shown that this law mostly benefited former employees who were aged sixty to sixty-five in 1912, and who could request immediate payment of their pensions (see "Les retraites en France au cours de la période 1895–1945," part 3, *Droit social*, September–October 1965, 515.

36. The CGTU had been hostile to the bill, but was relatively isolated in its opposition to the law, as the strike action that it initiated against Social Insurance was unsuccessful. By contrast, Léon Jouhaux's CGT campaigned actively in its favor from 1921 to 1930.

37. Antoine Prost notes that older workers were sometimes being retired early in the mines from 1927, and on the railways from 1931, as retirement became a "substitute for unemployment": "Jalons pour une histoire des retraites et des retraités," 267. Retirement was becoming an increasingly important means of controlling the size of the workforce.

38. Guy Perrin defines social insurance as a limited form of solidarity for the lowest-paid wage earners, who had finally been obliged to look after their own interests in the name of social responsibility; this was after they had been encouraged, with little success, to do so in the name of individual freedom. Perrin, "Pour une théorie sociologique de la Sécurité sociale dans les sociétés industrielles," *Revue française de Sociologie* 8 (1967): 310.

39. Estimates for this are taken from Patrice Grevet, *Besoins populaires et financement public* (Paris: Éditions Sociales, 1976), 440–60.

40. For the exact provisions of the law, see Netter, "Les retraites en France, 1895–1945," part 3, 515–17. In an effort to spread the cost of introducing old age insurance, the Law on Social Insurance only allocated a full pension of 40 percent of average pay to those

who had been insured for thirty years—in other words, to those who had been aged thirty in 1930 and would not be able to draw their pension until 1960. For other workers, provision was even less generous, and the conditions for obtaining even the minimum pension were extremely strict.

41. These calculations are taken from Antoine Prost, "Jalons pour une histoire des retraites et des retraités," 264; and L. Legrain, *La retraite nationale des vieux travailleurs*, 1939, quoted by ibid.

42. Francis Netter gives a higher figure, as he includes 322,000 recipients of a complementary social insurance pension on 31 December 1937. Netter, "Les retraites en France, 1895–1945," part 3, 517).

43. Even retired wage earners on small pensions from favored sectors did not remain idle. Antoine Prost describes them as part-time workers who supplemented their income from small pensions with income from small jobs.

44. Source: J. Daric, *Vieillissement de la population et prolongation de la vie active* (Population aging and extending active life), INED, Travaux et Documents, cahier no. 7 (Paris: Presses Universitaires de France, 1948), 85, 92.

45. In this book, "social security" refers only to the French system. See the glossary.

46. For an interpretation of the ideal social security system, and a typology of the different systems, see Perrin, "Pour une théorie sociologique," 311 et seq.

47. Apart from the CGPME (Confédération Générale des Petites et Moyennes Entreprises—General Confederation of Small- and Medium-Sized Companies), there was no organization that represented employers at this time. The CNPF (Confédération Nationale du Patronat Français—National Confederation of French Employers) only came into being in December 1945, and was not formally constituted until June 1946.

48. J.-D. Reynaud, *Les syndicats en France* (Paris: Armand Colin, 1963), 1:56.

49. Charles de Gaulle, *Mémoires de Guerre. Le Salut, 1944–1946* (Paris: Plon, 1959), 121.

50. H. Ehrmann, *La politique du patronat français, 1936–1955* (Paris: Armand Colin, 1959).

51. Henry C. Galant, *Histoire politique de la Sécurité sociale française, 1945–1952* (Paris: Armand Colin, 1955), 59–60.

52. De Gaulle, *Mémoires de Guerre*, 28.

53. In de Gaulle's view, for France to achieve cohesion, workers had to feel once more part of the nation. He also believed that the idea that workers might again distance themselves from the nation was unacceptable to the country. Public opinion was in favor of rebuilding the economy so that service to the community came before private individuals making profits, and at the same time improved the condition of the working class. See ibid.

54. De Gaulle believed that the flood of passions, hopes, and pains lavished on the combatants, the immense human intermingling to which they had been subjected, and the effort required for reconstruction placed the social question at the forefront of all the problems that the state had to solve. He had no doubt that there would be no lasting order without profound and rapid changes in this area.

55. This theme is developed in particular by T. H. Marshall, *Social Policy* (London: Hutchinson University Library, 1965); and R. M. Titmuss, *Essays on the Welfare State* (London: Unwin, 1963).

56. H. Michel and B. Mirkine-Guetzevitch, *Les idées politiques et sociales de la résistance* (Paris: Presses Universitaires de France, 1954), 217. On the National Resistance Council and its program, see also J.-P. Rioux, *L'ardeur et la nécessité, 1944–1952,* vol. 1 of *La France de la Quatrième République* (Paris: Le Seuil, 1980), 77.

57. Pierre Laroque, "La Sécurité sociale de 1944 à 1951," *Revue française des Affaires sociales*, April–June 1971, 12.

58. Ibid., 11.

59. This relationship is confirmed by international comparative analyses that establish correlations between the level of old age coverage and the power of the trade unions and the presence of the democratic parties in government. Cf. Mary Maguire, "Pension Policy: An Overview of Patterns of Development and the Impact of Party," a paper given at the European Consortium for Political Research, Lancaster, U.K., April 1981.

60. Social security had been mainly designed for workers: to preserve their health (health and industrial injuries insurance) and to ensure the restoration of their work ability and increase the birth rate through family allowances.

61. For an account of the employers' position on social security, see C. Bonifay and H. Sylvander, in CERS (Centre d'Étude des Relations Sociales), *Sécurité sociale et conflits de classes* (Paris: Éditions Ouvrières, 1962), 51–73.

62. Quoted by Reynaud, *Les syndicats en France*, 1:58.

63. It should be noted that the CGT, in focusing on the campaign for social insurance, did not at the time oppose the separation of sickness and old-age risks, or their management through either pay-as-you-go or funded systems.

64. The view taken by the representatives of employers' associations on the 1945 Social Security Special Commission is convincing evidence of this. Cf. Galant, *Histoire politique de la Sécurité sociale française*, 30–32. The employers' position never wavered and largely inspired the 1976 reform, which foundered on this very point.

65. On all these questions, see G. Lefranc, *Les expériences syndicales en France de 1939 à 1950* (Paris: Aubier Montaigne, 1950), 310–12.

66. On the campaign for family allowances and the single fund, see Galant, *Histoire politique de la Sécurité sociale française.* For a short summary, see J. Doublet, *Sécurité sociale* (Paris: Presses Universitaires de France, 1964), 36–37.

67. The CGT had been demanding the creation of autonomous funds managed by workers as part of social insurance since its 1923 Congress; the union was reluctant to allow employers to participate in the management of these funds (Galant, *Histoire politique de la Sécurité sociale française,* 13). At the time, the CGT was in favor of workers' contributions because it believed that they gave workers the right to be involved in management.

The CGTU opposed the idea of social insurance, but was in favor "of the management of the funds by workers alone, to the exclusion of all employer representatives, through their trade unions" (CGTU pamphlet "Les Assurances sociales et la classe ouvrière," quoted by Lefranc, *Les expériences syndicales en France de 1939 à 1950*, 313.

68. The Soviet example exerted considerable influence after the Liberation. Cf. Grégoire Madjarian, *Conflits, pouvoirs et société à la Libération* (Paris: UGE, Coll 10/18, 1980), 342–43. While the Beveridge model in Britain directly influenced experts working with Laroque and Parodi on the administration plan, the Soviet experience had more impact on the Communist members of the National Resistance Council and on the various commissions that were consulted under the plan.

69. Laroque, "La Sécurité sociale de 1944 à 1951," 13. Social security funds achieved autonomy in practical terms by being set up as private-sector companies.

70. The ordinance of 4 October 1945 provided for the *appointment* of trade-union representatives and gave them two-thirds of the seats on the management committees. The 30 October 1946 act brought in the *election* of representatives, and altered the ratio of union seats to employers' seats to 3:1.

71. Those who ran the *mutualité* (mutual insurance) scheme were not insured members; they were executives, shopkeepers, industrialists, and members of the liberal professions; the uninsured therefore behaved in a paternalistic manner toward the insured. There was no true democracy.

72. At the April 1946 Congress, the first to be held after the war, the Communists

polled approximately 80 percent of the votes and controlled the seven biggest union federations (Rioux, *L'ardeur et la nécessité*, 115).

73. The following analysis of the role played by the unions in the initial stages and implementation of social security is based on Henry Galant's well-documented and detailed description of the political history of social security from 1945 to 1952, and on conversations with key observers of the period.

74. They were represented on the Special Commission, which was made up as follows: one state councillor, two representatives of the Consultative Assembly, ten ministry representatives, four representatives of employers' associations, four representatives of social insurance organizations, four representatives of family allowance compensation funds, three experts in industrial injuries, and two representatives of the Alsace-Lorraine social insurance schemes.

75. The results of the vote were as follows: the Communist Party won with 26 percent, and the MRP came second with 25.6 percent and rising fast; the SFIO took 24.6 percent, but had fallen back slightly compared with 1936. The Communists, Socialists, and MRP combined had an absolute majority: they had over three-quarters of the votes and over 80 percent of the seats. The moderates and radicals were routed, and the Right was nowhere in sight.

76. Galant, *Histoire politique,* 69.

77. Even *Le Monde* published articles on the plan under headlines such as "Pensions Extended to Older Workers" (13 April 1946) and "Croizat Addresses Council of Ministers on the Possibility of Extending Pension to All Elderly People in France as part of French Social Security Plan" (17 April 1946). On 20 April 1946 the same newspaper announced: "The bill making social security generally available has been adopted by the Council of Ministers at the request of Ambroise Croizat. It gives an old-age pension to all categories of French citizen over the age of sixty-five." See also *Le Monde* of 28–29 April 1946. It was not until 4 May 1946 that Marcel Tardy, in an article entitled "Compulsory Social Insurance for All French Citizens," made it clear that, contrary to what most French people believed, the law not only provided for an extension of the old-age pension but also made insurance compulsory for the whole population.

78. The law also provided for the immediate interim payment of a temporary benefit to all unwaged older workers who were "économiquement faibles" (on very low incomes).

79. Henri Raynaud, an outspoken opponent of the 1930 law on social insurance, stated during the Confederal Congress of April 1946 that the CGT wholly subscribed to the social security plan: "Even though the current social security legislation is not perfect, the Confederal Congress of the CGT reiterates our union's full support."

80. The CGT had eight times more members than the CFTC. It claimed 6 million members in 1946 at a time when CFTC membership was about 700,000.

81. Pierre Laroque, preface to Galant, *Histoire politique,* 14.

82. On all these matters, see Antoinette Catrice-Lorey, *Dynamique interne de la Sécurité sociale* (Paris: Economica, 1981), 36 et seq.; and Laroque, "La Sécurité sociale de 1944 à 1951," 13–14.

83. For details of the CGT strategy to take control of social security, see Galant, *Histoire politique,* 69–75, and J. Doublet, *Sécurité sociale* (Paris: Presses Universitaires de France, 1964), 37.

84. Quoted by Catrice-Lorey, *Dynamique interne de la Sécurité sociale,* 38.

85. Quoted by ibid.

86. The term "self-employed" *(travailleurs indépendants)* is used to describe craft workers, shopkeepers, small industrial employers, and members of the liberal professions.

87. Cf. Henry Roson in his chapter on the middle classes and their representation in *Succès et faiblesses de l'effort social français,* ed. P. Laroque et al. (Paris: Armand Colin, 1961), 219–43.

88. René Mathieu (CGC), "Les cadres," in CERS, *Sécurité sociale et conflits de classes*, 85. "Cadres are very disturbed by cases of senior members who built up good pensions in 1938, but had to ask for the older workers' retirement pension in 1945."

89. This phrase ("seuil de respectabilité") is used by Guy Perrin to describe the line of social respectability drawn by the Social Insurance earnings ceiling. Perrin, "Pour une théorie sociologique," 309.

90. The collective agreement of 14 May 1937, signed by the UIMM and the Fédération Nationale des Syndicats d'Ingénieurs (National Federation of Engineering Unions), set up a generous savings scheme for cadres not covered by social insurance. It was an employer initiative. By responding in this way to the need of their "collaborators" to provide for their own and their families' security, the large employers had two aims in mind: firstly, during the days of massive trade-union recruitment in 1936, they wanted to prevent the cadres from getting too close to the unions; secondly, they wanted to strengthen the ties that these "collaborators" had with management. The cadres were thus covered by voluntary group insurance, whereas the lowest-paid wage earners were dependent on social insurance.

91. Cf. Luc Boltanski, *Les cadres. La formation d'un groupe social* (Paris: Éditions de Minuit, 1982).

92. *Cadres de France,* August 1945, quoted by ibid., 149–50.

93. "We need to form a bloc to oppose a uniform pension for all French citizens. Let us not forget that we support a hierarchy of both salaries and pensions, but not everyone shares our point of view." Speaker at the CGC Congress, August 1946, quoted by Mathieu, "Les cadres," 86.

94. "We are opposed to any extension of social insurance to people who will be obliged to pay, and pay dearly, when practically nothing will be done for them for a very long time." "La voix des cadres," *Le Creuset*, quoted by Mathieu, "Les cadres," 82.

95. Hatzfeld, *Du paupérisme à la Sécurité sociale*, 302.

96. For an analysis of how small employers changed their view on social benefits between 1945 and 1978, see François Gresle, "Indépendance professionnelle et protection sociale. Pratiques de classe et fluctuations idéologiques du petit patronat," *Revue française de Sociologie* 18, no. 4 (October–December 1977): 577–99.

97. In its early days, the CGC recruited mainly among Catholic engineers.

98. The cartel strongly supported the principles of the social security plan, and above all wanted to ensure that the system was as widely available as possible. It therefore came out in favor of a complementary plan for cadres that ensured their involvement in collective solidarity within the limitations of the ceiling.

99. In an account of the history of the cadres' supplementary pension funds, its president significantly described it as "a joint effort on the part of employers and salaried cadres." A. Milan, "Le régime complémentaire des cadres," in *Les régimes complémentaires de retraites par répartition,* ed. François Piketty (Paris: Documentation française, 1965), 31–40.

100. In the view of René Mathieu, if the employers had not intervened, the CGC would probably have lost the battle, and the cadres would eventually have been completely integrated into the social security plan. Mathieu, "Les cadres," 87.

101. ORGANIC: Organisation Autonome de l'Assurance Vieillesse de l'Industrie et du Commerce (Autonomous Organization for Old-Age Insurance in Industry and Commerce). See the glossary.

102. CANCAVA: Caisse Autonome de Compensation de l'Assurance Vieillesse Artisanale (Craft Workers' Autonomous Old-Age Insurance Compensation Fund). See the glossary.

103. The 17 January 1948 act could not be applied to farmers until the new 10 July 1952 act provided for a financial contribution from the state.

104. The Communist Party remained the biggest party in France, with 28.8 percent of the votes, but the SFIO received only 18 percent; the MRP held steady with 26.8 percent. The Right and the Center made a comeback with impressive support (15.4 percent for the independents and 11.4 percent for the radicals).

105. The Christian Democrats had always been ardent defenders of plurality of funds, and were behind the bill of 12 December 1946, which was designed to set up a special social security fund for each of the professional categories.

106. H. Ehrmann characterizes the position of the CNPF social commission until 1955 as purely defensive. The employers were cutting their losses, and it was not until the late 1960s that they adopted a more positive position and moved onto the offensive. Ehrmann, *La politique du patronat français*.

107. "Living conditions have deteriorated to such an extent that you would have to be very optimistic to imagine that older workers are at last heading for that hard-earned rest they deserve in the few months remaining to them." "Les sacrifiés de la vie," *Le Peuple,* 29 January 1948.

108. The slow progress, even the regression, in the rate of contributions from wages devoted to expenditure on old age over this period clearly shows the narrow limits within which the general old-age insurance scheme operated.

Changes in the rate of contribution from wages devoted to expenditure on old age

1947	1948	1949	1950	1951	1952	1953	1958
4.79	4.41	5.75	7.21	6.99	6.40	6.80	5.30

109. Results by socioprofessional category show that working-class people had the highest level (48 percent) of dissatisfaction; only 31 percent of higher-graded employees in industry and shopkeepers were dissatisfied. Cf. the survey introduced by Alain Girard in Daric, *Vieillissement de la population,* 195.

110. Quoted by *Les régimes complémentaires de retraites par répartition,* ed. Piketty, 42.

111. The destitution of the elderly population was underlined by the administration's figures for the number of potential recipients of the complementary allowance under the Fonds National de Solidarité (National Solidarity Fund). They were estimated at 4.5 million in 1955, the 1954 census having revealed that there were 5,184,000 people aged sixty-five and over. Approximately 80 percent of the elderly population at the time did not have an income above the ceiling fixed for the complementary allowance (2,850 francs for a married couple). Of all retirees living on the general scheme, 55 percent received benefits from the National Solidarity Fund in 1958, although the allowance was distributed much less generously than had been originally projected: there were only 2,550,000 recipients, less than half the number forecast.

112. *Le Peuple*, 29 January 1948.

113. This can be verified by reference to the number of members of National Solidarity Fund plans in 1958: 55 percent of beneficiaries of the general scheme were in receipt of Solidarity Fund benefits, but this proportion rose to 67 percent in the farmers' plan and 89 percent in the craft workers' and shopkeepers' plan. Source: Laroque Report, 93.

114. *Vie ouvrière*, 2 March 1960.

115. These demands were submitted in identical form by the three confederations, and were regularly restated from 1950 onward in Confederal Congress resolutions.

116. The resurgence of this traditional working-class demand, now freshly phrased in the context of the new social security system, also signified that trade unions had returned

to classical forms of action, following hiatuses during the immediate postwar period and the "battle for production." In her thesis, "La CGT et les revendications ouvrières face à l'État (Septembre 1944–Décembre 1947)" (Paris-I, 1981), Annie Lacroix-Riz notes that, at the end of 1947, trade unionists returned to "classic" practices of class struggle when they resumed their prewar campaign against overexploitation brought about by the drive for productivity.

117. *Le Peuple*, 1 October 1957, 12.

118. Roger Mario (CGT), "Table ronde sur l'âge de la retraite," *Esprit*, no. 5 (May 1963): 875–76. Normal retirement age under the 1930 social insurance scheme was sixty.

119. The same position was defended in similar terms by the CFTC and the CGT-FO. Cf. speeches made by Charles Gatinel (CFTC) and André Bergeron (FO) in the course of the aforementioned "round table."

120. According to the 1954 census, half the male population aged sixty-five to sixty-nine (i.e., those of pensionable age) were still working. As a result, the general availability of the right to retirement, which was established under the social security system, did not encourage widespread adoption among older workers. Between 1936 and 1954, there was only a 23 percent drop in men aged sixty-five to sixty-nine still working; percentages of this age group still working fell from 65 percent in 1936 to 50 percent in 1962. The proportion still working began to fall more rapidly in 1962, when the figure stood at only 38 percent (October employment survey and censuses). See table 5.1 in the appendix.

121. Cf. research findings in A.-M. Guillemard, *La retraite, une mort sociale* (Paris: Mouton, 1972).

122. This result was obtained by tabulating the "issues occurring in the debate" item with the locutors, and by examining the different issues presented by the trade unions as locutors between 1946 and 1975.

123. There will be further examination of this question in chapter 3 in the context of employment.

124. For a summary of this issue, which figured frequently in the trade union press during the period, see Henri Raynaud's detailed article in *Le Peuple* of 15 October 1957: "Comment lutter pour l'amélioration des rentes, pensions, et allocations vieillesse tant à l'intérieur qu'à l'extérieur des régimes existants." See also the article on Roger Mario's speech to the FNOSS (Fédération Nationale des Organismes de la Sécurité Sociale—National Federation of Social Security Organizations) (1 December 1954). The CFTC position is covered in the historical background supplied by Mathevet in his report to the Economic and Social Council on the balance and management of complementary pension plans (Session of 10 July 1962), and an article entitled "L'évolution des retraites complémentaires" in the 25 July 1962 issue of *Syndicalisme*.

125. At the "Trois Journées pour l'Étude Scientifique du Vieillissement de la Population" (22–24 April 1948), Mme Poinso-Chapuis, the minister of public health and the population, spoke in favor of the development of family policy and extension of the working life. During the "Journées d'Étude sur l'Amélioration du Sort des Gens Agés" (Lille, 18–20 October 1952), Paul Ribeyre, the new minister of public health, declared that "it was difficult to disagree with the need to defer the age of retirement," and that "the extension of working life needed to be organized in such a way as to ensure a more satisfactory balance between working and nonworking people, and take account of such factors as the type of work carried out and the degree of aptitude required for the job at a given age."

126. There were several indicators of this change in attitude. Examples include:

- Henri Raynaud's (CGT) resignation as president of the FNOSS at the end of 1949;
- the CGT's plea, during the 1947 election campaign, that electors be patient about inadequate benefits and imperfections in the legislation, followed by a call in 1950 urging insured employees to press for the "reconquest" of social security by workers.

127. In the matter of relations between social security and the supervisory structure, this book relies on the penetrating analyses of Antoinette Catrice-Lorey, and in particular her *Dynamique interne de la Sécurité sociale* and "La Sécurité sociale et l'État en France: Quelle autonomie de gestion pour l'institution?" *Revue internationale de Sécurité sociale*, no. 2 (1983): 213–28.

128. Catrice-Lorey, "La Sécurité Sociale et l'État," 219.

129. The CGT said it issued 6,369,000 membership cards in 1946, while the CFTC claimed 800,000 members in the same year; total trade-union membership in France was approximately 7–8 million. In 1950, it was estimated to be around 4 million, and there were probably more nonmembers than members. (Source: Lefranc, *Les expériences syndicales en France, 1939–1950*, 367.) Jean-Pierre Rioux estimates that no more than 15 percent of the workforce were in trade unions in 1955 (*L'ardeur et la nécessité*, 256).

130. Cf. Reynaud, *Les syndicats en France*, 100.

131. "L'insuffisance du système vieillesse," *Le Peuple*, 15 January 1957.

132. The headline of an article in *Le Peuple*, 15 February 1957. Policy statements issued by the CGT Administrative Commission on 27 June 1956 clearly show that the union was in favor of complementary plans at the time: "Push at all times for an increase in the number and general availability of complementary old-age plans, on the basis of the best of the implemented programs; use every available means and try to implement all plans according to the available possibilities—the company, the locality, the industrial sector, the region, and the national plan." An article in *Le Peuple* of 1 July 1956 states that, in the view of the CGT, action had to be taken on two fronts—the general scheme and complementary plans: "It has become obvious to everyone that, while developing the general scheme to obtain satisfaction for the workers as a whole, action also had to be taken to extend complementary pension plans."

133. "La retraite c'est la vie au rabais," *Vie ouvrière*, 2 March 1960.

134. Quoted by Jean-Pierre Dumont, "L'anarchie des retraites," *Le Monde*, 5 February 1971.

135. During this period, a new issue made its appearance in the public debate: this was the policy of integrating the elderly, and it featured in 16 percent of articles. The next chapter will examine this question in greater detail.

136. Interestingly, the issue of pensions does not appear under "policy," but under "negotiating demands." Negotiations clearly win the day over demands, as the locutor most frequently referred to was "joint." Cf. results of the analysis of articles in *Le Monde*.

137. François Sellier has highlighted the links between pension provision and salary, noting that social supplements increase during periods of strong pressure on wages. Sellier, "Les retraites comme les autres compléments sociaux sont des substituts des augmentations de salaire," in *Dynamique des besoins sociaux* (Paris: Éditions Ouvrières, 1970), 241.

138. Daric, *Vieillissement de la population*, cahier no. 7.

139. "Opinions et attitudes des chefs d'entreprise à l'égard des travailleurs âgés dans l'entreprise," in *Les personnes âgées et l'opinion en France*, ed. High Consultative Committee on Population and the Family (Paris: Documentation française, 1962), 93–164.

140. The view of a company director in the metallurgy sector employing a workforce of two hundred; interviewed in the 1961 IFOP survey in *Les personne âgées*, ed. High Consultative Committee, 117.

141. The old-age pension plan provided for 40 percent of salary up to a ceiling; the complementary plans gave an average of 20 percent.

142. High Consultative Committee on Population and the Family, ed., *Les personnes âgées et l'opinion en France*, 118.

143. On this point, see in particular Piketty, ed., *Les régimes complémentaires*, 42. He notes that "the Renault agreements attracted attention in all parts of the economy, and with

both employers and workers." On the employers' side, the agreements certainly disturbed the contractual vacuum (Bernard Brizay) that had characterized the period 1950–55. The CNPF expressed reservations at the time, fearing that company agreements might trigger developments in the most prosperous companies, and would unsettle those in a more precarious situation if they were adopted more widely. Notwithstanding, the episode paved the way for the 1961 agreement on the general availability of ARRCO.

144. On the tactical value of company agreements, see François Sellier, *Stratégie de la lutte sociale en France, 1936–1960* (Paris: Éditions Ouvrières, 1961).

145. This situation was acknowledged by the CGT. The union stated that "it would not only be ineffective but mistaken and, to an extent, dangerous to imagine that the struggle for the right to manage could be won within the framework of existing complementary plans. All of them, even the least bad, like the AGRR, are still usually initiated and managed by employers. There is therefore no hope of putting workers in as managers in the prevailing social climate simply by referring to our contribution in the plans." "Les régimes complémentaires vieillesse répondent à une nécessité vitale pour les travailleurs," *Le Peuple*, 15 February 1957.

146. Steve Cohen thought that the question of industrial competitiveness was one of the causes of permanent crisis in the French social security system. In Cohen's view, this had its origins in the increasingly deep contradictions between the industrial imperative defended by the modernizing alliance formed by the plan and large companies and the workings of the traditional political system. "From Permacrisis to Real Crisis in French Social Security: The Limits to Normal Politics," in *Stress and Contradiction in Modern Capitalism,* ed. L. Lindberg et al. (Lexington, Mass.: Lexington Books, 1975), 57–98.

147. Before UNIRS came into being, four hundred thousand salaried noncadres qualified for a supplementary pension plan.

148. Cf. Bernard Brizay, "Le Plan: Le rachat patronal," in *Le patronat* (Paris: Le Seuil, 1975), 69 et seq.; and idem, "Les patrons au gouvernement," in *Le patronat,* 25 et seq.: "

149. The employers felt they could not take management responsibility for Social Security institutions with only a quarter of the seats. See CERS, *Sécurité sociale et conflits de classe*, 61.

150. Cf. Pierre Birnbaum's analysis of the upper echelons of the state structure; this underlines how the strength of the middle classes in Parliament and government grew during the Fourth Republic.

151. Jacques Doublet, director general of Social Security from 1951 to 1960, also recognized these limitations: "For years, maintaining the ceiling below the legally required level deprived social security of several billion francs a year. There was also a systematic tendency to relieve local authorities of the task of making certain payments that had hitherto been ascribed to classical systems of public assistance; this was achieved by generalizing and fixing uniform contributions that had previously been means-tested according to needs and financial resources." Jacques Doublet, "La Sécurité sociale et son évolution," *Revue française des Affaires sociales*, April–June 1971, 30–31.

152. In 1956, there were as many as six hundred unregulated complementary pension funds of various kinds.

153. UNIRS (Union Nationale des Institutions de Retraites des Salariés—National Union of Employees' Pension Institutions) was founded on 15 May 1957 by the CNPF, FO, and CFTC. The CGT joined on 22 July 1958. Its objective was to bring order to the anarchy that then reigned among complementary pension plans by setting up an optional plan "which, through extended compensation and coordination and proper financial rules, provided greater security in the management of pension plans and a firmer guarantee of the durability of contributions." Proceedings of the foundation of UNIRS, quoted by Piketty, ed., *Les régimes complémentaires de retraites par répartition*, 42. ARRCO (Association des Régimes de

Retraite Complémentaires—Association of Complementary Pension Plans) was set up on 8 December 1961 under an agreement between the CNPF, FO, and CFTC; the CGT and CGC joined in 1962. It extended complementary pensions to virtually all employees, and made it possible for plans to be coordinated.

154. There is evidence for this in the different levels of contributions in different sectors; this resulted in retirees in different sectors receiving different levels of pensions.

155. Contributory service rose from thirty to thirty-seven and a half years, average salary was calculated on the basis of the best ten years, and the pension was increased to 50 percent (up from 40 percent) of salary up to a ceiling of the best ten years.

156. The 1967 social security ordinances were largely influenced by employer opposition to social security. They particularly provided for the separation of risks and equal representation on management committees.

157. The first full pensions under the general scheme were paid out in 1960 to retirees who had been insured since 1930.

Chapter 2. Old Age and Ways of Life

1. Studies carried out under the aegis of the Commission d'Étude des Problèmes de la Vieillesse (Study Commission on the Elderly) showed that elderly people living in rural areas were better off than those living in urban areas. First, there were major food and housing problems in the towns, and these were less acute in the country. Second, the proportion of elderly people living alone was higher in the towns: in the Paris region, 40 percent of homes inhabited by elderly people contained only one person in this category, while 43 percent contained an elderly couple; in the country, 42 percent of retired agricultural workers lived with their children. Source: *Les personnes âgées et l'opinion publique* (Paris: Documentation française, 1962), 18.

2. Mr. Roclore, president of the Commission on the Family, the Population, and Public Health, minutes of the debate, *Journal officiel*, National Assembly, 31 May 1949, p. 2932.

3. Elie Alfandari, *Aide sociale* (Paris: Dalloz, 1977), 195.

4. This percentage is calculated on the basis of figures in the Laroque Report (p. 107). See table of public assistance expenditure for the elderly living in towns in 1959 (ibid.).

5. Despite considerable regional and organizational variations (e.g. ,sections of hospitals given over to the elderly, and community-based old people's homes), the percentage of patients under the age of sixty never rose above 19 percent during 1963, and even dropped to around 16 percent in 1965. During the same period, the average admission age climbed to seventy-eighty. In the Seine Region, it rose three to four years on average compared with the period 1945–60. (Source: IGAS Report, 1968–69, pp. 233–34).

6. Confusing figures relating to old people's homes and retirement homes in the public sector make it difficult to chart the progress made by these two forms of housing. At all events, 90.7 percent of old people's homes were built before 1945, and 40 percent of retirement homes were put up between 1945 and 1959 (Caisse Nationale d'Assurance Vieillesse des Travailleurs Salariés, *Recensement des réalisations immobilières en faveur des personnes âgées* (Paris: CNAVTS, 1960).

7. M. Mayen, "La population des hospices et des maisons de retraite," *Population*, no. 1 (1972): 70–82.

8. For a historical analysis of the way in which old people's home policies and public-assistance policies for the destitute elderly acted as a moralizing instrument for all age groups, see Carmen Bernand, *Les vieux vont mourir à Nanterre* (Paris: Ed. du Sagittaire, 1978), 196–251.

9. Fluctuations in the proportions of people aged sixty or over living in community housing (per 1,000) between 1946 and 1962 are as follows: 1946: 27.9; 1954: 21.2; 1962: 23.9. Source: Santé et Sécurité Sociale, *Statistiques et commentaires*, no. 6. Interpreting the causes of variations in these figures is a delicate matter. There are doubts about the numbers of households questioned for the 1946 census, but two other factors also need to be taken into account. First, there were alterations in the demographic structure of the elderly population by gender, age group, and marital status; there is no doubt that housing demands are greatly influenced by changes of this sort. Second, changes in the supply of accommodation were able to contain or reduce the rate at which the elderly were housed.

10. Report on the organization of medical and other forms of public assistance for the elderly, *Bulletin d'information du Ministère de la Santé Publique de la Population*, no. 2 (1960): 19.

11. In 1949, the ceiling for receiving the poverty card was an income of 75,000 francs per year for a single person and 100,000 francs per year for a couple.

12. Concerns articulated during the debate on the Poverty Card were very similar to those that had been expressed in 1871 during the debate on the law on the hospices. The following statement from a Socialist representative is an illustration of this: "We believe that if a nation has a duty towards lower-income groups, their children have an even greater duty. The state should intervene only when the children are unable to help their parents. An excess of welfare should not cause children to forget their most sacred duty." Proceedings of the National Assembly, 31 May 1949, p. 2938.

13. In the Chamber of Deputies debate on the poverty card, one member referred to it as the "card that entitles you to nothing" and that "in no way solves the problem of the wretchedness endured by the elderly in this country." Proceedings of the National Assembly, First Sitting, 31 May 1949, p. 2940.

14. On this point, see the excellent analysis of the abortion question and the Bobigny trial by Maurice Mouillaud et al., *Stratégies de la presse et du droit* (Lyon: Presses Universitaires de Lyon, 1979), 213–35.

15. Each article was coded according to the images of old age that it portrayed.

16. Taken from a paper delivered by Health Minister Paul Ribeyre to the *Journées d'Étude sur l'amélioration du sort des gens âgés* (*Le Monde*, 17, 18, and 19 October 1952).

17. Congrès National de la Protection de la Vieillesse (National Congress for the Protection of the Elderly) organized by the Association Nationale d'Entraide à la Vieillesse (National Association of Mutual Aid for the Elderly) (*Le Monde*, 24, 27, and 28 October 1946).

18. The shortage of beds in old people's homes and retirement homes, the overpopulation of these institutions, and building programs adopted in the sector were often cited in this connection. In 1951, the prefect of the Seine Region announced the opening of a 250-bed home in Chevilly-Larue. When he discovered that the Bicêtre home held 3,872 people, although its maximum capacity was 2,500, he announced a ten-year plan for the Paris Region that would provide housing for 6,000 old people. This was to allow "the elderly Parisian poor with no means of support to be allowed to lead decent lives until the end of their days" (*Le Monde*, 18 October 1951).

A study carried out in 1958 of the housing situation of elderly people on low incomes by the Municipality of Paris identified a need for 3,000 beds in retirement homes and 4,000 in old people's homes. Plans were adopted by the Public Assistance Department to provide 4,300 beds (*Le Monde*, 19 November 1958).

19. Extracts from a short article in *Le Peuple* (12 October 1946) on old people's homes illustrate this admirably—and show that the old parish poorhouse formula had not been completely buried:

What we need is:

(1) homes where the elderly can spend time with their peers, as if they were in their own homes (this is vital);

(2) clean, healthy, well-ventilated buildings;

(3) we want to see:

a. sufficient tables and chairs;

b. a library;

c. games;

d. materials for elderly women who want to do knitting; also, and without overdoing the abstract considerations, some mutual solidarity between men and women to bring them together, based on soling shoes;

(4) a good fire;

(5) hot drinks;

(6) a home set up by the local council and managed by the local branch of the Union Nationale des Vieux Travailleurs de France (National Union of French Former Workers).

A lot of good will is going to be needed, but we will see to that; suburban local authorities have already been asking questions.

20. The title of the Study Commission's report was *Politique de la Vieillesse* (Old-age policy) (Paris: Documentation Française, 1962).

21. Laroque Report, 262.

22. Ibid., 9.

23. Ibid., 208.

24. Ibid., 4.

25. Ibid., 215.

26. Ibid., 247.

27. Ibid., 245.

28. Ph. Ariès, *L'enfant et la vie familiale sous l'Ancien Régime* (Paris: Le Seuil, 1973), 21.

29. Article 1 of the decree that set up the commission.

30. Intergroup Report: *Problèmes relatifs aux personnes âgées* (Paris: Documentation Française, 1971),13.

31. The other three were improving the job market, perinatal care, and new towns.

32. The Intergroup Report expressly stated that "the state's initiative should ensure that provision is not restricted to those in receipt of compulsory public assistance; this objective might be achieved by asking for a monetary contribution. Such a contribution should reflect their financial situation" (*Problèmes relatifs aux personnes âgées,* 107).

33. *Journal officiel*, 31 January 1960.

34. Report on the organization of medical and other forms of public assistance for the elderly, *Bulletin d'Information du Ministère de la Santé Publique et de la Population*, no. 2 (1960).

35. Established under a public decree in the *Journal officiel* of 5 January 1961.

36. The construction of forty thousand places in old people's homes and retirement homes was written into the Fourth Plan. The increase in the number of retirement and nursing homes during the period 1939–72 also highlights the rapid growth in beds between 1958 and 1962.

37. The issue of demands had previously fluctuated, according to the bands of years examined, between 2 percent and 15 percent.

38. Criticism of elderly people's material living conditions first appeared in the press in 1955; until 1960, fewer than 10 percent of articles were devoted to the subject.

39. This shift was well documented by the content analysis of *Le Monde* when looking at the various beneficiaries. The elderly people referred to during the period 1946–60 were mainly from lower-income groups or were extremely poor; depending on the year, they featured in 36 to 56 percent of articles. From 1960 onward, the press saw all elderly people as the targets and beneficiaries of social action. In 1959, this category of beneficiaries rose to second place with 29 percent of articles. After 1962, it occupied first place and accounted for 35 to 50 percent of articles.

40. *Journal officiel*, session of the National Assembly, 20 May 1960, 1027.

41. Representative for the Union pour la Nouvelle République, 20 May 1960.

42. Laroque Report, 3–4.

43. *Les personnes âgées et l'opinion publique,* 91–197.

44. These new concerns were expressed in discussions that took place during preparations for the Fourth Plan. They were also echoed in Pierre Drouin, "Le progrès social ne doit plus être un sous-produit de l'expansion," *Le Monde*, 12 December 1962.

45. This formula has been borrowed from Pierre Laroque, who stated that "the disparity between, on the one hand, the ambitions of social endeavor and the means required to achieve its objectives, and the psychological behavior of the population, on the other, is the main obstacle to that endeavor bearing fruit. This disparity may be erased or attenuated only by continuous effort over a long period aimed at solidarity education." *Succès et faiblesses de l'effort social français*, ed. Pierre Laroque (Paris: Armand Colin, 1961), 349.

46. Laroque Report, 5.

47. The development of social sciences in France clearly influenced both this new formulation of the problem of old age and the development of this new definition. The involvement of these disciplines is evident from the composition of the commission, in that four of its nine members were academics who specialized in this field.

48. The Caisse Interprofessionnelle de Prévoyance des Cadres (CIPC—Interprofessional Provident Fund for Cadres) opened rest and holiday homes for its members in 1950. A holiday service was added in 1955, and residential homes were built in 1960. In 1962, the president of the Social Funds Commission of AGIRC (Association Générale des Institutions de Retraite des Cadres—General Association of Executive Pensions Institutions) wrote that the social action provided by complementary schemes "concerned itself with providing retirees with a choice of the best living conditions. Contacts with members, which has been systematically carried out in interviews by some of the funds, has revealed that their difficulties are not necessarily anything to do with a shortage of money, but are often linked to their age and state of health, and to social changes that make it impossible for them to lead normal lives." J. Fréville, "L'action sociale des régimes complémentaires," *Droit social* 7–8 (July–August 1962): 452.

49. The Association Village-Retraite (Retirement Village Association) was founded in 1958. Membership was by election, and it financed its activities with money from the Caisses Cadres (Cadre Funds). The formula developed rapidly after 1962, and by the mid-1980s there were as many seventeen retirement villages altogether.

50. *Le Monde* of 30 January 1961 described the opening of a new retirement home in Montereau as follows: "The building, whose foundation stone was laid fourteen months ago, resembles a large, welcoming hotel with its spacious hall, snack bar, library, telephone, and mail room, unisex hairdresser's, four hundred–seat theater, and newspaper and book stand ."

51. *Syndicalisme*, June 1962. Elsewhere, the CGT spoke of "workers cruel disillusionment with the commission's deliberations that reject all their demands," while the FO deplored the fact that the commission "challenges the principles that the union holds dear by encouraging aging workers to continue working."

52. Roger Thierry and Vincent Dominique, "Problèmes actuels de la vieillesse,"

Economie et politique, March 1963, 34. This article argues that the Laroque Report supported the philosophy of the Gaullist state, and promoted capitalist interests.

53. National Assembly, 15 June 1962.

54. Source: IGAS Report, 1968–69, p. 197.

55. The commission report states: "The elderly have reduced mobility, and are a heavy burden on the overall housing market because they occupy underinhabited accommodation where the rent is high and maintenance difficult. This partly explains why accommodation inhabited by young people is overcrowded. The result is that accommodation occupied by the elderly is inadequately maintained" (ibid., 199).

56. Article 12 of the law of 7 August 1957 had opened up new possibilities for this type of housing. Administrative circulars published in January 1960 and April 1963 further elaborated this formula by specifying community-based facilities and services that should be incorporated for optional use.

57. See table 10. Evolution in the numbers of retirement and nursing homes—public and private sectors, 1939–1972.

58. Source: IGAS Report, 1968–69, p. 28.

59. Laroque Report, 135–36.

60. The Agence Nationale pour l'Emploi (National Employment Agency) was not set up until July 1967.

61. Lucien Nizard et al., *Changement social et appareil d'état* (Grenoble: CÉRAT, 1974).

62. Analysis of the trade-union press reveals that, in the period 1962–67, *Le Peuple* (CGT) carried no articles at all on the way of life of the elderly; all articles on the elderly dealt with pensions (i.e., complementary pension schemes and social security minimum benefits). *Syndicalisme* (CFTC-CFDT) launched several campaigns focusing on the material well-being of the elderly, but only once during the entire period (in October 1965) dealt with the kind of social action that should be promoted in favor of the elderly. Articles in *FO Hebdo* covered the minimum old-age benefit (several times every year) and improvements to complementary pensions; only two articles (in June 1964 and October 1965) were devoted to social action for the elderly.

63. At the 35th Congress of Hygienists in October 1955 (the theme was the problems of old age), all three elements were represented and provided rapporteurs. It was attended by Jean Daric for INED, with Léon Binet and Professor François Bourlière representing the medico-hospital group, and Dr. Roger Wibaux and Dr. Jean-André Huet speaking on behalf of the medical-political axis.

64. It seems to have been Dr. Huet, the leader of the third section, who coined the term "third age" around 1955. The first publication to use the term in its title was by another doctor, H. Destrem from Bordeaux, who might also be counted as a member of the medical-political group. Dr. Destrem's work was entitled *A la conquête du troisième âge ou les secrets de la longévité* (Paris: Gallimard, 1958).

65. The International Association of Gerontology was founded in 1951.

66. Michel Philibert, "Le rôle et l'image du vieillard dans notre société," *Esprit,* no. 5 (May 1963): 928–51. See also his book based on his thesis: *L'Échelle des âges* (Paris: Le Seuil, 1968).

67. For further evidence of this, see references to the work of Robert J. Havighurst and his school in Aline Ripert's article on leisure in *Esprit,* no. 5 (May 1963): 899–911. Michel Philibert, who wrote his complementary thesis on social gerontology in the United States, draws the main points from this in a critical article in the same edition (pp. 994–99).

68. Guillemard, *Old Age and the Welfare State*.

69. In the conclusion to his contribution, François Bourlière stated: "The real enemy is not illness; it is isolation, boredom, and loss of interest when employment comes to an

end. These days, job specialization suffocates secondary interests, and people no longer know how to relax. The result is that, when we reach the age when we have to stop work, we run up against a void. Hobbies and pastimes are the best cure against accelerated aging of the intellect." "Qu'est-ce que vieillir," *Esprit,* no. 5 (May 1963): 730.

70. Founded by Dr. Wibaux (then the health director) and Dr. Huet.

71. This organization, founded by Dr. Huet, was intended to take over from the CERG (Centre d'Étude et de Recherches Gérontologiques—Center for Gerontological Study and Research). It mainly brought together practitioners from the private sector who worked as doctors in old people's homes. These doctors were on the fringe of the hospital hierarchy, but usually had close connections with the public authorities.

72. Xavier Gaullier, *Une politique municipale de la vieillesse. La région grenobloise (1965–1975).* (Paris: Fondation des Villes, 1975). The following analysis is based on Xavier Gaullier's work, other research in the field, and original documents collected for the purposes of writing this book.

73. The very first was probably carried out by the CIPC (Caisse Interprofessionnelle de Prévoyance des Cadres—Interprofessional Provident Fund for Cadres). It took place in 1963, and was published in collaboration with the ISST (Institut des Sciences Sociales du Travail). The study was entitled *Les cadres retraités vus par eux-mêmes* (Paris: CIPC-ISST, October 1965).

74. It should be remembered that the first full pensions under the general scheme were only available from 1960 onwards. They were paid to workers who had joined the scheme in 1930, and who thus benefited from thirty years of insurance contributions.

75. For an account of the establishment of the study of geriatrics, see Nicole Benoît-Lapierre, "Guérir la vieillesse," *Communications* (Paris), no. 37 (1983): 149–65, and her research report (in collaboration with R. Cevasco), *La politique de la santé à l'égard des personnes âgées,* DGRST Report (Paris: EHESS-CETSAS, 1981).

76. The analysis is based on some ten case studies that describe the early days of local integration policies; in addition to Grenoble, there were examples in Saint-Étienne, Bar-le-Duc, Poitiers, Boulogne-Billancourt, Elboeuf, and Montargis. Apart from a few small variations, and disregarding the political affiliations of the local authority, the same groups of protagonists and the same alliances were involved in each case.

77. "The various elements of the action program just outlined are, in the commission's opinion, completely interdependent. It is only by working together at every level that we can possibly hope to provide a satisfactory solution eventually to the problems of old age in France." Laroque Report, 275.

78. For further information, matter, see Xavier Gaullier, *Une politique médico-sociale de la vieillesse: le 13e arrondissement de Paris (1965–1975)* (Paris: Fondation des Villes, 1975).

79. For example, engineers as a proportion of the entire population rose from 2.9 percent to 4.8 percent between 1954 and 1968. In the same period, the proportion of middle-range cadres rose from 5.8 percent to 9.9 percent.

80. This is an approximate assessment, as a true projection would have to have taken account of certain other issues, such as mortality rate (which has a differential effect on professional categories) and the differences to be found in the employment participation rates of older workers (which show how different proportions of people, particularly those aged sixty to sixty-five and in certain jobs, go on retirement). This in turn leads to distortions in observations made of the employed population at a given age. However, the concept of bringing the retirement age down to below sixty-five is a recent phenomenon. In 1962, the percentage of men aged fifty-five to fifty-nine still working was 85.1 percent, and for those aged sixty to sixty-four it was 71.1 percent. This shows that the degree of error concerning men taking early retirement is of relatively little importance in the assessment

that this book makes. To all intents and purposes, early retirement at that time was only to be found among certain socioprofessional groups such as miners, deep-sea fishermen, primary school teachers and railway workers. It has also been decided to study only the employed male population so as to ensure that those variations in changes in the level and nature of female employment do not appear in the comparisons made in this book. These last two elements underwent major modifications during the period in question.

81. INSEE (Institut National de la Statistique et des Etudes Economiques—National Institute of Statistics and Economic Studies) does not register retired people according to their last occupational category. Their statistics are merely entered in relation to the sector in which they worked: public, private, or agricultural.

82. Workers aged fifty-five to sixty-four in 1954 formed the majority of the retired population in 1964 or thereabouts; by then, they were aged sixty-five to seventy-four and represented 64 percent of the elderly population. According to the 1962 census, the breakdown of the elderly male population by age, together amounting to 64 percent, was as follows:

- 65–70 years of age: 37%
- 70–74 years of age: 27%

Those aged 55–64 in 1962 prefigured the dominant age band of elderly people in 1972. The 1968 census shows the structure of the elderly male population by age as follows:

- 65–70 years of age: 41%
- 70–74 years of age: 27%
- 75 years of age or over: 32%

From 1968 onwards, however, almost half of these were retired. In other words, workers aged fifty-five to sixty-four in 1962 consisted of 42 percent of older workers aged sixty to sixty-four (and who were therefore aged sixty-six to seventy in 1968).

83. Guillemard, *La retraite, une mort sociale*.

84. *Consultation sur les problèmes d'action sociale en faveur des personnes âgées*, Ministry of Public Health and Social Security conference, Paris, 23–27 June 1969.

85. Ministry of Public Health and Social Security, *Aspects médicaux du vieillissement*, September 1970.

86. Named after the then secretary of state, Marie-Madeleine Dienesch.

87. An analysis of the debate on old age that took place in the pages of *Le Monde* reveals how vigorously the trade unions campaigned. The claim for an improved social right to retirement in the period 1968–70 relegated the issue of integration into second place, but during 1971 and 1972, concerns relating to the pension system were easily the most widely discussed and they completely dominated the debate. By that time, the issue of an integration policy had dropped to fourth place.

88. Five Intergroups were set up under the Sixth Plan: Local Finance, Training and Vocational Skills, the Handicapped, the Elderly, and Leisure.

89. Quoted from an introductory paper given by Francis Pavard, the director of Mme Dienesch's cabinet, at *Consultation sur les problèmes d'action sociale en faveur des Personnes âgées,* Ministry of Public Health and Social Security conference, Paris, 23–27 June 1969.

90. The conference dealt with five issues altogether: opportunities for the elderly to remain in their own homes, accommodation, health and social services workers, information, and documentation and research.

91. Robert Castel, *L'ordre psychiatrique* (Paris: Éditions de Minuit, 1973). Also idem, "Genèse et ambiguïté de la notion de secteur en psychiatrie," *Revue de sociologie du travail*, no. 1 (1975): 55–57.

92. A figure who was both dominant in, and typical of, the new coalition of modernizers inside the state system was Bernard Lory. Lory, a senior civil servant and public auditor

at the Revenue Court, was director of Social Action until 1965. He always argued for a progressive social action policy that restricted its activities to public assistance and was free from the narrow dictates of economic policy. See Bernard Lory, *La politique d'action sociale* (Toulouse: Privat, 1975). In 1969, as president of the Social Action Commission and involved in preparations for the Sixth Plan, he vigorously defended his ideas. During the same period, he was president of the Gerontology Association of the Thirteenth Arrondissement (Paris); the work of this body was a pilot scheme, much of whose practice, as later pages will show, was the inspiration for government action.

93. Michel Philibert in *Gérontologie*, no. 1 (November 1970): 5.

94. Pavard, introductory paper, 4.

95. Two specific surveys were carried out by the officials responsible for these experiments at the request of the Intergroup. The results are attached to the Final Report.

96. Research carried out by the Gerontology Association of the Thirteenth Arrondissement and published in 1973 under the title *Un service social: Le club de loisirs pour personnes âgées, Essai de définition* contained a finalized form of the club as a venue for building up the confidence of elderly people.

97. Articles by Claude Balier, Michel Philibert and Robert Hugonot in *Gérontologie*, no. 2 (February 1971): 5–23 deal with sectoral gerontology. All three were senior gerontology officials in the thirteenth arrondissement and Grenoble, and each explains the importance of this kind of organization in gerontological practice.

98. Guillemard, *Old Age and the Welfare State.*

99. "The opening of more old people's homes cannot be countenanced in any circumstances" (administrative circular no. 1575 of 24 September 1971, Ministry of Health, 8). The Hospital Law of 31 December 1970 provided for the conversion of old people's homes into long-term care facilities over a period of fifteen years.

100. Ibid., 6, 7.

101. See analyses by Bruno Jobert in *Le social en Plan* (Paris: Ed. Ouvrières, 1982), 133 et seq.

102. This idea is borrowed from Nizard et al., *Changement social et appareil d'État*, 108 et seq.

103. The Bureau Réadaptation Vicillesse (Office for the Rehabilitation of the Elderly) was part of the DAS.

104. The elderly and the handicapped are the only sectors for which the Directorate-Plan alliance was activated within the framework of the Sixth Plan and through a final program.

105. Studies into the planning process have provided many instances of its poor impact on decision making.

106. See Nizard et al., *Changement social et appareil d'État.*

107. In 1968, it was estimated that, by 1980, there would be a 19 percent increase in the number of people aged sixty-five and over (a rise of over a million in absolute terms) and a 34 percent increase in those aged seventy-five and over. It was acknowledged that they would have a major impact on housing demand.

108. Intergroup Report, p. 106.

109. Annual Report of the General Inspectorate of Social Affairs 1976, p. 253.

110. There were four types of sector; they varied according to their facilities: (1) two community centers providing food, two clubs, and one day center; (2) one community center providing food, two clubs, and one day center; (3) one community center providing food, one club, and one day center; (4) one sector to be completed: one modernized community center providing food and one club.

111. For a detailed, statistical picture, see Guillemard, *Old Age and the Welfare State.*

112. It should be remembered that, when the Sixth Plan was published, the number of

elderly people who received assistance from home carers was below target. In 1976, there were only about 190,000 beneficiaries instead of 700,000.

113. See Jacqueline Devouassoux-Merakchi and Danièle Martin, "La population des hospices et des maisons de retraite." Part of this study was published in *Statistiques et commentaires*, no. 6 (1975): 5–18.

114. Annual Report of the General Inspectorate of Social Affairs 1976, 2:215.

115. "Rapport général du VIe Plan de Développement économique et social" (Law on the Sixth Plan), *Journal officiel,* no. 1371 (1971): 91. The lost was shared out as follows among bodies that provided funding for facilities: the state, 40 percent; CNAVTS, 40 percent; local authorities, 20 percent. The CNAVTS was to take over responsibility for operational budget when state subsidies stopped after two years. See above.

116. All reports on the implementation of the final program from the DRASS (Direction Régionale des Affaires Sanitaires et Sociales—Regional Directorate for Health and Social Affairs) support this view. They highlight the difficulties caused by the Old-Age Fund in respect of (1) the burden on running costs triggered by loans to purchase equipment; and (2) procedural delays prior to giving its required agreement to sign the sectoral contract. *Note sur l'exécution du programme finalisé* (in the three Aquitaine *départements* of Landes, Lot et Garonne, and Pyrénées Atlantiques), 4 June 1974.

117. For instance, the Old-Age Fund only donated funds to those sectors where retirees coming from the General Scheme in that sector represented 60 percent of the entire elderly population.

118. This strategy for change was so strikingly unsuccessful that it was changed under the Seventh Plan; this was an initiative that developed into a more administrative exercise. In addition to the PAP 15 delegates, a program leader was appointed in each DDASS and was systematically sent on a PAP 15 (Programme d'Action Prioritaire no. 15) training course.

119. Theodore Lowi, *The End of Liberalism* (New York: Norton, 1969).

120. Intergroup Report on the Elderly by the Sixth Plan (Paris: Documentation française, 1969), 15.

121. Congrès national des Offices d'Information et d'Action Gérontologiques, Nancy, 25–26 April 1974. Rapports du deuxième congrès des offices d'information et d'action gérontologiques (GLOPA), Nancy, April 1974. *Les offices et le programme finalisé,* Grenoble, Travaux gérontologiques et gériatriques, CHU of Grenoble, 103 p.

122. This is similar to Robert Castel's view of the New Frontier antipoverty programs in the United States. "La guerre à la pauvreté aux États-Unis," *Actes de la recherche*, 19 January 1978, 47–60.

123. This is an estimated average percentage, and is based on some twenty French urban local authorities with a gerontology center. It would not have been helpful to calculate a percentage for the whole of France, as these specific facilities and services did not exist, or else continued to be inadequate.

124. Ministry of Health and Social Security, Directorate of Social Action, Bureau RV2. *Programme d'action prioritaire no. 15 du VIIe Plan en faveur du maintien à domicile des personnes âgées*, Bilan d'exécution (Paris: Ministry of Health, 1980).

125. The list of specifically encouraged programs was as follows:

(a) information/prevention: information services; action on preparation for retirement and bringing the generations closer together;

(b) improvements to the home environment and living conditions: adapting the home environment to the disabilities associated with old age; home help; washing clothes and other heavy domestic duties; food preparation;

(c) running activities for the elderly: physical activities, developing cultural activities; telephone services;

(d) health service: home-care service; day centers; gerontological consultations.

126. Work on shaping public opinion also figured in the administration's analysis of the program. The PAP 15 assessment report concluded with a statement that the program "did much to give the public and the elderly themselves a 'positive' image of old age."

127. North Americans use the phrase "senior citizens" rather than "third age," and have given a clearer focus to the redefinition of citizenship that underlies this new classification of individuals.

Chapter 3. Old Age and Employment

1. See table 7: Retrospective-Prospective Changes in Age Structure of the Population in France over Two and a Half Centuries.

2. The same political shifts were taking place at the same time in the United Kingdom, as Chris Phillipson shows in chapter 3 of his *Capitalism and the Construction of Old Age* (London: Macmillan, 1982). In place of the "virtues of retirement" that characterized the period of high unemployment during the 1930s, the "dangers of retirement" became the keynote of the full employment era in the 1950s. The theme of an "industrious," as opposed to an "idle," old age became dominant.

3. A survey carried out among business people by the Institut National d'Études Démographiques (INED) in 1946 demonstrates this position clearly: "Employer resistance to the employment of older workers is greater where the company is more important or is more mechanized or rationalized. Where standardized norms of production are the rule, the employment of older workers is seen as difficult, if not undesirable." The authors conclude: "Although the shortage of workers, and above all the shortage of skilled workers, impedes many companies from operating normally, any rational desire to give employment to older workers is almost nonexistent." Daric, *Vieillissement de la population.*

4. The general strike by civil servants in August 1953 paralyzed all public services and demonstrated the strength of this defensive position. The main aim was to show that civil servants rejected the government's move to raise the retirement age by two years as a way of extending their working lives.

5. These study seminars included three days on a scientific study of population aging, organized by the Alliance Nationale contre la Dépopulation (National Alliance against Underpopulation), under the patronage of the president of the Republic (22–24 April 1948), and Seminar on Improving the Lot of the Aging, held in Lille, France, October 1952.

6. See Claude Thomas and Dominique Balmary: "Le fonds national de l'emploi," *Droit social* 12 (December 1969): 575–83. Between 1964 and 1968, the regions of Nord, Lorraine, and Pays de Loire had easily the largest number of agreements on special allowances; they accounted for 55 percent of all recipients.

7. By 1969, when it had been in existence for six years, the FNE had paid out three times more special (i.e., preretirement) allowances (22,838) than training grants (7612); other types of intervention attracted even less interest. Cf. Thomas and Balmary, "Le fonds national de l'emploi."

8. This agreement was introduced for the benefit of dismissed workers; it guaranteed a sum equal to 66 percent of gross salary during the first year of application, 68 percent during the second year, and finally 70 percent. The reference salary was what had previously been used to establish contributions to the unemployment insurance scheme during the three calendar months prior to dismissal. The guaranteed income provided beneficiaries with guaranteed social security rights, including the old-age allowance, and required no contribution on their part.

9. Employees unfit for work, manual workers, working mothers, and mothers who claimed the right to a pension at sixty were excluded from entitlement to the guaranteed income that was available to workers who had resigned. This highlighted the consequences

and inequities of the confusion surrounding unemployment and retirement during the final stage of life, because the pension to which all the above categories were entitled paid out, on average, less than the guaranteed income for dismissed workers.

10. The unions demanded a full pensionable rate of 55 percent. It should not be forgotten that the rate obtaining at the time was 40 percent of salary over the final ten years. The SMIC *(salaire minimum interprofessionnel de croissance*—minimum wage*)* level was demanded for minimum allowances. (In 1971, these allowances were less than half of SMIC.)

11. In their letter of 29 March 1971 to the president of the CNPF, the two unions wrote: "You cannot have failed to notice that in an industrially developed country such as France, scientific and technological advances, increased productivity, and higher profits provide an opportunity to bring access to full pension rights down to sixty, particularly as current conditions of employment are causing workers' strength and health to decline more quickly." *Le Peuple*, 14–30 April 1971.

12. CFDT, "Le droit à la retraite c'est possible," *Syndicalisme*, June 1971. Robert Bono's analysis in *Gérontologie*, no. 7 (June 1972): 22 states: "Many workers, including the most disadvantaged, suffer the accumulated effects of excessive demands on their bodies when very young: they start work at a very young age and therefore do unskilled jobs, most of which are arduous; another problem is that these jobs are the lowest-paid, and this affects their level of pension. What is more, these are the very people who have the shortest life expectancy. We are faced with an intolerable contradiction of the most disadvantaged benefiting scarcely, if at all, from retirement, and contributing to other people's pensions!"

13. *Syndicalisme*, 21 December 1968, 12. In the course of its Thirty-eighth Congress in 1971, the CGT argued that "Retirement age, which was fixed twenty-five years ago at a time when the economy was in poor health, is no longer consistent with the legitimate right of workers to enjoy their retirement or with the opportunities opened up by our country's current levels of production and productivity."

14. Robert Bono, general secretary of CFDT, in *Gérontologie*, no. 7 (June 1972): 22.

15. Michel Frossard has demonstrated in a rigorous analysis that, traditionally, older workers were not especially vulnerable to unemployment, although the trend went into reverse during 1967–68; this was the beginning of a period when unemployment rose rapidly for fifty to fifty-nine-year-olds and sixty-year-olds, and even more quickly than for workers aged twenty-five to forty-nine. *L'emploi des travailleurs âgés et la crise. Le cas français* (Grenoble: IREP [Institut de Recherche Économique et de Planification], Faculty of Economic Sciences, September 1980).

16. *Journal officiel* of 19 May 1971, p. 1981. Intervention by a Communist Party deputy in the National Assembly.

17. Two quotations will suffice on this issue. First, "There is also a need to give way to young people: tens of thousands of them are unemployed even before they have started work." "La retraite à 60 ans, une aspiration normale," *Syndicalisme*, December 1968. Second, "There is no longer any justification for keeping the age of entitlement to a full pension at sixty-five. On the contrary, it seems incompatible with the risk of unemployment that can now be foreseen as a result of developments in more advanced industrial mechanization, and the ever-increasing numbers of young workers who will be entering the labor market in the years to come." Speech by Georges Séguy, March 1969.

18. Minimum old-age pensions rose by 164 percent in Sweden and by 120 percent in the United Kingdom between 1955 and 1967, while national per capita incomes rose by 135 percent and 85 percent, respectively, during the same period. Exactly the opposite happened in France, where minimum pensions only rose by 101 percent while national per capita income rose by 165 percent.

19. See "Retraite: les positions de la CFDT," *Syndicalisme*, 10 December 1970.

20. Georges Séguy in *Le Peuple*, 1–15 April 1970.

21. This matter was raised at the colloquium organized by the secretary of state for social action, Marie-Madeleine Dienesch, entitled Social Action in Favor of the Elderly, Paris, 23–27 June 1969.

22. *Le Peuple*, 1–15 September 1969.

23. Several articles in *Syndicalisme* during the late 1960s testified to an increased awareness that was not matched in the CGT's journal, *Le Peuple*. An article entitled "Retraités et Problèmes de la vieillesse"' in the 11 February 1967 issue of *Syndicalisme* stated that, "the pension is only one of a number of problems raised by old age. What is more, retired people are often isolated. . . ."

24. According to a survey carried out by the Fondation Nationale des Sciences Politiques (National Foundation of Political Sciences) in 1970, this was the most important of all workers' demands (*Le Monde*, 12–13 April 1970).

25. In the unions' postcard campaign designed to put pressure on the government, the postcards read: "If I live to be sixty, I want to be able to put my feet up."

26. Company preretirement packages proliferated spectacularly between 1968 and 1972. They took a wide variety of forms, but there were two main types (for the diversity of formulas, see Phillippe Latty, "Les systèmes de préretraite en France," in *Droit social*, no. 4 (April 1973): 255–67, and idem, *Réunions sur les travailleurs âgés dans l'entreprise, l'emploi et la retraite* (Paris: OECD, 20 April 1977). First, formulas that allowed for early exit. These covered three categories of beneficiary:

• The beneficiary who draws his or her retirement pension and receives from the company a "complementary" allowance that wholly or partly compensates for the abatements lost through taking early pension (early retirement).

• The beneficiary who is deemed unemployed, for whom the company adds a "complementary" differential compensation to UNEDIC benefits until the age of sixty-five. The employment contract is broken, but the pension is not paid out.

• The beneficiary who remains a company employee and receives career-end leave compensation.

These measures were used by Chrysler France (September 1971), SNIAS (November 1970), Thomson CSF (September 1970), IBM (1969), and Citroën (1972).

Second, formulas that allow the employee to disengage gradually from the contract of employment, either through gradual leave schemes designed to give the pensioner-to-be a chance to experience life in retirement, or through a reduction in the working week. This system of gradual retirement was used by Turboméca (1968), Gillette France (February 1971), SNECMA (1971), SEB (1973), and Merlin Gérin (1970). The history of some of these agreements, and an analysis of the impact they had, is set out in Mars Audras, "Vers la retraite progressive," in *Documents d'information et de gestion, Gérontologie* (Cagnes-sur-Mer: Caisse Nationale de Retraite des Ouvriers du Bâtiment [CNRO], 1973).

27. Robert Bono, head of the "Action Sociale Cadre de Vie" department of the CFDT at a hearing before Groupe Prospective "Personnes Âgées," Commissariat Général du Plan, 14 June 1979.

28. A summary of the employers' arguments on the cost of lowering the retirement age may be found in the CNPF journal, *Notes et arguments*, May 1971.

29. The president of the CNPF in "A la veille des journées d'action CGT/CFTC. Le gouvernement consulte les partenaires sociaux sur ses projets visant à améliorer les retraites," *Le Monde*, 23–24 May 1971.

30. Statement by CGT spokesperson, 10 July 1971.

31. When the agreement on job security between employers' associations and the trade unions was finalized on 10 February 1969, the signatories agreed to meet again to discuss a lowering of retirement age for older workers who had lost their jobs. In this sense, a formal undertaking had been given, and all that remained was to put it into practice.

32. Statement by CGC spokesperson, *Le Monde*, 4 April 1971.

33. In "Le processus est engagé," *FO Hebdo*, 25 May 1971.

34. Statements made by employer representatives when the agreement on guaranteed income was signed on 27 March 1972 confirmed these fears—if confirmation were needed; the employers believed that it was an important agreement and, through it, they "were becoming realistically involved in third-age politics."

35. The development of these schemes was abruptly halted by the agreement on guaranteed income; this was either because they were invalid or because they had been turned into simple measures that complemented the new initiative. The analysis of preretirement policies in twelve companies in the Rhône-Alpes Region demonstrates this quite clearly. The "in-house" schemes introduced at the time of the great union mobilization of 1968–69 fell into disuse, or were amended, after 1972.

36. The events leading up to the implementation of the social-integration policy were designed to defuse the union mobilization around pensions. This was very clear from an intervention that Robert Boulin, then minister for public health and social security, made in the National Assembly on 1 December 1971 in a debate on draft legislation to improve pensions. He was anxious to relocate improvements to pensions "in the context of the whole problem posed by old age." He insisted at some length on the importance of a way-of-life policy: "We should not, in the current situation, simply talk about the problem of retirement as an aspect of age. We must give those who are so inclined the opportunity to carry on working, and give them enough money on which to live if they retire. We must therefore concern ourselves not only with the level of pensions, but also, as I was saying a few moments ago, with housing, a chance for them to carry on living in their own homes, and access to home carers, hospital departments, and geriatric clinics, and social workers. We therefore have to invest in these areas, and not simply do something about revaluing the level of pensions. . . . We need to support the elderly with a technical and human infrastructure so that we do not end up with a catastrophe." *Journal officiel,* 6243.

37. IGAS Report, 1968–69, p. 8. Report of the Elderly Persons' Intergroup, p. 13.

38. Report of the General Inspectorate of Social Affairs, p. 40: "All workers must have their jobs guaranteed so long as they do not endanger the security of the enterprise or their own health."

39. Report of the Elderly Persons' Intergroup, pp. 72, 77.

40. General Inspectorate of Social Affairs, Annual Report 1968–69, p. 8.

41. Ibid.

42. "There therefore arises the question as to whether the effect of certain company policies, as far as older workers are concerned, is sometimes to cast a slur on their dignity, while at the same time triggering expenditure that no economy can tolerate" (IGAS Report, 1968–69, p. 8). "The number of employees 'sent on early retirement' is reported in victory bulletins, but it really means that older workers can no longer have any dignity as producers. . . . This tendency to systematically dismiss older workers, and even get rid of them even earlier, does not always suggest a well-thought-out personnel policy" (ibid., p. 39).

43. Ibid., 40.

44. Note published by the Ministry of Labor, Employment, and Population, 14–20 June 1971.

45. Association Nationale pour la Formation Professionnelle des Adultes (National Association for Adult Vocational Training).

46. These efforts did not completely fail to hit their mark. The "Entreprise et Progrès" Association, which had been set up in 1970 by a group of senior managers, two of whom were on the CNPF Executive, used a press release dated 30 November 1971 to propose the drafting of a general policy on third-age employment—the very terms used by the Ministry of Labor. Companies like Gillette, which were operating in the association's sphere of influence, later took part in experiments involving gradual and partial retirement.

47. This failure was confirmed by the fact that after one final, and somewhat timid, attempt by the government in May 1972 to promote a policy enabling older workers to remain in employment (the setting up of a task force), the issue totally ceased to figure among the Ministry of Labor's preoccupations.

48. National Assembly, minutes of debates, *Journal officiel*, p. 6242.

49. The level of pension had previously been fixed at 40 percent of average salary over the final ten years; between 1972 and 1975, it rose in stages to 50 percent.

50. See the Report of the Elderly Persons' Intergroup, p. 76.

51. Trade unionists were alive to this statistical sleight of hand, and later criticized the guaranteed-income scheme as little more than "disguised unemployment."

52. This refers to conclusions reached by Michelle Durand in her study of workplace disputes, *Les conflits du travail,* CRESST (Paris: Paris-Sud, 1977). This study showed that retirement was a confrontational issue and a frequent negotiating claim, but that talks were often blocked: strikes and claims do not lead to successful negotiations. Durand concluded that as far as retirement was concerned, the system of social change could work only through long-term social mobilization. Several CGT and CFDT representatives expressed a similar view after the agreement was signed. See "Retraites: pour le développement et la permanence de l'action," *Syndicalisme*, 10 February 1972, and "L'accord sur la garantie de ressources," *Le Peuple*, 1–15 April 1972.

53. *Journal officiel,* 8 June 1972, 2351–52.

54. Under the 27 March 1972 agreement, an unemployed worker could leave work and take preretirement from the age of fifty-eight years four months onward by drawing the unemployment benefits consecutively.

55. G. Adam and J.-D. Reynaud, *Conflits du Travail et Changement Social* (Paris: Presses Universitaires de France, 1978).

56. The supplementary clause of 25 June 1973 reduced from fifteen to ten years the period that workers had to be members of the social security scheme in order to qualify for the guarantee. In addition, it brought the waiting period for assistance qualification down from nine months to six months, lowered the minimum age from fifty-eight years four months to fifty-seven years, provided for an option to take a reversion pension, and raised the minimum guarantee.

57. The Renault preretirement agreement signed in January 1973 allowed employees to qualify for retirement rights from the age of sixty-two onward. It became a model for early retirement and was quickly imitated by many companies that wanted to bring down their employees' retirement age.

58. The most important schemes included those at the La Ciotat shipyard and Air France. Restructuring at the French broadcasting service ORTF (Office de la Radio et de la Télévision Française), which also led (not without a dispute) to the introduction of special measures for older workers who had been laid off.

59. *Syndicalisme*, 6 November 1975.

60. The period of insurance required by manual workers to benefit from this measure was a minimum of forty-five years; during the fifteen years preceding the application, they had to have been employed on manual work for five years.

61. The government later proposed to Parliament an "à la carte" retirement formula that allowed everyone to choose between employment and a pension at the age of sixty. The level of pension drawn at the age of sixty was gradually reduced to 40 percent of salary after five years. Speech by Pierre Messmer at Provins, 7 January 1973, and in the National Assembly on 10 April 1973.

62. See articles by Jean-Pierre Dumont: "Budget 1976 et pensions au Conseil des Ministres. Le gouvernement souhaite un relèvement des retraites versées à soixante ans," *Le Monde*, 25 September 1975; "Bénéficiant d'abord aux travailleurs manuels, la retraite à

soixante ans ne serait pas généralisée avant 1980," *Le Monde*, 9 October 1985; and "Le gouvernement fera des propositions sur l'âge de la retraite et la durée du travail," *Le Monde*, 6 September 1975.

63. *Le Monde*, 9 October 1975.

64. Sixteen French francs per claimant per day in 1977.

65. Examples include the aforementioned December 1975 reform, as well as the 12 July 1977 reform, which from 1979 onward offered retirement at sixty to women who could show proof of thirty-seven and a half years' insurance contributions to the general scheme.

66. A survey carried out in 1979 and 1980 of twelve major companies in the Rhône-Alpes Region.

67. It was mainly large companies such as Renault V.I. *(Véhicules Industriels)* and Rhône Poulenc Textiles that made use of this procedure and stimulated massive job losses by giving workers (both those who had been laid off and those who had retired) a small payment or pay supplement. The survey also revealed that the measure was used only by employers to cut jobs. The twelve companies examined made heavy use of guaranteed income, but the only employees taken on since 1977 had been temporary staff. Available evidence showed that no employees who left on early retirement were replaced.

68. These practices were frequently criticized in the union press, e.g., the CGT's *Le Peuple,* no. 464 (15 April 1977): 3, 4.

69. One of the classic forms of negotiations of this type relied on the logic of unemployment insurance, which calculated compensation on the basis of salary in the final three years. When extended to a five-year preretirement scheme, this rule became flexible and the door was opened to all kinds of negotiations between employer and employee. By substantially raising workers' salaries for a long enough period, an employer could urge an employee to resign with a particularly advantageous early retirement package paid for by UNEDIC. Jean-Jacques Dupeyroux described this practice as "fraudulent misuse," since measures for dealing with unemployment were being made to perform functions traditionally carried out by pension schemes. He also emphasized that the systems should not be mixed together. "Préretraite ou retraite à soixante ans, les inconséquences du mélange des genres," *Le Monde*, 30 August 1977, 11–12.

70. A study of a sample of early retirement schemes in the Rhône-Alpes Region confirms this view.

71. In this respect, this author's interpretation differs from Michel Frossard's otherwise flawless analysis of early exit. Frossard establishes a close link between the economic crisis and early-retirement measures. He believes that these measures were linked to the improved occupational health standards demanded after the crisis was over. This kind of analysis expresses the situation in terms of natural relations and imputes to the crisis a new social definition of the older worker. This should be understood as the climax of a long process of negotiating the definition; it involved unions, employers, and the state, and the employers' definition finally won the day. All the crisis did was to provide a context that was favorable to employers by adjusting the balance of forces and altering the issues underlying the dispute. See Michel Frossard, "Crise et cessation anticipée d'activité: une comparaison internationale," *Travail et emploi*, no. 16 (April–June 1983): 9–26.

72. Employees dismissed after the age of fifty-five qualified for guaranteed income, although they did not receive further compensation on their sixtieth birthdays. Furthermore, the FNE reforms put in place in 1979 allowed workers dismissed for economic reasons after the age of fifty-six years two months to qualify for guaranteed income until they began to draw their pensions.

73. This demand was turned down by the employers' associations.

74. These comparisons are of only relative value for three reasons:

(a) The inquiry carried out by the Institut National de la Statistique et des Études Économiques (INSEE) into employment was a survey and not a census. The results were estimates, and this distinguishes them from the UNEDIC figures.

(b) The definition of the private sector adopted for the purposes of the INSEE inquiry was not identical to that used by UNEDIC.

(c) The reference periods for the two sources were not the same: the employment investigation used the March figures (these are less subject to seasonal variations than the October figures), while the number of people on guaranteed income was calculated on 31 December.

75. This exercise did not take into account any INSEE, UNEDIC, or CNAVTS data on possible concurrent drawing of salary and pension.

76. Annual Report of the General Inspectorate of Social Affairs (1980), pp. 115, 116.

77. Louis Roussel and Alain Girard, "Régimes démographiques et âges de la vie," in *Les âges de la vie*, Colloquium Proceedings, Travaux et documents, no. 96 (Paris: Presses Universitaires de France), 1:13–23.

78. For the purposes of calculating this participation rate, people available for work were counted in with those who actually had jobs.

79. Michel Lévy, "L'âge de la retraite s'abaisse," *Population et société*, no. 117 (October 1978).

80. Cf. SOFRES 75 for *Notre Temps*, SOFRES 72 for the CFTC and *Notre Temps*, IFOP 77 for *Nouvel âge*, CREP 1978 for *La vie française*, INED. A. Monnier, "Les limites de la vie active et la retraite," *Population*, nos. 4–5 (1979): 801–24. All available information qualifies this position to a greater or lesser extent, however, as individual wishes for a lowering of retirement age varied according to socioeconomic category, age, and gender.

81. A survey on retirement based on a sample of two thousand people representing French people over the age of fifteen. It was carried out by SOFRES for the periodical *Notre Temps*.

82. The 1982 reform that lowered the retirement age was marked by the incorporation into the pension system of the new unemployment philosophy; this included new regulations covering the concurrent drawing of pension and pay.

83. In her article "Droit au repos et droit au travail, retraite de crise et marginalisation des travailleurs âgés," *Revue française des Affaires sociales*, no. 1 (January–March 1982): 10–38, Yvette Harff demonstrates that choice in respect of retirement age is conditional upon the right to work.

84. There were many workers on preretirement schemes who came to understand the precariousness of their situation only through the decree of 24 November 1982; this revised downwards the benefits accorded by guaranteed income and its conditions for qualification. This was followed by the setting up of a large number of associations for the defense of the rights of workers who had gone on preretirement.

85. The survey took place in 1980 and was based on a questionnaire handed to a sample of 342 individuals out of the 2700 on the survey database. Fieldwork was carried out in collaboration with Dominique Motte, researcher at Groupe Lyonnais in industrial sociology, economics, and humanism.

86. For more of Dumazedier's ideas on this subject, see "Nouveaux problèmes du temps libre dans la crise des valeurs," *Temps libre* (Paris), no. 4 (1981).

87. "Health problems" included medical reasons that had led to the taking of sick leave, or to a doctor's recommendation to take retirement. "Fatigue" encompassed all subjective health assessments.

88. A survey carried out by *Le Monde* on freedoms in March 1981 provided confirmation (as if confirmation were needed) of the extent to which this principle had penetrated

people's consciousness. The survey indicated that almost one reader in two (48 percent) considered that forcing early exit on older workers as a way of cutting unemployment was unremarkable, despite the fact that *Le Monde* readers belong to socioeconomic categories (e.g., senior management and the intellectual professions) that are, on the whole, traditionally more in favor of continuing to work until a more advanced age than are working-class or white-collar groups.

89. See Françoise Cribier, "Le temps de la retraite," *Temps libre*, no. 4 (1981).

90. This was undoubtedly because describing the scheme as "preretirement" concealed the element of social exclusion, and because many workers in this situation refused to be referred to as "preretirees" *(préretraités)*. They preferred to be known as unemployed.

Chapter 4. The Elaboration of Policies for Old Age, and the Crisis that Ensued

1. This included the *carte d'économiquement faible* (poverty card), an allowance to compensate for rent rises, and a special allowance for older people who did not qualify for any payment such as old-age benefits.

2. Alain Touraine, *Production de la société* (Paris: Le Seuil, 1973), 260.

3. The virtual nonexistence of a home-care service seriously impeded the implementation of the policy to enable the elderly to carry on living at home. In the absence of any political will in this area, and in a climate dominated by the establishment of a health and social protection scheme, the *caisses régionales d'assurance maladie* (regional health-insurance funds) were able to obstruct their development.

4. PAP 15 was the Seventh Plan's Priority Action Program 15, which was implemented at a time when planning had been virtually abandoned.

5. As far as social policy is concerned, the thesis developed by Patrice Grevet in *Besoins populaires et financement public* is central to this position.

6. Touraine, *Production de la société*, 274.

7. The link between the state and society that underpinned this system of action was based directly on the welfare state's type of sociopolitical organization. It is therefore hardly surprising that the role played by the state within this system of action was close to the Social Democratic conception of the state as an arbiter encouraging a confluence of interests in civil society. It made use of agreements of the type described in Jean-André Bergougnoux and Bernard Manin, *La Social-Démocratie ou le compromis* (Paris: Presses Universitaires de France, 1979).

8. This idea was developed by René Lenoir, then director of Action Sociale, in his book *Les exclus*.

9. Émile Lévy and his team. In particular, see "L'Évolution des conceptions et des modalités de la politique d'action sociale en France au cours de la période 1960–1980," in *4e Journées d'Économie sociale* (Paris, 1984).

10. Ibid. Lévy specifically discerns a new model for managing deviance. See also Michel Vingré, *Le social c'est fini* (Paris: "Autrement" Collection, 1980).

11. In 1981, pensions accounted for almost 40 percent of social expenditure in the seven main OECD countries; France was ranking high over 40 percent (see table 1 in the appendix). However, this figure underestimated the overall proportion of social benefits devoted to old age, as it did not include the money spent on preretirement or on health and in-patient care for the elderly, despite the fact that they are the main consumers. If the cost of preretirement is taken into account, and if a third of health expenditure on older people is added, well over half of social expenditure for 1984 (over 55 percent) is estimated to have been for the elderly (calculation by J.-C. Chesnais, in *Revue française des Affaires sociales*, July–September 1985, 58).

12. Expenditure on the elderly in France rose by 9 points between 1960 and 1980. It therefore climbed more steeply than money spent on unemployment (+5.8), the funding of health programs (+2.4), and expenditure on maternity and the family (–15.4). From 1975 onward the annual growth rate in expenditure on the elderly in OECD countries was as high as that on unemployment compensation (+16.8 percent).

13. Average annual rate of growth in France (*Source:* OECD):

	1960–75	1976–81
GDP	+5.0%	+2.8%
Social benefits	+7.4%	+7.6%

14. It should be remembered that the main factor in population aging is a slowdown in fertility rates, and not a drop in mortality rates.

15. By the end of the century, the proportion of people in France over the age of sixty will remain more or less constant, moving from 18.9 percent in 1975 to 19 percent in the year 2000, assuming constant mortality and fertility rates. However, it will rise appreciably during the early decades of the twenty-first century, reaching 24 percent in 2020 (see table 8 in the appendix); the baby boomers cohorts will begin to reach their sixtieth birthdays from 2005 onward. Falling mortality rates among adults after 1975 encouraged the hypothesis that there was an underlying fall in mortality rather than a trend in the direction of stable rate of mortality. On the basis of that more likely assumption, and using the same fertility hypothesis of 1.8, people aged sixty and over will account for over 20.6 percent of the population in 2006 and 26.1 percent in 2020.

16. André Babeau's *La fin des retraites?* (Paris: Hachette, Pluriel, 1985) and the original French version of this book were published in France at approximately the same time. The author offers an economic diagnosis of the wide-ranging questions being asked of pension systems, and its conclusion is similar to the one that the end of this chapter reaches by means of a sociological approach. Demographic and economic crises certainly hastened the emergence of problems in pensions, but the biggest problem was unquestionably the introduction of a new form of compulsory early exit.

17. The deficit for the old-age element of the general scheme alone was over 5 billion francs in 1970 and over 10 billion in 1980; in 1982, it was approaching 17 billion.

18. It is important to remember that the population of working age (i.e., twenty to fifty-nine) remained, and will continue to remain, relatively unchanged. (see table 8).

19. Jean-Claude Chesnais, "Évolution démographique et charge de financement des retraites," *Revue française des Affaires sociales*, June 1984, 85–112.

20. From a demographic standpoint, four major periods stand out:

(a) 1984–92: slight accentuation due to the fact that the large cohorts of the 1920s reached their sixtieth birthdays;

(b) 1993–2005: respite caused by the small cohorts of 1933–1945 reaching retirement age;

(c) 2006–33: an abrupt and significant increase in the ratio as the full age cohorts of 1946–73 will be reaching their sixtieth birthdays;

(d) 2034–43: slight decrease (small birth cohorts of 1974–83).

Source: ibid. The ratio rose to 34 percent in 1985; it is estimated that it will reach 38 percent in 2006 and it will be close to 51 percent in 2020.

21. Report of the Groupe Quantitatif sur la Protection Sociale (Ninth Plan), 30.

22. A redistributive analysis of pensions carried out by the Direction de la Prévision underlined the antiredistributive nature of pension-scheme transfers. In fact, the amount of money that the most needy sections of the population were receiving in pension payments during the latter part of their lives was less than the contributions they had previously paid in. The ratios between pensions received and contributions paid in were lower than 1 for

skilled manual workers (0.83), skilled workers (0.85), and laborers (0.66), and above 1 for foremen (1.19), middle managers (1.36), and senior managers (1.40). This inequality was mainly due to the fact that less highly skilled workers died younger.

23. Chesnais, *Évolution démographique et charge de financement des retraites.*

24. Source: *Vieillir demain*, (Paris: Documentation française, 1980), 118. These estimates, which were made in 1980, may turn out to be a little optimistic, as adult mortality has fallen much more quickly than predictions at the time were suggesting.

25. The increase in women's employment, a phenomenon that has been observed now for many years, will also contribute in time to an increase in the volume of pensions as full pensions come to replace reduced schemes.

26. The sixty to sixty-five age group was at its least populous in 1980, but doubled between 1980 and 1985. This demographic shift was not unconnected to the very favorable conditions for early exit that had previously been negotiated, particularly in 1977 within the framework of an extension to the 1972 agreement.

27. Compensation for workers on preretirement and unemployed workers aged fifty-five to fifty-nine who had definitively quit work.

28. Source: "Groupe quantitatif sur la protection sociale pour la préparation du 9e Plan, contribution aux comptes publics de l'emploi."

29. Source: François Lenormand and Gerard Magnier, "Le développement des dispositifs de cessation anticipée d'activité: aspects sociaux et conséquences financières," *Travail et emploi*, January–March 1983, 51.

30. The reason for this was that the compensation rate was high (70 percent), and the incomes of individuals affected were large because they were at the ends of their careers. For an analysis of the absurd, antiredistributive way in which UNEDIC worked, see ibid.

31. This share was estimated at over 40 percent of UNEDIC expenditure in 1987.

32. Associations of preretirees were quick to register concern on seeing their members described in the press as people who "cost more than unemployment" (*Le Monde*, 23 June 1985). This, the associations felt, made them out to be "selfish profiteers of the crisis," whereas many of them felt that they had performed an act of solidarity by contributing toward the employment of younger colleagues.

33. Under the terms of preretirement solidarity contracts for workers who had left their jobs voluntarily—these were the only contracts to include a replacement clause, and therefore to encourage the hiring of new workers—there was approximately one new employee for every three departures. A study into the effect of these contracts concluded that the exercise cost public funds a substantial amount of money, and achieved a short-term impact on unemployment that "fell short of what might have been expected." However, the authors went on to say that "in the medium term, a company's increased efficiency resulting from this reorganization, and the improved competitiveness that will flow from it, could have a substantial effect on employment." Franck, Hara, Magnier, and Villey, "Entreprises et contrats de solidarité de préretraite-démission," *Travail et emploi*, no. 15 (July–September 1982): 88.

34. Jürgen Habermas, *Raison et légitimité. Problèmes de légitimation dans le capitalisme avancé* (Paris: Payot, 1978).

35. This contradictory aspect of the development of the welfare state has been highlighted by Claus Offe. Offe claims that the welfare state is largely definable by its skills at crisis management and by its ability to develop multifunctional interventions that can provide the necessary regulation at different levels. He believes that what he calls the "crisis of crisis management" is mainly based on the inability of the welfare state to introduce coherence into the many objectives traditionally assigned to it. Claus Offe, *Contradictions of the Welfare State* (London: Hutchinson, 1984).

36. This is how Nicole Questiaux describes the failure of a number of global social-policy projects, including the project defined within the framework of the Laroque Commission. Questiaux, *Le pouvoir du social* (Paris: Presses Universitaires de France, 1979), 90.

37. In a way, Janowitz makes the same point when he supports the notion that the development of the welfare state was not accompanied by a new social consensus, but, on the contrary, that it was the source of political fragmentation. He pursues this argument by showing how the welfare state helped to reduce the political legitimacy of the state, and how in western industrialized countries it has supported the introduction of weak political systems. Morris Janowitz, *Social Control of the Welfare State* (Chicago: University of Chicago Press, 1976).

38. Pierre Grémion has highlighted how the networks of partners, which were allowed to discuss matters with the state and formed "exclusive bureaucratic and representative islands," went through a process of increasing rigidification. Grémion mainly attributed this process to the systems of mutual control that grew up among the different agents.

39. Guillemard, *La retraite, une mort sociale*.

40. The money devoted to social action in 1976 came to scarcely more than 4 percent of all spending on the elderly.

41. Guillemard, *Old Age and the Welfare State*.

42. Habermas believes that there may be a crisis of legitimation "if the system encourages expectations that cannot be met . . . with forms of compensation that conform to the system." *Raison et légitimité*, 107.

43. Denis Kessler, "Les retraites en péril?" *Revue française des Affaires sociales*, June 1984, 69–83.

44. This is one way of interpreting the results of surveys that clearly show that retirement is a youthful dream: the more certain we feel that it is a long way off, the sooner we want it to happen. Those under thirty-five see retirement as a time when aspirations can easily be realized (72 percent as against 58 percent for fifty- to sixty-four-year-olds), but people over fifty see it as a time of isolation and money problems. IFOP, 1978, for *Le Nouvel Age*.

45. In 1900 life expectancy at birth was forty-five years; as people entered the labor market at a much younger age in those days, working-life expectations were therefore on the order of thirty years.

46. Louis Dirn and Henri Mendras, "Le 3e âge animera la société française" *Futuribles*, no. 80 (September 1984): 3–28.

47. A.-M. Guillemard, "Conduites et attitudes en préretraite," chapter 4 of "Dynamique et crise des politiques de la vieillesse. Contribution à une sociologie des politiques sociales" (Ph.D. thesis, Ecole des Hautes Etudes en Sciences Sociales, 1984).

48. For many people a desire for a lower retirement age was closely linked to the principle of being able to choose when to stop work. A COFREMCA survey (Study 3 SC) in 1979 showed that in answer to the question "Should retirement age be brought forward for everyone, or should each person have a degree of freedom in choosing retirement?," 59 percent of those questioned chose freedom, while only 33 percent opted for equality. This showed that there was a link between the prominence given to free time and the demand for individual control.

49. It should be remembered that early exit was more often imposed than chosen, and that most preretirees and retirees had to give up the freedom to have a job as pension entitlement increasingly excluded the right to work. (See recent measures related to concurrent drawing of pension and pay in chapter 3.)

50. These dire straits have been highlighted by research into the way of life of preretirees. They also appear in other indices, however, such as the relative position of the fifty to sixty-four age band on the morale scale, which is constructed by COFREMCA and

measures the morale of the French population every year. This age band had been the only one since 1979 to see its position on this scale drop regularly and rapidly toward 0, moving away from other age bands whose positions on a scale of 0–20 oscillated between 13 and 11.

51. Alain Touraine, *L'après-socialisme* (Paris: Grasset, 1980), 143.

52. The rapporteurs of the *Vieillir demain* task force preparing for the Eighth Plan wrote: "If the public authorities and the social partners continued to be satisfied with these disconnected and limited actions, if global society was not organizing to take more account of aging, the prospects for the elderly would be gloomy. French society would be preparing for difficult times, and the country would be seriously undermined by the disputes and discords caused by relations between the elderly and the country." Report "Vieillir demain" (Aging tomorrow), 149. This task force contained many who would later become members of the new ruling élite; they included Robert Lion, who was president of the group and later cabinet director to Prime Minister Pierre Mauroy, and Nicole Questiaux, who became minister of national solidarity in the same government.

53. The reform was not equitable in all respects, as it aligned the rights of all socioprofessional categories at the same age, thereby aggravating inequalities linked to different life expectancies for different categories, inequalities for which the law of 1975 on early retirement provided remedies. Furthermore, it should be emphasized that the social intentions of the reform did not eliminate financial anxieties. According to calculations by the Direction de la Prévision, the insecure situation that guaranteed income at sixty occupied within the pension system made it possible to divide the cost of unemployment between sixty and sixty-five almost in half by 1985.

54. Contracts issued by the National Employment Fund were also added to this measure. This moved entitlement to guaranteed income for dismissed workers to fifty-six years and two months, and even fifty-five years in some cases.

55. It was also symptomatic of the government's wish to relaunch the welfare state in its traditional form that it did not attempt to link the two sets of negotiations (period of employment and retirement age) that were taking place at the time. By failing to dovetail preparations for these two reforms, a marvelous opportunity was missed for slowing down the segregation of age bands and for giving shape to new ways of distributing jobs among them.

56. The CGT representative later stated, in the course of government consultations on reform of the retirement age, that his organization wished to draw the government's attention to the impact of retirement at sixty: because it was rigid and inequitable, there was a danger that it would benefit employers, as the system was now mainly associated with employers' freedom to cut the workforce.

57. All of these ideas were summarized in a circular of 7 April 1982. It dealt with the social and medicosocial policy for pensioners and the elderly that was being produced by the secretary of state with responsibility for the elderly.

58. Ian Gough, *The Political Economy of the Welfare State* (London: Macmillan, 1979).

59. Pierre Rosanvallon, *La crise de l'État-Providence* (Paris: Le Seuil, 1981).

Glossary

AFPA	(Association Nationale pour la Formation Professionelle des Adultes) The National Association for Adult Professional Training was created in 1949 under the supervision of the Labor Ministry and is the main public organization for continuing education in France.
AGIRC	(Association Générale des Institutions de Retraite des Cadres) The General Association of Pension Funds for Cadres oversees the supplementary pension funds for cadres and is to them what AARCO is to wage earners.
Air France	The French state-owned national airline.
ANPE	(Agence Nationale Pour l'Emploi) Created on 13 July 1967, the National Employment Agency has offices throughout the country to help people look for work, training, or professional career counseling. The ANPE also compiles unemployment statistics and publicizes job and training offers.
ARRCO	(Association des Régimes de Retraite Complémentaires) The Association of Supplementary Pension Funds, created on 8 December 1961, oversees the supplementary pension funds for wage earners.
ASSEDIC	(Association pour l'Emploi dans l'Industrie et le Commerce) The Association for Employment in Industry and Commerce consists of local organizations that manage unemployment benefits and is under the direction of the "social partners." These local organisms are under the umbrella of UNEDIC.
Assurances Sociales	Social insurance, adopted between 1928 and 1930, covered only blue-collar workers whose incomes were under a fixed

ceiling for affiliation. It was the precursor of the Social security system.

AVTS — (Allocation aux Vieux Travailleurs Salariés) The Elderly Wages Earners' Benefits was created in 1942 to ensure a minimum assistance income for retirees by making up for the shortcomings of the Assurances Sociales retirement system.

Boulin Act — Named after the French labor minister who sponsored the December 1971 law that substantially raised retirement pension payments.

cadres — Private-sector white-collar workers in management positions: managerial staff, decision makers, executives. They are represented by special unions, such as CGC, and enjoy specific benefits (for example, cadres have a separate complementary retirement plan from those of noncadre wage earners. (See AGIRC.)

CANCAVA — (Caisse Autonome Nationale de Compensation de l'Assurance Vieillesse Artisanale) The National Autonomous Fund for the Compensation of Crafts Industry Retirement Pensions is a supplementary fund for artisans and craftsmen.

CE — (Comité d'Entreprise) Businesses in France are required by law to create a structure directed by employee representatives to administer social works for the company's employees (leisure activities, Christmas parties for staff children, trips, price reductions or other advantages for retail goods). But Comité d'Entreprise also serves as the channel for dialogue over decisions concerning the entire company, such as what arrangements to make for those affected by mass layoffs.

CES — (Conseil Economique et Social) The Economic and Social Council is an institution that was created by the Constitution of the Republic. It assembles representatives of the unions, employers, and major national associations in order to solicit their opinions on various social questions and to enlighten the government.

CFDT — (Confédération Française Démocratique du Travail) The French Democratic Labor Federation is a union that was created in 1964 after the split with the French Confederation of Christian Workers (CFTC). The CFDT abandoned all religious references.

CFTC — (Confédération Française des Travailleurs Chrétiens) The French Confederation of Christian Workers is a Christian union founded in 1919.

CGC (Confédération Générale des Cadres) The General Confederation of Cadres is a union that was created in 1946 and rechristened CFE-CGC (Confédération Française de l'Encadrement—CGC).

CGPME (Confédération Générale des Petites et Moyennes Entreprises) The General Confederation of Small and Medium-Sized Businesses is an employers' organization.

CGT (Confédération Générale du Travail) The General Labor Confederation is a Communist-leaning union founded in 1895 and affiliated with the French Communist Party (PCF).

CGT-FO (Confédération Générale du Travail-Force Ouvrière) The General Confederation of Labor-Workers Force is a splinter union that broke away from CGT in 1948. Often referred to as the "FO."

CGTU (Confédération Générale du Travail Unitaire) The United General Labor Confederation, a union created in 1921 after breaking away from the CGT, represented the revolutionary wing of the workers movement and was closely affiliated with the French Communist Party. It reunited with the CGT in 1936.

Chaban-Delmas administration Fifth Republic administration that bears the name of the prime minister from 20 June 1969 to 7 July 1972 under President Georges Pompidou. Mr. Chaban-Delmas was a major figure in the Resistance movement under de Gaulle. The project slogan "The New Society" summarizes his efforts to put France on the path to social and economic modernization.

CNAVTS or CNVAT (Caisse Nationale d'Assurance Vieillesse des Travailleurs Salariés) The National Retirement Pension Fund for Wage Earners, the old-age branch of the French social security system, manages the first tier of retirement benefits for wage earners (the second tier being the supplementary scheme) and is under the direction of "social partners."

CNPF (Conseil National du Patronat Français) The National Council of French Employers, created in 1946, is the main group to which most employers' federations in the different sectors of the French economy belong.

CNR (Conseil National de la Résistance) The National Resistance Council was the seat of the major movements comprising the French Resistance during German occupation. The council's task

	was to coordinate the Resistance and to assess what actions would lead to liberating France.
CNRPA	(Comité National des Retraités et Personnes Âgées) The National Committee of Retirees and Elderly People was created in 1982 and brings together various experts, representatives of the major national organizations for retirees, members of Parliament, and representatives from local communities in charge of old-age policy. The committee puts forward advisory opinions on all questions related to old-age policy. This structure also exists on the local level of decision making: the Departmental Committee of Retirees and Elderly People (Comités Départementaux des Retraités et Personnes Âgées, CODERPA) in the *départements,* and the Regional Committee of Retirees and Elderly People (Comités Regionaux des Retraités et Pérsonnes Âgées, CORERPA) in the *régions*.
COFREMCA	(Compagnie Française d'Etudes de Marché et Conjonctures Appliquées)
Commissariat au Plan, or Plan	The Plan Commissionership is a public organization responsible for studying and orienting the priorities and objective of future governmental action. Unlike the former Soviet Union, where planification was imperative and fixed quantified mandatory objectives, French planification is purely indicative. Its role was greatly reduced in the mid-1970s and with the 1982 decentralization laws that reinforced the powers of local communities.
Conseil d'Etat	The Council of State is the highest French administrative court.
Conseil Géneral	The General Council is an assembly elected by citizens at the departmental level (third level of government after the national and regional levels); it manages a part of the infrastructure and the social services within the département.
Conseil Régional	The Regional Council is an assembly elected by the citizens of a *région* (second level after the national level); it manages a part or the infrastructure and the social services within the *région*. A *région* is composed of several *départements*, but does not hold as much power in social matters as *départements* do.
Cour des Comptes	The Revenue Court is an institution responsible for verifying the proper use of public finances. It is the French equivalent of the General Accounting Office in the United States.

DAS — (Direction de l'Action Sociale) The Social Action Office, within the Health and Social Affairs Ministry, deals with social questions.

DDASS — (Direction Départementale de l'Action Sanitaire et Sociale) The Departmental Office of Sanitary and Social Action.

DRASS — (Direction Régionale de l'Action Sanitaire et Sociale) The Regional Office of Sanitary and Social Action.

FNE — (Fonds National de l'Emploi) The National Employment Fund was created in 1963 to furnish funds for the modernization of the French industrial apparatus. All of its interventions are submitted to a convention between the state and business that organizes the implementation of a range of benefits. Among the fund's interventions was the creation of an early-exit scheme (pre-retirement) for wage earners aged sixty and over who have been laid off by their employers. It has remained an essential instrument for financing pre-retirement.

FNOSS — (Fédération Nationale des Organismes de Sécurité Sociale) The National Federation of Social Security Organizations was responsible for the collection of social security contributions. Now called URSSAF (Union de Recouvrement de la Sécurité Sociale et des Allocations Familiales).

FNS — (Fonds National de Solidarité) The National Solidarity Fund was created in 1956 as one of the entities that financed minimum welfare benefits for the elderly.

FNV — (Fonds National Vieillesse) The National Old-Age Fund was created in 1955 to financially support the old-age minimum retirement pension. In 1956, it was transformed when the FNS was created.

FO — See CGT-FO.

Front Populaire — The Popular Front was an alliance formed in 1935 between left-wing parties (mainly Socialists, Communists, and Center-Left). The alliance also got the support of around one hundred left-wing political-cultural organizations and two major labor unions (CGT and CGTU, which reunified in 1936). The coalition won legislative elections and governed from May 1936 to November 1938 under the leadership of the Socialist Léon Blum. The Communists decided to support the government but did not join the coalition government. It was in 1936 that the first paid vacations were instituted and that the work week was limited to forty hours. The alliance progressively dissolved from 1937 on until finally breaking up on 30 November 1938.

GRD (Garantie de Ressources Démission) Guaranteed Income Resignation.

GRL (Garantie de Ressources Licenciement) Guaranteed Income Dismissal.

Grenelle See Mai 68.

IFOP (Institut Français d'Opinion Publique et d'Études de Marché) The French Institute of Public Opinion and Market Study is an opinion-poll institute.

IGAS (Inspection Générale des Affaires Sociales) The General Inspection of Social Affairs is a body attached to the Ministry of Social Affairs that verifies and evaluates the administration of social affairs.

IGSP (Inspection Générale de la Santé Publique) The General Inspection of Public Health is a body that inspects and evaluates public-health policies.

INED (Institut National d'Études Démographiques) The National Demographic Studies Institute is a public institution in charge of demographic studies.

INSEE (Institut National de la Statistique et des Études Économiques) The National Institute of Statistics and Economic Studies is a public institution in charge of compiling statistics (the equivalent of United States Bureau of the Census).

Journal officiel (JO) The *Official Journal* publishes all laws and decrees.

Laroque Commission A commission, created on 8 April 1960 at the request of the prime minister, that studied the problems of old age to provide an overall view of the questions related to population aging and to elaborate a general action scheme for old-age policy. It was presided over by Pierre Laroque (after whom the final report was also unofficially named) and composed of high-level civil servants. The Laroque Report marked an essential turning point in the conception of age policy by giving priority to the integration of retirees into society. Up until then, old-age policy had been primarily limited to reducing pockets of poverty and placing the most dependent individuals in institutions.

Le Monde — National daily newspaper founded in 1944 by a former member of the French Resistance, Hubert Beuve-Méry. Although pluralist and not affiliated with any particular party, it is generally considered to be of Center-Left inclination.

Mai 68 — In May 1968 a major student protest was followed by massive strikes led by wage earners and civil servants, thus plunging France into a quasi-insurrectionist situation and completely paralyzing the country. Georges Pompidou's government was compelled to negotiate numerous social reforms and to raise the minimum wage within the framework of the Grenelle Accords (Accords de Grenelle), named after the street in Paris where the Labor Ministry was located.

MRP — (Mouvement Républicain Populaire) The People's Republican Movement was a political party created in November 1944. It belonged to the Christian movement and modeled its doctrine after Social Catholicism, though it had no organic or structural ties to the Church. The involvement of Christian Democrat groups in the Resistance facilitated its creation after the Liberation. One of the leaders of the prewar Christian Democrat movement, Georges Bidault, was also the president of the National Resistance Committee. The movement was situated at the Center-Right of the political spectrum, but its voters ranged from Center-Left to Center-Right. Just before the war, the MRP recuperated a part of the electorate that had deserted the right-wing parties implicated in the Vichy collaborationist regime. It became the second biggest party in France and remained a political force to be dealt with throughout the Fourth Republic (1946–58) along with the French Communist Party (PCF) and the SFIO Socialists. The MRP supported both left-wing and right-wing governments. The party was based on several key ideas:
• economically, the MRP asserted the importance of free enterprise, but within the framework of an economy at the service of man and social progress;
• socially, the MRP supported mechanisms of solidarity from the strong to the weak;
• in foreign policy, the party was a strong advocate of constructing the European Union and rather in favor of strengthening ties with the United States against the Soviet Union. The MRP slowly broke up between 1966 and 1969. The 1967 elections intensified existing divisions and the various constituents of the MRP

	rejoined groups on the Left and Right. A large fraction of its members finally joined together in the centrist Social Democrats Center (CDS). Explicit references to Christian doctrine were abandoned, and in the mid-90s the CDS was rechristened the Force Démocrate.
Notre Temps	The leading monthly magazine for the elderly since its inception in 1968 (similar to *Modern Maturity* in the United States).
ORGANIC	(Organisation Autonome de l'Assurance Vieillesse de l'Industrie et du Commerce) The Independent Federation of Supplementary Retirement Pensions in Industry and Commerce is a supplementary pension fund for self-employed workers.
ORTF	(Office de Radio et de Télévision de France) French Radio and Television Office.
PAP 15	(Programme d'Action Prioritaire) The Priority Action Program of the Seventh Plan (1976–80). Its aim was to "favor keeping elderly people in their homes" and financing operations to that effect.
Parti Radical	The Radical Party, created in 1901, had at its roots the ideal of secularism and republicanism inspired by the ideas of Enlightenment philosophy. It defended human rights, the democratic system, and universal suffrage. Thus, the Radical Party was opposed to all forms of absolutism, both monarchic and imperial. Its second tenet was a struggle against the power of the Church, the affirmation of the primacy of secularism, and the strict separation of church and state. Freemasonry played an important role in the party and greatly influenced its political and philosophical positions. It was considered a moderate left-wing party and it took part in numerous coalition governments during the Third Republic as well as allying itself with right-wing republican parties. When the SFIO Socialists freed themselves from the Communists in 1920 they progressively attracted a group of Radicals to their party. The Radicals participated in the Popular Front but progressively lost influence. The party was weakened by World War II and was discredited by France's military defeat at the hands of the Germans in 1939, for which they were held responsible. In 1972 the party split into two branches. They represented opposite ends of the political spectrum, and the party thus lost all influence.
PCF	The French Communist Party was created in 1920 after a schism within the SFIO (at the Tours Congress). The PCF represented

the revolutionary branch of the Left. A short time after the schism a separation occurred within the labor movement between the majority CGT faction (which remained for the most part faithful to the SFIO) and the minority close to the Communists (which formed the CGTU). The PCF had close ties with the Soviet Communists and thus supported the Popular Front (1936–39) without actually joining the government. The PCF was dissolved by the government on 26 September 1939. The August 1939 pact between Hitler and Stalin delayed Communist participation in the French Resistance; it only became actively involved after Germany attacked the Soviet Union. Just after the war, the PCF became the biggest party in France and took part in the government. It pushed for the nationalization of big industry while infiltrating the top levels of the government; it also took the control of the CGT union. With the beginning of the cold war in 1947 the Communists left the government. During the Fourth Republic the PCF generally remained the biggest party in France. But the institution of the Fifth Republic and the increased popularity of the Gaullist right-wing party that supported de Gaulle's candidacy for president of the Republic considerably weakened the PCF. Its influence over the CGT allowed it to support numerous social conflicts. In 1972 the Communists signed a common program with the Socialists, who in 1981 asked them to join their administration under the newly elected Socialist president, François Mitterand. However, they quit the government in 1984 and the decline of the PCF's popularity accelerated in elections throughout the 1980s, a trend that continued into the early '90s. However, in 1997 the Socialists once again asked the PCF to join their government.

Pinay administration — A Fourth Republic administration in office from March to December 1952. It bore the name of the council president (equivalent to the prime minister), Antoine Pinay.

Plan — See Commissariat au Plan.

PRL — (Parti Républicain de la Liberté) The Liberty Republican Party.

PS — At a turbulent congress at Epinay in June 1971 François Mitterand took control of the party created from the defunct SFIO and began to renovate it, leading to a reconciliation with the Communists. Moreover, associations and clubs contributed considerably to expanding the Socialist network. The number of Socialists elected at the local level (especially municipal) also furthered the expansion of a vast network of militants who contributed to

Mitterand's victory over the economically liberal Valéry Giscard d'Estaing in 1981. The PS was the biggest French political party during much of the 1980s, winning 36 percent of the votes in the legislative elections of 1981, 30.8 percent in 1986, and 34.8 percent in 1988. But like many parties in power, the PS became the victim of its own success and underwent a major electoral erosion. A number of political and financial scandals broke out in the early '90s that tarnished the party's image. Unemployment continued to rise and social unrest set in. The French were greatly disappointed by the PS, of which they had expected so much as the "party of change" in 1981. The Fifth Republic entered a new phase marked by alternating majorities in the Assembly, swinging from the Right (1986–88 and 1993–97) back to the Left (1988–93), and finally participating in the return of the Left in 1997, led by the ex-secretary of the PS, Lionel Jospin, supported by the Greens and Communists.

PSU — (Parti Socialiste Unifié) The Unified Socialist Party is a left-wing party characterized by its ideas on decentralization and self-management. Most of its members joined the PS in the 1970s.

Ramadier administration — Named after the council president (equivalent of the prime minister) in 1947. This administration was in office at the beginning of the Fourth Republic (early postwar period, very beginning of the cold war). The Communists quit this government in May 1947, putting an end to the alliance between the major parties of the postwar period (see *tripartisme*).

République, IVème — The Fourth Republic (1946–58). After the period of collaboration (see Vichy), France undertook reforms of its institutions and adopted a new constitution. Constituent Assemblies prepared and then submitted a referendum to French voters on constitutional projects under consideration. One project supported by much of the Left (and in particular the Communists) attempted to institute a parliamentary system but was rejected by French voters, who feared giving too much power to Parliament (since the Communists constituted the biggest party at the time, they would have dominated the French government). The Gaullists favored a strong executive branch and thus were opposed to the first project. A second project aimed at a compromise by balancing the powers of the executive and legislative branches. It was approved by the French without great enthusiasm and promulgated on 27 October 1946. The constitution then adopted gave birth to the Fourth Republic, which was characterized by the dominance of the legislative branch over the executive and by a proportional voting method. This was a period when France was grappling with the thorny problem of decolonization. The voting method, the number of political parties and their lack of discipline, and even the fragility of the alliance between parties—all greatly contributed to a fundamental political fragility that led to overturning the government. This state of great instability played itself out in a high number of resignations of heads of governments and their teams. A new government was formed every six months on the average (twenty-two governments fell in twelve years' time). The Fourth Republic was incapable of resolving the problems of decolonization and the war between France and the Algerian independence movement, and it was thus replaced by the Fifth Republic.

République, Vème — The Fifth Republic (1958–). Instituted in 1958 by a new constitution, this new Republic reinforced executive power and notably conferred on the president the powers to dissolve the Assembly and to organize national referendums (with the prime minister's agreement). General de Gaulle favored strong presidential powers and was the main inspiration behind the constitution (he was president from 1958 to 1969). The voting method adopted by the Fifth Republic is no longer completely proportional but rather is determined by majority in the second round. As of 1962 the president was elected directly by the people (direct universal suffrage), which grants greater legitimacy to the system. Several presidents have succeeded de Gaulle: Georges Pompidou (1969–74), Valéry Giscard d'Estaing (1974–81), François Mitterand (1984–88; 1988–95), and Jacques Chirac (1995–).

ROP — (Retraites Ouvrières et Paysannes) Workers' and Farmers' Retirement was a contributory retirement system set up by the decree of 5 April 1910 which for the first time made retirement insurance mandatory by organizing a three-party financing system (wage earners, employers, and the state). The system met much opposition and ultimately failed when the Conseil d'Etat (State Council) annulled the compulsory nature of the insurance. (See Conseil d'Etat.)

RV2 (Bureau) — A governmental social action office that is responsible for matters related to old age.

RVI — Renault Industrial Vehicles is a state-owned truck and van manufacturer.

Securité Sociale — See social security.

SFIO — (Section Française de l'Internationale Ouvrière) The French Section of the Workers' International was created in 1905 and combined different branches of the French Left, including radical Marxists and the moderate Left. But Marxists who were opposed to a gradual social transformation of society and compromise with the capitalist system caused a schism at the Tours Congress in 1920 in their pursuit of a brutal revolution without concessions. For its part, the SFIO wanted to be a party for the masses that defended the interests of the people against the ruling class and embraced the traditional themes of the Left: the fight against inequality, secularism, pacifism, and a certain degree of internationalism. Moderate Marxist ideology allowed this party to work with other reformist parties, as the Popular Front period illustrated. Some of the Socialists voted for granting full power to Marshal Pétain during the German invasion (1939–40). Like the Communists, the Socialists profited from their opposition to Nazism and the occupiers: the SFIO won 23.8 percent of the votes during the first Constituent Assembly after the war, and the party had some 350,000 members in 1946. But this popularity didn't last. It won only 14.3 percent of the votes in the 1951 legislative elections and 15.2 percent in the 1956 elections. The SFIO participated in a number of coalition governments, including with right-wing parties. One part of SFIO even went so far as to support de Gaulle's return to power in 1958, causing a split within the party over the danger of "Caesarism à la de Gaulle." However, support for de Gaulle was short-lived and the bipolar division in French politics got the upper hand, particularly in 1962 when the Socialists vigorously opposed the idea of electing the president by the universal direct suffrage so dear to de Gaulle. In 1965, François Mitterand ran for president for the first time. But after General de Gaulle resigned in 1969, the SFIO suffered a stinging defeat in the presidential elections and the Socialists were quick to learn their lesson: the SFIO was disbanded and the Socialist Party was created. (See PS.)

SMIC — (Salaire Minimum Interprofessionel de Croissance) The guaranteed minimum wage.

SNCF — (Société Nationale des Chemins de Fer) The French National Railroad Company, created in 1945 when French railways were nationalized, is state-owned and has a monopoly on train transportation in France.

social partners — In the French political context, "social partners" is a term used to refer to the three parties that negotiate major work-related policies: employers' federations, trade unions, and the government.

social security — (Sécurité Sociale) French social security, established in 1945, is a comprehensive system of public insurance that covers three categories of risk: (1) old-age pension and work disability; (2) national health insurance; (3) family and child allowances. French social security thus covers more than American social security. Originally it was to constitute a universal, generalized system for all, but although the public-health system effectively became generalized, the same was not true for old-age pensions and work disability. Pensions were segregated into different systems according to professional categories (civil servants, farmers, small businesses, self-employed workers, etc.). Old-age security pension is now reserved for wage earners, since other categories have kept their own systems.

SOFRES — (Société Française d'Enquêtes et de Sondages) An opinion-poll institute.

tripartisme — (Three-party government) A government alliance just after the Second World War that brought together the three major political parties : the PCF (Communists), SFIO (Socialists), and MRP (Christian Democrats).

UIMM — (Union des Industries Métallurgiques et Minières) An employers federation in the metallurgical and mining industries.

UNEDIC — (Union Nationale Interprofessionnelle pour l'Emploi dans l'Industrie et le Commerce) The National Interprofessional Union for Employment in Industry and Commerce is a joint organization (directed by unions representing wage earners and employers) responsible for the management of unemployment insurance. ASSEDIC is the related organization at the local level.

UNIOPSS — (Union Nationale Interfédérale des Oeuvres et Organismes Privés Sanitaires et Sociaux) The National Interfederal Union of Charitable Organizations and Private Sanitary and Social Organisms is an organization that brings together the sectors of social action that are outside state-run public service (associations, non-profit and charitable organizations, etc.).

UNIRS — (Union Nationale des Institutions de Retraite des Salariés) The National Union of Wage Earners' Retirement Funds Institutions is an organization that was created in 1957 to organize and coordinate the multitude of small supplementary pension schemes for wage earners. The UNIRS is one of several institutions under the authority of the ARRCO.

UNR (Union pour la Nouvelle République) The Union for the New Republic was a Gaullist party at the beginning of the Fifth Republic.

Vichy government Vichy is the name given to the French government under Marshal Pétain during the German occupation. It collaborated with the occupying power. In 1939, when France was at war, the Parliament (short of some of its members) voted to grant Marshal Pétain full powers so he could prepare a new constitution. Pétain took advantage of the situation and monopolized executive, legislative, judiciary, and constituent powers (which he later shared in 1942 with Pierre Laval). This authoritarian collaborationist regime ended with French Liberation and the installation of a provisional government mainly composed of members of the Resistance.

Bibliography

General Books on Old Age and Old-Age Policy

Les Ages de la vie. Actes du VIIe colloque national de démographie, Strasbourg, 5–7 Mai 1982. Tomes I et II, Cahiers no. 96 et 102. Institut National d'Etudes Démographiques. Paris: Presses Universitaires de France, 1982, 1983.

Andréani, E. *Indicateurs sociaux pour la population âgée*. Paris: Caisse Nationale de Retraite des Ouvriers du Bâtiment (CNRO), DIG-Gérontologie nos. 27–28, September–November 1974.

Beauvoir, S. de. *La vieillesse*. Paris: Gallimard, 1970.

Communications, no. 37 (1983). Special issue: "Le continent gris."

Cribier, F. *Une génération de Parisiens arrive à la retraite*. Laboratoire de Géographie humaine, CNRS. Paris: Report CORDES, June 1978.

Esprit, no. 5 (May 1963): 721–1025. Special issue: "Vieillesse et vieillissement."

Futuribles, no. 88 (May 1985). Special issue: "Le vieillissement de la société."

Gérontologie, no. 1 (November 1970) and no. 23 (June 1976). Special issue: "Politique de la vieillesse."

Guillemard A.-M. *La retraite, une mort sociale*. Sociologie des conduites en situation de retraite. Paris and The Hague: Mouton, 1972.

———. *La vieillesse et l'Etat*. Paris: Presses Universitaires de France, 1980.

———, ed. *Old Age and the Welfare State*. London: Sage, 1983.

Imhof, A.-E. *Le vieillissement: Implications et conséquences de l'allongement de la vie humaine depuis le XVIIIème siècle*. Lyons: Presses Universitaires de Lyon, 1982.

Philibert, M. *L'échelle des âges*. Paris: Le Seuil, 1968.

Sociologies et Sociétés 16, no. 2 (October 1984). Special issue: "Sociétés et vieillissement."

Official Reports on Old Age and Old-Age Policies

Arreckx, M. *L'amélioration de la qualité de la vie des personnes âgées dépendantes*. Rapport. Paris: National Assembly, 1979.

Brudon, J. *Les conditions de vie à l'âge de la retraite*. 2 vols. Paris: Economic and Social Council, 1 February 1976.

General Commissariat of the Plan

Sixth Plan (1971–1975)

Personnes Agées: Rapport de l'Intergroupe. *Problèmes relatifs aux personnes âgées.* Paris: Documentation française, 1971.

Rapport de la Commission *Action Sociale.* 2 vols. Paris: Documentation française, 1971.

Rapport général du VIe Plan de *Développement économique et social.* (Introduction: "Les choix du VIe Plan," pp. 11–30.) *JO*, no. 1371 (1971).

Seventh Plan (1976–1980)

Rapport de la Commission *Emploi et travail.* Paris: Documentation française, 1976.

Rapport de la Commission de *l'Inégalité sociale.* Paris: Documentation française **[DATE?]**.

Rapport de la Commission *Santé et Assurance maladie.* Paris: Documentation française, 1976.

Rapport de la Commission *Vie Sociale.* Paris: Documentation française, 1976.

Rapport de la Commission *Vie Sociale. La politique de la vieillesse.* Paris: Documentation interne, 1976.

Eighth Plan (1981–1985)

Rapport de la Commission *Emploi et relations du travail.* Paris: Documentation française, 1980.

Rapport de la Commission *Protection sociale et famille.* Paris: Documentation française, 1980.

Rapport du Groupe Prospective *"Personnes Agées." Vieillir demain.* Paris: Documentation française, 1980.

Public Reports

General Inspectorate of Social Affairs (IGAS)

Annual Report 1968–1969: *Les problèmes sociaux des personnes âgées.* Paris: IGAS, 1969.

Annual Report 1973: *La Prévention.* Paris: IGAS, 1974.

Annual Report 1975: *Les formes complémentaires de la protection sociale.* Paris: IGAS, 1975. Initial title: *Les régimes complémentaires de retraite et de prévoyance.*

Annual Report 1976. Vol. 2: *Les Dépenses sociales.* Paris: IGAS, 1976.

Annual Report 1977–1978: *Les Etablissements sanitaires et sociaux.* (Fifth part : "Les établissements pour personnes âgées," pp. 447–541.) Paris: IGAS, 1978.

Annual Report 1980: *Protection sociale et mutations socio-économique.* Paris: IGAS, 1980.

Other Reports

Laroque, P. *Politique de la vieillesse.* Rapport de la Commission d'Etudes des problèmes de la vieillesse. High Consultative Committee of Population and the Family. Paris: Documentation française, 1962.

High Consultative Committee of the Population and the Family. *Les personnes âgées et l'opinion en France.* Paris: Documentation française, 1962. Surveys conducted in 1961.

Ministry of Public Health and Social Security. *Consultation sur les problèmes d'action sociale en faveur des personnes âgées.* Paris, 23–27 June 1969 (Colloque Dienesch).

Ministry of Public Health and the Population. Rapport sur l'organisation de l'aide médicale et sociale aux personnes âgées. *Bulletin d'information du Ministère de la Santé Publique et de la Population,* 1969, 10–63.

Ministry of Public Health and Social Security. *Aspects médicaux du vieillissement.* Paris, September 1970.

Ministry of Public Health and Social Security, Division des études et du plan. Rapport de la Commission Santé Assurance maladie. *Les personnes âgées.* Paris, September 1975.

Ministry of Public Health and Social Security. Direction de l'Action Sociale. Bureau RV2. *Programme d'action prioritaire no. 15 du VIIe plan en faveur du maintien à domicile des personnes âgées.* Bilan d'exécution, Ministry of Health, 1980.

Moreau Y. *Le vieillissement de la population.* Report to M. Matteoli, High Committee of the Population. Paris, June 1980.

Chapter Sources

Chapter 1. Old Age and Retirement

Aron-Schnapper, D., D. Hanet, S. Deswarte, and D. Pasquier. *Histoire orale ou Archives orales?* Rapport d'activité sur la constitution d'achives orales pour l'histoire de la Sécurité Sociale. Association pour l'étude de l'histoire de la Sécurité Sociale. Paris, 1980.

Aznar, G. *Non aux loisirs. Non à la retraite.* Paris: Galilée, 1978.

Baudus de Fransures, P. de. *L'évolution du régime de retraite et de prévoyance des cadres de 1947 à 1969.* **Paris:** Published privately, 1970.

Boltanski, L. *Les cadres. La formation d'un groupe social.* Paris: Ed. de Minuit, 1982.

Catrice-Lorey, A. *Dynamique interne de la Sécurité sociale.* 2d ed. Paris: Economica, 1982.

———. "La Sécurité Sociale et l'Etat en France: Quelle autonomie de gestion pour l'institution?" *Revue Internationale de Sécurité sociale,* no. 2 (1983): 213–28.

CERS (Centre d'Etude des Relations Sociales, University of Aix-Marseille). *Sécurité sociale et conflits de classes.* Paris: Ed. Ouvrières, 1962.

Cloward, R.-A., and F.-F. Piven. *Regulating the Poor: The Functions of Public Welfare.* New York: Pantheon Books, 1971.

Cohen, S.-S., and Ch. Goldfinger. "From Permacrisis to Real Crisis in French Social Security: The Limits to Normal Politics." In *Stress and Contradiction in Modern Capitalism: Public Policy and the Theory of the State,* ed. L.-L. Lindberg et al., 57–98. Lexington, Mass.: Lexington Books, 1975.

Doublet, J. "La Sécurité sociale et son évolution (Oct. 1951–June 1960)." *Revue française des Affaires sociales,* no. 2 (April–June 1971): 27–60.

Dumont, J.-P. *La Sécurité sociale toujours en chantier.* Paris: Ed. Ouvrières, 1981.

Dupeyroux, J.-J. "Introduction aux problèmes juridiques des régimes complémentaires de vieillesse." *Droit social,* nos. 7–8 (July–August 1962): 387–95.

———. *Sécurité sociale.* 5th ed. Paris: Précis Dalloz, 1973.

Ehrmann, H.-W. *La politique du patronat français, 1936–1955.* Paris: A. Colin, 1959.

Ewald, F. "Formation de la notion d'accident du travail." *Sociologie du travail,* no. 1 (1981): 3–13.

———. "Old Age as a Risk: The Establishment of Retirement Pension Systems in France." In *Old Age and the Welfare State,* ed. A.-M. Guillemard, 115–26. London: Sage, 1983.

Galant, H.-C. *Histoire politique de la Sécurité sociale française (1945–1952).* Paris: A. Colin, 1955.

George, V. *Social Security and Society.* London and Boston: Routledge and Kegan Paul, 1973.

Graebner, W. *A History of Retirement: The Meaning and Function of an American Institution, 1885–1978.* London and New Haven: Yale University Press, 1980.

Gresle, F. "Indépendance professionnelle et protection sociale. Pratiques de classe et fluctuations idéologiques du petit patronat." *Revue française de Sociologie* 18, no. 4 (1977): 577–99.

———. "Les travailleurs indépendants et la protection sociale." *Droit social,* no. 4 (April 1983): 259–68.

Grevet, P. *Besoins populaires et financement public.* Paris: Ed. Sociales, 1976.

Hatzfeld, H. *Du paupérisme à la Sécurité sociale: Essai sur les origines de la Sécurité sociale, 1850–1940.* Paris: A. Colin, 1971.

Kohli, M. "Retirement and the Moral Economy: An Historical Interpretation of the German Case." *Journal of Aging Studies,* nos. 1–2 (1987): 125–44.

Lacroix-Riz, A. "La CGT et les revendications ouvrières face à l'Etat: De la Libération au début du Plan Marshall (sept. 1944–déc. 1947), Deux stratégies de la reconstruction." History thesis, Université de Paris I, 1981.

Lafargue, P. *Le droit à la paresse.* Paris: Maspero, 1975.

Laroque, P., et al. *Succès et faiblesses de l'effort social français.* Paris: A. Colin, 1961.

Laroque, P. "La Sécurité sociale de 1944 à 1951." *Revue française de Affaires sociales,* no. 2 (April–June 1971): 11–26.

Lefranc, G. *Les expériences syndicales en France de 1939 à 1950.* Paris: Aubier-Montaigne, 1950.

———. *Le mouvement syndical de la Libération aux événements de mai–juin 1968.* Paris: Payot, 1969.

Lion, H. "La convention de 4 Mars 1947 et son évolution." *Droit social,* nos. 7–8 (July–August 1962): 396–402.

Marshall, T.-H. *Social Policy*. London: Hutchinson University Library, 1965.

Mathieu, R. "Les Cadres." In *Sécurité sociale et conflits de classe*, ed. Centre d'Etude des Relations Sociales, Aix-en-Provence, 75–99. Paris: Ed. Ouvrières, 1962.

Melchers, R. "La vieillesse ouvrière 1836–1914. Les origines de la retraite ouvrière." Thesis of 3e cycle, Univ. Aix-Marseille II, Laboratoire d'Economie et de Sociologie du Travail, 1984.

Myles, J. *Old Age in the Welfare State*. Toronto: Little, Brown, 1984.

Netter, F. "Evolution historique des régimes privés de vieillesse." In *Les régimes complémentaires de retraites par répartition,* 9–19. Recueils et Monographes, no. 54. Paris: Documentation française, 1965.

———. "Retraites des non-salariés." *Droit social*, no. 1 (January 1967): 45–51.

———. "Les retraites en France au cours de la période1895–1945" (part 1). *Droit social,* nos. 7–8 (July–August 1965): 448–55.

———. "Les retraites en France au cours de la période1895–1945" (part 2). *Droit social,* nos. 9–10 (September–October 1965): 514–26.

———. "Les retraites en France avant le XXe siècle." *Droit social*, no. 6 (June 1963): 358–73.

Perrin, G. "Pour une théorie sociologique de la Sécurité sociale dans les sociétés industrielles." *Revue française de sociologie* 7, no. 3 (July–September 1967): 299–324.

Perrot, M., and J.-L. Guglielmi. *Salaires et revendications sociales en France, 1944–1952.* Paris: A. Colin, 1953.

Prost, A. "Jalons pour une Histoire des retraites et des retraités, 1914–1939." *Revue d'Histoire moderne et contemporaine* 11 (October–December 1964): 263–89.

"Les Régimes complémentaires de retraite." *Droit social,* nos. 7–8 (July–August 1962): 383–476.

Les Régimes complémentaires de retraite par répartition. Recueils et Monographes, no. 54. Paris: Documentation française, 1965.

Rollet, Ch. *Les systèmes de retraite en France*. Dossier constat no. 4, Commissariat Général du Plan, Groupe prospective personnes âgées, September 1978.

"Sécurité sociale et santé." *Prévenir*, no. 5 (March 1982).

Sellier, F. *Dynamique des besoins sociaux.* Paris: Ed. Ouvrières, 1970.

———. *Stratégie de la lutte sociale en France, 1936–1960.* Paris: Ed. Ouvrières, 1961.

Stearns, P.-N. *Lives of Labor. Work in a Maturing Industrial Society.* London: Croom Helm, 1975.

———. *Old Age in European Society: The Case of France.* New York: Holmes and Meier, 1976.

Teissier, G. "La CFTC et le plan actuel de la Sécurité sociale." *Droit social,* no. 5 (May 1946): 205–15.

Titmuss, R.-M. *Essays on the Welfare State*, London: Unwin, 1963.

Touraine, A. *La conscience ouvrière.* Paris: Le Seuil, 1966.

Trempé, R. *Les mineurs de Carmaux, 1848–1914.* 2 vols. Paris: Ed. Ouvrières, 1971.

———. "The Struggle of French Miners for the Creation of Retirement Funds in the Nineteenth Century." In *Old Age and the Welfare State*, ed. A.-M. Guillemard, 101–14. London: Sage, 1983.

Veillon, Charles. "L'accord du 8 décembre 1961." In "Les régimes complémentaires de retraite." *Droit social*, nos. 7–8 (July–August 1962): 415–18.

PARLIAMENTARY DOCUMENTS, MINISTERIAL DECREES, AND CIRCULARS

Bill no. 2029. Discussion on "Retraites du régime général de Sécurité sociale." Session of 1 Dec. 1971. *JO*, pp. 6237–56. Session of 2 Dec. 1971. *JO*, pp. 6295–312. Session of 16 Dec. 1976. *JO*, pp. 6841–42; Session of 18 December 1976, *JO*, pp. 6950–51.

Conseil Economique et Social. Avis et Rapports. *Institution d'un Fonds National de Vieillesse.* Session of 9 March 1955. *JO,* 16 March, 201–9.

Journal officiel. Loi no. 71-1132 of 31 Décember 1971 on increase in public pensions of the Regime General of the social security and for wage earners in agriculture, too. *JO,* 5 January 1972, 140–41 (Boulin Law).

Journal officiel. Parliamentary debates. National Assembly. *Fonds National de la Vieillesse.* Presentation of a bill, 1st and 2nd sessions, 16 November 1955. *JO*, pp. 5737–63. Second reading of a bill, 1st session of 22 March 1956. *JO*, pp. 1164–72.

Mathévet, R. *Equilibre et gestion des régimes de retraites complémentaires.* Avis et Rapports du Conseil Economique et Social, no. 17. Session of 10 July 1962. *JO*, 24 August 1962, 720–36.

Projet de loi portant institution d'un Fonds National de Solidarité. Presented to National Assembly on 23 March 1956; adopted on May 1956, as "Projet de loi portant institution d'un Fonds National de Solidarité." Session from 24 April 1956 to 30 June 1956.

Retraites du personnel des entreprises. Discussion, second reading of proposed legislation aimed at preventing certain abuses in company-board staff pension plans. Session of 9 October 1956. *JO*, p. 4069.

Chapter 2. Old Age and Ways of Life

Ariès, P. *L'enfant et la vie familiale sous l'Ancien Régime.* Paris: Le Seuil, 1973.

Attias-Donfut, Cl., and A. Rozenkier. *Vieillir chez soi: Enquête sur l'aide ménagère à domicile.* Paris: Caisse Nationale d'Assurance Vieillesse des Travailleurs Salariés, April 1981.

Auriol, V. *Mon septennat, 1947–1954.* Paris: Gallimard, 1970.

Balier, C. "La place de la personne âgée dans le cadre d'une gérontologie de secteur." *Gérontologie,* no. 2 (1971): 5–12.

Balier, C., et al. "Le centre de traitement de jour pour personnes âgées." *Revue française des Affaires sociales,* no. 3 (July–September 1972): 79–110.

Barrère, D. "Le maintien à domicile des personnes âgées." *Gérontologie,* nos. 31–32 (October–December 1975) and *Documentation d'Information et de Gescian.* Paris: CNRO (Caisse Nationale de Retraite des Ouvriers du Bâtiment), n.d.

Benoît-Lapierre, N. "Guérir de vieillesse." *Communications,* no. 37 (1983): 149–65.

Benoît-Lapierre, N., et al. *Vieillesse des pauvres: Les chemins de l'hospice.* Paris: Ed. Ouvrières, 1980.

Bernand, C. *Les vieux vont mourir à Nanterre.* Paris: Ed. du Sagittaire, 1978.

Berthod, M. *Action sanitaire et sociale en faveur des personnes âgées.* Commissariat Général du Plan. Groupe Prospective Personnes Agées. Dossier constat no. 8. Paris, November 1978.

Bing, J. "L'évolution de la politique gouvernementale en faveur des personnes âgées." *Questions de Sécurité sociale,* no. 1 (January 1971): 11–17.

Birnbaum, P. *Les sommets de l'Etat.* Paris: Le Seuil, 1977.

Boétard, Y., and F. Pallez. *Le maintien à domicile des personnes âgées.* Paris: Centre de gestion scientifique de l'Ecole des Mines de Paris, January 1977.

Bourlière, F. "Qu'est-ce que vieillir?" *Esprit,* no. 5 (May 1963). In the special issue "Vieillesse et vieillissement."

Castel, R. "Genèse et ambiguités de la notion de secteur en psychiatrie." *Revue de Sociologie du travail,* no. 1 (1975): 57–77.

———. *La gestion des risques.* Paris: Ed. de Minuit, 1981.

——— "La "guerre à la pauvreté" aux Etats-Unis: Le statut de l'indigence dans une société d'abondance." *Actes de la Recherche,* no. 19 (January 1978): 47–60.

Castells, M. "Vers une théorie sociologique de la planification urbaine." *Sociologie du travail,* no. 4 (1969): 130–43.

Centre Lorrain de Gérontologie Sociale. *Bilan du PAP 15 en Lorraine.* (V11e Plan.) Nancy, November 1979.

Chauvet, J. "L'action sanitaire et sociale de la Caisse Nationale d'Assurance Vieillesse des Travailleurs Salariés." *Droit social,* no. 5 (May 1975): 322–34.

———. "FamilleVieillesse." *Droit social,* nos. 9–10 (September-October 1974): 437–42.

———. "Le programme finalisé pour le maintien à domicile des personnes âgées." *Vie sociale* (Cahiers du CEDIAS), no. 5 (May 1973).

Chauvet, J., and M. L. Pitois. "La politique de la vieillesse." *Revue française des Affaires sociales,* no. 4 (October–December 1980): 327–50.

Comité National d'Entente pour la Journée des Vieillards. *Personnes âgées: Valeur sociale.* Paris: Collection CLEIRPPA (Centre de Liaison, d'Etude, d'Information et de Recherche sur les Problèmes des Personnes Agées), Feb. 1971. Supplement to *Union sociale,* no. 196 (1971).

Commission du Bilan. *La France en mai 1981.* Vol. 3 of *La vie collective et les politiques sociales.* Bilan de la politique de la vieillesse. Paris: Documentation française, 1981.

Congrès national des Offices d'Information et d'Action Gérontologiques, Nancy, 25–26 April 1974. *Rapports du deuxième congrès des offices d'information et d'action gérontologiques* (GLOPA), Nancy, April 1974. "Les offices et le programme finalisé." Travaux gérontologiques et gériatriques, CHU de Grenoble, Grenoble.

Correspondance municipale, nos. 159–60) (July–August 1975). Special issue: "Le Maintien à domicile des personnes âgées."

Crozier, M. "Pour une analyse sociologique de la planification française." *Revue française de Sociologie* 6 (June 1965): 147–53.

Crozier, M., et al. *Où va l'administration française?* Paris: Ed. d'Organisation, 1974.

Dessaint, L. "Le point sur le programme finalisé." In *Années-Documents* CLEIRPPA, 9–75 p. 312.

Devouassoux-Merakchi, J., and D. Martin. "La population des hospices et des maisons de retraite." *Statistiques et commentaires,* no. 6 (1975): 518.

Droit social, nos. 4–5 (April–May 1972). Special issue, edited by J. J. Dupeyroux: "Aspects sociaux du VIe Plan."

Estes, C.-L. *The Aging Enterprise.* San Francisco: Jossey-Bass, 1979.

Fréville, J. "L'action sociale des régimes complémentaires." *Droit social,* nos. 7–8 (July–August 1972): 450–56.

Friedberg, E. "Insaisissable planification: Réflexions à propos de quelques études sur la planification française." *Revue française de Sociologie* 16 (1975): 605–23.

Gaullier, X. *Une politique médico-sociale de la vieillesse: Le XIIIe arrondissement de Paris (1965–1975).* Paris: Fondation des villes, 1975.

———. *Une politique municipale de la vieillesse: La région grenobloise (1965–1975).* Paris: Fondation des villes, 1975.

Gérontologie 71, no. 2 (1971). Special issue: "Gérontologie de secteur."

Gillette, A. *Votre commune et les personnes âgées.* Paris: Ed. du Moniteur, 1978.

Guillemard, A.-M. "Social Policy and Ageing in France." In *Ageing and Social Policy: A Critical Assessment,* ed. C. Phillipson and A. Walker, 263–79. London: Gower, 1986.

———. *La Vieillesse et l'Etat.* Paris: Presses Universitaires de France, 1980.

Houplain, Y., and F. Petit-Liévois. *Le point de la politique de la vieillesse 10 ans après la Commission Laroque.* Paris: Centre de Liaison d'Etude, d'Information et de Recherche sur les Problèmes des Personnes Agées (CLEIRPPA), November 1973.

Hugonot, R., C. Mollard, and Y. Billon-Tyrard. "Le réseau d'information et de formation." *Gérontologie* 71, no. 2 (1971): 20–23.

Jobert, B. *Le social en Plan.* Paris: Ed. Ouvrières, 1982.

Keene, J.-L. "Le programme finalisé pour maintien à domicile des personnes âgées." *Revue française des Affaires sociales,* no. 1 (January–March 1972): 65–78.

Lautman, J., and J.-C. Thoenig. "La planification, agent du changement dans quelques administrations publiques françaises." In *Tendances et volontés de la société française,* ed. J. D. Reynaud, 229–47. Paris: SEDEIS, 1966.

Lenoir, R. *Les exclus.* 2d ed. Paris: Le Seuil, 1976.

———. *Le temps de vivre un 3e âge heureux.* Paris: Documentation française, 1978.

———. "Un véritable plan pour les personnes âgées." *Le Monde,* 9 November 1972.

Lowi, T. *The End of Liberalism.* New York: Norton, 1969.

Massé, P. *Rapport sur l'adaptation des équipements et services sanitaires et sociaux aux besoins des personnes des troisième et quatrième âges.* Paris: Commissariat Général au Plan, May 1977.

Mayen, M. "La population des hospices et des maisons de retraite." *Population,* no. 1 (1972): 70–82.

Mizrahi, A., and D. Moyse. *Les personnes âgées vivant en institutions. Caractères socio-démographiques, autonomie et handicaps.* Paris: Centre de Recherche pour l'Etude et l'Observation des Conditions de vie (CREDOC), June 1977.

Nizard, L. "Nécessaires régulations planificatrices de l'appareil d'Etat dans la France capitaliste d'aujourd'hui." *Revue française de Sociologie* 16 (1975): 625–52. Supplement 1975.

———. *Planification et société.* Grenoble: Presses Universitaires de Grenoble, 1974.

Nizard, L., et al. *Changement social et appareil d'Etat du 5e au 6e Plan.* Rapport d'étude. Grenoble: Centre d'Etudes et de Recherches sur l'Administration Economique et l'Aménagement du Territoire (CERAT), 1974.

Philibert, M. "L'aspect politique de la gérontologie de secteur." *Gerontologie* 71, no. 2 (1971): 13–18.

———. "L'essor de la gérontologie sociale aux Etats-Unis." *Esprit,* no. 5 (May 1963): 994–99. In the special issue "Vieillesse et vieillissement."

———. "Le rôle et l'image du vieillard dans notre société." *Esprit,* no. 5 (May 1963): 928–51. In the special issue "Vieillesse et vieillissement."

Questiaux, N. "L'Intergroupe personnes âgées et la préparation du VIe Plan." *Gérontologie* 70, no. 1 (November 1970): 16–18.

——— "La politique de la vieillesse dans le VIe Plan." *Droit social,* no. 45 (April–May 1972): 192–97.

———. "Réflexions sur la politique de la vieillesse." *Gérontologie* 73, no. 13 (December 1973): 32–36.

Sallois, J., and M. Crétin. "Le rôle social des hauts fonctionnaires dans la crise de l'Etat." In *La crise de l'Etat,* ed. N. Poulantzas, 233–59. Paris: Presses Universitaires de France, 1976.

Schnapper, D. *Le système administratif.* Vol. 2 of *Morphologie de la haute administration française.* Paris and La Haye: Mouton, 1972.

Sociologie du Travail, no. 3 (1966). Special issue, edited by M. Crozier: "L'Administration face aux problèmes du changement."

Thierry, R., and V. Dominique. "Problèmes actuels de la vieillesse." *Economie et Politique,* no. 104 (March 1963): 25–36.

Van Lerberghe, R.-W., and S. Paul. *Les soins aux personnes âgées.* Rapport du groupe de travail soins aux personnes âgées. Paris: Ministry of Health and Social Security, December 1980.

PARLIAMENTARY DOCUMENTS, MINISTERIAL DECREES, AND CIRCULARS

Discussion sur les personnes âgées. Session of 20 May 1960. *JO*, pp. 1027–35. Second session of 7 June 1962. *JO*, pp. 1582–83. First session of 14 June 1962. *JO*, pp. 1697–98. Session of 15 June 1962. Oral questions in debate on "Situation des personnes âgées." *JO*, pp. 1755–67. Session of 20 July 1962. Oral questions in debate on "Organismes spécialisés pour la construction et la gestion des logements foyers de vieillards." *JO*, pp. 2737–41.

Journal officiel. Parliamentary debates. National Assembly. *Carte sociale des économiquement faibles.* First session of 31 May 1949. *JO*, pp. 2932–45. Third session of 30 July 1949. *JO*, pp. 5634. First session of 23 March 1950. *JO*, pp. 2275–84.

National Assembly. *Rapport d'Information au nom de la Commission des affaires culturelles, familiales et sociales sur la prolongation du temps moyen de la vie face aux problèmes de l'emploi et de la retraite,* by M. J. R. Debray. National Assembly, 4 July 1961, no. 1300.

Chapter 3. Old Age and Employment

Adam, G., and J.-D. Reynaud. *Conflits du travail et changement social.* Paris: Presses Universitaires de France, 1978.

"L'Age de la retraite." *Gérontologie* 72, no. 7 (June 1972).

Alliance Nationale contre la Dépopulation (in collaboration with INED, INSEE and the Institut d'Hygiène). *Compte rendu des trois journées pour l'étude scientifique du vieillissement de la population.* 5 parts. Paris, 22–24 April 1948.

Association des Ages. *Attitudes et aspirations face au travail.* Paris: Association des Ages, January 1980.

Audras, M. "Vers la retraite progressive." *Gérontologie* 23–24 (July–October 1973): 23–

24. Special issue: *Documents d'Information et de Gestion.* Paris: CNRO (Caisses Nationale de Retraite des Ouvriers du Bâtiment), n.d.

Barfield, R., and J. Morgan. *Early Retirement: The Decision and the Experience.* Ann Arbor: University of Michigan, Institute for Social Research, 1969.

Béranger, T. "La garantie de ressources aux travailleurs sans emploi âgés de 60 ans et plus: préretraite ou prestation de chômage améliorée." *Droit social,* nos. 9–10 (September–October 1978): 67–77.

Bergeron, A., Charles Gatinel, Ph. Madinier, R. Mario, P. Naville, and P. Paillat. "L'âge de la retraite." *Esprit,* no. 5 (May 1963): 874–93. In the special issue "Vieillesse et vieillissement."

Boullot, M., et al. "L'âge de la retraite." *Revue française des Affaires sociales* 2 (July–September 1986): 457–532. In the special issue "Perspectives de la Sécurité sociale."

Brouard, N., and M.-A. Lévy. "La durée d'activité professionnelle." *Population et Sociétés,* no. 152 (November 1981).

Casassus Montéro, C. *Les syndicats et l'emploi.* Paris: Centre de Recherches en Sciences Sociales du Travail, Université Paris-Sud, 1980.

CNPF (Conseil National du Patronat Français) The National Council of French Employers. "Abaissement de l'âge de la retraite." *Notes et Arguments,* no. 20 (May 1971).

Cribier, F. "Itinéraires professionnels et usure au travail: Une génération de salariés parisiens." *Le Mouvement social,* no. 124 (July–September 1983): 11–44.

Daric, J. *Vieillissement de la population et prolongation de la vie active.* INED, Travaux et Documents, Cahier no. 7. Paris: Presses Universitaires de France, 1948.

"De nouveaux inactifs." *Gérontologie et Société,* no. 24 (April 1983).

Dumazedier, J. "Nouveaux problèmes du temps libre dans la crise des valeurs." *Temps libre,* no. 4 (1981): 55–71.

Durand, M. *Les conflits du travail.* Paris: Centre de Recherches en Sciences Sociales du travail, Université Paris-Sud, 1977.

Evans, A.-A. *Temps et vie de travail.* Paris: OECD, 1973.

Frank, D., R. Hara, G. Magnier, and D. Villey. "Entreprises et contrats de solidarité de préretraitedémission." *Travail et Emploi,* no. 13 (July–September 1982).

Frossard, M. "L'âge de la retraite, le coût de la vieillesse et la rationalité économique." *Gérontologie et Société,* no. 23 (1982): 14–22.

———. "Crise et cessations anticipées d'activité: Une comparaison internationale." *Travail et Emploi,* no. 16 (April–June 1983): 9–20.

———. *L'emploi des travailleurs âgés et la crise: Le cas français.* Grenoble: Institut de Recherche Economique et de Planification (REP), Université des Sciences sociales de Grenoble, 1980.

Galland, O., J. Gaudin, and P. Vrain. "Contrats de solidarité et stratégie des entreprises." *Travail et Emploi,* no. 22 (December 1984): 7–20.

Grossin, W. "L'abaissement de l'âge de la retraite." *Revue française des Affaires sociales,* no. 4 (October–December 1974): 19–48.

Guillemard, A.-M. "Changes in Withdrawal from the Labor Force: An International Trend." In *States, Labor Market, and the Future of Old Age Policy,* ed. J. Myles and J. Quadagno, 209–26. Philadelphia: Temple University Press, 1991.

——— (with M. Rein). "Comparative Patterns of Retirement: Recent Trends in Developed Societies." *Annual Review of Sociology* 19 (1993): 469–503.

———. *Le déclin du social: formation et crise des politiques de la vieillesse.* Paris: Presses Universitaires de France, 1986.

———. "France: Massive Exit through Unemployment Compensation." In *Time for Retirement: Comparative Studies of Early Exit from the Labor Force,* ed. M. Kohli, Martin Rein, Anne-Marie Guillemard, and Herman van Gunsteren, 127–80. Cambridge: Cambridge University Press, 1991.

———. "Pathways and Their Prospects: A Comparative Interpretation of the Meaning of Early Exit." In *Time for Retirement: Comparative Studies of Early Exit from the Labor Force,* ed. M. Kohli, Martin Rein, Anne-Marie Guillemard, and Herman van Gunsteren, 362–87. Cambridge: Cambridge University Press, 1991

———. "Préretraite et mutations du cycle de vie." *Futuribles,* no. 88 (May 1985): 31–38.

———. "The Social Dynamics of Early Withdrawal from the Labor Force in France." *Ageing and Society* 5, no. 4 (1985): 381–412.

Harff, Y. "Droit au repos et droit au travail." *Revue française des Affaires sociales,* no. 1 (January–March 1982): 19–38.

Heller, J. L. "La retraite anticipée: Choix ou contrainte?" *Economie et statistique,* November–December 1986, 97–109.

———. "Les retraites anticipées." *Données sociales,* 1987, 133–41.

Institut de l'Entreprise. *Sortir de la vie professionnelle: Application des concepts de la stratégie du temps rémunéré.* Paris: January 1985.

Kerschen, N., and H. Réminiac. "Les systèmes de 'préretraite': Classification juridique et pratique." *Droit social,* no. 2 (February 1981): 175–201.

Kirchberger, A. *Emploi des travailleurs âgés.* Commissariat général du Plan, Groupe prospective personnes âgées, dossier constat no. 2. Paris, 1978.

Kohli, M., Martin Rein, Anne-Marie Guillemard, and Herman van Gunsteren, eds. *Time for Retirement: Comparative Studies of Early Exit from the Labor Force.* Cambridge University Press, 1991

Latty, Ph. "Les systèmes de préretraite en France (garantie de ressources pour les salariés entre 60 et 65 ans." *Droit social,* no. 4 (April 1973): 225–67.

Lenormand, F., and G. Magnier. "Le développement des dispositifs de cessation anticipée d'activité: Aspects sociaux et conséquences financières." *Travail et Emploi,* no. 15 (January-March 1983): 47–62.

Lévy, M. "L'Age de la retraite s'abaisse." *Population et sociétés,* no. 117 (October 1978).

———. "Relativité de l'âge." *Population et sociétés,* no. 164 (December 1982).

Magnier, G. "Les sorties de la vie active en 1981." Supplement to *Bulletin mensuel des statistiques du travail,* no. 95.

Malabouche, G. "Retraites: les périls de l'an 2030." In *Etudes et Recherches, 5.* Paris: Documentation française, 1987.

Marbach, G. *Aménagement des postes de travail pour les travailleurs âgés.* Paris: OECD, 1968.

Mercereau, F. "La retraite à 60 ans." *Droit Social,* June 1982, 452–64.

Ministry of Labour, Employment, and Population. "Le travail des plus de 60 ans: Emploi et retraite anticipée." *Notes du Ministère du Travail,* no. 17 (14–20 June 1971).

Monnier, A. "Les conditions du passage à la retraite: réalités et projets." *Population,* no. 1 (1980): 109–36.

———. "Les limites de la vie active et la retraite." *Population,* no. 45 (July–October 1979): 801–24.

Morisot, M. "Flexibilité de l'âge de la retraite en France." In *Flexibilité de l'âge de la retraite,* 89–129. Paris: OECD, 1980.

OECD (Organisation of Economic Cooperation and Development). *Le Placement des travailleurs âgés.* Paris: OECD, 1967.

Paillat, P., and J.-C. Chesnais. "L'âge de la retraite aujourd'hui et demain." *Gérontologie et Société,* no. 14 (October 1980): 59–92.

Philipson, C. *Capitalism and the Construction of Old Age.* London: Macmillan, 1982.

Ragot, M. *La cessation anticipée d'activité salariée.* Report presented on behalf of Labour Section, Economic and Social Council. Paris, 1985.

SEDES (Société d'Etudes pour le Développement Economique et Social). *Etude sur les conventions et accords de préretraite.* Paris, December 1977.

Sociologie du travail, no. 2 (April–June 1981). Special issue: "Le Chômage, Politiques d'emploi et action collective."

Sueur, J. P. *Changer la retraite: Propositions pour le développement du volontariat des préretraitées et retraités.* Report to the Prime Minister's Office. Paris: Documentation française, 1985.

Thomas, Cl., and D. Balmary. "Le Fonds National de l'Emploi." *Droit social,* no. 12 (December 1969): 575–85.

Treanton, J.-R. "Travail et vieillissement, état des questions." *Revue de Sociologie du travail,* no. 1 (1964): 84–87.

Valentini, A. "Licenciement et Départ en retraite." *Droit social,* no. 11 (1978): 346–67.

Villebrun, J. "La loi du 18 décembre 1963 et le Fonds National de l'Emploi." *Droit social,* no. 2 (February 1965): 86–96.

Vimont, Cl. "L'attitude des employeurs face aux travailleurs âgés." In *Cahiers du Centre d'Etudes de l'Emploi,* no. 2, 3–32. Paris: Presses Universitaires de France, 1972.

Vrain, P., and G. Gontier. "Les ouvriers vieillissants de la région parisienne." In *Cahiers du Centre d'Etudes de l'Emploi,* no. 17. Paris: Presses Universitaires de France, 1979.

PARLIAMENTARY DOCUMENTS, MINISTERIAL DECREES, AND CIRCULARS

Journal officiel. Act 72-635 of 5 July 1972 on "guaranteed income for unemployed older workers aged less than 60." *JO,* 11 July 1972, 7235.

Journal officiel. Opinions and reports of the Economic and Social Council. Sessions of 8 and 9 February 1961. *Problème du reclassement et de la réadaptation des travailleurs dits "âgés ,"* no. 7, 15 March 1961, pp. 348–65.

Journal officiel. Parliamentary debates. National Assembly. Discussion on the bill on "guaranteed income." Session of 8 June 1972. *JO,* pp. 2349–58. Discussion and adoption. Session of 28 June 1972.

Journal officiel. Parliamentary debates. National Assembly. Oral questions in debate on "lowering the retirement age." Session of 19 May 1971. *JO*, pp. 1980–97.

National Assembly. Bill no. 2310 on "guaranteed income" *(garantie de ressources)* presented on behalf of Prime Minister J. Chaban-Delmas by J. Fontanet, Minister of Labour, Employment and the Population, 16 May 1972.

Ratification of an agreement of 13 June 1977 concerning "unemployed workers aged over 60 years." Ministry of Labor. *JO*, 10 July 1977, 3666–67.

Chapter 4. The Elaboration of Policies for Old Age, and the Crisis that Ensued: Clues for an Interpretation

L'Avenir de la protection sociale: Préparation du IXe Plan, 1984–1988. Paris: Documentation française, 1983.

Babeau, A. *La fin des retraites?* Paris: Hachette, 1985.

Bergougnoux, J.-A., and B. Manin. *La Sociale Démocratie ou le Compromis.* Paris: Presses Universitaires de France, 1979.

Blum-Girardeau, C. *Les tableaux de la solidarité.* Paris: Documentation française, 1981.

Bono, R., ed. *Sécurité sociale: L'Enjeu.* Paris: Syros, 1983. Interviews with B. Brunbes, M. Foucault, R. Lenoir, and P. Rosanvallon.

Buci-Glucksmann, Ch., and G. Therborn. *Le défi social-démocrate.* Paris: Maspero, 1981.

Cazes, B. "L'Etat-Protecteur contraint à une double manoeuvre." *Futuribles,* no. 40 (January 1981): 5–29.

Chesnais, J.-C. "Evolution démographique et charge de financement des retraites." *Revue française des Affaires sociales,* June 1984, 85–102. Supplement entitled "Population, équilibres économiques et systèmes sociaux."

———. "Sécurité sociale et Population." *Revue française des Affaires sociales,* July–September 1985, 45–61. Special issue: "Quarante ans de Sécurité sociale."

Commissariat Général du Plan. Groupe administratif sur les transferts sociaux. *Rapport du sous-groupe Retraites.* Paris, July 1979.

Commissariat Général du Plan. *Rapport du groupe quantitatif sur la protection sociale.* Paris, October 1982.

Commission du Bilan. Etudes et rapports. *La France en mai 1981: 1. Les grands équilibres économiques.* Paris: Documentation française, December 1981. 3. *La vie collective et les politiques sociales.* Paris: Documentation française, December 1981. *La France en mai 1981: Forces et faiblesses.* Paris: Documentation française, 1981.

Dahrendorf, R. "L'Après-social-démocratie." *Le Débat,* no. 7 (1980): 18–36.

Donzelot, J. *L'invention du social.* Paris: Fayard, 1984.

Estes, C.-L., R. J. Newcomer and Associates. *Fiscal Austerity and Aging: Shifting Government Responsibility for the Elderly.* London: Sage, 1983.

Fournier, J., and N. Questiaux. *Le pouvoir du social.* Paris: Presses Universitaires de France, 1979.

Gough, L. *The Political Economy of the Welfare State.* London: Macmillan, 1979.

Grémion, P. *Le pouvoir périphérique.* Paris: Le Seuil, 1976.

Guillaume, H. *Faire gagner la France.* Paris: Hachette, 1986.

Guillemard, A.-M. "Jalons pour une sociologie des politiques sociales: Le cas de la politique française de la vieillesse." *Sociologie et Sociétés* 16, no. 2 (October 1984): 119–28.

———. "La production des politiques de la vieillesse. Débats, enjeux rapports sociaux sous-jacents." *Communications,* no. 37 (1983): 105–22.

Habermas, J. *Raison et légitimité: Problèmes de légitimation dans le capitalisme avancé.* Paris: Payot, 1978.

Hirschman, A.-O. *Bonheur privé, action publique.* Princeton: Princeton University Press, 1982; Paris: Fayard, 1983.

———. "L'Etat-providence en difficulté; Etats-Unis: Crise de système ou douleurs de croissance?" *Le Débat,* no. 7 (December 1980): 58–63.

Janowitz, M. *Social Control of the Welfare State.* Chicago: University of Chicago Press, 1976.

Kessler, D. "Les retraites en péril?" *Revue française des Affaires sociales,* June 1984, 63–83.

Lévy, E. "L'évolution des conceptions et des modalités de la politique d'action sociale en France au cours de la période 1960–80." Quatrièmes Journées d'Economie Sociale, "L'évaluation des politiques sociales," 27–28 September 1984.

Mendras, H., and L. Dirn. "Le 3e Age animera la société française." *Futuribles,* no. 80 (September 1984): 3–28.

Minc, A. "France: L'inéluctable réforme du régime social?" *Le Débat,* no. 7 (December 1980): 63–66.

Neugarten, B.-L. *Age or Need? Public Policies for Older People.* London: Sage, 1983.

O'Connor, J. *The Fiscal Crisis of the State.* New York: St. Martin's Press, 1973.

OECD. *Dépenses sociales, 1960–1990: Problèmes de croissance et de maîtrise.* Paris: OECD, 1985.

———. *L'Etat-Protecteur en crise.* Paris: OECD, 1981.

Offe, C. *Contradictions of the Welfare State.* Edited by J. Keane. London: Hutchinson, 1984.

Padioleau, J.-G. *L'Etat au concret.* Paris: Presses Universitaires de France, 1982.

Ravel, J. *Le temps choisi.* (Ninth Plan.) Paris: Documentation française, January 1983.

Rosanvallon, P. *La crise de l'Etat-Providence.* Paris: Le Seuil, 1981.

Schmitter, P.-C., "Modes of Interest Intermediation and Models of Societal Change in Western Europe." *Comparative Political Studies* 10, no. 1 (April 1977): 7–37.

———. "Still the Century of Corporatism?" *Review of Politics* 36, no. 1 (January 1974): 85–131.

Sfez, L. *Critique de la décision.* Cahiers de la Fondation Nationale des Sciences Politiques. Paris, 1973.

"La Solidarité mal en point?" *Economie et humanisme,* no. 271 (May–June 1983): 9–34.

Sueur, J.-P. *Changer la retraite.* Rapport au Premier Ministre. Paris: Documentation française, 1985.

Touraine, A. *L'après-socialisme.* Paris: Grasset, 1980.

———. *Production de la Société.* Paris: Le Seuil, 1973.

Vingré, M. *Le social, c'est fini!* Paris: Collection "Autrement," 1980.

Wilensky, H. L. *The Welfare State and Equality: Structural and Ideological Roots of Public Expenditures.* Berkeley: University of California Press, 1975.

Index

Adam, G, 200
age debate, 99
age discrimination, 39, 42, 45, 119; origins of, 41
aging, 100, 249, 250; demographic and economic data on, 277–86; occupational, 41, 42; physiological, 41; and public assistance, 96–100; public management of, 233–43
alienation, 38, 265
amenities: cost of, 104; subsidized, 104
Ariès, Philippe, 102
ARRCO, 30, 82, 114; agreement, 79, 80, 83
ASSEDIC (Association pour l'Emploi dans l'Industrie et le Commerce [Association for Employment in Industry and Commerce]), 224
assembly, 81
Association de Gérontologie (Gerontology Association), 128
Association Village-Retraite, 98
assurance sociale, 34. *See also* social insurance
autonomy: and retirement, 45
AVTS *(allocation aux vieux travailleurs salariés),* 57, 70, 71

baby boomers, 181
BAS (bureaux d'aide sociale [welfare agencies]), 245
Beveridge Plan, 10
big businesses, 36, 39, 45, 63, 66, 69, 81, 114, 122; and cadres, 67–68; control of workers, 43; needs of, 40; and pension funds/schemes, 43, 44, 80; and social benefits, 44; and workforce, 39, 44
Binet, Léon, 126
Birnbaum, Pierre, 107
birth cohorts, 252, 253
birth rate, 90, 92, 170
Blanzy Mining Co., 42, 43
Bloch-Lainé Report on the Handicapped, 246
Boulin, Robert, 142, 189
Boulin Act/Boulin Law (1971), 30, 75, 85, 86, 143, 190, 202
Bourlière, François, 126
Buisson, Georges, 54, 56, 59
Bureau RV 2, 104, 156, 159

cadres, 67, 114, 117, 118, 126, 139, 160; pensions of, 64, 83; and the self-employed, 63
Caisse Nationale d'Assurance Maladie (National Health-Insurance Fund), 157
Caisse Nationale de Retraite pour la Vieillesse [National Old-Age Retirement Fund]), 31
capital: for old-age coverage, 35
capitalism, 180; French, 172
career-end employment, 176–200
Carmaux coal mines, 42
cash benefits, 91, 92
Castel, Robert, 147
Catrice-Lorey, Antoinette, 75
CDIC (Comité de Défense du Personnel des Ingénieurs et Cadres bénéficiant d'un Régime Particulier [Defense Committee for Engineers and Cadres belonging to a Special Plan]), 67
center, the, 68

Centre de Gérontologie de la Caisse Nationale de Retraite des Ouvriers du Bâtiment (Gerontology Center of the National Retirement Fund for Construction Workers), 128
Centre Pluridisciplinarie de Gérontologie (Multidisciplinary Gerontology Center), 132
CFDT, 143, 173, 176, 177, 180, 181, 182, 184, 185, 189, 190, 191, 201, 207, 208, 210, 271
CFTC, 54, 57, 59, 60, 66, 67, 70, 71, 77, 79, 110, 178, 185
CGC (Confédération Générale des Cadres [General Confederation of Cadres]), 64, 65, 67, 73, 177, 178, 185, 189, 190, 207, 208
CGT (Confédération Générale du Travail), 10, 37, 55, 56, 58–61, 63, 64, 67, 70–72, 74, 77, 80, 99, 111, 143, 173, 176, 177–80, 181, 182, 184, 185, 189, 190, 191, 201, 207, 208, 210, 271: and CFDT, 178; pension objectives, 178–79; and social insurance funds, 54
Chaban-Delmas government, 151
Chamber of Deputies, 32
charitable institutions, 112
charity, 92
Chirac, Jacques, 204; government of, 202
Christian Democrats, 56, 68, 81
CNAVTS, 156, 157
CNPF (Conseil National du Patronat Français), 67, 178, 187, 188, 190, 194, 202, 205, 207, 208
clubs, 145, 148, 155; for the elderly, 121; statistics for, 121
Cold War, 62
collective agreements, 114
Comité d'Entraide Sociale, 59
Comité National de la Vieillesse de France (National Committee for Old Age in France), 106
Comités Départmentaux d'Information aux Personnes Âgées, 150
Commissariat Général du Plan, 149, 150, 195; Social Affairs Service of, 146; Commission de l'Emploi (Employment Commission), 194
Commission du Travail des Affaires Sociales (Workers Social Affairs Commission), 56
Common Market, 182
Communist Party, 10, 66, 68
community centers, 106, 118, 120, 148, 149, 155
community housing, 161
company loyalty, 43; and pensions, 78; and retirement, 40–41, 43
compensation funds, 54
complementary pension plans, 69, 70
compulsory insurance, 66
Comte, Auguste, 33
Constituent Assemblies, 234
consumerism, 108
craft workers, 64
crédits d'équipment, 155
crédits de fonctionnement, 155
Creusot Co., 45
crisis of legitimacy, 261–63
"crisis of motivation," 255
crisis of rationality, 255–61
Croizat, Ambroise, 56, 57, 58
Croizat Act, 57

Daric, J., 78
DAS (Direction de l'Action Sociale [Social Action Directorate]), 146, 148, 157
day centers, 98, 145, 148, 155, 164
DDASS, 163
Debré, Michel, 115
definitive exit, 217, 221; age of, 218–20
de Gaulle, Charles, 10, 50
Delors, Jacques, 151
demographics, 249, 254
devaluation, 65
Dienesch, Mme., 148
Dienesch Colloquium, 142
Directorate of Social Security, 69, 150
disability legislation, 144
disability scheme, 214
droit à l'existence, 37. *See also* right to subsistence
Dubois, Jean, 179
Dumazedier, Joffre, 225
Du Pont Co., 40
Dupont-Fauville Report on Childhood and Families, 246

early exit, 186, 190, 203–5, 206, 210, 211, 214, 215, 216, 217, 223, 224, 225, 227, 232, 239, 253, 271; schemes, 169–227, 202, 208; uses of, 172, 206

East Germany, 111
Economic and Social Council, 77
economic crisis, 249, 250, 252, 254–56
economic growth, 51, 248
economic security: as collective responsibility, 29; as property-based right, 34; as work-based right, 33
elderly: daily lives of, 74, 92–95, 112; employment of, 119, 123; home care of, 105, 142, 143, 148, 260; homes for, 93–94, 98; housing benefits, 120; incentives for employment, 170–72; income of, 120, 122; income policies for, 135; laws for, 135; lifestyle of, 73; living conditions of, 109–10, 112; management of , 133; medical care for, 101, 123, 258; numbers of, 74; in own homes, 152, 153, 154, 158, 156, 159, 161, 164; poverty of, 92, 98, 113; public assistance for, 90–100, 139; reintegration of, 128; social actions/services for, 105–7, 110, 117–19, 139, 172, 274; social clubs for, 118; social integration, 100–105, 123, 125, 134, 262, 276; spiritual needs of, 131; and the state, 113; way of life, 89–102, 105–7, 128–29, 135, 191; way-of-life policy, 191, 230; well-being of, 146
Elderly Persons' Intergroup (Intergroupe Personnes Âgées), 121, 142, 151, 152, 155, 162, 192, 194
employees, male: socioprofessional shift in, 140
employer-employee relations, 46
employers, 207: and older workers, 193, 238; and retirement, 186, 189; and social security, 54–55
employment: contract, 43–44; incentives for, 170–72; issues, 200–210; offices for, 123–24, and old age, 169–227; for older workers, 205–10, 230, 232; policies, 170, 210; rates, 48; and retirement, 186; right to, 36, 38, 143, 153, 193, 197, 223, 271; strategies, 39–44
Employment Ministry, 122
Esprit, 127, 128
European Union, 18
exploitation: campaign against, 180–81
Ewald, François, 43
Factory and Agricultural Workers' Pension Act: (1905), 47; (1910), 32, 37, 39, 44, 46–48
family allowances, 54, 56, 70, 82
Family Commission of the National Assembly, 91
family unions, 124
Fifth Plan, 121
Fifth Republic, 85, 172, 235
First Constituent Assembly, 57, 58
FNE (Fonds National de l'Emploi [National Employment Fund]), 172, 175, 186, 191, 197, 205, 231, 232, 253; mission of, 173
FO (union), 110, 173, 177, 178, 185, 189, 190, 207, 208
Fondation Nationale de Gérontologie (National Gerontology Foundation), 128
Fondant, Joseph, 197
Foucault, Michel, 235
Fourteenth Plan, 121
"fourth age," 135, 250
Fourth Plan, 121, 122, 135, 142
Fourth Republic, 81–82, 84, 85, 107, 165, 166, 171, 235
France, 221, 222; elderly population in, 111
funding system, 53

Gaullist state, 85, 107, 108, 114, 115, 203, 235, 236, 238, 239
General Directorates of Health and Social Security, 152
General Electric, 40
General Inspectorate of Social Affairs (Inspection Générale des Affaires Sociales), 122, 194
General Social Security Scheme, 99, 171, 179, 196, 230, 250
Germany, 222
gerontology: dynamics in, 128–29; elements of, 126. issues in, 125
Girard, Alain, 220
Giscard d'Estaing, 219; Giscardian state, 203
Goffman, E., 93
Gough, Ian, 274
Graebner, William, 40
Grandval, Gilbert, 173

Grémion, Pierre, 245
Grenelle Agreements, 177
Grenoble: as case example, 130, 133, 135; social policies in, 130
Grievance Register (1882), 38
gross domestic product (GDP), 248, 249, 252
Groupement National d'Action en Faveur de la Vieillesse (National Action Group for the Elderly), 110
guaranteed income *(garantie de ressources),*174, 176, 185, 191, 197, 198, 201, 206, 210, 213, 214, 215, 227, 271; scheme, 219, 270
Guesde, Jules, 37
Guillemard, A-M: "Old Age and the State," 8; *Retirement: A Social Death,* 8, 10

Habermas, Jürgen, 255
Hatzfeld, Henri, 34, 45, 66
health insurance, 70, 82; deficits in, 74
Holland, 222
home care, 159: programs, 106, 120, 121, 124, 130, 155, 163; workers, 101, 102, 161
hospices, 90
hospitals, 90, 93, 101
housing, 109; allowances for, 142
Huet, Dr., 126, 132

IFOP, 79, 112
individualism, 46, 66
industrial injuries, 54, 56; and social insurance, 43
Industrial Injuries Act (1898), 44
industrial proletariat, 30–35; and savings, 31, 32
industrialization, 32, 36; effects on workforce, 33, 44; in Europe, 42; process of, 43
inflation, 64
Institut National d'Études Démographiques (National Institute of Demographic Studies), 126
insurance: companies, 82; fight for, 37, private, 54
insurance schemes: old-age, 120
integration policy, 273, 276
Interoccupational Agreement, 176

Japan, 251
Jean Moulin Club, 246
job: alienation, 185; control, 39; cuts, 186; defense of, 201–3
Journal Officiel, 105

Kessler, Denis, 263
Keynes, John Maynard, 52

labor: intensification of, 41
Labor Inspectorate, 172
labor unions, 50, 55, 63, 66, 70, 72, 74, 82, 83, 85, 88, 99, 110. 112, 114, 117, 118, 119, 125, 126, 171, 173, 176, 177–86, 194, 196, 197, 203, 206, 207, 209, 233, 234, 244, 257, 270; and birth of social security, 60–61; and cadres, 67; Christian, 59; disillusionment with, 69; in France, 50, and jobs, 201–3; and pensions, 177–78, 182; philosophy of, 52, 53–55; power of, 52, 75–76; press, 73, 99; and retirement, 143, 200; and social security, 55–60; and work week, 180–81
Lafargue, Paul, 38
Laniel government, 76
Laroque, Pierre, 10, 56, 60, 100, 114, 128
Laroque Commission, 13, 103, 115–20, 191, 236, 245; composition of, 115–16
Laroque Report, 102, 106, 122, 117–19, 121, 123–25, 127–29, 132, 139, 141, 142, 146, 148, 151,154, 159, 167, 183, 246; recommendations of, 119–20
Law of the Sixth Plan, 143–44
layoffs, 198; guaranteed income during, 174; and older workers, 199
left-wing parties, 50, 56, 60, 76
Lenoir, Réné, 150
Liberation, the, 50, 52–55, 61, 62, 67, 76, 80–82, 84, 85, 88, 172, 230, 271; sociopolitical context of, 49–52
life expectancy, 18, 220
life hazards, 43, 49
Lowi, Theodore, 159
Lucas, Mr., 77

Maire, Edmond, 179
"manager state," 246–47
manual workers, 202, 204, 271

Mario, Roger, 77
Mathevet, Mr., 77
Mauroy government, 273
mechanization, 41
medicine: curative, 101; preventive, 100, 101, 108
Melchers, Ronald, 42, 43
Mendras, Henri, 265
Messmer, Pierre, 202
metallurgy industry, 79
middle classes, 11, 63, 64, 66, 68, 69, 84, 149; interests of, 81; retirement of, 141; salaried, 141
miners, 38, 39; of Carmaux, 40; and pension funds, 38, 44–45
minimum wage, 73, 91
Ministry of Labor, 197
Monde, Le, 73, 75, 77, 96, 97, 99, 109, 125, 129, 130
money, 114
MRP (Mouvement Républicain Populaire), 49, 54, 56, 57, 66, 76
mutual benefit societies, 35
Mutuality Charter, 35

National Agreement, 67
National Assembly, 63, 69, 85, 109, 115, 120, 124, 190, 197, 203; and old-age debate, 99
National Employment Fund. *See* FNE
National Interoccupational Agreement, 174, 205
National Middle-Class Liaison and Action Committee, 68
National Old-Age Fund (Fonds National Vieillesse), 71, 75, 120, 121, 133, 156, 182, 218
National Old-Age Insurance Fund for Salaried Workers (Caisse Nationale d'Assurance Vieillesse des Travailleurs Salariés), 120, 155. *See also* General Social Security Scheme
National Old-Age Retirement Fund (Caisse Nationale de Retraite pour la Vieillesse, 1850), 31, 32, 33
National Resistance Council, 50, 51, 55, 59
National Sickness Insurance Fund, 163
National Solidarity Fund (Fonds National de Solidarité), 75, 81, 82, 91, 92, 106, 109, 111, 120, 182
noncadres, 69, 78, 79; and old-age insurance, 70; pensions of, 83
non-Communists, 74
noncontributory allowances, 75, 92
Non-Governmental Organizations, 104
"Nouvelle Société" Project, 151

old age, 7, 20, 86–88, 107, 127, 209, 220, 226, 227, 260; and ability to work, 42; cash benefits, 130; debates on, 119, 125, 129; defined, 41–42, 117; economic views of, 249, 251; and employment, 169–227; image of, 113; implications of, 108–13, pension schemes, 130; post- 1945 employment, 170–76; provisions for, 31; and public assistance, 48; and retirement, 48; as social entity, 109, 119, 226 132, 226, 263–69; social integration of, 239, spending on, 73, 249; and state control, 108, 114, 229, 230–33; as way of life, 86, 88, 114
"Old Age and the State" (Guillemard), 8
old age benefits: in Canada, 18; in France, 18; in Germany, 18; in Italy, 18; in Japan, 18; in the United Kingdom, 18; in the United States, 18
old-age insurance, 62, 63, 64, 70, 75–76, 81, 82, 84, 85, 214, 231, 234, 252, 253, contributions toward, 70; improvement of, 72; problems of, 69–70, 74; "naturalization of, " 127
old-age policies, 100, 114, 130, 134, 135, 141, 147, 165, 167, 228–76
old people's homes, 101, 105, 106, 113, 118, 120, 132, 156
older workers, 57, 58, 186, 191, 192, 194, 195, 197, 206, 207, 222, 223; compensation for, 164– 76, 196, 200; dismissal of, 191; employment of, 122, 188, 189, 192, 193, 203–5, 230, 231, 232; guaranteed income of, 176, 190, 197, 198, 199; laying off, 209; living standards of, 71; prejudice towards, 78–79; right to retirement, 244; unemployment policy for, 260, 264; vs. younger workers, 207

Paris: thirteenth arrondissement, 135, 148
PCF (Parti Communiste Français), 49, 55, 57, 58, 59, 60, 61, 64,

PSU (Parti Socialiste Unifié), 130
Parliament (French), 69, 81, 85, 104, 107, 188
Parliamentary Group on Problems of the Third Age, 182
pay-as-you-go system, 53, 65, 66, 263
payment methods, 39
"pedagogy of interdependence," 152
pension legislation: nineteenth century, 29; by occupation group, 231
pension levels, 88, 143, 177, 179
pension plans, 11, 62, 73, 81, 109, 114, 168, 173, 177, 183, 188, 206, 214, 215, 224, 230, 237, 244, 249, 250–53, 255, 263; autonomous, 68; and company loyalty, 41; complementary, 67, 77, 79–80, 82, 83, 110, 111, 114, 117–18, 123, 125, 129, 130, 131, 134, 135; as compulsory insurance, 46; contributory, 91; debates on, 20, 77–78; emergence of, 44, forms of, 83; funds for, 50; general scheme, 83, 91, 110, 114; improvement of, 76; as management tool, 43–43, and the needy elderly, 99; noncontributory, 70; private, 33, 82; problems with, 75–78; qualification for, 180; as recruitment tool, 40; reforms to, 183, 185, 186; right to, 44–45; state control of, 113–14; two-tiered, 30, and the working class, 33, 76, 78
pensioners, 48
Perrin, Guy, 47
Peuple, Le, 58, 70, 71, 77, 182
Philibert, Michel, 127
Pinay government, 76
Pinel School, 147
"policy of the elderly": defined, 19
political and administrative system: changes to, 107–8
Pompidou, Georges, 124
population: aging of, 77; distribution of, 213
Poulot, Denis, 40
poverty card *(carte d'économiquement faible)*, 81, 93–95, 99
"preretirement" *(préretraite)*, 169, 170, 175, 203, 212, 214, 216, 226; reasons for, 225; vs. retirees, 266; and stages of life, 220–26
preretirement plans, 173, 176, 187, 191, 210, 211, 218, 223, 224, 261, 264
Priority Action Program (PAP) no. 15 (1976–80), 162–64, 238
PRL, 57
productivity, 42, 122; decline in, 43; and retirement, 42; standards, 72; and workers, 41
Prost, Antoine, 35
Provins Program, 202, 203
Provisional Consultative Assembly, 56
public actions, 261–63
public assistance, 49, 89, 104, 105, 106, 108, 112, 134, 139, 147, 149, 161, 175, 230, 231; for the elderly, 113, 156; 1953 reform, 91; and old age, 125; policy of, 109

Questiaux, Nicole, 103, 142, 148

Ramadier government, 68
Raynaud, Henri, 60, 72
recession, 188
reconstruction, 69
redistributive state: financial crisis in, 249–55
Renault agreements, 79, 80
replacement income, 258, 260
Resistance, the, 49, 50, 52, 62, 64
resource centers, 98
retirees: income of, 182–83; organization of, 183–84, vs. preretirees, 266
retirement, 29, 43, 191, 201, 257, 258; age for, 39, 72, 73, 74, 76, 79, 88, 122, 143, 144, 151, 173, 177, 180–85, 187–89, 192, 194, 196, 197, 200–202, 203, 204, 218–19, 233, 252, 255, 271–72, 274; agreement on, 46; aspiration to, 45; attitude toward, 35, 36; and class strength, 37; vs. employment, 186–87, 222; and industrial society, 268, institutionalization of, 33, insurance, 46, 47; and labor union philosophy, 61–62, 73, 184–86; as management tool, 41, 45, 47; and the middle classes, 62; planned, 34; as a right, 46, 47, 49–62, 176–86, 200, 201, 209, 234, and "social death," 185; work-related, 30–49; and worker discipline, 40
Retirement: A Social Death (Guillemard), 8, 10
retirement homes, 93, 100, 105, 106, 120, 121, 156

revenues: distribution of, 51, 52, 53, 86
Revue de Gérontologie d'Expression Française, 128
Reynaud, J. D., 200
Right, the, 68, 81
"right to charity," 70
"right to poverty," 69
"right to rest," 38, 39, 47–48, 69, 72, 73, 108, 117, 119, 122, 268
"right to retirement," 39, 45, 48, 55, 63, 70, 71, 72, 74, 75, 77–78, 80, 82, 83, 85, 87, 99, 110, 119, 143–46, 166, 169, 171, 176, 185, 196, 231, 234, 235, 261, 265, 268, 270, 272, 274; defeat of, 63; and occupational categories, 69; segmentation of, 62–82
right to security, 36, 37, 234; work-based, 44
right to subsistence, 37, 38, 72, 73, 74, 80, 87
risks: separation of, 53–54
Roussel, Louis, 220

savings: voluntary, 31; and the working class, 31
Sauvy, Alfred, 126, 230
Schneider Co., 43
scientific management, 41, 268
Second Constituent Assembly, 58
Second World War, 11, 50, 66, 170; and pensions, 48
sectorization, 148–49
security: wage-related, 43–44, 46
self-employed, the, 64, 65, 66; and the cadres, 63, 68
Seventh Plan, 104, 162, 164, 203, 232, 238: Priority Action Program, 166
SFIO (Section Française de l'Internationale Ouvrière), 49, 55, 61, 62, 81
Sixth Plan, 103, 104, 123, 142, 143, 146, 148, 151, 153, 155, 156, 159, 162, 163, 191, 192, 194, 196, 203, 232, 237; and social reform, 144
small businesses, 37, 39, 66
SMIC (Salaire Minimum Interprofessionel de Croissance [Guaranteed Minimum Wage]), 183
social action: for the elderly, 105–7, 260; expenses for, 259
Social Action Fund, 155
social administration, 53, 124, 257
social benefit funds, 44, 247, 248, 250, 252
social dynamics, 179, 210, 211, 228, 229, 244
social exile/segregation, 191, 261
social insurance *(les assurances sociales)* (1930), 34, 43, 47, 49, 51, 52, 53, 54; and the elderly, 48; system, 60, Soviet model, 54; and the working class, 48
Social Insurance Act (1930), 34, 47, 54, 84
social integration, 105–42, 153, 191, 192, 193, 199, 204, 255; program assessment, 154–64; state initiatives for, 100–103
social legislation, 90
social mobilization, 182
social needs, 53
social planning, 259–60, 262
social proletariat, 250
social protection system, 248, 260–74
social renewal: need for, 50–51
social rights, 52, 257
Social Security, 74–75, 80, 82, 108, 110, 111, 234; development of, 49–62; legislation for, 91, 92; 1945 ordinance, 51–52; property-based, 30–34; reform, 75; and social pact, 52; unified, 62
Social Security Act, 222
Social Security General Direction, 55
Socialist government, 81, 174, 206, 269–74
Socialists, 66, 68, 130, 210, 218
Société de Gérontologie (French Gerontological Society), 128, 132
society: and workers, 36
solidarity, 49, 53, 55, 92; contracts, 174–75, 219; fragmentation of, 68
Spain, 222
State, the, 63, 89: as agent of change, 193; building programs of, 119–42; and initiatives for the elderly, 100–103; and management committee, 74; and old age, 114; and way-of-life policy, 191
State Council, 100
State Secretariat, 148; for the Elderly, 269, 272, 273
Stearns, Peter N., 36, 42
Study Commission on Old Age, 121, 122, 123, 125, 126, 142, 165. *See also* Laroque Commission
Syndicalisme, 59, 71

Taylorism. *See* scientific management
textile industry, 79
"therapeutic seclusion," 147
"third age," 102, 117, 126, 134, 135, 141, 143, 144, 149, 226, 250, 264, 265, 267, 276; categories of, 152; citizens, 166; clubs, 160, 161, 163; described, 265
Touraine, Alain, 45, 235, 243, 267
transfers: system of, 74
Treaty of Rome, 111
Trempé, Rolande, 34, 37, 38, 40
tripartisme, 235

UIMM (Union des Industries Métallurgiques et Minières), 53
UNEDIC, 197, 198, 205, 211, 253, 272.
unemployment, 55, 202, 224, 249, 251–52, 272; benefits, 169, 192, 196, 218; and older workers, 175; scheme, 194, 206; transition to, 223–26
Unemployment Compensation Fund, 216, 219
unemployment insurance, 174, 205, 216–18, 232
Union Confédérale des Retraités (Confederal Union of the Retired), 184
UNIRS (Union Nationale des Institutions de Retraités des Salariés [National Union of Employee Pensions Institutes]), 77, 79, 80, 82, 83, 114
urban proletariat, 36

Vichy government, 92
Voluntarism, 107, 113
voluntarist state, 114

wage: earners, 64, 65, 66; negotiations, 45; of older workers, 42; and right to security, 44
way-of-life, 235, 255, 257; of the elderly, 191; global model for, 90; policies for, 89, 117, 133, 134, 142–54, 157, 165, 166, 167, 192, 193, 196, 201, 203–5, 230, 231, 233, 237, 238, 244, 245, 260, 261
Weber, Max, 46
welfare, 40, 51, 89, 90, 247, 248, 257, 258, 261, 266, 270, 273, 274
women: employment of, 171
work, 258; issues in, 39; organization of, 40; pace of, 72; and retirement, 222–24; scientific management of, 42
workforce: aging of, 41, 43; exploitation of, 37; male, 137–38; older, 41, 41, 83; retirement demands of, 44; security needs of, 44
workforce mobility, 43, : and retirement in large companies, 41–43
work week: length of, 41, 179, 181
working class, 64, 69, 83, 84, 87, 136, 204; expectations of, 53; interests of, 234; occupations of, 139, and pensions, 35–39; and property, 33; regard for, 50; retirement development of, 34; and social security, 55
working conditions, 73